W9-CTW-121

DATE DUE

DEMCO 38-296

Governing the White House

STUDIES IN GOVERNMENT
AND PUBLIC POLICY

Contents

GOVERNING THE WHITE HOUSE
From Hoover Through LBJ

Charles E. Walcott
Karen M. Hult

University Press of Kansas

Published by the University Press of Kansas (Lawrence, Kansas 66049), which was
organized by the Kansas Board of Regents and is operated and funded by Emporia
State University, Fort Hays State University, Kansas State University, Pittsburg
State University, the University of Kansas, and Wichita State University

Library of Congress Cataloging-in-Publication Data

Walcott, Charles Eliot, 1943–
    Governing the White House : from Hoover through LBJ / Charles E.
  Walcott and Karen M. Hult.
      p.   cm.—(Studies in government and public policy)
    Includes bibliographical references and index.
  ISBN 0-7006-0688-2 (cloth)—ISBN 0-7006-0689-0 (pbk.)
      1. Presidents—United States—Staff.   2. Organization.
  3. Organizational behavior.   I. Hult, Karen Marie.   II. Title.
  III. Series.
  JK552.W35   1995
  353.03′13—dc20
                                                        95-1108

British Library Cataloguing in Publication Data is available.

Printed in the United States of America

10 9 8 7 6 5 4 3 2 1

The paper used in this publication meets the minimum requirements of the
American National Standard for Permanence of Paper for Printed Library
Materials Z39.48-1984.

Preface

In this book we continue a project that has occupied most of our scholarly efforts for the better part of a decade. In that time we have sought to do two related things. The first is to develop a variant of organization theory grounded in an understanding of organizations as inherently political systems, or "polities." The second is to employ that perspective—which we call a "governance" model of organizations—in analyzing the White House Office.

These two interests developed almost simultaneously. Our ideas about organizational governance clearly were inspired by our familiarity with organizations like the White House Office: structurally fluid, responsive to both environmental and leadership change, yet also pursuing a growing number of similar tasks. At the same time, it seemed to us that organizationally based discussions of the White House suffered from theoretical and empirical underdevelopment. Much of this work focused on formalisms such as pyramidal versus spokes-in-the-wheel organization of the staff, confining attention mostly to the very top of the White House and to concerns with presidential control of White House aides. Meanwhile, many of these analyses were aggressively prescriptive without being based on as strong a descriptive foundation as one might like. An empirical research project employing an organizational governance approach, we thought, could help enrich our understanding of how and why the White House has evolved in the ways it has, in part by asking different questions and in part by providing more detailed answers.

In electing to take on the White House Office, we followed, wittingly or not, the injunction to test theory on "hard" cases. The White House is sometimes thought to have properties that defeat organizational analysis or at least render such an approach not particularly relevant. The White

House Office is, after all, "reinvented" every four to eight years by presidents who have their own theories and preferences about how to organize a staff. Moreover, it is enmeshed in a turbulent environment that requires considerable flexibility. Thus the question arises: Is the White House enough of an "organization" for organization theory to explain? Not surprisingly, our suspicion was that it is, especially if one approaches it with analytical tools that are well adapted to dealing with an organization that is not, for the most part, a simple, stable hierarchy. The bulk of this book represents, then, our efforts both to explore the contributions of organizational analysis to an understanding of the White House staff and to informally "test" several aspects of the governance model.

Our initial version of the governance model was openly normative. Here, in contrast to that and in contrast to much of what has been written about the White House, we stress the empirical. This book does not seek to offer advice to presidents about how to organize their staffs. One could argue—persuasively, we think—that the governance model still has implicit biases, such as its rejection of purely hierarchical understandings of organization and its enthusiasm for the creative potential of politics. We confess to these charges but also note that no social theory is completely free of bias. Nonetheless, in what follows, we concentrate on description and especially on explanation of the organizational dynamics of the White House Office, not on prescription.

In choosing to focus our analysis on the "early modern" presidency, which we date from 1929 and the advent of a plural professional staff in the White House to the end of the Johnson administration, we have consciously sacrificed coverage and immediate relevance for descriptive and explanatory depth. But we also believe that this era saw the White House Office develop (and not develop) in ways that shaped, or at least greatly limited, the options for future White House organization. An appreciation of the evolution of the early modern White House thus seems necessary to a fuller understanding of more contemporary staff organization. At the end of each substantive chapter, therefore, we try to sketch how later White Houses developed, paying particular attention to the administrations of Richard Nixon (under whom the size of the White House Office exploded) and Bill Clinton (who, at this writing, works in the newest version).

A project of this scope creates many debts of gratitude. The research was supported by numerous sources. Charles Walcott appreciates the funding he received from the Bush Foundation; the National Endowment for the Humanities; the Conflict Research Project, the Graduate School, and the Department of Political Science at the University of Minnesota; and the Department of Political Science at Virginia Tech. Karen Hult is grateful for the support she received from the American Association of University Women, the American Political Science Association, the National Endowment for the Humanities, the Center for Politics and Policy at the Claremont Graduate School, Pomona College, and the Department of Political Science at Virginia Tech.

Many individuals also contributed significantly to the research. Throughout, our colleagues and students at Virginia Tech, the University of Minnesota, Pomona College, and the Claremont Graduate School challenged us to clarify and systematize our ideas. Throughout the course of our research we benefited greatly from conversations with many colleagues, notably Robert Holt, Lawrence Jacobs, David Elliott, Richard Harrison, Kim Spiezio, and Daniel Mazmanian. Frank Tugwell shared his expertise in data base management and helped us avoid being overwhelmed by mounds of information. We are grateful as well for the research assistance of Jennifer Tice, James Melcher, Donald Dresser, and Bruce Snyder. Maxine Riley, Kim Hedge, and Terry Kingrea provided efficient and remarkably patient clerical support.

Because of our extensive reliance on the papers and files of White House staffers, we especially appreciate the help of archivists at the libraries of the early modern presidents—in particular, Dale Mayer and Robert Wood at the Hoover Library, Susan Bosanko at the Roosevelt Library, Erwin Mueller at the Truman Library, Tom Branigan at the Eisenhower Library, Ron Whealan at the Kennedy Library, and Nancy Smith at the Johnson Library. Scott Parham, the supervisory archivist for the Nixon Presidential Materials Project, aided us with some initial work on the Nixon White House. Bradley Patterson shared with us not only his recollections of the Eisenhower White House but also his sharp insight into presidential staffing more generally.

Comments on the manuscript by Peri Arnold and Joseph Pika were of immense help in strengthening (though hardly perfecting) the work. Last but scarcely least, we are deeply grateful for Fred Woodward's support of the project, for his skill at soliciting constructive reviews, and for his patience as we struggled to keep the work on track. We also have come to admire his commitment to encouraging serious scholarly work.

Finally, we should note that throughout this was a genuinely collaborative effort. Since our first joint work listed us alphabetically, this time we reversed the order.

Introduction

The framers of the U.S. Constitution showed remarkable wisdom and fore-sight concerning most of the main structural features and problems of gov-erning a vast republic. Not surprisingly, though, they failed to anticipate a large array of particulars, many of them products of a kind of economic and governmental expansion that the framers could neither have imagined nor approved. This book explores one of the details the founders missed—the structuring of the president's closest group of advisers and aides, the White House staff.

The Constitution provides for no such entity as the White House staff. Article II briefly discusses "executive departments" but is mute on the sub-ject of presidential staff. Early Congresses, taking that silence as their guide, appropriated no money for presidential aides. Nevertheless, all presi-dents have required at least one such assistant. But until the administration of James Buchanan (1857–61), presidents either paid out of their own pockets or recruited volunteers, sometimes relatives, for the job.

Although presidential aides were occasional sources of controversy and, far less often, admiration, they were not objects of sustained concern to journalists, scholars, or, by extension, the American public prior to 1929.[1] But ever since Herbert Hoover elected to expand the number of pro-fessional White House staffers beyond the traditional single secretary, alarms have been going off periodically. Even Hoover's modest move, ap-pointing three secretaries and an administrative assistant, provoked a skep-tical writer in the *American Mercury* to observe:

> It was to be expected that the appearance in the White House of a Big Executive should see an accompanying enlargement of office quarters,

expansion of equipment and massing of secretarial help. In bygone days, the President had *a* secretary. Good, bad or indifferent, but only one. But that was before the era of the Super-Administrator, before Efficiency came to the White House. Now there is a whole machine-gun squad to handle the work.[2]

Since then, every president has had to cope with similar criticism, or worse. Thus, some of Franklin Roosevelt's aides, such as Rexford Tugwell and Harry Hopkins, were viewed in some circles as dangerous radicals; Harry Truman's staff was widely seen as full of corrupt cronies; Dwight Eisenhower's staff system inspired the joking query: "What if [Sherman] Adams died and Ike became President?" In contrast, individual aides such as Clark Clifford and Bill Moyers have been lionized by the press and the public or have basked in the golden aura of a few revered administrations ("the Brains Trust," "the Best and the Brightest"). White House staffs have not only shared in the fate of their leaders, they have also helped bring it about and symbolize it.

For all this attention, however, our understanding of the White House staff as an organization is incomplete. Questions of how and when the staff grew and developed as it has have not been fully answered. We currently lack a full account of exactly what White House staffs, especially those prior to Richard Nixon's administration, have contained and what they have done. We lack a detailed account of the personnel, the organizational structures, and the decision-making and other routines that have defined the White House and helped give that metaphorical building its political importance.[3] This book's first task is to sketch the details of White House staffing from 1929 through 1968, from the administration of Herbert Hoover through that of Lyndon Johnson.

In our view, however, description is not enough. Beyond questions of how much the staff has grown and what jobs it has performed lie issues for explanation and evaluation. An understanding of what the White House staff has been, and how it became that way, is vital to an appraisal of the strengths and weaknesses of the organization of the modern presidency. Such an understanding also may provide insights into what the staff can yet become. Our primary emphasis here is on explanation, and only secondarily on evaluation. In what follows, we seek to account for the emergence of new staff structures and responsibilities and to suggest why certain tasks and structures have come to have a stable residence in the White House and others have not. We do not mean to shrink from assessing the organization of the presidential office, but rather to contend that sensible evaluation must be both based on a solid descriptive foundation and informed by a theoretically grounded understanding of such staff structuring.[4]

APPROACHES TO UNDERSTANDING WHITE HOUSE STAFFING

Any explanation of the structure and operation of a complex organization like the White House Office must, of course, be guided by some general theoretical ideas about both organizations and the presidency. Chapter 1 details the theoretical framework that animates our analysis. Here we anticipate that discussion by briefly reviewing some of the theoretical arguments about the staff that have already been advanced and that inform much of the scholarship on the organization of the presidency. Our purpose is both to outline the nature of theoretical ideas that have guided recent presidential scholarship and to point to promising avenues that have not yet been fully explored. One such avenue marks the path we intend to follow.

Although it has become relatively commonplace to lament the paucity of theory in presidential scholarship,[5] the charge is not altogether a fair one. Theory is not wholly lacking in studies of White House organization. Indeed, in a sense there is a great deal of theory, even if much of it is implicit rather than explicit, and some of it is perhaps overly simplistic.[6] For example, many attempts to deal theoretically either with the White House staff over time or with particular presidencies settle for essentially single-factor explanations. The two factors most commonly stressed are organizational structure and presidential personality. Such studies range from those that posit the central importance of structure and offer advice about what constitutes the best organizational form, to arguments asserting or assuming that structure matters far less than the personal characteristics (e.g., the "character" or "style") of individual presidents.[7]

Near the structural end of the spectrum, for instance, is the ongoing debate over whether the modern White House requires a strong chief of staff or can be run using more of a "spokes-of-the-wheel" arrangement.[8] Other analyses focus on single presidencies, as the continuing discussion over the extent and desirability of Dwight Eisenhower's "formalistic" leadership style illustrates.[9]

Toward the opposite end of the spectrum are many historical studies of particular presidencies,[10] as well as some critical analyses of the Reagan, Bush, and Clinton administrations.[11] These sorts of accounts emphasize the idiosyncratic strengths and weaknesses of presidents and their advisers. In this view, the characteristics of the chief executive determine the makeup and working of the White House staff and largely dictate the administration's success or failure.

Between these poles lie other works, some of which advance more complex theoretical formulations. What might be called the "personal contingency" approach, for instance, stresses the importance of matching staff structures to the management style and personality of the chief executive.[12] If any perspective comes close to being the conventional wisdom on presidential staffing, it is probably this one. Among the virtues of this approach is that it explicitly addresses the question of the relative importance of some of the variables that might be included in a theory about the evolution of the White House staff.

Regardless of the number of explanatory variables these works on presidential staffing discuss, however, most share two critical weaknesses: an overemphasis on presidential control of staffers and a general neglect of the environment in which the presidency operates. First, many discussions of the White House staff seemingly cast presidents and their aides in a principal-agent relationship. Clearly, this concern with control—typically manifested through discussions of staff supervision, coordination, or management—is not misplaced. The desire for policy coherence and effectiveness and for democratic accountability highlights the significance of presidential control. Staffers may abuse their power, alienate key presidential supporters, and overload or dangerously isolate presidents.

Even so, a focus principally on *control* is incomplete, for it threatens to underplay the *substance* of what presidents do. Presidents do more than control their staffs; they also use aides to cope with the complexity, ambiguity, and controversy inherent in national politics and policy making. Moreover, this primary concern with control reinforces the tendency of most analysts to focus principally on top-level White House staffers.[13] These senior aides are the people whom presidents can try to directly supervise and who themselves have the responsibility for controlling the rest of the staff. Often neglected as a result of this emphasis are the diverse responsibilities, activities, and structures at lower levels of the increasingly large and complex White House Office.

A second element that is missing from many analyses of White House staffing is explicit consideration of the political and institutional *environment* in which the White House is embedded. In part, this neglect reflects the dominant emphasis on controlling presidential staff, which restricts analytical and prescriptive attention to internal White House matters. Relatedly, legitimate concern for the impact of presidential personality on staffing has tended to minimize concentration on environmental matters.

Recently, scholars such as Terry Moe and Samuel Kernell have reintroduced environmental influences into analyses of staffing by arguing that White House staff development should be seen as a strategic response by presidents to the political and policy problems their administrations confront.[14] This perspective views presidents as interjecting not their personalities but rather their objective needs into their decisions about the creation and utilization of staff. Organizational structures, in turn, are seen as reasonable responses to circumstances rather than generically "right" or "wrong" approaches to staffing the presidency. And presidents, rather than bringing unique bundles of style and substance to the presidency, are treated instead as rational decision makers who seek to protect and enhance their own power and effectiveness.

Such rational-choice analyses pose problems, not the least of which is the difficulty of determining the "objective" needs of presidents in a manner that does not render the analysis circular. Moreover, focusing on structures purely in light of presidential goals hews closely to the conventional concern for staff structures only as facilitators of presidential control.

Nevertheless, there is much value in such a "problem-contingency" logic. The essential claim of this approach is that organizational change to a significant extent reflects the external conditions an organization faces. Although the processes through which environmental characteristics compel organizational response may be more varied and complex than the hypothesized rational president calculating his or her political needs, the logic of the argument points to many interesting analytical possibilities.

A problem-contingency analysis need not be reduced to a single-factor explanation. Neither must it accept the limitations inherent in an emphasis on control as the central fact of organizational life in the White House. In our interpretation of the organizational evolution of the White House, we adopt an analytical perspective that accepts and proceeds from the premise that staff structures emerge primarily from strategic responses by presidents to environmental demands. Then, following Moe, we add an organizational dimension.[15] Once organizational structures are in place, even in such volatile settings as the ones the White House faces, structures can exercise an independent effect on the subsequent recognition and definition of problems that impinge from the external environment. Moreover, in most cases these organizational responses begin to manifest many characteristics long identified with bureaucracies: the creation and maintenance of routines, members' claiming and protecting turf, and the development of relationships with external constituencies. In other words, as the White House becomes more organizationally complex, that complexity itself shapes perceptions of and responses to the environment, and often constrains presidential choices.

In order to trace these dynamics, we first focus our attention on some of the areas that have been somewhat neglected in White House scholarship to date. Most importantly, perhaps, we take a close look at White House structuring below the top staff level. It is not enough simply to debate the possible arrangements for consultation with senior advisers (e.g., spokes of the wheel versus chief of staff versus troika) or to examine only those aspects of organization that come in for the president's personal attention (as, for instance, the rational-choice version of problem-contingency theory tends to do). If we are to deal with—indeed stress—the more *enduring* features of White House organization, we must encompass more of that organization within our scope. In this way, the demands of our theoretical approach and the requirements of our other task, more comprehensive description, dovetail nicely.

Second, we move theoretically beyond an emphasis on presidential control. Much of the policy-relevant work done by the president's staff is handled outside the chief executive's immediate supervision. If anyone ever doubted that, the Iran-contra affair in the Reagan administration provides a striking counterexample. Moreover, our inspection of earlier, simpler administrations strongly suggests that modern presidents have never been in all the loops all the time. In moving beyond control as the central theoretical element in understanding the staff, we need to offer a substitute. Our proposal, outlined in Chapter 1, is a perspective that emphasizes organizational politics and governance.

ORGANIZATION OF THE BOOK

Broadly speaking, we organize our analysis by examining the evolution of staff structures to handle three sorts of presidential tasks: outreach, policy processing, and coordination and supervision. *Outreach* refers to the management of relations between the president and the rest of the government and the public. The first hints of organizational structuring in the White House were directed toward outreach: Herbert Hoover had aides whose primary responsibilities were dealing with the press, working with Congress, and overseeing the executive branch bureaucracy. In one way or another, all subsequent presidents likewise arranged for the location of these tasks in or around the White House Office.

Presidential aides who specialized in handling *policy processing* did not call the White House home until the early 1940s, when Franklin Roosevelt persuaded Samuel Rosenman to leave the New York State Supreme Court and come to work in the White House full time. Since then, the White House has grown to be a central forum for policy discussion and decision within the executive branch, though the precise issue content and the nature of the relevant structuring have varied from one administration to another.

Emphasis on *coordination* and *supervision* within the White House directs attention to tasks that span the boundary that separates policy and outreach. Presidential speeches, for example, provide the opportunity for both outreach and policy articulation. As demands for presidential speeches increased, presidents beginning with Roosevelt turned to senior policy advisers for assistance; with Eisenhower, specialized White House writing aides first appeared. Under Johnson, writing experts were pushed further down in the White House hierarchy and interacted little with the president, anticipating the disjunction between writing and policy deliberation that would appear in later White Houses. Focusing on coordination and supervision returns us as well to an explicit issue of control: how to manage a larger, more complex White House. This latter concern, though present in all White Houses, was not addressed systematically until the administration of Dwight Eisenhower.

In the years since Hoover, organizational structures for the performance of various aspects of outreach, policy processing, and coordination and supervision have proliferated. Even before the number of White House staffers and staff complexity exploded under Richard Nixon, one can identify a large array of structural arrangements that were tried and, in many cases, incorporated into the seemingly permanent organizational landscape of the White House. After laying the conceptual foundations for studying the White House Office in Chapter 1, the rest of the book analyzes the evolution and dynamics of staff structuring from 1929 through 1968. Part I explores outreach, examining structures for congressional liaison, press and public relations, patronage and civil service, relations with executive branch agencies, and liaison with interest groups and subnational government officials. Part II concentrates on staffing for policy formulation and implementation, focusing on the arrangements that developed for working in different policy arenas. Part III highlights structures whose primary purposes cut across the distinctions between outreach and policy processing, those for presidential speechwriting, scheduling, and staff management. The discussion concludes with a consideration of the prospects for explaining White House staff structuring.

SCOPE OF ANALYSIS

Before beginning our detailed examination of White House staffing between 1929 and 1969, the boundaries—and potential limitations—of the investigation must be briefly sketched. First, the study focuses on the White House Office[16] rather than on, say, the National Security Council staff, the Council of Economic Advisers, or the Bureau of the Budget. Clearly, these latter three units (and others) are important components of the institutional presidency; as such, they will be mentioned frequently in the story that follows when they are relevant to understanding the structuring and dynamics in the White House Office itself. In part, this decision to confine our attention to the White House Office was a pragmatic one; even with this restriction, one risks being buried in mountains of detail. More importantly, examining the White House Office allows us to zero in on structural evolution within a relatively bounded setting. While doing so we can add to descriptive knowledge about the presidency.[17]

Second, as we have already pointed out, this volume covers the Hoover through Johnson administrations. We begin with Hoover, since he was the first president to rely on a plural professional staff. Confining attention to the period from March 1929 through January 1969 adds to the information available on White House staffing; much more descriptive material exists on the White House staff from the Nixon administration to the present.

More importantly, limiting the analysis allows us to concentrate on the first of two evident "eras" in White House staffing. During the first era—corresponding roughly to the Hoover through Kennedy administrations—the White House staff became institutionalized. That is, a plural professional staff with specialized responsibilities came to be an expected feature of the presidency. Institutionalization was never complete; as we shall see, certain tasks were lodged in the White House only for short periods, and many structures survived for limited times. Nor did institutionalization happen all at once. As John Burke argued, the Hoover and early Roosevelt staffs, although novel in their size, are perhaps better considered "precursor[s] to the institutional presidency." Only after 1939 and the formal creation of the Executive Office of the President (and in it the White House Office) did institutionalization begin in earnest.[18] Even so, one should not overstate the sharpness of the change. During both the Hoover and the Roosevelt administrations, the tasks of key advisers were relatively loosely defined, and the boundaries that separated the staff from the cabinet and, later, from other units in the Executive Office of the President were shifting and unclear. Lines became more sharply drawn and roles more formalized under Truman and, especially, Eisenhower. The Kennedy and Johnson administrations tried to move away from such formalization, but by the time Lyndon Johnson left office, much of what Eisenhower had introduced to the White House Office remained—and persists today.

In many ways, the Johnson White House can be seen as the transition between the two eras of the modern presidency: it both continued the activities of the first era and anticipated some of the new uses of the staff with which second-era administrations would experiment (for example, a separate domestic policy unit). After the Johnson administration, the size of the staff again became an important factor.[19] The second era begins with what Richard Neustadt called "a quantum jump" in the number of staff in the Nixon White House.[20] According to Neustadt's figures, which estimated the number of "full-time civilian officials in the White House . . . with some continuing concern for the substance of policy,"[21] Roosevelt had 11 aides at the end of his administration; by the beginning of 1952, Truman had 22, and Eisenhower had 34 by 1959. By 1963, Kennedy had cut back to 22 aides, and Johnson raised the number to 29 by 1967.[22] Even according to an earlier, more conservative count by Neustadt, the number for Nixon grew to 52.[23]

These numbers come far closer to defining the size of the White House staff that we are interested in. Our operational definition of "staff" will be somewhat broader, extending to a handful of "unofficial" staff members in the early years, some noncivilians, and a few persons with significant administrative but not policy tasks.

Descriptively, as Neustadt himself noted, the increase in staff size during the Nixon years makes it "almost impossible to work out comparability between the roles of the junior staff . . . in Truman's time and junior staff in the 1970s."[24] Analytically and substantively, too, this "swelling of the presidency"[25] seems likely to be significant—for example, complicating the tasks of linking staffers both to the president and to one another, and providing presidents increased opportunities for direct White House involvement in policy formulation, executive branch oversight, and public outreach. Moreover, Richard Nixon's systematic efforts to centralize authority in both the White House and the Executive Office of the President and to use them to pursue presidential goals have for the most part been followed, and in some cases intensified, by his successors.[26]

A careful exploration of the first, or early modern, era of the presidency is essential to a fuller appreciation of the foundations it laid for the later evolution of White House staffing beginning with Nixon. This first era also merits attention in its own right, as the basis for an enhanced understanding of the presidency during the middle part of the twentieth century.

1
Analytical Framework

ORGANIZATIONAL GOVERNANCE

Despite the fact that the White House Office has become an increasingly prominent feature of the institutional landscape of the U.S. government, organization theory has contributed relatively little to an analysis of the growth, evolution, and performance of the staff. Traditional organization theory tends to view organizations as "control systems," as devices for enhancing the efficiency and reliability of human activity.[1]

Implicit in such an understanding of organizations is that both organizational goals and the means for achieving them are clear and agreed upon. The crucial task, then, becomes to find ways of using the prescribed means for achieving shared goals that are as reliable and cost as little as possible.[2] To be sure, these ideas are consistent with and may have informed many scholars' concerns with presidential supervision and coordination of staffs.[3] Such notions also highlight the very real worries about maintaining staff accountability to presidents.

Yet these emphases largely ignore the *politics* that pervades an organization like the White House Office and tasks such as constituency liaison and domestic policy formulation. When politics is considered, it typically refers to the Machiavellian scheming and maneuvering of self-interested individuals, groups, and coalitions, where most relationships are fluid and conflictual.[4] Viewed in this light, politics often appears pathological, for such dynamics seem likely to threaten an organization's control over its members and their activities, and thereby to undermine reliability and efficiency and to undercut accountability. It is this notion that politics is somehow corrupting or at least inconsistent with the pursuit of organizational—especially public organizational—objectives that Terry Moe and other scholars find so troubling in the theories of management and public administration that are often applied to the presidency. Grounded in an understanding of organizations as control systems, these theories share a "jaundiced view of politics" and too frequently offer nonpolitical "solutions" to the political challenge of White House governance.[5]

Even when politics is not demonized, understanding it as merely the interplay and conflict among narrowly self-interested actors gives short shrift to other equally political notions such as cooperation, collaboration, and authority. At the same time, few generalizations can emerge from a view of organizational life that stresses idiosyncratic exchanges between ever-changing actors.

In our view, a more useful understanding of organizational politics starts with the assumptions that organizations are inherently political and that politics taps something beyond the politicking and gaming just described.[6] In contrast to the control-system perspective, we contend that organizations must work continually to establish and define their orienting goals and to discover and choose means for achieving them. Coping with the attendant uncertainty and conflict is at the very heart of organizational politics, much as it is for politics in nation-states. These efforts at coping, in turn, involve an organization in a range of recognizably political tasks—allocating values, distributing benefits and burdens, and generating commitment to and a sense of the legitimacy of the organization—with implications for those inside and outside the organization.

Many, if not most, organizations face a continuing stream of demands to address prevailing uncertainties and controversies (which can be generated both within and outside an organization). Organizations must be *governed,* and they can be conceived of as *governance systems.* Yet even when viewed from this perspective, organizations seek to enhance reliability and efficiency. They are typically pushed by top officials or external stakeholders to be accountable. Organizational actors tend to respond in the same way in which they handle most demands: through routinization.[7] Standard ways develop for deliberating over goals, for addressing questions about priorities, and for developing plans for actually pursuing objectives. We call these routine responses organizational *governance structures.*

Governance, then, refers to politics within a relatively orderly, rule-bound setting. The governance approach used here aims at focusing the analysis on organizational purposes beyond control and on an organizational politics that encompasses more than the micro-level maneuvering of self-interested individuals.

Nevertheless, we hasten to point out that this emphasis on structured politics is only one possible theoretical lens through which an organization may be viewed. The governance approach is not necessarily the most useful for all purposes.[8] Stressing control, for instance, might be a more helpful approach to analyzing the problem of staff leaks to reporters or the misuse of White House perquisites. A more Machiavellian view of politics might provide better insight into the waxing and waning of the fortunes of individual presidential advisers. Our theoretical perspective is not, therefore, the only way to describe or explain an organization like the White House Office. Nonetheless, we offer it as potentially a highly useful one. Presidents and their aides strive constantly to discover and articulate political and policy goals and priorities as well as to formulate strategies for pursuing them. White House staffers often work feverishly to find ways to, for example, respond to growing unemployment, mobilize potential supporters of presidential health care legislation, secure cooperation from recalcitrant executive branch officials, or generate public support for the president. The structuring that results from the repeated performance of such tasks is precisely what the governance approach seeks to examine.

STAFF STRUCTURING

In this study, attention centers on the structuring of the White House Office.[9] As we use the term, structure refers to "recurring interactions in organizations."[10] Such patterned relationships may be either formal or informal.[11] Dwight Eisenhower, for example, presided over official weekly meetings with legislative leaders and invited members of Congress, among others, to his less formal "stag dinners" for discussing politics and policy. Similarly, some structures are relatively permanent, such as staff meetings to prepare to brief presidents before press conferences; other structures—the ExCom during the Cuban missile crisis comes quickly to mind—are more temporary. (A full list of the more important governance structures that we identify can be found in Table 4 in the epilogue.)

Of greatest interest are those structures most clearly dedicated to governance in its most manifestly political (i.e., goals- and means-seeking) sense. For example, before press conferences, senior White House aides (and frequently others in the executive branch) typically meet to determine the issues and response tactics on which they should brief the president. The structures for performing this fundamentally political task are collegial, bringing together individuals with varying areas of expertise and often differing views; these structures typically provide a forum for exploration, argumentation, and deliberation. When sharp disagreements arise and persist—as they did, for example, over how Eisenhower should respond to questions about Sen. Joseph McCarthy—the president is the ultimate adjudicator.

At the same time, we also pay attention to structures charged primarily with control and supervision, such as those associated with the staff secretariat and many of the activities of the chief of staff or equivalent. Such structures often influence the conduct of more overtly political tasks, serving, for instance, as mechanisms for assigning, coordinating, and overseeing work. Thus, in most White Houses, structures such as staff meetings emerged to ensure that top staff members were informed about the relevant activities of their colleagues on a routine basis. More generally, the governance perspective considers these control routines a key component of organizational governance, for they permit work to proceed when both ends and means are agreed upon.

Dependent Variables

Discussion of the structuring of the White House staff involves distinguishing among various structural dimensions. We seek to identify and explain three key properties of governance structures: the emergence, the stability, and the particular forms of the structures through which aides carry out given tasks. In addition, we seek both to explain and to examine the consequences of the differentiation of governance structures within the White House Office.

Emergence. Structures emerge when relationships and decision processes begin to fall into routines. It is difficult to state in the abstract exactly when a structure can be considered to first appear, since what counts as routine is highly context specific. Yet when problems (e.g., how to mobilize support in Congress for presidential legislation, how to fill appointive positions in the executive branch) recur and are responded to in similar ways, structures can be said to have emerged.

Stability. Such structures, of course, can be more or less stable. Least stable are those structures that fail to be relied on throughout a single presidential term; most stable are those that remain today in the White House Office. Other structures persist through more than one administration but ultimately disappear. Scholars often refer to structures that last through more than one presidency as having become "institutionalized."[12] In what follows, we consider a structure to be institutionalized when it persists through at least two presidencies.[13] Evidence of institutionalization is especially compelling when the two administrations are of opposing parties. Without evidence of this latter degree of stability, the structure's persistence may reflect idiosyncratic presidential preference or partisan imitation rather than longer-run persistence.

Nature. The third dependent variable explicitly acknowledges that structural form may vary, making the determination of the nature of prevailing structures an important consideration. Governance structures can (and, we argue later, should) take on a variety of forms.[14] Table 1 describes several types of structures that we use as we explore staff structuring. It is crucial to underscore at the outset that hierarchy is by no means the only structural form that has characterized the White House. Of course, the White House Office as a whole must be viewed as a hierarchy, with the president at its apex. Within that hierarchical skeleton, however, a diverse array of subordinate structures has emerged. Structures for control do tend to be hierarchical, since their chief purpose is to ensure accountability to specified superiors.

Yet also present, as we shall see, are a variety of collegial structures. *Collegial-competitive* structures bring together parties with differing points of view on, for example, appropriate policy directions for an administration or the most effective strategies for lobbying members of Congress. Such structures allow for debate among the participants and for developing compromises; since neither consensus nor compromise may emerge, formal decision rules such as majority vote may be invoked to reach decision closure. In the Johnson White House, the staff meetings sporadically called by Cabinet Secretary Robert Kintner typically were arenas for such discussion.

Collegial-mediative structures are quite similar, though they include a party that helps other participants explore and attempt to resolve their differences. White House staffers often served this mediative function as they sought to work out disputes among agency officials.

Last, *collegial-consensual* structures permit more nonconflictual brainstorming about values or strategies for addressing perceived problems. During the Kennedy administration, for instance, White House staffers established and worked with the Subcabinet Group on Civil Rights, with representatives from several executive branch agencies, to develop strategies aimed at eliminating racial discrimination in federal programs.

In addition, arrangements that rely on intervention by a party not involved in the debate are possible. *Adjudicative* structures are designed to handle recurring disputes between, say, White House staffers or executive branch officials with overlapping responsibilities. The parties in effect submit their disputes to an uninvolved "judge" for settlement. Typically, disputes handled by such structures are reducible (or reduced) to two competing positions, one of which is finally determined to be the "correct" one. Presidents frequently find themselves serving in such an "appeals courts" capacity when they must decide between the arguments advanced, for example, by substantive policy staffers and congressional liaison aides who disagree over whether the president should accept a proposed legislative compromise.

Much like adjudicative structures, *adversarial* mechanisms rely on parties not

Table 1. Characteristics of Selected Governance Structures

Governance Structure			Characteristics		
	Participation	Expertise	Decision Rule	Conflict Management	Uncertainty Management
Hierarchy	Following or giving orders	Technical knowledge, organizational position	Preference of top decision maker	Resolution avoidance	Resolution avoidance
Collegial-Competitive	Advocacy of interests	Political expertise, skills in persuasion and bargaining	Majority vote, extraordinary majority	Competition, collaboration, compromise	Competition, collaboration, compromise
Collegial-Mediative	Argument before neutral third party	Skills in mediation, argumentation	Parties' acceptance or rejection of mediator's advice and proposed settlement	Guided compromise	Guided compromise
Collegial-Consensual	Cooperative search	Skills in persuasion, collaboration	Consensus	Collaboration, avoidance (groupthink)	Collaboration, avoidance
Adjudicative	Two-party advocacy	Skills in marshaling evidence, persuasion	Burden of proof	Two-party competition	Reduction: issues cast as right or wrong; correct or incorrect
Adversarial	Multiparty advocacy	Skills in marshaling evidence, persuasion	Judgment of decision maker (not included among advocates)	Multiparty competition	Competition; may exacerbate uncertainty
Market	Separate pursuit of different objectives	Little guaranteed; varies by party and situation	Epiphenomenal coordination	Competition, avoidance	Acceptance as inevitable

directly involved in a dispute to make a final resolution. Unlike adjudicative arrangements, however, adversarial structures do not treat conflicts as having only two sides, with the ultimate decision in effect declaring a "winner" and a "loser." On numerous occasions, Sherman Adams's staff meetings in the Eisenhower administration took on the character of an adversarial structure, with the chief of staff listening to debates among other aides before rendering a final decision.

Finally, White House decisions may be handled using *market*-like mechanisms. Such structuring appears when changing participants pursue their own varied interests; how decisions are made is neither explicit nor consistent.[15] Market structuring pervaded, for instance, the handling of White House public-relations efforts during most of the period to be examined, as diverse staffers worked to design ways to mobilize public support for presidents and presidential initiatives.

It should be emphasized that any White House as a whole will have more than one type of structure within it, and any organizational unit in the White House may display a diversity of governance structures. For example, by the Johnson years, the legislative liaison office responded to requests for favors from members of Congress by following simple routines outlined by the liaison head and carried out by support staff—an arrangement relying on hierarchy; at the same time, strategies for mobilizing support for key legislation elicited more collegial-consensual efforts by top professionals. Still other structures may link organizational units in the White House with each other or with external entities. Legislative liaison staffers on occasion meet in collegial-competitive settings with White House policy aides to set strategy for moving particular presidential bills through Congress. At the same time, liaison aides work to guide the activities of their counterparts in executive branch agencies by incorporating the latter into hierarchical structures directed from the White House.

Differentiation. Finally, we must note that no organization and few organizational units contain only one structure. The fourth dependent variable—differentiation—directs attention beyond single structures to the extent of structural elaboration in the organization as a whole or in its subdivisions.[16] The multiplication of structures is primarily the result of two other dependent variables: emergence and, to an extent, stability. Differentiation is of interest mainly because of its possible consequences. As governance structures multiply, this in itself may generate a need for additional structuring; as staffers struggle over turf or face difficulties coordinating their activities, increased conflict or uncertainty may result. We refer to this tendency of governance structure to beget governance structure as the *differentiation dynamic.*[17]

Explanatory Variables

The chapters that follow search for possible explanations for the emergence, stability, nature, and differentiation of staff structures. Three clusters of explanatory factors are examined: environmental, presidential choice, and organizational.

First, the environment surrounding the White House Office encompasses myriad possible influences, including technology, other governmental actors both in the United States and abroad, and the public. For example, technological changes (the advent of radio, newsreels, and television; advances in transportation) affected the demands and expectations confronting presidents, offered them new strategic opportunities, and placed additional responsibilities on the White House staff. Moreover, from 1929 until 1969, presidents and staffs faced a growing and diversifying executive branch bureaucracy, a changing global economic and political arena, and shifting public and congressional expectations. Meanwhile, presidential politics itself changed; for example, national party organizations weakened, and direct links between the White House and constituency groups grew and were seen as more legitimate.

The second cluster of variables having to do with presidential choice taps the influence of particular presidents. Two dimensions of presidential choice seem especially significant. First, the salience and nature of presidential objectives may affect staff structuring. For example, Dwight Eisenhower, with a relatively small policy agenda, might have been willing to permit a great deal of staff deliberation in collegial settings, trading time spent for more careful staff work. Lyndon Johnson, with a burgeoning set of policy objectives, would be far more impatient with such arrangements.

Presidential strategy also may be important in shaping staff structures. Many scholars have focused their discussions of strategy on the development of an essentially administrative or control capacity in the White House, de signed to provide the president with the sort of help the Brownlow committee advised FDR he needed.[18] Yet, as the introduction suggested, presidential strategies may also be understood in the manner proposed by Moe[19] and harking back to Neustadt[20]—as presidential efforts to shape the influences of the environment. These efforts in turn might be reflected in reliance on particular governance structures.

Perhaps surprising to many, we pay little systematic attention in what follows to the impact of presidential personality and management style.[21] In part, this lack of emphasis reflects dissatisfaction with prevailing definitions of and indicators for these concepts.[22] It is not always easy to determine what is a matter of style as opposed to goal or strategic preferences. Indeed, appeals to such an idiosyncratic explanation of presidential staffing (which the introduction referred to as a personal contingency perspective) may tend to obscure presidential intent. In examining the issue of presidential *agency*—the extent to which presidents have impacts, especially intended ones—it is generally more useful to think in terms of objectives and strategies.

Nonetheless, presidents do have styles, in the sense of preferred arrangements with which they are most comfortable. When explanations in terms of clearer and more obviously instrumental variables seem inadequate, we fall back on style as a residual explanation.

The third and final cluster of explanatory variables is organizational, tapping dynamics within the White House Office. The potential importance of such factors stems from the expectation that structures designed at one point in time will affect later organizational patterns. When organizing their staffs, for example, new presidents may model them after those of predecessors of the same party, a response that might be termed "partisan learning." Kennedy, for example, sought assistance from Truman staffers Clark Clifford and Richard Neustadt. More recently, the Eisenhower White House served as a model for Richard Nixon and George Bush. Presidents also may jettison approaches used by their immediate predecessors, thereby underscoring the change in administrations and, in some cases, a change in presidential parties. Thus, John Kennedy promptly dismantled Eisenhower's complex structures for formulating and implementing national security policy.

On other occasions, structures become institutionalized, persisting across administrations, even those of different parties. By the end of the Johnson administration, most of the activities that one now associates with the White House staff—domestic policy advising, handling presidential press relations, maintaining relationships with varying constituencies—were in place to stay. To an extent, institutionalization is simply a kind of "nonpartisan learning" that reflects an understanding of successful experience on the part of the preceding administration, regardless of party. But institutionalization also can occur because of environmental forces. Over time, significant actors come to expect particular tasks to be performed and certain structures to be in place. Presidents tend to challenge such precedents cautiously, typically pursuing only incremental change.[23]

Other sorts of dynamics are inherent to complex organizations. The White House Office, like most organizations confronting mounting numbers of increasingly complex demands, has responded with increased differentiation, developing structures to handle particular tasks such as formulating domestic policy and monitoring executive branch activities. As mentioned earlier, increased differentiation itself can produce a self-sustaining differentiation dynamic. Thus, the emergence of a chief of staff, a chief of staff's office, and the staff secretariat can be viewed as responses to growing needs within an expanding White House for coordination and guidance.

Organizational change is rarely this neat, of course. New structures designed to enhance the pursuit of some goals may trigger resistance from those focusing on other objectives or working to protect existing relationships and responsibilities. These new structures, then, may set off struggles over both policy direction and organizational turf. The result may be the emergence of additional structures to resolve conflict, persistent turf battles, or even the disappearance of the new structures. During the Eisenhower years, for example, a fledgling communications structure first emerged, as the administration experimented with ways of influencing public support for the president and his policies that went beyond the day-to-day work of the press secretary. Press

Secretary James Hagerty worked hard—and ultimately succeeded—at under-cutting these efforts, which he saw as a direct threat to his operations.[24]

In addition, the nature of an existing structure may affect perceptions of both the environment and the activities in the White House itself (once more making structure an independent as well as a dependent variable). Hierarchical structuring, for example, may operate to screen out conflict and uncertainty. Similarly, collegial-consensual structures may encourage participants to focus on external threats while papering over internal disagreements and uncertainties (as, for example, discussions of the dangers of "groupthink" would suggest).[25]

In sum, three clusters of factors—environmental, presidential choice, and organizational—are likely to be important in explaining White House staff structuring over time. Such a diversity of potentially relevant factors threatens to bury one in possible explanations. One might hypothesize, however, that certain types of variables will be more relevant in explaining structuring for particular kinds of responsibilities. Environmental variables are likely to be most helpful in examining the structuring of outreach tasks, as presidents try to respond to and shape the demands of key external actors. Policy and especially coordination and supervision responsibilities may be easier to buffer from the environment, suggesting that organizational factors may well be more significant to an understanding of their structures. Presidential choice variables probably both influence the effects of and are themselves affected by environmental and organizational factors.

COPING WITH UNCERTAINTY AND CONTROVERSY

Clearly, all three clusters of explanatory variables can significantly affect the perceived levels of uncertainty and controversy in the decision settings confronted by the White House.[26] Uncertainty and controversy constitute intervening variables, mediating the relationship between the explanatory variables—environment, presidential choice, and organization—and the dependent variables—the emergence, stability, nature, and differentiation of governance structures. Coping with prevailing uncertainty and controversy, of course, is at the center of our understanding of White House politics. Paying attention to the sorts of structures that emerge and persist in these circumstances is critical to understanding presidential staffing. Moreover, since our analysis seeks to move—albeit tentatively—from the explanation to the evaluation of White House staff structuring, it also seems important to suggest the types of structures that might be most congruent with particular decision settings.

Yet, as the introduction contended, insufficient emphasis has been given to exploring the implications of such a problem-contingency approach to

White House staffing. In earlier work, we sketched the outlines of a framework that relies on problem-contingency logic to generate predictions of and prescriptions for organizational structuring.[27] This framework—called the governance model—directs attention to the decision settings that organizations (or their subunits) confront as they strive to set goals and priorities and to determine means for pursuing them. Such settings can be distinguished by the extent of certainty (or consensus), uncertainty, or controversy over ends (goals) and means for achieving those ends (technologies). As the terms are used here, "*[c]ontroversy* implies that two or more actors are to some extent 'certain' of their positions, but have differing views. . . . *[U]ncertainty* refers to circumstances in which participants are genuinely in doubt."[28] During the Truman and Kennedy administrations, for example, senior staffers waged pitched battles over domestic policy goals and priorities; in contrast, especially toward the end of Roosevelt's and Johnson's terms in office, domestic policy goals were more uncertain and diffuse. Similarly, White House staffers may disagree over or be uncertain about ways of achieving various ends. This often happened, for instance, in pre–press conference sessions in the Eisenhower White House, as staff aides discussed possible ways for the president to respond to anticipated questions.

Decision Setting and the Emergence and Stability of Particular Structural Forms

Prevailing levels of uncertainty and controversy can be expected to affect each of the dependent variables identified earlier. The governance model uses characteristics of the decision setting—the extent of goal uncertainty, controversy, or consensus and of technical uncertainty, controversy, or certainty—as the basis for advancing empirical contentions about White House structuring as well as some tentative normative analysis. Empirically, the model hypothesizes that in many cases the structures that emerge will be roughly congruent with the prevailing decision setting.[29] Moreover, the model suggests that as congruence between structural type and decision setting increases, structural stability will increase, since congruent structures will best meet organizational needs. When congruent structures do not emerge or persist, one has the basis for invoking more normative concerns and assessing the structuring of decision making in particular cases.[30] Normatively, the model proposes that, given a particular decision setting, the most congruent structural response will generally be the most preferable.[31] Table 2 contains predictions and prescriptions that link decision settings and the governance structures introduced in Table 1.

We derive our expectations of when particular governance structures will be more congruent with their decision settings from the following premises:

Table 2. Decision Settings and Congruent Structures

Beliefs about causation (technologies)	Preferred Outcomes (Goals)		
	Uncertainty	Consensus	Controversy
Uncertainty	1. Inspiration/market: "transforming" leadership or structure allowing decisions to emerge	2. Collegial-consensual: consensus seeking, collaboration	3. Collegial-competitive/collegial-mediative: representation of experts and stakeholders; formal decision rules
Certainty	4. Collegial-consensual: brainstorming techniques (Delphi, Nominal Group)	5. Hierarchical: programmed decision authority	6. Collegial-competitive/collegial-mediative: stakeholder representation; formal decision rules
Controversy	7. Adversarial: multiparty advocacy with judgment by disinterested party; some concern for stakeholder or expert representation	8. Adjudicative: formal rules of argumentation and decision, with judgment by disinterested party	9. Indeterminate: structure must be perceived as legitimate; either hierarchy or structure facilitating representation is likely

1. When an organization must cope with uncertainty, it will (should) search extensively for alternative sources of information and diverse judgments.
2. When an organization must cope with controversy, it will (should) seek to discover and bring together representatives of contending parties and viewpoints.
3. When an organization faces certainty, its central problems are those of control; thus, the hierarchical structures suggested by classical organization theory are most likely and most congruent with the decision setting.

Two initial points should be made about this framework. First, structures become more congruent as they incorporate relevant information and expertise into deliberation or decision making, enhance the ability to achieve decision closure or to take action, increase representation of relevant interests, and heighten accountability to the president. Structuring that takes such values into account may well generate legitimacy for the operation or action being affected as well as for the organization as a whole, which in turn may enhance stability.[32] Clearly, these values will often be in tension with one another. For example, making a structure more representative of affected interests may complicate efforts to reach decision closure. Balancing such values may itself be a significant source of controversy and uncertainty in organizations and a catalyst for additional structural development (for instance, the emergence of appeals structures). Moreover, which value is most important may depend in part on the task at hand. Structuring for White House outreach activities, for instance, may need to pay particular attention to the importance of preserving presidential accountability where centrifugal forces are likely to be intense. In contrast, aides with substantive policy responsibilities may be well-advised to turn to structures that encourage consideration of a wide range of information and points of view as a way of decreasing the risks of presidential isolation and miscalculation.

Second, as these comments indicate, this view of structuring focuses on *process,* not outcome. Clearly, results (a widely approved decision, effective coordination of executive branch activities) will be the ultimate bottom line for most observers. Yet, especially under conditions of uncertainty or controversy, desirable results may be difficult to specify. Moreover, structures themselves rarely if ever guarantee particular results. They can, however, affect the probability of achieving more or less desirable outcomes. Had there been mechanisms in place to encourage more searching and critical review of the CIA's plans to overthrow Fidel Castro in 1961, for example, President Kennedy might not have ordered the ill-fated Bay of Pigs invasion—a lesson he learned well and clearly applied in the subsequent Cuban missile crisis.

We briefly discuss the predictions and prescriptions contained in each cell of Table 2.[33] It should be noted that characterizations of the decision setting need not hold for the White House Office as a whole. Like any complex organization, it probably faces settings of each type virtually all the time—which is why its governance structures ought to be and, as we will see, typically are multiple and diverse.

Cell 1: Inspiration and Market Structures. Presidents and their aides often confront situations in which neither orienting values nor the means for achieving them are clear. One possible response is what organization theorist James Thompson called "inspiration"—individual or group processes for choosing purposes and exploring ways of meeting them.[34] Indeed, one interpretation of presidential leadership is the capacity to act when there are no firm answers. Such "transforming leadership"[35] may promote goal redefinition and move the problem out of cell 1 altogether.

In the absence of such activity, the White House may elect to drift in certain areas. For example, as presidents and staffs focus on other priorities, they may turn to more decentralized market structures in certain problem areas. Such mechanisms allow decisions to "emerge," with the president receiving scant blame or credit.

Cells 2 and 4: Collegial-Consensual Structures. Collegial-consensual structures encourage joint efforts by "experts" to search for means of achieving agreed-upon goals (cell 2) or for ways of better defining goals and priorities (cell 4). Such structures permit the free exchange of ideas and have decision rules and norms that stress collaboration and the forging of consensus.

Cells 3 and 6: Collegial-Competitive or Collegial-Mediative Structures. When there is conflict over goals, the governance model counsels reliance on structures that permit the airing of diverse points of view. At the same time, there must be ways to reach closure if no consensus emerges— voting rules in collegial-competitive structures, the presence of a mediator in collegial-mediative arrangements.

Cell 5: Hierarchical Structures. In contrast, when there is agreement on ends and means are certain, the control aspects of governance rise to the fore. Activities can be fully routinized, and hierarchy becomes more congruent and may be expected to emerge.

Cell 7: Adversarial Structures. Such structures permit conflict over means to be explored by the relevant "experts," without allowing any of those experts to capture the decision process. Because goals are also uncertain in cell 7 decision settings, the final decision on means is left to another party, presumably one who can make authoritative statements about both goals and acceptable relationships between means and ends.

Cell 8: Adjudicative Structures. Unlike adversarial structures, adjudicative structures are proposed for decision settings where there is goal consensus. These agreed-upon goals determine the "burden of proof" used by a third party (in the White House, typically the president or the chief of staff) to judge the validity of disputants' arguments.

Cell 9: Indeterminate. When conflict erupts over both ends and means, efforts at negotiation or compromise may prove unworkable. No particular structure seems particularly likely to be most congruent with this decision setting. Perhaps the only irreducible requirement is that the way in which such problems are handled be seen as legitimate by the key players, by others in the White House, and, ultimately, by those to whom the president is accountable—the voters and their elected representatives.

Influences on Differentiation

Finally, organizational decision settings can influence the extent of structural differentiation. Previous work on White House governance predicts that differentiation will increase as environmentally induced uncertainty and controversy increase.[36] Under such conditions, White Houses often experiment with new structures to address the heightened challenges from the environment, to attempt to buffer existing structures and practices from external volatility, and to cope with any disruption generated by changes in activities and priorities.

Furthermore, over the course of a president's term in office, unresolved problems typically mount in number, goals and strategies for pursuing them frequently are called into question and must be reexamined, and conflicts both within the White House Office and between the White House and external actors may rise. Often, demands for improving the coordination of existing decision processes are also made. Additional structures for responding to such pressures might be expected to emerge, and the degree of differentiation to increase.[37] Moreover, to the extent presidents are reluctant to completely dismantle their predecessors' governance arrangements (fearing, among other reactions, external objections), one would anticipate that differentiation would increase across presidential administrations.[38]

CONCLUSIONS

The varying decision settings confronted by modern presidencies may well point to the need for diverse structural responses. The chapters that follow describe and try to account for the emergence, stability, nature, and extent of differentiation of governance structures in White Houses from Hoover's through Johnson's, comparing the findings to the ones the governance model predicts and prescribes. Such comparison, in turn, lays the foundation for evaluating White House staffing.

Quite clearly, the analysis rests on a critical assumption: that the organization of the presidency matters. As in so many instances, Dwight Eisenhower succinctly expressed what seems to us to be the critical insight about the importance of organization: "Organization cannot make a genius out of an incompetent. On the other hand, disorganization can scarcely fail to result in inefficiency"[39] and, we would add, ineffectiveness and lack of accountability.

PART I
Outreach

2
Congressional Liaison

Presidential skill in dealing with Congress one of the most important targets of presidential outreach—is a sine qua non of a successful presidency. During the early modern era, White House structures emerged to abet presidential efforts at legislative leadership.

In this chapter, we encounter perhaps the most striking example of White House structures that became institutionalized. Even so, little structuring for congressional liaison emerged until the Truman administration, and structures stabilized only after both experimentation and considerable presidential agonizing over potentially conflicting White House goals. For the most part, the relevant governance structures were hierarchical and collegial in nature. Although most of these structures were congruent with the decision settings they confronted, their presence did not spell the end of jockeying within the White House for influence over legislative outreach.

Presidential objectives, in the form of Herbert Hoover's relatively ambitious policy agenda, first propelled congressional liaison into the White House, but an increasingly demanding environment soon made its presence there virtually mandatory. Franklin Roosevelt and Harry Truman nonetheless resisted locating such structures in the White House proper, fearing that they would likely infect the presidency with congressional goals.

During this same period, however, Congress members' expectations of presidents underwent significant change. Congress increasingly looked to the presidency for leadership, first during the depression and then through World War II. That such presidential guidance would require staff channels linking the White House and Capitol Hill was underscored by FDR's preoccupation with national security during the last several years of his term and his virtual replacement in domestic affairs by presidential aides such as Samuel Rosenman. Easing acceptance, too, may have been the substantial legislative liaison efforts undertaken by the War Department during World War II, which other executive branch agencies began to imitate in the late 1940s.[1]

Finally, in Truman's second term, the outlines of White House structuring began to emerge. Eisenhower, with his preference for formal structuring, built on Truman's beginnings and placed legislative outreach in the Office of Congressional Relations (OCR). Several structures for legislative liaison emerged during the Eisenhower years. Hierarchical, collegial-consensual, and collegial-competitive in nature, these structures were generally congruent with the prevailing decision settings. Since the demands and expectations of the political environment in which congressional liaison was embedded were relatively stable, the structures likewise exhibited great stability.

Such structures were not set in stone, however. Considerable differentiation occurred within OCR as well as in its ties with others in the White House and in the larger executive branch. Environmental influences also shaped the internal structuring of the legislative relations unit. To a significant extent, OCR's organization mirrored the institution with which it dealt. In the Eisenhower, Kennedy, and Johnson administrations, liaison staffers specialized in interacting with senators or House members. During the Kennedy and Johnson years, staff assignments further reflected the divisions and power distribution among House Democrats, with different aides emphasizing members from different parts of the country. The power of the southern Democrats and their general resistance to presidential objectives made them particular targets of attention. More generally, the concentration of power in committee chairs in the "unreformed" Congresses of the 1950s and 1960s, as well as senators' pretensions of being members of the "upper house," also had implications for the division of labor and allocation of authority within OCR: not only did congressional "whales" receive considerable attention, but they also tended to be ministered to by senior White House staffers. Thus, the internal OCR hierarchy that appeared in all three White Houses arguably was congruent with the task of dealing with members of a still hierarchical Congress.

Hierarchy also was congruent with decision settings in which OCR was less permeable to external influences, where its activities could be more easily programmed. Handling congressional correspondence and keeping records of votes and favors, for example, could be assigned to a particular staffer or subunit and largely routinized.

At the same time, the work of staffers who dealt with legislators could not be fully anticipated. Events often moved too quickly, members too frequently changed their minds, and the development of suitable responses evoked too much uncertainty for rules to determine all activities or for any one person to dictate tasks. OCR's internal hierarchy typically was supplemented by more congruent collegial-consensual structures that permitted not only information sharing among liaison aides but also exploration of possible strategies for advancing bills and maintaining cordial relations with key legislators.

Meanwhile, OCR staffers sought to bring legislative liaison operations elsewhere in the executive branch under White House control. From the White House perspective, hierarchical structuring of these relations was congruent, since presidential goals and strategies were assumed to dominate. Yet agency officials did not always agree, and a White House–dominated hierarchy sometimes failed to fully respond to uncertainty and controversy over priorities and strategies.

Organizational factors are also important for understanding structuring for congressional outreach. Presidential aides perform two kinds of activities relevant to legislative liaison.[2] Staffers with *policy* responsibilities (whose work is probed more fully in Part II) frequently were involved in efforts to pass (or block) legislation and offered presidents substantive policy advice on matters pending before and passed by Congress.[3] At the same time, White House aides engaged in more *representational* activities—for example, serving as information channels between members of Congress and the president, providing favors to or withholding them from members, and gathering intelligence on events and players on Capitol Hill.[4]

No matter how it was organized, the increase in size and differentiation within OCR did not mean that liaison staffers monopolized all White House staff dealings with Congress. Nor were liaison aides excluded from other activities. As we shall see, the extent to which structures or staffers specialized in policy or representational activities varied within and between administrations, and the lack of full specialization generated coordination problems and frequently ignited raging turf battles in the White House.

That full specialization of legislative liaison was never achieved probably reflects several factors. Again, environmental influences were part of the story. Members of Congress did not always respect the boundaries between subdivisions in the White House Office; they sought to deal with White House staffers with whom they had had previous contact or who had reputations for helpfulness or influence with the president.

More important were the organizational dynamics. The policy process itself is difficult to carve up into distinct stages such as formulation, adoption, and implementation, each to be handled by separate White House structures. White House staffers responsible for developing policies and drafting legislation tended to monitor the progress of and lobby for the bills they had worked on. Similarly, OCR aides often participated in executive branch discussions of possible proposals, giving their assessments of the bills' likely chances in Congress.

Not surprisingly, the goals of these policy and liaison staffers were not always compatible. Success for the former tended to be defined in terms of securing the passage of legislation as it was proposed and of assuring that any bills passed in Congress would advance important substantive objectives. Liaison aides, in contrast, had more of a "batting average" notion of success: they concentrated on getting legislation passed even with significant changes in content or clearly inadequate provisions for implementation.[5] The OCR staff was also concerned with establishing and maintaining cordial relations with members of Congress; at the very least, liaison aides sought to avoid major conflict. These divergent goals often produced sharp disagreement about reasonable strategies (or "technologies") for achieving them. Together, overlapping responsibilities and sometimes inconsistent objectives and strategies set the stage for often fierce turf struggles among White House units with some involvement in congressional relations. These battles, in turn, were the result of an ongoing White House differentiation dynamic and produced demands for additional governance structures.

It was at this point that presidential choice variables again appeared. Presidents experimented with a variety of mechanisms to address the uncertainty and conflict that often characterized congressional relations. Only rarely did they have the time, expertise, or interest to arbitrate among staffers who disagreed over legislative aims and strategies. Alternatively, presidents created collegial-consensual structures that brought together individuals representing varying interests to develop strategies for achieving important legislative objectives. Such structuring was largely congruent with decision settings characterized by agreed-upon goals but some uncertainty over the means of achieving them, though it hardly guaranteed presidential success. On still other occasions, presidents formed special units to formulate and work on the passage of particular proposals. These kinds of structures, however, frequently created additional problems, since they both competed and had to coordinate with existing policy and liaison staff.

For the most part, the nature of staff congressional relations activity depended on OCR's position in the overall White House staff hierarchy, which to a significant extent reflected presidential objectives and approaches to managing the White House. In the early modern period, legislative liaison tended over time to become more specialized, and OCR exercised greater control over White House–congressional relations as the unit and its senior staffers were drawn closer to the president in the White House hierarchy. As access to the president became more direct and as liaison aides received greater authority to speak for the president (as was true, for example, under Kennedy), OCR grew in influence both inside and outside the White House. The Johnson experience, however, suggests that too much direct presidential participation in congressional relations, unmediated by OCR, could undercut the liaison operation by obscuring its purpose and devaluing its activities—thus dramatically reducing its influence both in the White House and on Capitol Hill. Even more important, reliance on the White House hierarchy for determining who did what in legislative relations frequently was not congruent with decision settings shot through with uncertainty and controversy over both goals and means.

Under such circumstances, as Chapter 1 suggested, the differentiation dynamic often produces structures for coordination and conflict resolution. In the case of congressional liaison, however, this did not always occur. Instead, a pattern of continuing conflict and ad hoc adjustment ensued.

HOOVER THROUGH TRUMAN: KEEPING A LOW PROFILE

When Hoover named the first plural professional staff, complaints abounded. If there was general suspicion regarding presidential aides who were too powerful, the notion of those staffers lobbying Congress produced particular hostility. Indeed, presidents themselves had to be cautious about trying to exercise too much influence over Congress, whose members stubbornly insisted on the institution's independence and its (at least) coequal status with the president. Even though White House staffers worked with Congress during the Hoover through Truman administrations, little structuring for legislative relations emerged.

Hoover: Operating Behind the Scenes

Formally, the task of handling Congress on the Hoover staff was given to White House aide Walter Newton. Considerably more important in actuality, however, were the covert activities of an unofficial staffer, James MacLafferty.

Newton left the House of Representatives (where he had represented a district in Minnesota) to join Hoover's staff, hoping ultimately to position himself to run for a U.S. Senate seat or to land a judgeship.[6] The president evidently recruited Newton because Hoover "felt the need for better contacts with the House leadership."[7] Much of what Newton did in dealing with Congress was representational; he collected political intelligence and reported back to Hoover rather than seeking to persuade members to support the president's legislation.[8] Newton, though, was not considered particularly effective, never being "quite in the hurly-burly of things."[9]

Press Secretary George Akerson noted that Newton had an especially difficult job, given Hoover's distaste for logrolling and discomfort when dealing with members of Congress.[10] Arguably even more important, however, were environmental factors. Many members of Congress still preferred a more passive presidential approach to legislation.[11] Through much of his term, Hoover confronted significant opposition from members of Congress from his own party, especially from Old Guard Republicans.

The illegitimacy of active presidential leadership in Congress also explains the shroud of utter secrecy under which Hoover's more active (but still little known) legislative liaison, James MacLafferty, worked. A businessman and former House member from California, MacLafferty had been a Hoover assistant at the Commerce Department and an active campaigner in the 1928 presidential campaign. In mid-1930, he became virtually a full-time, unpaid White House staffer.

MacLafferty assiduously hid his frequent contacts with the president: he "knew more back doors than anyone in Washington."[12] MacLafferty confided to his diary that such secrecy was important for maintaining his influence and credibility with his former colleagues in Congress (where, as an ex-member, he had open access to the cloakrooms, floors of the House and Senate, and member dining rooms).

Although MacLafferty also was a key link between the White House and the Republican National Committee, many of his activities anticipated those of later congressional liaison units. Much of MacLafferty's work involved serving as a covert intelligence channel between Hoover and Capitol Hill Republicans. MacLafferty sought as well to influence the strategies and bolster the morale of Republican members of Congress. At Hoover's request, for example, MacLafferty sought to organize Republican members who would actively and vocally express support for the president.[13] Several times he recorded in his diary that he had spent a day at the Capitol "bracing up Congressmen, Republicans, who seem to take it for granted that we are to be defeated next year."[14]

Although most of MacLafferty's activities are best described as representational, on occasion he engaged in policy-related efforts. For example, he sought to help block a veterans' pension bill pending in June 1930 and met with Hoover to determine which pieces of pending legislation he should try to stop in committees.[15] Other times, MacLafferty attempted to influence legislation to keep it in line with administration policy.[16]

Roosevelt: Entering the Fray

White House–congressional relations became far more central during the Roosevelt years. A rough division of labor for dealing with Congress emerged during FDR's presidency that has persisted in one form or another ever since. Policy advisers helped push key legislation, and more representational activities typically were performed by staffers with fewer responsibilities for substantive policy. Even so, there were no "congressional relations specialists" on the staff. And despite the fact that both Roosevelt and members of Congress considered presidential leadership to be more legitimate, aides who became too visible in their dealings with Congress did so at their own risk.

Those who were formally lodged elsewhere in the executive branch frequently acted as de facto White House aides as they proposed new programs, helped draft legislation, and sought to get it passed in Congress. During the first New Deal, for instance, Rexford Tugwell dealt with a range of agricultural policy issues as well as with unemployment insurance and the revision of the Pure Food and Drug Act.[17] During the second New Deal, aides such as Tommy Corcoran and Ben Cohen rose to the fore, drafting and lobbying for the 1935 Holding Company and Social Security Acts. Later on, Harry Hopkins and especially Samuel Rosenman followed pending legislation and advised the president on it.[18]

At some point, most of these men faced considerable environmental hostility, and critics blasted their "victimization" of the president in their advocacy in Congress. Tugwell, for example, became a ready target for conservative opponents of New Deal legislation, who directed their attacks at a too powerful and manipulative adviser: "Rex the Red" was embarked on a relentless quest to "sovietize America."[19]

Throughout the Roosevelt administration, White House staffers also engaged in a range of representational activities.[20] On occasion, they worked together to push particular presidential initiatives through Congress. A good example is the notorious "court packing" legislation proposed in 1937, which also illustrated the dangers of White House violations of prevailing congressional norms. The president assigned his son to coordinate strategic planning. James Roosevelt established what amounted to a collegial-consensual structure to develop legislative strategy for this highly charged bill. The committee of executive branch and party officials met daily at the White House,[21] but most of the intense interaction in planning the legislative campaign took place among James Roosevelt, Corcoran, and unofficial White House staffer Charles West.[22] Yet, for all this coordinative effort, no enduring structure emerged.

Meanwhile, Corcoran and Cohen were publicly identified as the "authors and successful vendors" of the court packing plan,[23] despite their actual exclusion from the drafting of the bill. Vilified as "Bolsheviks and headless Rasputins," they withdrew from the public eye—until the final onslaught triggered by Corcoran's alleged orchestration of the "purge" of Democratic members of Congress during the 1938 campaign.

Although James Roosevelt was the target of somewhat less public brutalization, he too endured considerable criticism for his role in the court packing fiasco. His dealings with Congress declined precipitously, and he became less visible after the defeat. In his fervor to get the bill passed, the younger Roosevelt had "made promises that seemed to have special authenticity but in fact did not . . . [and] Congressional friction and bitterness increased."[24] On the whole, the outcomes experienced by Cohen, Corcoran, and James Roosevelt could only have reinforced FDR's reluctance to formally ensconce congressional liaison responsibilities in the White House.

Nonetheless, legislative outreach stepped up following the appointment of six administrative assistants in 1939,[25] and later as FDR devoted more attention to the conduct of the war. At the same time, congressional expectations of White House attention were mounting, and by 1941, FDR was receiving reports of ongoing problems with legislative outreach. Administrative Assistant James Rowe wrote to the president, for example, that he

> hear[d] time and time again that no one in the White House will listen. . . . The 203–202 Selective Service vote can be explained in a number of ways. But one interesting point is that I counted at least 10 men who never vote against the Administration. Casual and discreet inquiry indicates there is some minor irritation in practically every case.[26]

Rowe recommended that Marvin McIntyre, who wished to return to the White House after a long illness, be given the job of staying in touch with members of Congress. FDR agreed, asking McIntyre to "create a medium for [members] to register their complaints."[27] But Roosevelt refused to call McIntyre the "liaison man with the Hill." "I do not want to see you 'murdered' as some of our friends have been in the past."[28] Meanwhile, other aides continued to deal with members of Congress.

Unlike his predecessors, Roosevelt "brought legislative lobbying out into the open."[29] At the same time, he clearly resisted the title of "congressional liaison" for any of his aides, the creation of structures for coordinating staff activities, and the notion that anyone other than the president should authoritatively deal with legislators.

Although presidential objectives and strategies were clearly relevant here, they operated within marked environmental constraints. Roosevelt appreciated the limits that prevailing congressional and public norms placed on staff liaison. First, FDR was well aware of congressional resistance to dealing with such aides and of the congressional resentment and public pillorying that staffers such as Tugwell, Corcoran, and Hopkins had confronted. Second, the president correctly anticipated that the presence of a permanent legislative liaison staff in the White House would lead members of Congress to come to those aides for service rather than going to the appropriate executive branch agencies.[30] Finally, Roosevelt believed in what James Rowe dubbed the "obsolescence theory."[31] On the one hand, the president feared that "as soon as his staff began to deal with congressional requests and complaints, they would be working for members of Congress as well as for him."[32] On the other hand, FDR knew that if staffers refused to grant such requests, they would rapidly lose credibility among members.[33] More than anything, this sensitivity to conflicting goals and political pressures led Roosevelt to veto formal structuring for congressional outreach.

Truman: Edging Toward Specialization

The initial signs of a distinct liaison operation appeared in the Truman White House, although the president steadfastly resisted any efforts that members of Congress might have perceived as "arm twisting."[34] Still, when legislators demanded additional White House attention, there was some effort to respond. Most of the president's senior professional staff were involved to some degree in dealing with Congress, and unlike most Roosevelt aides, they typically performed both policy and representational tasks. In addition, specialized staff capacity for performing routine representational activities emerged toward the end of the administration.

Who became involved in legislative liaison, and when, "depended on the subject."[35] Although John Steelman and his aides were formally assigned to handle "operational" issues (see Chapter 5), they frequently interacted with members of Congress. Most of Steelman's activity was representational in nature. He saw himself as a virtual caseworker for individual members of Congress concerned about public works and federal grants for their districts.[36]

Other Steelman aides focused on matters relevant to their substantive policy specialties. For example, Harold Enarson, Milton Kayle, and David Stowe were involved with a range of economic and labor issues.[37] In addition, staffers with more narrowly focused responsibilities dealt with Congress when their particular assignments called for it. Within Averell Harriman's special foreign policy staff (see Chapter 8), for instance, Theodore Tannenwald spent considerable time on legislative relations.

Most of the Congress-related activity, however, was centered in the special counsel's office, as it had been by the end of the Roosevelt administration. Samuel Rosenman continued his dealings with Congress until he resigned in early 1946. Clark Clifford, who took over as special counsel, worked closely with the legislative leaders in the House and Senate.[38] When the Marshall Plan was being considered in Congress, for example, Clifford served as an intermediary between the president and Robert Lovett at the State Department as they developed a strategy for getting the legislation passed.[39]

It was Charles Murphy, however, both as a Clifford assistant and later as special counsel, who devoted the most systematic attention to White House interaction with Congress. Murphy recalled being stunned to discover on arriving at the White House that there was no structure in place for tracking pending legislation on a daily basis, leading him to initiate such monitoring as well as to systematically follow the fate of Truman's bills.[40] Murphy regularly discussed such intelligence with the president, who in turn encouraged executive branch departments and agencies to share intelligence with the White House. Murphy did more than report on pending legislation; he also included his own political and policy analyses, focusing on domestic policy.[41] In addition, Murphy on occasion offered Truman advice for lobbying particular members of Congress and for meeting with legislative leaders, and he briefed the president before some of these sessions.[42]

It should be understood, however, that Murphy saw his role as being quite circumscribed, restricted to behind-the-scenes reporting and advising. Murphy himself did no lobbying. Rather, the president did considerable personal lobbying for particular bills.[43] Also, the Bureau of the Budget (BOB) maintained its own liaison with members of Congress as well as contacts on both Murphy's and Steelman's staffs.[44]

In addition, the other aides in the counsel's office were heavily involved in legislative liaison activities. Stephen Spingarn, for example, was brought to the unit from the Treasury Department in 1948, in large part because of his expertise in legislative drafting and congressional relations.[45]

In matters involving congressional relations, the special counsel's office operated mostly as a hierarchy, much as later legislative liaison units would. This was especially true under Murphy, who both directed most of the unit's activities and received reports from its other staffers. Clifford had headed a much smaller staff; formally, his only assistant was George Elsey, even though Murphy and others frequently worked for him and reported to him. Clifford, too, had tended to act on his own agenda. In contrast, ties among staffers were stronger and closer under Murphy. There also was evidence of differentiation. Murphy (as his successors would) supplemented the internal hierarchy with more collegial-consensual structuring. Material was widely shared within the office, and staffers frequently discussed priorities and activities.

The special counsel's office under Murphy was the focal point for legislative activity elsewhere in the White House. For the most part, this meant that the unit assumed the top position in the staff hierarchy when White House–congressional relations were involved. Tannenwald, for instance, kept Murphy informed about his activities and funneled his recommendations for the president through Murphy.[46] Other times, more collegial structures linked White House units. Junior staffers in both Steelman's and Murphy's offices, for example, sometimes collaborated on formulating legislative strategy and then reported the results to their respective bosses.[47]

For all the activity in the counsel's office, however, perhaps the clearest formal predecessor to what we now recognize as the White House congressional liaison unit appeared under Appointments Secretary Matthew Connelly. Throughout the Truman years, Connelly was the White House contact point for individual members of Congress with specific requests and complaints.[48] In mid-1949, with the president's approval, he hired Charles Maylon and Joseph Feeney to help with this increasingly demanding task.

Sander probably best summarized these aides' tasks as legislative "handholding."[49] Feeney, the Senate liaison, and Maylon, the House contact, were "largely leg men"[50] who worked with "individual members of Congress on individual problems"[51]—typically involving patronage or pork. "Messengers rather than responsible political agents," they could neither "commit the President [n]or . . . speak authoritatively for him."[52]

Congressional dissatisfaction with White House liaison persisted. The expectations of presidential leadership generated during the Roosevelt years also produced general legislative acceptance of and significant demands for interaction with White House aides who could serve as emissaries to the president. Recalled Hechler: "There was a thirst for new ideas, a desire to check developments with knowledgeable people in the White House, and a reluctance to disturb the President to test emerging strategies."[53] Senior staffers such as Connelly and Murphy were too overloaded to perform these tasks, and Feeney and Maylon had neither the status nor the experience to fill the gaps.[54]

Finally, in 1951, John Carroll—a Colorado House member who had lost his bid for a Senate seat in 1950—was hired. Initially, at Murphy's behest, Carroll worked on the congressional hearing investigating Gen. Douglas MacArthur's dismissal. Then Truman asked Carroll to handle a range of economic policy issues. Although Carroll left in early 1952 to attempt a political comeback, Hechler credits him with giving the congressional relations operation "a more realistic and more effective issue-oriented direction."[55]

In sum, by the end of the Truman years, the rudiments of what would become the dominant patterns of relations between the White House staff and Congress were established. Presidential aides performed both policy and representational tasks, with some specialization and structural differentiation. Surfacing, too, was the potential difficulty of linking governance structures. Members of Congress, meanwhile, clearly had come to expect some staff involvement in presidential-legislative relations and to demand staff channels into the White House.

EISENHOWER THROUGH JOHNSON: CONGRESSIONAL RELATIONS COME OUT OF THE CLOSET

Reflecting this altered environment, the Eisenhower administration ceased treating White House dealings with Congress members as a "closet operation"[56] and created a separate legislative liaison unit. This operation—which we refer to as the Office of Congressional Relations (OCR)—has appeared in White Houses ever since.

Moreover, by the end of the Eisenhower administration, several continuing themes concerning the White House staff's participation in congressional relations could be identified. First, structuring for congressional outreach emerged and differentiation began. Second, specialization was incomplete, and ambiguities about who directed and who participated in legislative relations pointed to the potential for turf battles among the players. Third, the prospect for such struggles was sharpened by the recognition that OCR and other staffers often had varying, not fully consistent interests and objectives. This pointed, fourth, to an incomplete differentiation dynamic in the White House: as tasks became more specialized and the structures for handling them multiplied, the need arose for additional governance mechanisms both to coordinate the activities of these diverse structures and to quell conflict among them. Underscored, finally, was the impact of OCR's position in the overall White House hierarchy on the dynamics of these conflicts.

Eisenhower: The Emergence of OCR

For most of his administration, Eisenhower's OCR was headed by the second in command in the White House. Yet substantive policy staffers and other senior aides remained involved in congressional relations. Although top OCR staffers also participated in policy discussions, much of the unit's work revolved around routine representational activities such as tracking legislation, counting votes, and keeping in touch with key members of Congress.

The liaison office was designed to provide the White House with "early warning" about problems in its dealings with Congress.[57] Eisenhower and his senior aides assembled a team that had considerable experience dealing with Congress.[58] Both of OCR's heads—first Wilton Persons and then Bryce Harlow—had worked in the War Department's legislative liaison operation during World War II. Persons had gone on to perform similar tasks for Eisenhower at NATO, and Harlow had served as a staffer on the House Armed Services Committee. Virtually all the other members of the liaison unit had legislative experience as well.[59]

According to Harlow, the OCR had several objectives, ranging from

> sell[ing] the President's program [and] . . . keep[ing] the Congress from doing something different [to the] care and feeding of members, plus also the blunting, thwarting, discouraging harmful congressional activities—spiteful investigations, spiteful speeches, spiteful actions, excessive partisanship.[60]

Pursuing these goals involved liaison staffers in a variety of activities. For example, they provided Eisenhower with political intelligence and tactical advice on when and how to deal with particular members of Congress and updated him on the status of legislation.[61] Monitoring the progress of the president's program occupied considerable time. "Each Administration bill [was] listed on a huge chart, and its progress [was] followed in detail. . . . Bills lying dormant or otherwise in trouble [were] marked by red flags."[62]

In addition, OCR staffers joined other White House aides in collegial-competitive structures in which pending legislation and other congressional actions were discussed in more substantive terms. Persons and legislative liaison aides Jack Martin and Gerald Morgan, for instance, were involved in the often heated White House debates about appropriate administration responses to the Army-McCarthy hearings.[63]

OCR aides met frequently with members of Congress or their staffers. Typically, this was to discuss particular bills and proposed amendments or to handle requests for favors. Although, like his predecessors, Harlow "felt the need to remain inconspicuous" and rarely ventured to Capitol Hill, he did stay in frequent touch with members of Congress by phone—sometimes making and receiving more than 125 phone calls a day.[64] On occasion, liaison aides worked directly with party leaders.[65] Harlow, for example, reported to the president on his success at convincing Senate Majority Leader Lyndon Johnson to intercede with Speaker Sam Rayburn in order to get the House to accept the Senate's appropriations for the administration's mutual security program.[66] Toward the end of his administration, Eisenhower encouraged OCR staffer Jack Z. Anderson to try to seek the cooperation of Speaker Rayburn: "tell him that we were desperately in need of assistance and ask him to give us all the help he could."[67]

The liaison staff also performed more routine tasks in dealing with legislators. Much like Murphy's staff, the unit sought to place itself at the top of a hierarchical structure inside the White House. Although OCR on occasion requested other aides to provide lists of members of Congress with whom the staffers were friends and could discuss particular bills, it tried to monitor such contacts and asked staffers either to check with the office first or to report any discussions after they took place.[68] In addition, all letters from members of Congress were supposed to be directed to OCR, which would then pass them on to the appropriate place in the White House or elsewhere in the executive branch; a liaison staffer would draft an acknowledgment letter for the president to send to the legislator. Similarly, all correspondence to members of Congress from White House staffers was to be sent first to OCR. The fact that non-OCR staffers had to be reminded so frequently of these rules (especially on outgoing correspondence) suggests that not everyone in the White House always followed them.[69]

For the first time, the liaison unit oversaw what departmental liaison officers were doing, seeking to bring executive branch officials into a White House–headed hierarchy. Although the White House wanted departments and agencies to push for their own bills in Congress, OCR staffers tried to ensure that such efforts were consistent with administration objectives and stepped in to guide dealings with Congress on certain key issues or when the departments "ran into trouble."[70] In an attempt to improve coordination, White House liaison aides brought their departmental counterparts to the White House for regular Saturday conferences. At these meetings, participants discussed pending legislation and various strategies and tactics, and White House staffers offered advice.[71] Additionally, there was a fair amount of informal interaction between the White House and liaison officers in at least some of the departments.[72]

These efforts produced problems throughout the administration. The State Department, for instance, resisted White House attempts to deal with Congress on trade legislation in 1954 and 1955.[73] A year later, Persons complained about the ineffective strategies being used by department liaison officers in working with members of Congress and asked an aide to " 'brief' those without congressional experience on how to do the job."[74] Persons's dissatisfaction continued, focusing in particular on the Defense Department and BOB.[75] Such White House efforts foundered at least in part because, from the departments' perspective, the problems involved controversies about which they were interested and in which they had expertise, and hierarchical subordination prevented their input.

Although most members of OCR performed most of these tasks at some point, aides differed in authority and primary job responsibilities. Internally, the liaison unit, which contained four or five professional staffers throughout the administration, was organized as a loose three-tiered hierarchy, similar to Murphy's special counsel operation. Persons was the formal head for much of Eisenhower's time in the White House, although Persons also served as deputy chief of staff. When Sherman Adams was forced to resign in September 1958, Persons became chief of staff, and Bryce Harlow took Persons's place. Persons and Harlow directed much of OCR's work; typically they were among the staffers who were involved in substantive policy discussions, accompanied congressional leaders when they came to see the president, and arranged for special meetings between Eisenhower and legislators on major issues or during crises.[76] The two third-tier aides— Homer Gruenther and Earle Chesney, Jr.—performed almost entirely routine work.[77]

More important were the second-tier aides, including Harlow (when Persons headed the office), Gerald Morgan (before he became special counsel in 1955), Jack Martin, Jack Anderson, Fred Seaton, and Edward McCabe. These staffers also accompanied members of Congress who had appointments with Eisenhower, worked to get particular pieces of legislation passed, and on occasion participated in substantive policy discussions. In general, their involvement was dictated by the subject being discussed; when assigned to follow particular pieces of legislation, for example, they would participate in all relevant activities.

Throughout the administration, the second-tier staffers experimented with various ways of dividing up their work, none of which was fully satisfactory. Although there was a short-lived effort at the beginning of Eisenhower's second term to divide liaison work by congressional committees,[78] most of the time staffers were assigned to concentrate on either the House or the Senate. Initially, Harlow recalled, he was responsible for the House and Morgan for the Senate, "although we were really kind of across the board."[79] Later, Anderson and OCR aide Clyde Wheeler also covered the House, and McCabe and Martin mostly handled Senate liaison.[80] McCabe remembered the limitations of the ongoing attempts at a House-Senate division of labor:

We thought we finally got this thing licked . . . were sort of organized and within a month there may have been nothing much going on in the Senate which called for a lot of work, and all hell breaking loose in two or three places in the House. And so everybody pitched in. So, we really were like a fire brigade.[81]

The liaison staff also specialized to an extent by subject, generally reflecting particular aides' past experience and expertise. Harlow, for instance, tended to follow defense issues,[82] and Anderson usually handled agriculture and natural resources issues.[83] Meanwhile, Martin, as Robert Taft's former administrative assistant, dealt only with "the right wing side of the Senate and House."[84] Ultimately, however, neither structural nor substantive specialization could be strictly followed: "you kicked the dog who's closest to biting you."[85]

Despite the clear lines of authority within OCR, the staff worked together. According to Persons, his "office door was always open. . . . [I]t was a very informal sort of a proposition, but we kept each other thoroughly advised of what was going on."[86]

However, OCR by no means monopolized White House relations with Congress. Substantive policy staffers remained active participants in developing strategies for dealing with legislators and in working to get bills passed (or blocked) in Congress. Policy aides also frequently met with the president to discuss bills, to update him on legislative progress, and to brief him before meetings with members of Congress. As in earlier administrations, the involvement of most policy staffers reflected their particular areas of specialization.

In addition, ad hoc units occasionally were formed to formulate particular pieces of legislation and to gain its passage in Congress. Clarence Randall, for example, worked on trade legislation (as Chapter 9 elaborates). Randall's office had its own congressional specialist, Jack Stambaugh, who kept in careful touch with the liaison staff.[87] Randall and his staff also were part of a collegial-competitive structure that included executive branch officials, White House policy aides such as economic policy staffer Gabriel Hauge, and OCR aides to plot legislative strategy and hash out possible compromise positions.[88]

Despite the activity of some non-OCR staffers, actors who had been key participants in legislative relations in earlier administrations became less significant during the Eisenhower years. Although the special counsel's office was active at first, it was never as central as it had been under Truman, and its involvement decreased over the course of the administration. In this period, too, BOB became a less significant player in legislative relations than it had been in the Truman White House. Harlow remembered "incessant" contact and "constant interchange" with BOB, but he had to request that a BOB representative be invited to the legislative leaders' meetings with the president.[89]

During the Eisenhower years, then, the congressional relations structures became important parts of the White House Office. Exactly where OCR fit in the overall White House hierarchy, though, is somewhat less clear. Holtzman has argued that OCR was always subordinate to Adams, who "largely controlled" access to the president.[90] One should not push this observation too far, however. The OCR head and the second-tier staffers met frequently with Eisenhower, as did most of the substantive policy staff. Both Persons and Harlow recalled that they had easy access to the president.[91] And, Greenstein notes, "While Persons did coordinate with Adams to prevent organizational confusion and out of courtesy, he worked for and reported directly to Eisenhower."[92] Moreover, according to Jack Z. Anderson, Adams rarely intervened in the process of developing legislative strategy: "[There was] greater participation by Persons throughout the process; Adams looked more at the final staff package."[93]

Adams's activities, though, cannot be overlooked. He attended all White House meetings with legislative leaders, cleared OCR's agendas for those sessions, on occasion requested that liaison aides gather specific information or respond to particular members' complaints, and met with some members of Congress.[94] Adams also joined in discussions of domestic policy issues in which he had some interest or that generated particular controversy between the White House and Congress.[95] Of course, a good deal of Adams's Congress-relevant activity came at the president's direction.[96]

The Eisenhower years also demonstrated FDR's prescience in resisting congressional relations specialists. Just as Roosevelt feared, questions arose about the loyalty and objectives of liaison staffers—suspicions that are perhaps inevitable for those who regularly deal with external actors.[97] At least some members of the White House staff believed that OCR aides' primary focus on avoiding conflict with members of Congress undermined administration interests. John Bragdon complained that the liaison staff was an "inner circle group"[98] that was "never interested in a *new idea objectively*" and whose concerns drove out consideration of substantive policy goals.[99] Likewise, James Hagerty disagreed sharply with Jack Martin's willingness to compromise on the Bricker Amendment and with Martin's and Persons's objection to the White House taking a public stand against the proposed amendment.[100] The press secretary was deeply concerned as well about what he saw as Persons's advocacy of "disastrous appeasement" in his recommendations for responding to Sen. Joseph McCarthy's attacks.[101] Similar concerns would surface in subsequent administrations.

Kennedy: The Institutionalization of OCR

The Eisenhower liaison operation served as the foundation for Kennedy's and Johnson's dealings with Congress. Because of the higher volume of legislative initiatives in the latter administrations, White House–congressional liaison became more important. Although the Kennedy OCR performed most of the same tasks that its predecessor had, the special counsel's office in the Kennedy White House again assumed importance. Specialization declined as the two units worked closely together and performed many of the same activities.

Despite advice from Clark Clifford not to continue the specialized liaison operations of the Eisenhower years and counsel from Richard Neustadt to move very slowly and unobtrusively should he decide to keep the unit, President Kennedy concluded that he needed an active, visible OCR and appointed Lawrence O'Brien to head it.[102] O'Brien's background, like that of most of the staff he recruited, was in partisan politics. A long-time Massachusetts party activist, O'Brien had been heavily involved in Kennedy's general election campaign as director of organization for the Democratic National Committee.[103]

Despite the differences in background from their Eisenhower counterparts, Kennedy's liaison aides engaged in similar tasks.[104] They devoted considerable effort to gathering information about legislative activities. O'Brien and his staff "maintained an exhaustive card index that provided up-to-date information about every member's needs, interests, whims—and, of course, voting record."[105] Like their predecessors, too, members of the Kennedy OCR were "substantially involved in policymaking."[106] They kept detailed records on the status of bills proposed and opposed by the president, on the support of individual members of Congress, and on liaison staffers' contacts with members.[107]

The liaison operation benefited a great deal from a key environmental factor: the president's party controlled Congress. Compared to members of Eisenhower's OCR, Kennedy's liaison aides "openly lobbied for the President's program. On days when the House was voting on Kennedy's bills, O'Brien and his assistants . . . normally worked right out of the Speaker's office off the floor and in the corridors around the House."[108]

Much of the hierarchical structuring linking OCR to others in the White House and the broader executive branch remained. Kennedy's liaison staff sought to monitor other White House aides' contacts with members of Congress.[109] Even more than under Eisenhower, OCR tried to incorporate agency officials into its hierarchy and direct their activities. OCR, for example, pushed agencies to make sure that Democratic members of Congress were notified first about any projects or grants being awarded in their districts so that they could make the announcements themselves.[110]

In addition, O'Brien's so-called team approach to working with the executive branch involved several new elements. First was weekly reporting by agency liaison officers on the status of particular bills and on other congressional intelligence they had picked up from their discussions on Capitol Hill.[111] Second, OCR staff held monthly meetings at the White House for all agency liaison staffers. According to O'Brien aide Charles Daly, although these meetings, which generally entailed briefings on particular bills, contributed little to "the detail of daily operations," they did "create feeling among liaison people that they were part of Kennedy's team."[112]

Internally, the Kennedy OCR was organized much as it had been under Eisenhower. For most of the administration, it had six professionals.[113] O'Brien was clearly at the top of an internal hierarchy, directing the other staffers and receiving reports from them on the status of particular bills and individual members' positions and openness to further persuasion.[114] O'Brien also was typically the unit's direct link with JFK, summarizing for him the intelligence and reporting from the rest of the liaison staff.[115] In addition, O'Brien was responsible for dealing with both parties' congressional leaders and with committee chairs. By all accounts, he was authorized by the president to act and negotiate on Kennedy's behalf. O'Brien worked tirelessly to establish cooperative working relations with members of Congress—for example, inviting virtually all of them to a series of cocktail parties at the Capitol and to Sunday brunches at his home.[116]

Second-tier OCR staff included Charles Daly, Henry Hall Wilson, Richard Donahue, and Mike Manatos. On occasion, they too communicated directly with the president.[117] Daly praised Wilson, for example, for persuading JFK that "in these tight Congresses we could break a dozen or more [southern Democrats] away from a pattern of automatic conservatism."[118] As under Eisenhower, some division of labor among second-tier aides was attempted. Because of his 23 years as a Senate aide, Manatos concentrated on the Senate. Still, "O'Brien continued to consider the Senate his special responsibility in view of the status of the senators and their insistence in many cases upon dealing personally with the most respected executive leaders."[119]

The other second-tier staffers focused on the House. Here, the internal OCR hierarchy was elaborated, and the division of labor reflected the ideological factions in the legislative environment and the experience and expertise of the staff. Wilson, a former North Carolina state legislator and "a southern type in all but ideological orientation,"[120] was the first among equals. He concentrated on southern and border-state Democrats and worked with committee chairs and the House leadership. Donahue's specialty was urban Democratic members from the Northeast and Midwest, and Daly was added to the staff in early 1962 to maintain contact with other House Democrats from the North and the West who had felt neglected by the White House. In addition, some of the liaison aides specialized in policy substance, others in partisan politics. Wilson "knew more about the substance of legislation" than anyone else on the staff; Donahue was more interested in "some of the more political aspects of the work" and was an "expert" on public opinion and more involved in securing patronage and other favors.[121]

Finally, at the third tier was Claude Desautels, who formally was O'Brien's personal aide. Desautels did most of OCR's analyses of congressional votes, gathered intelligence at O'Brien's direction, arranged for bill-signing ceremonies, oversaw agencies' handling of approved projects to make sure that the appropriate members of Congress were notified, and was the White House contact for agency liaison officers.[122]

Even more than during the Eisenhower years, the Kennedy OCR did not monopolize White House dealings with Congress. Especially important was the special counsel's office, headed by Theodore Sorensen. Like staffers in Truman's special counsel's office, Sorensen and his assistants Myer Feldman and Lee White followed the progress of legislation in the substantive areas for which they were responsible (see Chapter 7) and worked to get bills passed or blocked.[123] Sometimes they worked with OCR aides in ad hoc collegial-consensual structures.[124]

O'Brien and Sorensen also shared responsibility for developing the agenda for the president's meetings with legislative leaders, and the two briefed JFK beforehand. White and Feldman suggested items for discussion at the meetings and, on occasion, sent memos directly to JFK as background for the sessions.[125] Similarly, members of the special counsel's office frequently briefed the president before his meetings with individual members of Congress; typically, the information and advice were about substantive policy and pending legislation.[126] Although sometimes such memos went through O'Brien, most often counsel staff communicated directly with the president.

In addition, Sorensen and his staff frequently dealt with members of Congress, many of whom approached the special counsel or his assistants directly rather than going through OCR.[127] Other times, Kennedy assigned a member of the counsel's office to work with a specific legislator on a particular issue. Others in the White House and executive branch also shared information with, offered advice to, and consulted with the counsel's office about the administration's relations with Congress.[128]

The involvement of the counsel's office in legislative relations was perceived to be heavy enough that its aides sometimes were subject to the same sort of criticism that liaison staffers received. Myer Rashish (an assistant in Howard Petersen's trade office), for example, complained that Feldman was "too prone to concede in bargaining with committees. . . . He's the kind of political animal who thinks in terms of buying votes by giving favors."[129]

Other White House staffers with policy responsibilities also followed congressional activities and had dealings with OCR. Arthur Schlesinger, Jr., for instance, monitored bills relevant to the arts, and Harris Wofford worked with both Sorensen's and O'Brien's offices on civil rights legislation. As Chapter 9 examines in depth, the Kennedy White House also had several specialized units to focus on particular policy issues and to draft and work to pass relevant legislation. Such offices—much like Clarence Randall's trade unit in the Eisenhower administration—typically had a staff member who was the congressional relations specialist and worked with members of O'Brien's and Sorensen's staffs.

For all the apparent interaction between congressional liaison and policy staffers, however, some observers believed that there needed to be more, implicitly pointing to the need for additional governance structures. Columnist Joseph Kraft reported, for example, that a common complaint was that "because the President deals bilaterally with his aides, there is insignificant coordination between White House offices." O'Brien, in this view, frequently lacked substantive knowledge about proposed legislation, making it hard to persuade members on its merits and perhaps pushing him to "hinge legislation to patronage more closely than ever before."[130]

Meanwhile, some members of Congress resisted the tone and forcefulness of White House liaison aides. Generally exempting Wilson and Manatos, critics charged that "some White House lobbyists display[ed] a lack of respect for their elders in the Congress and use[d] crude tactics more appropriate to the rough-and-tumble of party conventions than to the political process in a co-equal branch."[131] None of the legislators, however, objected to the existence of the White House OCR or to the services provided by its staff. OCR had become an accepted part of the White House landscape.

Johnson: Presidential and Staff Competition with OCR

The congressional liaison operation stayed essentially unchanged during 1964 and much of 1965, although the new president more avidly followed and became involved in OCR's activities than Kennedy had. At the end of the 1965 legislative session, O'Brien (who had been planning to leave government altogether) was appointed postmaster general but, at LBJ's insistence, agreed to continue as OCR head. The results were confusion and jockeying by others in the White House to move further into the legislative relations arena. After other OCR aides left, the Democrats lost congressional seats in 1966, and the president's political troubles grew, the legislative liaison operation deteriorated noticeably. Nonetheless, OCR staff were quite active throughout the Johnson years, concentrating mainly on routine operations and tactics. Meanwhile, policy aides continued to help plan legislative strategy and met with members of Congress to explain presidential objectives, seek support, and negotiate compromises.

Many of OCR's tasks and much of its structuring were identical to those it had performed in the Kennedy administration. Although liaison staffers continued to participate in White House policy discussions and senior OCR aides sat on all interdepartmental task forces,[132] most of the office's activities were representational in nature: routine information gathering, base touching, and reporting.[133]

The internal hierarchical structuring of OCR remained, but the size of the staff grew somewhat; a new specialized structure emerged, and authority relations grew less clear. Although definite numbers of OCR aides are difficult to determine because of the shifting responsibilities in the Johnson White House, for most of the administration, between eight and ten professional staffers worked full or part time at legislative liaison.[134] As in the Eisenhower and Kennedy administrations, different staffers dealt with the Senate and House.[135]

Differentiation within OCR continued with the establishment of a specialized writing structure in February 1967. This essentially systematized and expanded MacLafferty's efforts during the Hoover years and Corcoran's work under FDR to get materials to supportive members of Congress so that they could more adequately defend the president's programs and respond to attacks against the administration.[136]

Authority relations within OCR grew more ambiguous over the course of the administration. Until he became postmaster general, O'Brien without a doubt headed the operation. After he was named postmaster general, O'Brien continued to be involved in some of the unit's work.[137] Henry Hall Wilson attempted to take O'Brien's place. For example, Wilson summarized for the president his and other OCR aides' dealings with Congress, and he was designated the recipient of reports of White House staffers' contacts with members of Congress.[138] After O'Brien's formal departure from the White House, Wilson remembered seeing the president more frequently.[139] Johnson, however, steadfastly refused to name him as O'Brien's replacement, thus lowering Wilson's status both in the White House and on Capitol Hill.[140]

Johnson's reluctance to promote Wilson may have stemmed in part from the fact that Wilson was a holdover from the Kennedy staff. There was considerable suspicion and unease between the new president and OCR. Jake Jacobsen, for example, described his appointment as legislative counsel in April 1965 as an effort to help reduce the tensions. Given a West Wing office next to the OCR staff, Jacobsen remembered:

> I did good! I think I brought together the Kennedy legislative crowd and the Johnson people more than any other person had been able to do. They finally had someone they could talk to that they knew could talk to Johnson. They finally had someone in their crowd who was a real Johnson man, and therefore they were no longer a kind of offshoot Kennedy-type operation.[141]

Jacobsen began serving as liaison to House members from Texas and several northeastern and New England states. In his view, such activities "served to create a much, much better feeling between the holdover Kennedy group that was handling congressional relations and the Johnson incoming group."[142]

Soon, though, Jacobsen assumed other responsibilities in the White House.[143] Moreover, his arrival on the scene did little to quell worries about the absence of leadership in OCR or its place in the overall White House hierarchy. Senior White House staffers such as Joseph Califano, Bill Moyers, Harry McPherson, and Douglass Cater all expressed concern about the absence of clear authority over congressional relations.[144] Finally, Barefoot Sanders was named legislative counsel after Jacobsen left in 1967 and took on many of the responsibilities of head of OCR. Sanders, for example, called meetings of the OCR staff, assigned legislators other White House aides with whom they should maintain contact, and received information about those contacts.[145] Sanders also had routine, direct access to the president and attended legislative leaders' meetings with LBJ.

Still, lines of authority were not always clear. For example, several of those who worked at least part time at congressional liaison tasks were housed formally and seemed to report elsewhere in the White House. Jacobsen, William Blackburn, David Bunn, James Jones, and Sherwin Markman technically worked for Appointments Secretary Marvin Watson, and DeVier Pierson was a member of the special counsel's staff, where he had a range of policy responsibilities.[146]

The unclear authority within OCR and its perceived distance from the president in the White House hierarchy had several consequences. As the administration went on, agency liaison officers became less willing to follow White House directives.[147] Non-OCR staffers also passed on political intelligence and tactical advice to President Johnson and reported to him on their dealings with members of Congress. For senior aides such as Moyers, McPherson, and Cater, access to the president was direct rather than mediated by OCR.[148] Even the hierarchical structuring within the unit suffered, and Sanders faced growing difficulty managing OCR staffers. He discovered, for instance, that only he and Irving Sprague could be counted on to give the president timely and reliable reports on congressional activities.[149]

Instead, specialization in legislative affairs continued to drop, and market structuring flourished. As in past White Houses, policy staffers worked with OCR to get legislation passed in areas in which they had substantive expertise and had participated in policy formulation. More strikingly, though, on other occasions OCR was simply bypassed altogether. In 1968, for example, an ad hoc lobbying unit was created to handle the Supreme Court nominations of Abe Fortas and Homer Thornberry.[150]

Non-OCR aides duplicated the liaison staff's tasks, engaging in many representational activities. There was an extensive network of staff contacts with members of Congress, for example. Not surprisingly, the Texas delegation received special attention, a job eased by the surfeit of Texans on the White House staff. Walter Jenkins, Marvin Watson, and Larry Temple were assigned to stay in touch with fellow Texans in Congress.[151] Meanwhile, the White House also paid attention to other states. After hearing some complaints about Wilson, for instance, Watson took on liaison responsibilities with House members from North Carolina and Kentucky.[152]

Finally, other White House units on occasion undertook their own analyses of legislative situations rather than relying exclusively on OCR. As early as 1965, for example, Hayes Redmon followed congressional voting on several domestic issues for Bill Moyers.[153]

Especially important in presidential-congressional relations outside OCR was Joseph Califano's operation. Much of its involvement flowed from its substantive policy responsibilities. As Chapter 7 details, Califano's office essentially became a White House domestic policy staff. This led to participation in a range of legislative proposals. In addition, because Califano had worked for a time at the Defense Department, he also became involved in defense authorization debates in Congress.[154] Califano's office worked closely with members of Congress as it sought to identify the best times to introduce particular pieces of legislation, to develop the most persuasive presidential messages to accompany the administration's legislative proposals, and to negotiate any changes in those proposals in Congress.[155]

Additionally, Califano was a White House channel for more liberal members of Congress such as Edmund Muskie and Walter Mondale.[156]

This extensive participation in congressional relations generated both cooperation and conflict. In 1967, OCR and the Califano unit sent the president a joint review of the achievements of the 89th Congress, with an interim report on the 90th Congress.[157] Each office tried to keep the other informed on matters involving pending administration legislation.[158] Yet OCR staffers persistently complained that Califano and his aides were not keeping the liaison office notified of their legislative activities. In February 1968, Manatos wrote Califano:

> It would help me stay creditable [sic] if I could be advised direct by your staff of changes in scheduling messages—rather than to have me put in the embarrassing position of receiving a telephone call from Senator Mansfield's staff telling me that "according to Joe Califano there will be no Maritime message today." Whose side is your staff on?[159]

Although clearly needed, no additional structures for resolving such conflicts emerged: not only was Johnson too distracted to arbitrate, but after he withdrew from the 1968 election, the demand for conflict resolution plummeted.

CONCLUSIONS

By the end of the Johnson administration, OCR had clearly become institutionalized. Yet the Johnson years also brought into sharp relief the potential for conflict among White House staffers with diverse goals and differing views of appropriate legislative strategies. Highlighted, too, was the possible competition among staffers seeking to deal directly with Congress, as well as the potentially destabilizing role of a president who tried to supervise legislative relations.

Called for in such a setting were additional governance structures. Collegial-competitive mechanisms (such as those often relied on in the Eisenhower White House), for instance, would have provided forums for airing out and seeking compromises on competing goals and legislative strategies as well as for sharing accurate information and agreeing on joint action. On highly salient issues or when conflict remained irreducible, presidents or very senior staffers ultimately needed to step in as arbiters.

Much about the structuring of White House liaison with Congress, of course, is outside the reach of presidential manipulation. Since Eisenhower, members of Congress have come to expect a liaison operation; the organization, activities, and influence of such a unit are powerfully shaped both by the prevailing legislative environment and by the interplay among the numerous White House staffers in and out of OCR with congressional relations interests. Within these constraints, however, presidents *can* influence the degree and nature of their own involvement in legislative affairs, the location of the congressional relations operation in the White House hierarchy, and the other structures they rely on to try to harness and make constructive the differences among competing staffers.

3
Press Relations and Publicity

A second target of White House outreach is the U.S. public. Although the framers of the Constitution both anticipated and desired a presidency that was at some remove from the citizenry, presidents and the public have become quite closely tied. At the same time, presidential efforts to shape public preferences have multiplied.

During the early modern era, the White House staff became involved both in presidential dealings with the Washington press and in more direct public-relations efforts.[1] The dynamics of staff structuring for these tasks was quite different, however. In the area of press relations, there was some differentiation, and structures were generally both stable and congruent. Public-relations structuring, by contrast, was ad hoc and unstable even when congruent with the prevailing decision settings.

WHITE HOUSE PRESS RELATIONS

The exact timing of the emergence of White House structuring for press relations was dictated in substantial part by a presidential choice factor: Herbert Hoover's prior experience with strategic manipulation of the press. However, mounting press demands as early as the Hoover years, the proliferation of media representatives under Roosevelt, and much more profound environmental changes thereafter provided the major impetus and important reinforcement for the development of White House structures for press relations. The increasing complexity of the environment—especially the growth of the electronic media—also stimulated modest structural differentiation. It may be speculated, too, that the extent of controversy in the political environment—triggered by, for example, wars hot and cold, and the civil rights movement—heightened the importance of press secretaries as political and policy advisers. Since the nature of environmental demands remained roughly constant even as their magnitude grew, the fundamental structuring of the press office remained stable across all early modern administrations. Even so, despite the overall impact of environmental change, the character of press operations in each administration was importantly shaped by presidential preference, in part because the relationship between president and press secretary tends to be one of the closest in the White House Office.

Under Hoover, despite the designation of a press secretary, turmoil reigned at first, since the responsibilities of the press secretary and other advisers were not well defined. Gradually, a simple collegial-consensual structure emerged, providing a model for press operations under Roosevelt and Truman. During these years, the press secretary and no more than two assistants interacted informally with the president and his intimates in the White House. This was congruent with the prevailing decision setting: a consensus on the goals of press relations and technical uncertainty, reflecting the need to develop specific strategies, often on short notice.

Eisenhower's preference for formal organization produced some modification in structuring, with sharper definition of procedures and responsibilities, especially for the press secretary. Structural differentiation also continued. Ike's press aide, James Hagerty, sought to bring press officers throughout the executive branch into a hierarchical structure directed from the White House; he also formalized pre-press conference briefings, which operated within a hybrid collegial-consensual and adjudicative structure. In most respects, though, the Eisenhower White House continued the practice of working with a small staff unit that was designed to include collegial participation by the president. Much the same was the case for both Kennedy and Johnson, even though the level of formality dropped to something closer to the Truman era. Additional differentiation occurred under LBJ in response to the need to provide special services to television.

Finally, one encounters evidence of partisan learning. FDR's relative lack of interest in formal structures clearly influenced Truman, Kennedy, and Johnson. Eisenhower's conscious attention to creating White House structures roughly recalled Hoover and, more tellingly, served as a model for the next Republican president, Richard Nixon.

The First Press Secretary

In his mildly controversial move to expand the top White House staff, Herbert Hoover designated one of his new secretaries a "press secretary."[2] George Akerson, a former Washington correspondent and Hoover aide, was the first full-time press specialist to serve in the White House. The role of press aide to Hoover was not new to Akerson, who had joined then Sec-retary of Commerce Hoover in 1926 as a "public relations counsel."[3]

Although Hoover never fully explained why he decided to include a press secretary in his newly elaborated staff system, it is clear that he was more sensitive than his predecessors to the public outreach needs and op-portunities for executive politicians in general and for presidents in particu-lar.[4] Thus, Hoover's predilection toward public relations interacted with his own organizational experience to suggest the value of a press specialist. Moreover, the idea of locating presidential press relations in the White House was hardly new. In the days when presidents had only one secretary, it was normal for that aide to devote time to press relations.[5]

It is also apparent that presidential needs and opportunities in the realm of press relations were growing at about the time of Hoover's presi-dency. For instance, one estimate placed the number of Washington corre-spondents in 1930 at about 350, approximately 150 more than Woodrow Wilson faced 15 years earlier.[6] The environment was clearly changing: there were not only more outlets for a president to get his message to the public, but also more reporters demanding access to the president and fresh stories from the White House. Had Hoover not tried to respond positively to this environment, it seems likely that his successor would have.

Hoover's move was initially greeted with warmth by the Washington community. The appointment of Akerson promised much-needed access for the press, and Akerson himself was well liked. However, Herbert Hoover's administration was one in which much that initially seemed prom-ising ultimately soured. The performance of his first press secretary fol-lowed this pattern. Much of the fault lay with Hoover, who failed to deliver on promises to liberalize rules of attribution and open up the presidential press conference, which at the time required questions to be submitted in writing in advance. Akerson sought, without success, to make the president more available, but the press secretary himself came to be blamed for fac-tual confusion and favoritism in his briefings and other dealings with re-porters. Even the scheduling of routine appointments with the president, which Akerson assumed as an ancillary task, got him in trouble with those who could not get in when they wished.

In addition, governance analysis points to a structural reason for Aker-son's difficulties. The governance problem raised by press secretarial infor-mation gathering fits most comfortably in cell 2 of Table 2 (see Chapter 1): administration goals are assumed, at least by most press secretaries; the problem, from the secretary's point of view, is to discover how best to repre-sent them—for a press specialist, a "technical" issue. Congruent with such a setting, according to the governance model, would have been a collegial-consensual structure, which would have maximized free discussion, infor-mation dissemination, and participation within the White House. In this sort of structure, information is apt to be as complete as possible, contradictions or gaps can be discovered, and a wide range of strategic options can be explored. The Hoover White House was the opposite of this in most respects, reflecting both the president's general resistance to openness and the internal organizational dynamics. The relations among Hoover's aides were generally distant and often acrimonious, inhibiting communication and participation in decision making. Little structuring of any kind was in evidence during Akerson's White House career.

Finally, midway through the administration, Akerson resigned to take a job in the motion-picture industry. The resignation was prompted primarily by the press secretary's realization that he had lost a battle for White House influence with fellow secretary Lawrence Richey, who had resisted Akerson's efforts to make Hoover more accessible.[7] Still, Akerson had given initial definition to the office, especially in his institution of routine press briefings by a member of the White House staff.

When Akerson left in 1931, he was replaced by another White House correspondent, Theodore Joslin, who embarked on perhaps the least successful career of any presidential press secretary and underscored the significance of staff skill. A reporter for the *Boston Transcript,* Joslin was fervently pro-Hoover, to the point of antagonizing many in the press corps and seriously diminishing his credibility with them. One of his contemporaries summed up the prevailing sentiment by characterizing Joslin as "the first known instance of a rat joining a sinking ship."[8] Joslin got along well with Richey, however. This allowed the development of a more collegial-consensual relationship among the two and the president, which presaged press structuring to come.

White House Press Relations, 1933–52: Experimentation and Institutionalization

The position of press secretary became an established part of the White House staff when Franklin Roosevelt followed Hoover's precedent and appointed Stephen Early to the job, one of three professional positions that were in existence during the initial Roosevelt years. Early, also a former Washington reporter, presided over a highly successful operation and developed some of the activities that would endure, most notably that of briefing the president before press conferences. He also replaced "party hacks" in departmental press positions with experienced reporters—a move seemingly designed to achieve competence rather than to interject presidential (or press secretarial) control.[9] Early's success, of course, cannot be disentangled from Roosevelt's brilliant touch with the press, any more than his predecessors' failures can be wholly separated from Hoover's more hostile relationship with reporters. Like Hoover, but to vastly different effect,

Roosevelt was his own principal press spokesperson. The affable and experienced Early, however, was an ideal complement to FDR.

Early met daily with Roosevelt and was influential in advising him in his dealings with the press. Most accounts of the Roosevelt administration place him in FDR's inner circle, at least in the prewar years.[10] Early met regularly with the press and was credited with keeping them well informed by the standards of the time. His closeness to the president helped make Early a credible spokesman. Early also performed a variety of political functions, such as dealing with members of Congress and the Democratic National Committee, and he proffered occasional policy advice.[11] His last assistant, Eben Ayers, stressed, however, that Early "never considered himself a policymaker."[12]

Those aspects of White House business that routinely included the press secretary normally involved informal collegial-consensual structuring, which the Hoover operation lacked.[13] Indeed, the basic informality of these operations may have been the key to their success. In addition, the compatibility of the principals—Early, Roosevelt, and other key White House staffers—contributed immensely to the effectiveness of Early's performance.

The press office grew modestly in 1935 when William Hassett was detailed from the State Department to serve as Early's assistant.[14] Early and Hassett did not specialize according to function, except that Hassett was more likely to travel with the president while Early held the fort at home. When Early became appointments secretary near the end of FDR's administration, Jonathan Daniels, a North Carolina newspaper editor, was appointed press secretary for a brief time.

Harry Truman modified the Roosevelt model only minimally. Perhaps most importantly, he maintained not only the basic structuring but also the essential informality of interaction. At the same time, his press secretary, Charles Ross, a former high school classmate and Pulitzer Prize–winning journalist for the St. Louis Post Dispatch, became more of a policy adviser than Early had ever been.

Continuity with FDR was emphasized, as Ayers continued as Ross's professional assistant. And when Ross died in 1950, Steve Early returned briefly to fill in until he was succeeded by Joseph Short, Jr., a former Washington correspondent. Short appointed two assistants, Roger Tubby and Irving Perlmeter, both government press officers. With these appointments, a degree of substantive specialization appeared in the press office for the first time. Tubby, who came to the White House from the State Department, dealt mainly with foreign affairs; Perlmeter concentrated on domestic matters. When Short died in 1952, Tubby assumed his duties for the brief time remaining to the administration.[15]

The activities of press secretaries Ross and Short differed primarily as a result of their relationship to Harry Truman. Ross was "as close as any man" to the president,[16] not only meeting with Truman daily but also advising him on a wide variety of policy issues.[17] Indeed, Ayers complained that Ross was in meetings with Truman so often that the press secretary provided little direction to the business of the press office.[18] Reporters, although having no serious complaints regarding access, voiced similar criticism.

Short was much less close to Truman personally. Although Short saw himself as a policy adviser,[19] there is little evidence that he participated in many key policy decisions.[20] Yet Short, like Ross before him, attended the daily White House staff meetings with Truman; as a result, he had routine access to the president as well as knowledge of and some input into the activities of the rest of the staff. Moreover, Short initiated meetings of the "little cabinet." This collegial-consensual group, composed of departmental undersecretaries and assistant secretaries, shared information about issues and activities within the executive departments.[21]

The Hagerty Era: Formalization and Differentiation

Dwight Eisenhower continued the practice of selecting a veteran journalist as press secretary. James C. Hagerty had been a reporter before becoming press secretary to New York Governor Thomas E. Dewey. Hagerty named Murray Snyder, another reporter, as his sole assistant, interrupting Joseph Short's brief experiment with division of labor in the press office. When Snyder left in 1957, he was replaced by Anne Wheaton, a former journalist and long-time head of publicity for the Women's Division of the Republican National Committee.

Hagerty was a uniquely powerful press secretary, positioned at the very top of the White House hierarchy. Within the administration, "his word was law."[22] The press secretary was a regular figure at venues where policy was made, including some meetings of the cabinet and the National Security Council (NSC). Hagerty also had direct access to the president. Unlike most others, he did not have to go through Chief of Staff Sherman Adams to see Eisenhower.

More than a confidant and adviser, Hagerty was an organizational innovator as well, who "probably launched the modern growth of the office" of press secretary.[23] Although Hagerty did not increase the number of press aides, he did expand the tasks that the office performed. Beyond the by then routine duties of briefing the press and organizing the president's press relations, Hagerty paid considerably more attention to press operations in executive agencies and sought to place agency officials in a hierarchy directed from the White House. Going well past Early's concern for competence, Hagerty handpicked the press officers at State and Defense and met frequently with the information directors of other cabinet departments.[24]

Indeed, so concerned was the Eisenhower White House with guiding executive branch press operations that Hagerty's efforts were supplemented in 1955 when former governor Howard Pyle was brought into the White House to improve the publicity efforts of the departments[25]—a move that led to considerable tension with the press office.

Hagerty also did far more than his predecessors in formalizing the process of briefing the president before press conferences. This routine, performed on average every two weeks, included a breakfast meeting with top White House aides and cabinet members, regular conferences between Hagerty and other top advisers, and a meeting among Hagerty, Eisenhower, and others at which the president was thoroughly prepared.[26] Although such sessions were essentially collegial-consensual in nature, they on occasion served as forums in which staff disagreements over tactics and even policy were debated and sometimes adjudicated by Eisenhower himself.[27]

Hagerty also oversaw the editing of press conference transcripts for general release. Perhaps his best-known innovation in media circles, however, was the admission of television cameras to presidential press conferences. Indeed, television first became a major part of the environment during Eisenhower's presidency, and the White House response went beyond the press office. Robert Montgomery, the film actor, regularly advised Eisenhower on television dress and demeanor.[28]

Kennedy and Johnson: Further Institutionalization

Samuel Kernell contends that "the real break with the Roosevelt system [of press relations] came with John Kennedy."[29] Kernell's principal basis for this conclusion is Kennedy's frequent live, televised news conferences and his openness to reporters in other contexts. When it came to the work of the press office and the press secretary, however, the Kennedy administration was not especially innovative.

Like his predecessors, John Kennedy turned to the field of journalism for his press secretary. Pierre Salinger had been a newspaper and magazine reporter before joining the Kennedy presidential campaign. He brought in newspaper journalist Andrew Hatcher as his associate and later added an assistant—initially Jay Gildner, then Malcolm Kilduff—to handle the foreign press. Thus, the senior press office staff again grew to three, and some specialization was reintroduced. However, neither Gildner nor Kilduff spent all his time on matters pertaining to the foreign press or foreign policy.

Salinger, observers generally agree, was neither as well informed nor as autonomous a policy adviser as Hagerty had been. Kennedy, like Roosevelt, wanted to control his own press relations, and Salinger was, in Patrick Anderson's words, "someone who was hard-working, loyal, and who could keep the press happy."[30] Still, Salinger became involved in most of the activities that had occupied his predecessors.

Salinger did not continue Hagerty's formal governance structures for briefing the president or plotting issue strategies. Indeed, formal staff meetings of any kind were rare in the Kennedy White House, and Salinger did not regularly attend meetings at which substantive policies were discussed.[31] He did, however, maintain an office next to Kennedy's and had walk-in privileges, seeing the president several times a day.

At the same time, the press secretary retained the formal structuring Hagerty had established for working with other executive branch press officers.[32] Salinger served as the personnel officer for major executive branch jobs in public affairs, suggesting and clearing names. He met weekly with a coordinating committee composed of press officers from the executive departments. These meetings allowed those involved to survey initiatives and developments in the departments, agree on procedures for releasing such information, discuss issues in which journalists might be interested, and generate possible questions and responses for presidential press conferences.

When Lyndon Johnson assumed the presidency, Salinger stayed on for a few months. He was succeeded by veteran journalist and LBJ aide George Reedy. An outsider in the Johnson White House, Salinger needed an appointment to see the president. In contrast, Reedy and his successors, Bill Moyers and George Christian, had close relationships with Johnson, seeing him at least once a day and enjoying unrestricted access to the president. Indeed, one study of Johnson's conversations with others during his first 25 months in office found that 73 percent of the president's interactions were with only four staff members, among them Reedy and his immediate successor Moyers.[33]

Both Reedy and Moyers were personally close to Johnson, "part of a group of intimate cronies."[34] But that status failed to protect either man from the president's dissatisfaction with their performance or to shelter Moyers from LBJ's ultimate conclusion that policy disagreement was a sign of disloyalty. Still, it is clear that the personal relationship each enjoyed with the president—especially Moyers—made possible a role in the White House that went far beyond that available to less privileged press secretaries.

Reedy, Moyers, and Christian all were routinely involved in policy discussions. They attended the sporadic staff meetings as well as NSC and cabinet sessions. Moyers and Christian also were regular participants in Johnson's Tuesday lunch meetings on Vietnam.[35] The Johnson administration in many respects sought to move, albeit tentatively, toward more formal structures than had been present in the Kennedy White House. The press secretaries' involvement in regularized policy deliberations reflected that. All three likewise continued the now-routine functions of regularly briefing the press and preparing the president for his press conferences. These formalized opportunities facilitated each press secretary's performance of his job of informing the media.

Nevertheless, they do not account for the unusual policy role played only by Moyers. Of Johnson's press secretaries, Moyers came the closest to being an all-purpose adviser, one whom Stephen Hess called the "generalist-in-chief" of the Johnson White House.[36] In addition to being press secretary, Moyers, whose White House service as an aide preceded his appointment to the press office, was at various points a speechwriter, domestic policy adviser, link with the executive branch bureaucracy, and "foreign policy gadfly."[37] Even as press secretary, Moyers "continued to dabble in foreign policy, domestic programs, [and] speechwriting."[38] However, these activities declined once Moyers took over the press office.

Moyers was the only one of LBJ's press secretaries who seriously aspired to be a policy adviser to the president; the rest were "able mirrors."[39] Still, both Reedy and Christian pursued interests beyond a narrow job definition. For instance, Reedy was an informal liaison with labor,[40] and Christian was seen as a "senior adviser" on Vietnam by at least one key participant.[41] Nonetheless, historian Henry Graff expressed the consensus conclusion in commenting that Christian was "far less influential, far less emotionally involved in national and international issues" than was Moyers.[42]

Structurally, the press office experienced mild growth and differentiation in response to environmental demands. The sheer number of those with White House press credentials rose from around 350 when Hoover took office to 1,260 when Lyndon Johnson left office in 1969.[43] Nor, of course, were these only print journalists. By 1968, there were roughly 300 radio and television correspondents—up from zero in 1929.[44]

The electronic media produced both new demands on and unprecedented opportunities for presidents. Lyndon Johnson was the first president to formally incorporate expertise with nonprint media into the White House staff. Robert Fleming, formerly of ABC, served as deputy to both Moyers and Christian; among his duties was advising the president on television and radio appearances. When Robert Kintner, former president of NBC, joined the White House as cabinet secretary and speechwriting coordinator, his television expertise was likewise tapped.[45]

During the Johnson years, press office specialization increased more generally. Assistant Press Secretary Lloyd Hackler routinely tracked down information from the domestic agencies; at least some of the time, another press aide, Hayes Redmon, specialized in international matters. Close contacts were forged between the press office and the NSC staff during Christian's tenure, with two NSC staff members ultimately assigned part-time press duties. Nonetheless, the professional staff in the press office numbered at most five under LBJ—the press secretary and four assistants.

By the end of the Johnson administration, outreach to the press had become an expected White House task. For the most part, it was handled in stable structures that generally were congruent with prevailing decision settings.

PUBLIC RELATIONS

At the same time that structuring for press relations was stabilizing, the shifting Washington political environment led presidents to place a heightened premium on more direct interaction with the mass public. As Kernell argued, as key Washington actors multiplied and the political arena grew more heterogeneous and fragmented, presidents increasingly began to "go public" as they strove to achieve their policy objectives and maintain political support.[46] The more presidents went public, of course, the more potent a source of influence favorable public opinion became. Presidents and their staffs in turn devoted increased attention to public relations and to developing structures for reaching the public outside the channels routinely controlled by the Washington press corps.[47]

Throughout the early modern period, market structuring of White House public relations dominated—a generally congruent response in decision settings of transient goals and uncertain technology. Yet this structuring was not stable. More than ongoing environmental volatility was involved. Presidential press secretaries stubbornly resisted distinct public-relations efforts, generating intense turf battles that hindered the emergence and institutionalization of public-relations structuring.

The differentiation dynamic might have been expected to produce structures linking these domains, but during the period under examination, this seldom occurred and never endured. Mostly missing were either collegial-consensual linkage structures to enhance coordination or adjudicative structures designed to (quasi-) resolve the conflicts between the press and public-relations operations. Ultimately, such structuring did emerge, but not until the Nixon administration.

Environmental change, in the form of both the need for presidents to go public and the development of effective polling technology, also led presidents to pay increasing attention to tapping public opinion. But presidential responses were idiosyncratic and did not involve the White House staff until LBJ brought the first public-opinion analyst into the White House; the aide was incorporated into the overall staff hierarchy without significant additional governance structuring. This minimal White House response is noteworthy mainly because it, like public relations generally, anticipated more significant developments in post-Johnson administrations.

Hoover: Reluctant Publicist

As chair of the Commission for Belgian Relief and as commerce secretary, Herbert Hoover had been especially concerned with public relations and publicity.[48] Less of this was apparent during his White House years, probably because being president required Hoover to come out from behind the scenes, where he had always worked.[49] Staff aides struggled to pick up the slack: Hoover press secretaries George Akerson and Theodore Joslin tried desperately—and mostly futilely—to "humanize Hoover."[50]

Probably the greatest effort came from unofficial presidential aide James MacLafferty. In November 1930, for example, Vice President Curtis pleaded with MacLafferty to talk to the president and tell him that the "publicity . . . situation [in the West] is simply rotten."[51] MacLafferty discussed the message with Hoover and ended up securing the president's approval for MacLafferty to make a cross-country trip to shore up support for Hoover.[52] MacLafferty believed that he had "won many away from blaming Hoover for all of their problems."[53] In addition, MacLafferty made speeches for the president and, as Hoover's reelection prospects worsened in early 1932, joined Republican National Committee staffers in trying to persuade the president to issue statements defending his actions and in choosing speakers to appear on his behalf.[54]

Roosevelt: Competition Over Public Relations

Franklin Roosevelt also clearly understood the importance of public relations. From the outset, he worked to establish what Betty Houchin Winfield called a "publicity trust."[55] Like much of the rest of FDR's operations, the "trust" was characterized by overlapping, sometimes competing structures and individuals—a strengthening of the incipient market structuring that characterized the Hoover public-relations arrangements.

Among the key players were Roosevelt's White House advisers. Press Secretary Stephen Early "quickly made it apparent that he was going to do more than inform reporters about the activities of the President"; rather, he would be a "public relations manager."[56] He faced competition for a time from presidential secretary and political counselor Louis Howe, who also sought to be the president's adviser on public relations; through much of 1933, Howe had his own weekly radio show that spotlighted administration events and accomplishments.[57] The third professional White House aide, Marvin McIntyre, had relevant expertise as well: as publicity director for the Navy Department during World War I, he had worked for the Creel Committee.[58]

"The real beginning of formalized efforts to coordinate administration public relations," however, took place not in the White House Office but in the National Emergency Council (NEC).[59] Working with Early, the NEC "brought together the heads of the various recovery programs to plot strategies for using direct promotional campaigns and the media to bolster public support and offset negative reactions" to the New Deal.[60] As would happen repeatedly over the next several decades, the White House press secretary often saw competition coming from separate public-relations operations spread throughout the executive branch. In 1934, for example, Early wrote to Howe about an Executive Council proposal to publish a bulletin of official information:

> To date I have been but a mild zephyr, moving gently and creating only a slight and occasional disturbance. If the Government is to publish officially "The Federal Register," my barometer would drop immediately to new lows, registering in the cyclone or hurricane areas. In brief, I shall oppose the project with every ounce of energy and power I have.[61]

As the White House staff grew, Early also began approving aides' acceptance of invitations to speak, another early form of staff involvement in public relations.[62]

Additional structuring for public relations accompanied the naming of six administrative assistants in 1939. One of the new units in the Executive Office of the President was the Office of Government Reports (OGR), designed to be a "central public information office that would serve as a clearinghouse for the distribution of information about the activities of government agencies and as a tool for keeping the Roosevelt administration abreast of public opinion on government activities."[63] Lowell Mellett became both an administrative assistant and the head of OGR. Observers came to see Mellett as the "chief propagandist for the New Deal,"[64] who was charged with "overseeing administration public relations."[65] For a time, this provided a degree of hierarchical structuring, linking the White House, the Executive Office, and the rest of the executive branch.

With growing prospects of war in Europe, aides had more to worry about than intra-administration jockeying for position. Mellett worked to dispatch administration spokespeople across the country and to oversee newsreel reports on the war. Although Sander credits Mellett and Early with working together to execute Roosevelt's " 'informational' propaganda strategy" during the war years,[66] many others participated in the public-relations efforts as well. Through 1940, activities concentrated on coordinating speeches to discredit the growing isolationism in the United States.[67] According to Robert Sherwood, in the early days of the war, presidential confidants Samuel Rosenman and Harry Hopkins worked to promote

> an intensely pro-Britain, anti-Nazi sentiment in official Washington. There were very few of Roosevelt's most trusted advisers who agreed with this. The majority of them tried to persuade the President that support of beleaguered Britain would mean political suicide for himself and possible disaster for the nation.[68]

Such administration attempts to tie public support for the war with support for President Roosevelt generated controversy. Some members of Congress and some within the Office of War Information, for example, objected to playwright Sherwood's dual position as presidential speechwriter and director of the Office of War Information, fearing the apparent "politicization" of the informational activities.[69]

Truman: Continuing Involvement

One sees somewhat more public-relations activity during the Truman years, even though the president himself allegedly "missed the connection between policy and publicity."[70] Market structuring prevailed, with numerous players in and out of the White House working from time to time on public relations. Unlike in the Roosevelt era, however, the press secretary was far less active, significantly reducing the struggle for domination over publicity tasks.

Within the White House Office, specific events or perceived administration problems prompted aides to offer public-relations advice. Special Assistant Kenneth Hechler, for example, sought to advise the president on how to better handle the controversy over firing General MacArthur[71] and did an analysis of the timing and content of FDR's fireside chats; this latter task he shared with David Stowe of Steelman's staff and Special Counsel Charles Murphy.[72] In addition, Administrative Assistant George Elsey recommended that Truman travel to defense plants and military installations in early 1951 as part of an effort to "explain" the Korean War to the public.[73]

A more systematic approach to publicity, however, developed as White House aides helped officials from the Democratic National Committee (DNC) in efforts to promote the administration. The DNC initiated the publication "Twenty Years of Progress," designed to showcase the accomplishments of the past two Democratic presidents. William Loeb, a consultant to Murphy in 1951–52, was the coordinator for the project in the White House and worked closely with the research division at the DNC and several White House staffers.

Meanwhile, Truman's press secretaries participated less in public-relations activities than their predecessors had. "[Charles] Ross never attempted to 'sell' the President."[74] His successor, Joseph Short, at least occasionally recommended the use of department heads to more forcefully push and defend administration decisions.[75]

As during the Roosevelt years, few staffers worked to "sell" the administration by speaking publicly. Still, senior aides Averell Harriman and John Steelman did engage in a fair amount of speaking to service and partisan groups.[76] And Steelman introduced a weekly television show, "Battle Report—Washington," which showcased executive branch officials discussing their work.[77]

Eisenhower: Activism and Innovation

Far more evidence of public-relations activity can be found in the Eisenhower White House. Not only was the president more involved, but from the beginning his staffers pushed for a White House presence in public relations. Once more, market structuring of such activities dominated, and a strong presidential press secretary laid claim to directing public-relations efforts. Nonetheless, experimentation with additional structuring surfaced.

At the outset, most of the White House staff's public-relations activities were ad hoc. In March 1953, for example, Special Counsel Bernard Shanley wrote in his diary that he and Cabinet Secretary Maxwell Rabb had met with Chief of Staff Sherman Adams to discuss "the question of the human and broad approach to the problem of attempting to do something along the lines of social benefits to the country to indicate the leadership of the President."[78] Shanley pushed as well for more "political" discussions among key staffers.[79] By December, the president was convinced of the need for White House involvement and asked Shanley to discreetly select a person to go on the "Man of the Week" television show each week to support a particular part of the administration's legislative program.[80]

Other, more specialized activities also surfaced. For example, Clarence Randall's operation—set up to secure passage of foreign trade legislation (see Chapter 9)—established its own arrangements for communicating directly with the public. Similarly, White House aide C. D. Jackson was hired in part as a specialist in "psychological warfare" and charged with pursuing the "public relations aspects of the Cold War."[81] And far more than in previous administrations, most senior White House staffers engaged in public speaking of their own.[82]

The real innovation during the Eisenhower era, however, was the creation of the Executive Branch Liaison Office, which was intended to be a specialized public-relations unit. The office evidently grew out of a suggestion by Arizona governor Howard Pyle that the White House provide material to pro-Eisenhower speakers around the country "so that they could tell the Administration's story."[83] In late June 1953, Sherman Adams brought Undersecretary of Commerce Walter Williams and his assistant Stanley Rumbough to the White House to start the liaison office.[84] Williams—"one of the best salesmen"—returned to Commerce after a few months, and the unit continued under Rumbough's direction until 1954.[85] Rumbough and his assistant Charles Masterson worked to ensure that executive branch speakers were well distributed to groups across the country and suggested topics and provided information for their speeches.[86]

Under Rumbough and Masterson, the unit operated internally as a hierarchy. It had three tasks: issuing weekly "fact papers" to be used in speeches by agency and department officials, serving as liaison with the Republican National Committee (RNC), and coordinating executive branch speakers.[87] In addition, Masterson advised Appointments Secretary Thomas Stephens and others on which speaking invitations ought to be accepted by which administration officials. All these tasks assumed consensus on administration goals as well as substantial understanding of and agreement about the means of pursuing them, making the internal hierarchy congruent with the decision setting. Although it was limited in scope and in no way dominated administration public-relations efforts, the Rumbough operation was a relatively rare example of a serious attempt at non-market structuring in this area.

Rumbough resigned in 1954, amid some concern that his "type of operation was better out of the White House."[88] Almost immediately, other staffers moved in to fill the vacuum. In late 1954, legislative liaison aide Bryce Harlow and Bill Robinson of the RNC crafted plans to "sell" Eisenhower's program over the next two years—with Harlow, Stephens, and Adams directing the effort from the White House. Envisioned were activities that would be pursued independently of both the RNC and Citizens for Eisenhower.[89]

Finally, former governor Pyle, who had been defeated in a reelection bid, joined the staff on January 22, 1955. Shanley was delighted by his arrival: Pyle was "absolutely a top-notch individual [who] represents the other element of the party."[90] According to Press Secretary Hagerty, Adams informed him that "Pyle's job is going to be to work with the departments to get good publicity out of them and have the departments present their cases as forcefully as they can to the public."[91]

Masterson, who had remained in the White House after Rumbough's departure, served as Pyle's assistant. Masterson reported to Adams that his new boss believed that

the steps Stan Rumbough and I have taken to meet the need will serve as a basic structure for him in getting the Administration's story told. . . . Governor Pyle would expect to sit with the President and with you as the court of ultimate appeal on Public Relations for the White House, the Cabinet, and the RNC.[92]

Pyle spent much of his time speaking at fund-raisers and to trade associations and party groups.[93] In addition, the Pyle-Masterson unit was part of a collegial-consensual structure that helped link the RNC and executive branch agencies and also permitted White House officials to work with the RNC to develop responses to Democratic attacks.[94] Pyle breakfasted with Hagerty before press conferences, and either he or Masterson attended cabinet meetings.[95]

These efforts were not completely successful. Among the obstacles Pyle and the liaison office faced was competition from Hagerty. The press secretary, like some of those both before and after him, considered himself to be the White House public-relations expert and "spoke up vigorously on matters related to publicity in Cabinet meetings."[96] Meanwhile, Eisenhower paid little sustained attention to Pyle's efforts, and the perceived need for such an operation declined precipitously after the 1956 election.

In August 1957, John Eisenhower wrote a lengthy memo to his father outlining the administration's "political problems." Among his criticisms was the "failure to communicate important facts, issues to the people in general."[97] The younger Eisenhower's solution was to restructure the White House public-relations operation, creating an "informal committee whose job it would be to study the political situation, particularly as regards your fundamental issues and [to] recommend means of retaining the initiative."[98] He suggested that at least one staffer be assigned full time to this task. The president chose not to follow his son's recommendations for additional structuring. When Pyle left in January 1959, no replacement was assigned to take on his public-relations responsibilities, signaling Hagerty's victory.

Kennedy: Continued Market Structuring

Recognition of the need for public-relations efforts continued in the Kennedy administration. According to Sorensen, JFK was especially concerned with the need to educate and mobilize public opinion.[99] As during previous presidencies, however, most of the administration's activities were sporadic and not systematically pursued. This time, the explanation involves presidential choice factors rather than the opposition of the presidential press secretary: namely, the free-flowing approach to management generally characteristic of the Kennedy White House and JFK's reluctance to relinquish control over public relations.

Market structuring again appeared, and a range of White House aides took on tasks related to public relations. At the outset, Cabinet Secretary

Frederick Dutton urged the president to name a staff assistant to coordinate efforts to "marshall public support for our legislative proposals." Such a person "should be responsible not only for the overall program," which involved sending administration spokespeople around the country, but also "for making sure that the chief press representatives of the speakers participate in the program, plan ahead to make maximum use of local TV, local news angles, and other on-the-scene opportunities."[100]

Although such structuring never materialized, ad hoc efforts continued. Special assistant Brooks Hays was the closest to a public-relations specialist on the staff. He worked with fellow aides McGeorge Bundy, Lawrence O'Brien, Ralph Dungan, and Howard Petersen, spending most of his time giving speeches around the country.[101] In addition, Arthur Schlesinger attempted to get articles critical of Republicans or supportive of the administration placed in newspapers and magazines, and even wrote some himself.[102]

Other times, staffers became involved in particular issues. The most sustained effort was probably made by Howard Petersen's office, which, much like Randall's operation in the Eisenhower White House, was charged with mobilizing congressional, business, and public support for the president's trade program.[103]

Unlike in the Roosevelt and Eisenhower administrations, but reminiscent of the Truman era, the press secretary played only a minor role in public relations during the Kennedy years. Observers at the time noted that Pierre Salinger did "not make public relations policy nearly as much as Hagerty did."[104] Yet reduced competition from the press office failed to produce White House efforts to better coordinate press and public-relations activities. At least in part, this simply mirrored the more general approach to organization that was characteristic of the Kennedy White House. Key too, however, was the president's confidence in his own capacity both to effectively persuade in personal appearances and to develop appropriate strategies for gaining publicity.[105]

Johnson: Troubles Continue

Somewhat more staff specialization in public relations arose in the Johnson White House. Yet market structuring generally persisted, and no unit for handling public relations emerged. In part, this reflected the enormous tasks the administration took on and the mounting problems it faced—first in domestic policy and then in Vietnam. Under those conditions, many staffers had strong ideas about how the president might promote and defend his positions. At least as important, however, were Lyndon Johnson's approaches to public relations.

Early on, Horace Busby was the staffer most consistently concerned with the administration's "image."[106] He sought to interject a degree of hierarchical structuring into public relations—attempting, for example, to improve the volume and the quality of executive branch speeches given around the country, pushing cabinet members to submit advance statements "of major significance" for release after cabinet meetings, and suggesting that agencies work to make their accomplishments known.[107] Busby warned the First Lady's press aide, Liz Carpenter, to keep Lady Bird Johnson away from too close an association with Planned Parenthood, suggesting highway beautification as a more suitable concern.[108]

Also involved in public relations during this period was Paul Southwick, a special assistant for special projects who was a carryover from the Kennedy White House. Southwick helped compile information from executive branch agencies on their accomplishments since 1961.[109] Presidential assistant Ivan Sinclair developed and mailed speeches on the Great Society to key Democrats around the country, on Busby's recommendation.[110]

After Busby left the White House in late 1965, the aide most consistently involved in administration publicity efforts was Fred Panzer, a public-opinion specialist who referred to himself as "a public relations man."[111] Panzer performed a variety of tasks designed to help promote the administration, reporting to either Cabinet Secretary Robert Kintner or Appointments Secretary Marvin Watson.[112] He drafted materials on the accomplishments of the first three years of the Johnson presidency, generated telegrams of support for various presidential initiatives, produced materials for responses to attacks on LBJ, and worked with executive branch agencies to encourage them to develop a range of outreach channels to publicize their accomplishments. From his lower position in the White House hierarchy, Panzer also sought to serve as a White House public-relations consultant of sorts for more senior staffers. Thus, he advised Kintner on potential presidential television appearances and on ways of handling negative poll findings,[113] and he gave domestic policy aide Joseph Califano suggestions on how to respond to the Kerner Commission Report.[114]

According to Eric Goldman, LBJ immediately became engrossed in "what some of the less reverent members of his staff called 'the pollarama.'"[115] The president directly commissioned polls "to a much greater extent" than his predecessor had.[116] Oliver Quayle continued to do a great deal of the polling, as he had for JFK, and subjects ranged far beyond campaign issues to "monitor[ing] the 'political climate' in states and cities across the country."[117]

To deal with the mounting data, first Busby and Richard Nelson (assistant to Appointments Secretary Walter Jenkins), then Hayes Redmon on Bill Moyers's staff, and finally Panzer became the poll specialists.[118] Panzer—whom LBJ called his "poll cat"[119]—tracked mostly presidential approval levels as well as public views on key policy issues such as civil rights and Vietnam. He provided advance reports from Gallup and Harris (speaking with their staffs frequently) and examined other surveys taken around the country. Panzer not only described but also analyzed, criticized, and sought to explain the results. In addition, he reported "trying to cultivate Lou Harris," who in any case was quite willing to supply a steady stream of polling results and interpretations.[120]

Panzer, however, did not monopolize White House public-relations activities. Robert Kintner originally was brought to the White House in part to help improve the president's image.[121] Kintner sought to make greater use of cabinet members as speakers and tried to shield LBJ from overexposure.[122] In addition, Kintner "lunched frequently with Walter Lippmann, James Reston, and television executives in order to provide them with a sympathetic, insider's view of what was going on in an administration."[123] Other staffers likewise offered suggestions and worked in the administration's behalf.[124]

Not surprisingly, Vietnam was a frequent and increasingly painful subject. Especially those staffers who were not directly involved in foreign policy pled with the president to change his public strategies on the war. Early on, Busby paid considerable attention to how the larger public perceived the administration's activities in Vietnam. For example, he urged Johnson to give "better headline perspective" on the U.S. role in Southeast Asia and to encourage Secretary of Defense Robert McNamara to give people a better sense of "what he believes, not what he computes."[125] In 1967, Special Counsel McPherson begged the president to "present our Vietnam case more convincingly" and work to " 'de-politicize' your reports on Vietnam." McPherson hoped to make Johnson seem like "more of a commander-in-chief, and less of a beleaguered political figure trying to defend what is happening."[126] And just before LBJ decided not to seek reelection, economic policy assistant Ernest Goldstein advised the president to offer a cease-fire in order to demonstrate that he was "the peace candidate."[127]

Such recommendations and observations were typical of those offered by many in the White House who continually tried to paint Vietnam as a public-relations problem rather than a thorny and morally troublesome policy question. Staffers, for example, tended to approach the so-called credibility gap as though it were merely the result of poor publicity—a "communications gap."[128]

Although compared to the Kennedy years the Johnson White House paid more attention to public relations, there was considerably less staff speaking, mostly due to the president. LBJ had a well-known aversion to his aides' receiving more publicity than he did. McPherson tried to counter this as early as 1965 (following the infamous speech praising Johnson by presidential assistant Jack Valenti):

the public, if it thinks of [White House aides] at all, thinks of docile calves hustling around at the will of a singular bull. . . . I think there is a danger in the public belief that we are neutered, cowed by you, afraid to use whatever talents we have if our advice were to run counter to your views.[129]

McPherson thought that the solution was to permit the top staff to do more speaking, and the president evidently approved.[130] By 1968, however, Johnson blocked most of McPherson's requests to speak to outside groups.[131]

More generally, LBJ's insistence on dominating his administration affected the handling of public-relations activities in the White House. As his assistant press secretary later observed,

although Johnson wanted a public relations "genius" to do for him what he assumed Pierre Salinger had done for Kennedy, he was afraid that if he let subordinates such as Robert Kennedy get "too big," they would be a threat to him.[132]

CONCLUSIONS

Not until the Nixon administration did a White House public-relations unit, like the one that Eisenhower had experimented with, reemerge—as the Office of Communications. Communications structures became institutionalized, and they have appeared in one form or another in all subsequent administrations.[133]

Even with the creation of communications offices, however, the uneasy and volatile relations between press and public-relations operations that began to surface in the 1930s have continued. In some more recent White Houses, communications and press tasks have been placed in separate units with few formal links connecting them—as happened throughout the Nixon and Bush years and late in the Ford, Carter, and Reagan administrations. In other instances, some form of hierarchical structuring has been interjected. Both Ford and Carter at first experimented with placing communications under the press secretary, and communications chief David Gergen supervised the press office during the early Reagan years.[134] President Clinton initially followed the latter path, with Communications Director George Stephanopoulos even taking over the primary briefing responsibilities from Press Secretary Dee Dee Myers.[135]

The efficacy of relying on hierarchical structures to cope with the long-standing tensions between those involved in day-to-day dealings with the

Washington media and those responsible for longer-term and more unmediated efforts to shape public messages about the president is unclear. Undeniably, the strength, skill, and compatibility of the individuals responsible for press and public relations are likely to be important, as is the ability of the president and other senior White House officials to provide appropriate direction and support.

Even so, the nature of the linking structures themselves is a relevant consideration. For the most part, the situation confronting press and public-relations officials appears to involve fairly high goal consensus, with the primary objective being to promote the president and administration policies and programs. Yet significant uncertainty and controversy might well be expected over the selection of specific strategies and tactics for attaining that goal. Disagreements also are likely to erupt over how to distinguish in practice between "press" and "communications" tasks, reflecting differences over the relevant targets of and channels for information and persuasion. Press secretaries, for example, tend to pay more attention to and try to act consistently with the norms and expectations of the Washington media; those performing communications tasks are more apt to advocate going directly to citizens or to more malleable local media outlets.[136] Meanwhile, of course, competition among ambitious staffers over disputed, ambiguous turf promises to fuel any conflict.

If the decision setting that typically faces those with press and public-relations responsibilities can in fact be characterized as one of relatively high goal consensus and relatively low technical certainty (fitting into cell 2 or 8 of Table 2), then congruent structures would seem to be those with more collegial-consensual or adjudicative features rather than hierarchical ones. Collegial-consensual structuring appears to have been the kind of response that John Eisenhower was groping for when advising his father to rethink White House handling of public relations. The Blair House Group operation in the first-term Reagan White House, which brought together senior staffers to settle on overall directions and strategies for achieving presidential policy goals and boosting public approval, also had some of these characteristics; significantly, however, until David Gergen left in 1984, Acting Press Secretary Larry Speakes was conspicuously not a participant.[137] If participants in these sorts of collegial structures disagree, then either collegial-competitive structuring or some sort of additional adjudicative structuring could provide a useful conflict-resolution mechanism. The president or chief of staff, for example, could be appealed to to settle disputes over the means of achieving goals; such a person also could help ensure that participants stayed focused on and acted consistently with the shared objective of advancing presidential interests.

Remaining unresolved, of course, is the desirability of such activities for the U.S. political system.[138] If more and more White House time and energy are being devoted to efforts at shaping public opinion, then perhaps fewer resources are being focused on careful and sustained policy deliberation, development, and fulfillment.

4

Staffing the Executive Branch

Even as members of Congress and the public looked increasingly to the White House for leadership, presidents confronted another possible barrier to accomplishing their goals: the executive branch bureaucracy. Between 1929 and 1969, the executive branch grew in significance and complexity, and departments and agencies became targets of outreach by the White House staff.

Among the avenues for presidential influence in the executive branch are political appointments and oversight of the civil service. The former, of course, involves a key player (and, in many cases, another target) in the president's political environment: the political party. During the early modern era, with expanding presidential staffs, handling patronage moved from its traditional location in national party committees to the White House Office. For a period, it was joined by structuring for civil service liaison.

The addition of the secretary to the president gave early presidents some potential help in managing political appointments. The first secretary to be involved in patronage was Grant's aide Orville Babcock, whose legendary corruption was abetted by his considerable influence over presidential appointments.[1] The influence of subsequent secretaries varied. But with the development of the plural staff under Hoover, it was virtually inevitable that White House involvement would become institutionalized. Hoover gave this a push by assigning one of his staffers, Walter Newton, the responsibility of looking after patronage.

Yet the emergence in the White House Office of governance structures for processing political appointments was a consequence of Franklin Roosevelt's determination to wrest control of patronage away from Democratic party bosses. The general decline in the influence of political parties during the early modern period and the transfer of patronage expectations to presidents worked to keep the White House involved, despite the opposition of presidents such as Dwight Eisenhower. Compared with congressional liaison and press relations, however, White House structuring for handling patronage was less stable. Partly a consequence of divergent presidential choices, the reduced stability also reflected incompletely resolved goal conflicts, which escalated in the 1960s. Important as well during the Kennedy and Johnson years was an organizational factor: White House battles over control of political appointments. A term-cycle effect also contributed to lower stability. The importance of patronage matters and presidential attention to them declined as a term neared its end. Meanwhile, presidential goals typically focused more on loyalty to the administration and less on programmatic concerns.

Paralleling these efforts to cope with patronage pressures on presidents were attempts to link the White House with the other source of federal employment, the civil service. As with patronage, the emergence of such structuring in the White House Office can be traced to a strategic decision by FDR, albeit one encouraged by environmental factors. Gradually, the structures linking the White House and the civil service were combined with those for screening political appointments, reflecting the influence both of the environment and of presidential choice.

The early modern presidencies varied considerably in their handling of personnel matters. Despite the general congruence of Roosevelt's initial collegial-mediative structuring with the decision setting of the 1930s, the onset of World War II brought immense environmental volatility. Two additional kinds of collegial-mediative structures developed in response to these changes. Meanwhile, Roosevelt's attempt to involve the White House in civil service decision making produced only a single liaison official. Still, the interactions between this task and patronage led to additional structural elaboration—the differentiation dynamic at work.

After the war, organizational inertia led to the persistence of structuring for civil service liaison, but patronage fell into confusion. Truman ultimately tried a new strategy, placing patronage and civil service liaison in a single office. Like FDR, he experimented with collegial-mediative structuring, which was congruent with the prevailing decision setting.

With the change in administrations and in the party controlling the White House, however, this particular innovation did not endure. Eisenhower, concerned with maintaining a nonpartisan image, initially hoped to move both personnel tasks out of the White House altogether. During this period, presidential preference and environmental demands conflicted, with the latter typically prevailing. Environmental expectations precluded patronage from leaving, and new structures soon emerged for handling it, their details dictated more by the preferences of Chief of Staff Sherman Adams than by the president. Similarly, despite Eisenhower's reluctance, responsibility for civil service soon reentered the White House, again due mainly to environmental imperatives.

Presidential choices veered sharply again under Kennedy. At the outset, mostly incongruent patronage mechanisms emerged, with collegial-consensual structures operating in decision settings marked by goal conflict. A more congruent structure with links to key environmental actors soon supplemented the original structuring, but the tension between these two semi-independent White House structures was never fully resolved, even in the Johnson administration. Structures for mediating conflict among competing White House goals and aides failed to emerge.

HOOVER: THE CALM BEFORE THE STORM

Herbert Hoover's designated personnel aide, Walter Newton, added patronage to his other duties as liaison with Congress and with independent boards and commissions. Newton's primary credentials were his prior service in the House of Representatives and his active work for Hoover in the 1928 campaign. He had no involvement with civil service issues, which did not come into the White House in any significant way under Hoover.

As we have seen, Newton was not a particularly effective presidential staffer, despite his strategic position. In the case of personnel, this lack of influence was partly because, after eight years of Republican rule, there was not a great deal of patronage available to the new administration. Furthermore, patronage was a subject in which Hoover was generally uninterested.[2] His one major effort in this area was a "national patronage advisory committee," consisting for most of its existence of Newton and Postmaster General Walter Brown. It largely failed in its efforts to reform the "lily-white" southern Republican parties.[3]

In addition, Newton never had anything resembling full control over the administration's patronage decisions. At the outset of the Hoover years, Newton shared this responsibility with James F. Burke, general counsel to the Republican National Committee (RNC). This led a contemporary observer to note than Newton "feels that he is being slighted and that his importance and influence are not being sufficiently recognized and appreciated."[4] As the administration wore on, Brown became Hoover's key patronage official.[5] Even on the White House staff, Newton did not dominate patronage. Appointments Secretary Lawrence Richey, who was far closer to Hoover than was Newton, allegedly "sifted" patronage requests.[6]

Overall, patronage was not as central to the Hoover administration as it had been and would be to many others. Newton was unable to gain a clear foothold in this area in part because Hoover saw no major presidential interest to protect. As a result, primary responsibility remained outside the White House, with the postmaster general and the RNC.

ROOSEVELT: THE STORM, THEN REFORM

The early Roosevelt administration was the antithesis of the Hoover years in many respects, none more striking than patronage. The reasons are obvious. The Democrats had ascended to power after a 12-year drought, and they were led by politicians who had no distaste for political patronage. Moreover, the administration was frantically creating new entities to run its anti-depression programs, all of which it placed outside the civil service system. Roosevelt's initial arrangements for handling political appointments were traditional, with routine patronage placed under the control of Postmaster General Jim Farley. Burns describes what ensued: "Thousands of applicants besieged Farley in his office and hotel until the Postmaster General had to sneak back and forth to his office as if he were dodging a sheriff's writ."[7] It was business as usual, except for the remarkable volume of requests and openings.

Despite the magnitude of the personnel task, Roosevelt did not emulate Hoover in trying to formally shift some of this burden into the White House Office. None of his three original staffers was officially assigned to patronage work. In part, this was because FDR himself took an active interest in top-level patronage. Nor did he discourage the development of alternative channels for locating talent for important positions, such as the veritable pipeline from Harvard Law School operated by Felix Frankfurter, the "master employment manager for young lawyers seeking government jobs."[8]

Nevertheless, there was no way to keep Roosevelt's top secretary, the canny Louis Howe, entirely away from patronage matters. A White House generalist, Howe "was free to meddle wherever he wished,"[9] which definitely included staffing the administration. Although Farley later claimed that Howe never interfered in his patronage operation, Howe did "refer a steady stream of applicants," knowing that "his suggestion would be respected."[10] And Farley reciprocated, such as by sharing information about civil service openings with Howe.[11] Congressional complaints over patronage also were funneled through Howe. For example, in a letter to Howe's secretary, Agriculture's Julian Friant transmitted relevant data and noted, "No doubt quite a few Senators and Congressmen complain to Colonel Howe about not receiving any patronage. These lists show you what each of them has received through the Department of Agriculture."[12] Howe also paid special attention to Civilian Conservation Corps (CCC) appointments, urging that they be kept on a nonpolitical, merit basis.[13]

Strengthening the White House Role

Roosevelt's second term marked a change of circumstance and of presidential strategy. Frustrated by Democratic opposition to the New Deal, FDR sought to create an executive branch that would be more loyal to the president and his purposes.[14] Even before his attempted "purge" of disloyal Democrats in the 1938 election, Roosevelt had taken a smaller step in this direction by placing his son, James Roosevelt, in the White House and including in his portfolio substantial—if largely unofficial—involvement in routine personnel matters.[15] Franklin Roosevelt could not hope to fully separate patronage from the claims of members of Congress and elements of the Democratic Party, but he could at least seek stronger representation of the presidential point of view.

James Roosevelt was succeeded in late 1938 by his assistant, James Rowe, who proceeded to become even more involved in political appointments.[16] This was a time when FDR was turning "more and more to the so-called New Dealers . . . men who were supporters of the President and believed in what he was trying to do, but who were not Democrats in many instances, and in all instances were not organization Democrats."[17] Rowe became a central player in a collegial-mediative structure, responsible for "clearing all nominations with the DNC [Democratic National Committee] and on the Hill"[18] and working to overcome frictions between those elements of the party.

Rowe did not operate independently of the traditional patronage powers. Instead, his standard practice was to pull together a list of possible appointees, weed the list on behalf of the president, then send the surviving names to the DNC for comment. The list would then come back to FDR, who would make a choice and send that name to the DNC for clearance with relevant members of Congress. The understanding was that the name had to be acceptable to the members, but not necessarily their first choice.[19]

The prevailing decision setting changed dramatically as war loomed and the need for industrial mobilization began to overshadow all other domestic issues. Rowe became actively involved in the recruitment and clearance of "dollar-a-year men," those business executives who came to Washington to run the machinery of war production. Rowe and White House special assistant Wayne Coy developed a procedure in which names for such jobs were submitted by the Office of Production Management (OPM) to Coy, then sent to Rowe for preliminary clearance. Rowe sometimes referred these candidates to the FBI for checking. The names then went to FDR, who eliminated those that were unacceptable and sent the list back to Coy, who returned it to the OPM for final appointment. No partisan clearance was involved, and it would have been beside the point: virtually all these appointees were Republican businessmen whose contributions to the war effort were seen as indispensable. This effectively avoided a major source of potential goal controversy, thus making it possible for a hierarchical governance structure to emerge and function satisfactorily, though it was shaken by the OPM's occasional displeasure with the president's decisions, which tended to produce "a certain amount of yelling."[20]

Rowe left the White House in late 1941, moving to the Justice Department before joining the navy in 1943. Patronage and related matters lost their appeal as war began to appear inevitable: "I 'don't give a damn' who ought to be appointed to the D.C. Utilities Commission or the Muhlenberg College Memorial Commission," he wrote. "As is everyone else, I am interested only in national defense."[21] What remained of Rowe's patronage responsibility was transferred to Secretary Marvin McIntyre.[22]

In both routine patronage and the dollar-a-year process, one sees presidential purposes dictating the development of a White House capability. At the same time, environmental imperatives that raised at least the possibility of controversy over goals—the continuing interest of the party and Congress in patronage, the need to involve OPM and others in dollar-a-year appointments—guided the development of a collegial-mediative structure for obtaining clearance in the patronage realm and created at least modest discomfort with the operation of a more hierarchical, less consultative process for the dollar-a-year appointments. The collegial-mediative structure was congruent with a decision setting marked by goal conflict and technical certainty, and the hierarchy seemed reasonable if not fully congruent, given the crisis of looming war and consensus on the overarching goal of mobilization.

The Civil Service Connection

The second major thrust of White House involvement in personnel under FDR began with the creation of the liaison officer for personnel management in September 1939. Prior to this, the Brownlow Committee had recommended replacing the collegial, bipartisan Civil Service Commission with a single administrator, to serve at the pleasure of the president. This would have greatly enhanced presidential influence over personnel policy—which was one reason Congress had rejected the original Brownlow recommendations in 1938.[23] When presidential power over civil service was explicitly denied in the Reorganization Act of 1939, Roosevelt accepted a recommendation by Brownlow that a liaison officer be appointed to coordinate among the Civil Service Commission, the Bureau of the Budget (BOB), and the newly established Federal Personnel Council, a policy body that made recommendations to the president. "This was about as close as Roosevelt could come to centralizing authority for management of the federal personnel system in the absence of legislative support."[24]

William H. McReynolds, another of the original administrative assistants, was appointed liaison officer for personnel management in July 1939. McReynolds, a career civil servant from the Treasury Department, performed the requisite liaison duties. He also worked closely with Rowe and McIntyre on potentially controversial matters such as the blanketing-in, under the Ramspeck Act, of the approximately 125,000 persons appointed during Roosevelt's first term, four-fifths of whom had initially been appointed outside the civil service.[25] Rowe and McReynolds were required to work especially closely on matters that overlapped their primary areas of concern—for instance, how to handle lawyers who objected to being placed under civil service. When the two clashed, Roosevelt would be invited to adjudicate.[26]

With McReynolds's appointment, one again finds the emergence of a basically collegial-mediative structure designed to enhance presidential influence over the environment (in this case, the civil service system) by placing one element of the relevant governance structure in the White House. At the same time, it is clear that the roles carved out by Rowe and McReynolds overlapped, leading to occasions when mediative governance failed to produce an agreed-upon decision. In such cases, FDR, as the legitimate superior of both men, was the logical intervenor, an example of the differentiation dynamic at work.[27] Subsequent presidents would seek to clarify and, in most cases, simplify these structural arrangements.

TRUMAN: EXPERIMENTATION, THEN UNIFICATION

At the outset of the Truman administration, organizational inertia kept the civil service liaison in place, but the patronage task rather quickly plunged into controversy. With many players and uncertain, conflicting goals, market structuring for handling patronage prevailed. Truman ultimately responded by placing patronage and civil service in a single structure.

The First Two Years

When Harry Truman took office, the only remaining White House staffer with any continuing interest in personnel issues was McReynolds, who soon departed.[28] His successor for a short time was George Schoeneman, who soon vacated the administrative assistant position to become special assistant in charge of White House management. The position of liaison officer then went to Raymond Zimmerman, who served between September 1945 and March 1947.

Zimmerman, a veteran of the Civil Service Commission, pushed aggressively for modernizing the civil service in such areas as pay, health benefits, leave policy, productivity, and employee unionization while converting federal employment back to a peacetime basis.[29] He acted as the president's representative across the range of civil service matters, reporting formally to Truman but frequently communicating his ideas by transmitting them to military aide and presidential crony Harry Vaughan.[30] Zimmerman left the White House for "personal reasons" in 1947, eliciting sighs of relief from several on the White House staff, including Correspondence Secretary Bill Hassett, who proclaimed "V-Zim Day."[31] Personal considerations aside, Zimmerman's reformist objectives likely were not fully consistent with the more partisan political goals of some of his White House colleagues.

Prior to mid-1947, the president did little to systematize his consideration of patronage, and market structuring emerged. In the White House, responsibility for patronage involved such top advisers as Special Counsel Samuel Rosenman, Personal Representative George Allen, and Appointments Secretary Matthew Connelly. Meanwhile, outside the White House, the president tended to leave departmental personnel decisions in the hands of his cabinet officers.[32] Postmaster General Robert Hannegan, who was also DNC chairman, was sharply critical of some of these appointments and asserted—with some success—a stronger role for the party in patronage.[33]

After two years in office, then, Truman faced a patronage system largely unorganized and out of his control. Moreover, the civil service liaison operation fit uncomfortably in his White House. The personnel system that had been complex under Roosevelt had grown confused under Truman. Clearly change was in order.

Donald Dawson: Combining the Functions

In August 1947, Truman appointed Donald Dawson administrative assistant and liaison officer for personnel management, replacing Zimmerman. However, Dawson, formerly director of personnel for the Reconstruction Finance Corporation, did more than merely assume the duties of the liaison officer. He both combined and systematized personnel matters—patronage as well as civil service—in the White House. In his patronage work, Dawson essentially revived the central role played by Rowe under Roosevelt, even going beyond his predecessors in the degree to which he centralized the White House aspect of the patronage system in his own office.

Dawson routinized the keeping of patronage records; became the White House liaison with members of Congress, party officials, and others with patronage business; actively worked to place individuals recommended by partisan sources; and cleared presidential appointments with powerful Democrats.[34] In doing all this, Dawson worked cooperatively with the DNC, much in the manner that Rowe and Jimmy Roosevelt had pioneered.[35] In keeping with the practices of prior administrations, the White House was only one element—and not the most prominent one—of the collegial-mediative governance structure.

At the same time, Dawson and his assistant, Martin Friedman, also continued in the tradition of McReynolds and Zimmerman as civil service policy makers. Indeed, in an essay describing his duties, Dawson dwelt more on this task than on the patronage aspect of his work, noting that:

> I was responsible for the complete revision of the Classification Act in 1949, which set the grades and compensation of federal employees. . . . I recommended—and by Executive Order President Truman provided for—the appointment of career administrative assistant secretaries in certain of the departments to provide administrative continuity on a nonpolitical basis.[36]

Dawson also instituted the practice of running FBI checks on all new appointees.[37]

In retrospect, it may seem remarkable that Dawson and Friedman were able to preside over the highly partisan business of allocating patronage (in an administration alleged by its critics to be dominated by corrupt insiders) while simultaneously functioning as the president's representatives in the nonpartisan realm of civil service. Yet they did so, without offending the more politically minded in the administration or provoking any serious charges that they were undermining the merit system. In part, this was because Dawson and those who worked with him did not see these tasks as necessarily conflicting. After all, both had to do with recruiting the best people for the administration, though the rules of recruitment and the definition of "best" would vary according to type of position.

Truman did not attempt to dominate either the allocation of partisan patronage or the operation of the civil service system. It is reasonable to suppose that, had he tried, opposition from partisans on the one hand (who still ran, among other things, campaigns for president) and good-government advocates on the other would have frustrated his designs. Instructively, when Truman and his advisers briefly toyed with the idea of gaining more freedom from the national party through the creation of greater White House personnel capability, they had to abandon the plan in the face of opposition from elements of the Democratic Party.[38] Given such environmental constraints on presidential aspirations, the juggling act of Dawson and Friedman could be sustained.

Thus the governance structuring forged by Rowe and McReynolds had sprung back to life—simplified and rationalized, but not fully stabilized. The Truman approach would not survive intact into the next administration.

EISENHOWER: DIVIDING THE ROLES AGAIN

Following a suggestion by BOB Director Joseph Dodge, Dwight Eisenhower abolished the position of liaison officer for personnel management upon taking office in January 1953.[39] The chair of the Civil Service Commission, Philip Young, formally became the president's principal personnel management adviser. This arrangement endured into Eisenhower's second term. But it still left patronage to be handled in the White House.

Patronage: Staffing the Floodgates

Eisenhower was uncomfortable with patronage, wanted little to do with it, and chose initially to delegate as much responsibility for it as possible to the departments and the party. Nevertheless, a significant responsibility for handling political appointments remained in the White House. This was due primarily to environmental factors: after 20 years of Democratic rule, triumphant Republicans pushed hard to replace incumbent appointees with Republicans who would be loyal to the new regime. Thus, although Eisenhower personally had no taste for the matter, his staffers recognized the importance of patronage to the administration and essentially reproduced the patronage apparatus of Ike's predecessors.[40] Moreover, organizational inertia began to play a role at this point. By this time, the existence of some capacity for administering patronage from the White House was beginning to seem like a normal element of any presidency.

Responsibility for patronage was located in the office of Sherman Adams, assistant to the president and chief of staff. From the outset, Adams was heavily involved in this work, normally possessing the power of final approval or disapproval of an appointment.[41] Ultimately, Adams and his assistant Charles Willis wound up assuming as prominent a role in this realm as prior White House aides had, despite Eisenhower's initial hope that the whole business could be shunted off onto the Republican National Committee.[42] Willis was less independent than such predecessors as Rowe and Dawson, but he nevertheless followed in their footsteps as a "political troubleshooting liaison with the national committee"[43] and a buffer between the White House and Congress. To the latter end, he worked closely with the newly created legislative liaison staff. Thus, a kind of collegial-mediative structuring persisted. Yet the president's aversion to purely partisan demands, plus the aggressiveness of Adams, gave this version of the patronage governance structure a more hierarchical, less collegial tone than its predecessors.

Even so, the work of Adams and Willis was inadequate to stem the flood of requests from patronage-starved Republicans, especially senators. In response, Eisenhower created "Schedule C," a new category of "policy-determining" positions for political appointees. But reclassification of jobs into Schedule C was under the control of the Civil Service Commission and could occur only after departmental request. Worse, some of these new positions wound up being filled by Democratic careerists.[44]

Still seeking to cope with the demand, Willis, at the instigation of Adams and Young, went so far as to develop a comprehensive plan whereby the White House would act as a clearinghouse for Schedule C and top (GS 14–18) civil service jobs, notifying members of Congress of vacancies as they occurred. According to Thomas Weko, this approach never really worked, due to a lack of departmental cooperation, and it had to be terminated in late 1954 when news of its existence leaked out.[45] Its significance in retrospect is to highlight the powerful impact of the political environment, even on a White House that was initially committed to resisting such pressure.

The evident reason that the administration's response to patronage pressure was White House centered was the inescapable need to manage goal conflict. Eisenhower sought both competence and loyalty in his appointees, and he could not be assured that the people put forth by party politicians with their own objectives adequately fulfilled those criteria. The only apparent solution to the problem was to perpetuate a governance structure with a firm anchor in the White House itself.

Patronage: Settling Into a Routine

With the demise of the "Willis plan" and the departure of Willis himself about six months later, the Eisenhower White House settled into a pattern that much resembled its predecessors. Willis's successors—Edward Tait, Robert Gray, and Robert Hampton—performed the routine liaison functions but never became involved in any effort to strengthen the White House machinery or presidential control of patronage. Adams continued to preside, although his active involvement became more sporadic as the administration wore on. Other staff members advised in their areas of competence, as had been the case in previous administrations. The RNC continued to play a leading role in the dispensing of patronage.

By the conclusion of the Eisenhower administration, the responsibility for patronage can be said to have become institutionalized in the White House. The pressures of the political environment and organizational precedent overcame even presidential aversion. Still, presidential strategy was scarcely irrelevant. After all, presidents have many strategic goals, not all of them compatible. Eisenhower may have wanted little to do with patronage, but he did want an administration composed of right-thinking, competent individuals. His solution was to keep a strong White House presence, but with little direct presidential involvement in most decisions.

Civil Service: Reinventing a Governance Structure

Even though Eisenhower abolished the position of liaison officer for personnel management, the need for some White House liaison capability did not disappear entirely. Although Young was the principal adviser in this area, Willis also "kept abreast" of civil service developments.[46] Eisenhower always evinced a strong concern for management, as opposed to patronage, matters, and this concern became a recurrent theme of the administration. As early as August 1953, Adams tried to attack both personnel and management problems in the executive branch by allocating supervision of various departments among White House staffers.[47] After unsuccessful attempts at engineering management improvement through civil service and BOB,[48] Eisenhower finally resorted to virtually recreating the liaison officer's job, appointing Rocco Siciliano to be special assistant to the president for personnel management in September 1957.

Siciliano's job was carefully distanced from any involvement with patronage; he was "to advise and assist the president on personnel-management actions exclusive of presidential appointments," with emphasis on formulating a program for management improvement and carrying it to agencies and departments.[49] In fact, Siciliano, who had been assistant secretary of labor, occupied himself principally with such issues as employee morale, compensation systems, health insurance, job training, and management-employee relations.[50] The similarity between Siciliano's work and that of Zimmerman is obvious. Likewise, the regularized role carved out by Siciliano involved him in much the same kind of collegial-mediative interaction with civil service and the departments that his predecessors had had.

Eisenhower's initial attempt to move civil service responsibility out of the White House evidently reflected an assumption that such matters were nonpartisan and did not need to be handled by officials whose first loyalty lay with the president. Placing the liaison function back in the White House suggests that Ike came to see, as his predecessors had, that presidents have different interests, even in this area, than do other officials. They may need, as a consequence, not only to assert their own authority but also to create governance structures that guarantee a continuing White House involvement in policy.

KENNEDY: ACCENT ON PATRONAGE

John Kennedy entered the presidency feeling less dependent on or obligated to his party than his predecessors had, as well as being personally committed to creating what aide Theodore Sorensen called a "ministry of talent."[51] During his transition, JFK began a talent hunt that was better organized and placed more initiative in the incoming administration than had been the case in previous presidencies, and it included "intellectual" as well as political connections.[52] But in January 1961, the "talent hunt" expired and the pressures of patronage entered the White House.

The Kennedy administration wrestled hard with patronage and, although not fully mastering it, managed to make a degree of progress toward a fuller White House capacity. Civil service reform, however, did not rank high on the Kennedy list of priorities, with the result that little White House effort went in that direction.

The Early Months

At the outset, White House patronage responsibility was placed in a collegial-consensual structure. Participating were several members of the "Irish Mafia": congressional liaison head Lawrence O'Brien, appointments secretary Kenneth O'Donnell, staff secretary Ralph Dungan, and O'Donnell aide Richard Maguire. These four met weekly to review openings and recommend people to fill them.[53] The group's staff, housed within O'Brien's Office of Congressional Relations, was led by Maguire and O'Donnell aide Dorothy Davies, who sought both to maintain files and to provide clearances from the Democratic National Committee and Democrats in Congress.[54] But the structure worked badly, even though it was generally congruent with the decision setting. In part, this was because the group's members had other primary duties and because of a lack of staff skill: "O'Donnell, O'Brien and the others did not know anything more about how to run the government than a chair would."[55]

The collegial-consensual structure gradually developed an internal hierarchy. Ralph Dungan emerged as the effective manager of patronage, largely because he had fewer other pressing demands than his colleagues. Relying on Davies and her staff to handle referrals and routine clearances for lower-level jobs, Dungan presided over an operation that was soon viewed within the administration—even by Dungan himself—as inadequate, mainly because it was too oriented toward partisan political interests and insufficiently capable of locating outstanding talent. A number of people in the administration began to urge a return to something like the preinaugural talent hunt.[56]

Dan Fenn and the Search for Talent

O'Donnell and Dungan responded by recruiting Dan Fenn, a faculty member at the Harvard Business School and friend of O'Donnell's, to join the White House staff as an assistant to Dungan for personnel recruitment. Upon arriving in August 1961, Fenn was mildly appalled by the existing system, which he characterized as the " 'BOGSAT system'—a bunch of guys sitting around a table asking each other, 'Whom do you know?' "[57] Fenn and his small staff introduced another collegial-consensual structure, moving along lines that had been thought about but never really implemented in the Truman and Eisenhower administrations. Fenn established a talent bank, relying on a network of contacts that went beyond the usual political referrals, and he systematically inventoried high-level jobs.[58] In effect, he tried to create a presidential capacity to locate and appoint persons who would be more responsive to presidential goals in the personnel area (e.g., competence, loyalty) than to the goals of members of Congress or party workers.

The Fenn operation focused on high-priority, policy-level jobs, intentionally leaving lower-level appointments to the O'Brien-Maguire-Davies group. But this apparently neat division of labor worked unevenly at best in practice. As John Macy, then chair of the Civil Service Commission, recalled:

> Washington's sharpest politicians quickly came to realize that it was possible to circumvent the formal personnel operation and thus get their recommendations to the president directly before Fenn and his staff had geared up for their independent national search. Although it was obviously Kennedy's choice to permit this, it undermined much of the potential value that he might have derived from the much improved appointment procedures that Fenn and his staff had developed.[59]

Charles U. Daly of O'Brien's staff put the matter more colorfully. When a member of Congress was pushing for a candidate unbeknownst to Fenn, the legislative relations staff might go to bat for the member. If not, or if they were unsuccessful, they could use Fenn as a convenient whipping boy:

> We would screw Fenn—legitimately, because it certainly was Dungan's understanding that, trying to get votes and so on up there, we were not in the business of saying no to Congressmen. We'd say, "Jeez, I don't know, that goddamn Fenn has had that thing for a month."[60]

As Weko notes more generally, the competition Fenn experienced came not so much from the DNC, which had lost much of its earlier bite, but rather from within the White House and elsewhere within the administration, especially the departments.[61] Nevertheless, the Fenn operation won its share of victories and is generally given credit for improving the quality of top appointees. More important, it represented a significant enhancement of presidential influence, a "turning point" in White House capability.[62]

Competition and Disorder

These two overlapping governance structures sought different and, as Daly rightly noted, legitimate goals. The consequent controversy over goals generated turf struggles but no effective means of resolving conflicts. The differentiation dynamic appeared, and a kind of informal adjudicative structure emerged: final decisions rested with the president. But such a characterization is actually misleading, for nothing like an orderly presentation of alternatives was apt to occur, and Kennedy was not always involved. Rather, outcomes were dependent on who acted first, who got Kennedy's ear, or what short-term imperative seemed most pressing at a given time. Here, additional congruent governance structuring was called for but, mainly because of Kennedy's disbelief in obtrusive structures, did not develop.

Civil Service

The position of special assistant for personnel management was not filled at the outset of the Kennedy administration, but neither was the personnel liaison task formally ejected from the White House, as Eisenhower had initially tried. Rather, it was given to Maguire, which meant effectively reuniting the political patronage and civil service liaison roles, roughly following the Truman precedent.[63] The location of the civil service responsibility in a White House aide who was less prominent than Dawson had been reflected Kennedy's relative lack of interest in the subject.

When Fenn arrived, liaison with civil service drifted to him, and Maguire left the White House a few months later.[64] Fenn's relationship with John Macy, chair of the Civil Service Commission, was excellent. Macy offered Fenn staff and supported his efforts. This location of civil service liaison can be seen as a reasonable compromise between entrusting it to political operatives on the one hand or to civil service personnel specialists on the other. At the same time, it was evidently not much more of a major priority for Fenn than it had been for Maguire.

JOHNSON: ANOTHER SOLUTION, MORE CONFLICT

Lyndon Johnson inherited the personnel operation under Dungan but without Fenn, who left the White House in October 1963. LBJ also inherited many of Kennedy's other influential personnel advisers and brought several more into the White House with him. In short, in this area, as in so many others, he faced the new opportunities and the unsolved problems that were the Kennedy legacy. But Johnson also was inspired by an older legacy, that of Franklin Roosevelt. Like his erstwhile mentor, LBJ sought to shake free of the restraints of the Democratic Party,[65] another illustration of partisan learning.

The First Year

Johnson initially tried to work with Dungan much as JFK had, though less formally. Then, wanting to integrate his own staff into the process, he briefly tried a "personnel committee." This intendedly collegial-consensual structure was chaired by Dungan and included Johnson aides Walter Jenkins and Cliff Carter, along with O'Donnell, O'Brien, and Maguire.[66] The unease and distrust between Johnson staffers and former Kennedy aides kept this arrangement from working well. Dungan, beginning to feel left out, successfully requested appointment as ambassador to Chile. As he later put it, "What really happened was that I went out of business. . . . You go out of business very gently. All of a sudden there's nobody listening to you."[67]

What had developed to supplant Dungan was a "more informal, more intimate appointments process"[68] involving aides such as Jenkins, Bill Moyers, Jack Valenti, and Horace Busby, plus advisers and confidants outside the White House. The key was Jenkins, who devoted more time to appointments than to anything else during the first year.[69] Still LBJ was unsatisfied, especially when Jenkins was forced to leave in October 1964. At that point, Johnson announced a committee consisting of Secretary of Defense Robert McNamara, Commissioner of Education Francis Keppel, and Peace Corps Director Sargent Shriver to advise on both patronage and personnel management.[70] However, nothing seems to have come of this.

Clearly, the president was experimenting with structural forms. Johnson's initial committee made a certain amount of sense, since it pooled both expertise and loyalties at a time when both properties were crucial. His later idea seems mainly to have been for public consumption. Had it been seriously implemented, leaving nearly all political stakeholders on the sidelines, it would not have lasted long. What was clear at this point was that, after the 1964 election, Johnson would have to experiment some more.

John Macy: Combining the Functions in a New Way

A week after the 1964 election, Johnson asked John Macy, chair of the Civil Service Commission, to take on an additional duty as LBJ's adviser on political appointments. Johnson thus went Harry Truman one better: not only was his patronage adviser also a liaison to civil service, he was chair of the commission itself. Johnson's reasoning, as Macy recalled it, was that Macy had the expertise necessary to locate the best talent, and his lack of political identification served to stave off some political pressures:

> A number of times it was reported back to me that somebody would come in and complain about a particular appointment that the presi-

dent had made and he was quoted as having said, "Well, don't blame me. It's that goddamned Macy—he insists on merit."[71]

Macy's patronage involvement was limited to talent evaluation and recruitment. Political judgments were to be left to others. Macy proceeded to formally bring all existing White House machinery for patronage into his office.[72] He divided the government into segments, each assigned to a member of his staff.[73] The office proceeded, much in the manner of the Fenn operation, to develop talent pools, maintain records of positions, and cultivate relationships with people in the departments.[74] Macy described the meticulousness of this work:

> We developed in our records center a file on each of these positions, so that we had background information for the President on the statutory history of the position, on the individuals who had occupied the position previously, and then the correspondence relating to filling the position.[75]

The staff worked from a list of about 400 people they used as sources for identifying and evaluating candidates, building on a list inherited from Dungan and Fenn. The name file of possible appointees grew to 16,000. Working within a collegial-consensual structure, they put together lists of recommended candidates for LBJ, who would indicate those he was interested in or request more names. When Johnson had narrowed the field to one candidate, the FBI and the congressional relations office (or occasionally someone from Macy's staff) would begin doing clearance work.[76]

The principal difference between Macy's operation and that of Dungan and Fenn lay in the realm of presidential priorities. Clearly, Johnson was more committed at the outset to this White House–centered, merit-driven approach than Kennedy had ever been. When such luminaries as DNC Chair John Bailey, White House political aide Cliff Carter, and even James Rowe, LBJ's campaign director in both 1964 and 1968, became upset at Macy's resistance to their nominees, Johnson backed Macy.[77] The reasons for the president's attitude are debatable. He may have feared the DNC as a possible instrument of the Kennedys, or seen its influence as inconsistent with his efforts to transcend partisanship in his national leadership. At least as plausible is Sidney Milkis's suggestion that Johnson simply viewed the party as more of an impediment than an asset to the attainment of his ambitious policy goals, especially in the area of civil rights.[78]

Competence Versus Loyalty

Despite Macy's competence and Johnson's support, problems arose, somewhat reminiscent of those of the previous administration, but even more intense. By late 1965, Johnson was increasingly concerned with the loyalty of his appointees, especially as some of them began publicly to fall out with the administration over the Vietnam War. The president and some of his aides came to believe that the Macy operation was producing people who were competent and committed to their programs but loyal to neither the Democratic Party nor Lyndon Johnson.[79] Macy's influence began to be challenged.

LBJ had always received ideas from sources other than Macy and had run Macy's suggestions by other advisers. Schott and Hamilton describe a "surrogate appointments process," a kind of market structuring in which a "shifting constellation" of White House aides and other advisers had long influenced appointments outside of Macy's formal structure.[80] In the White House, people such as Jack Valenti and Bill Moyers had been especially useful to LBJ, their advice supplementing Macy's without undermining it. In late 1965 and early 1966, with Macy's project generating some suspicion, Johnson turned even more to other surrogates, especially Appointments Secretary Marvin Watson. The effect of this on Macy's position became corrosive.

Watson's influence on appointments acquired a formal aspect in early 1966 when he, rather than Macy, began receiving FBI reports on potential appointees and he assigned his aide, Doug Nobles, to serve on Macy's staff.[81] Watson's influence grew, especially over key appointments, as he stressed loyalty to LBJ over the competence-related criteria identified with Macy. Despite these conflicting goals, no additional governance structure emerged to sort out the responsibilities of the Watson and Macy operations. Instead, the changing influence dynamics in the White House drove personnel-related activities, reflecting the intensifying environmental pressures, the president's shifting priorities, and the normal tendency of an administration to come to favor loyalists as a term wears on. Accounts differ as to the effect of Watson's efforts on Macy's.[82] What is clear is that Macy's influence over top appointments was at least compromised, though his preeminence in the realm of mid-level appointments, as well as on policy matters involving civil service, remained largely unchallenged.

As the Johnson administration proceeded, the appointments problem became one of factoring in a growing emphasis on personal and programmatic loyalty. Previous administrations had faced a fairly straightforward conflict involving criteria of competence versus partisan loyalties, which could be addressed within collegial-mediative structures. In contrast, during the later Johnson years, the goals of the appointments process became uncertain because LBJ never addressed the general question clearly enough to untangle its elements. As Table 2 (see Chapter 1) suggests, a marketlike structure, allowing each decision to emerge as a consequence of particularistic concerns or circumstances, was arguably more congruent with such a setting than any form of collegial decision making, since the latter was too apt to produce stalemate and acrimony. Also indicated in Table 2 is "inspiration" or presidential leadership. This was not forthcoming.

Johnson mainly succeeded, then, in reproducing the kind of tangled governance that Kennedy had left behind. A merit-based patronage operation coexisted, increasingly uneasily, with a more conventionally political one. Seemingly understanding that all was not working well, Johnson continued to tinker with arrangements, for instance, assigning newly appointed Cabinet Secretary Robert Kintner to advise on appointments when he arrived in April 1966.[83] Such efforts simply underlined LBJ's sense that he needed an alternative or a supplement to Macy.

Thus, under LBJ as under JFK, the complex, somewhat dispersed business of political appointments frustrated presidential efforts at effective governance, leading in Johnson's case to clear presidential frustration with the outcomes achieved. A core part of the problem was the conflict of goals inherent in the process—competence, loyalty, party maintenance, programmatic commitment, and more. Any governance structure for patronage would need the ability to sort these out explicitly for a tremendous range of dissimilar cases. Macy's operation represented an admirable and partially successful attempt to do all this. It ultimately fell short in large part because the president did not act to clarify the relevant goals. To some extent, this reflected Johnson's strategy of cultivating an informal surrogate patronage system from the beginning as a means of preserving his options and satisfying demands for participation. It may have been tied as well to the aging of the administration. More than anything, though, the shifting environment—the war and its consequent protests—so changed the emphasis on the various goals for LBJ that, at least from his perspective, the Macy shop was no longer reliably producing the kind of product he required. And Johnson himself was not able to respond with the kind of leadership that might have saved the situation.

CONCLUSIONS

By the end of the Johnson years, efforts to distribute party patronage were securely ensconced in the White House, though its structuring had become unstable and problematic. By the middle of his first term, Richard Nixon would seek to exercise more systematic control over political appointments. It was left to Ronald Reagan, however, to fully centralize control over political appointments.[84]

Meanwhile, the ability of John Macy to wear two hats eliminated the need for a separate White House liaison with civil service. In fact, Macy's involvement marked the effective elimination of this as a White House task of any consequence. Richard Nixon would turn to the BOB (which he rechristened the Office of Management and Budget [OMB]) for expertise in matters of personnel management.

The story of civil service liaison, then, is one of several examples of a task that fell in the White House for a time and then left. It entered in this case due to presidential interest and the lack of another obvious place to put it. It finally found a home elsewhere, not because its importance declined but because its considerable significance to Richard Nixon helped provoke a broadening of the responsibility—and a politicization—of the former BOB. Thus, as the rest of the institutional machinery of government diversified and the president assumed greater control of the larger Executive Office, the White House Office was superseded as the institutional home for presidential involvement in personnel management.

5
White House–Executive Branch Relations

Presidents, of course, seek to do more than influence personnel policy in the executive branch. They strive as well to at least learn about—if not always shape—the activities of federal departments and agencies. As White House outreach to the executive branch persisted and intensified during the early modern era, aides strove to be the "spies, gumshoe artists, and needlers" that Richard Neustadt insisted every president needed.[1]

In dealing with the executive branch, White House staffers performed three additional kinds of tasks relevant to outreach.[2] Most frequently, they served as *liaisons*, monitoring agency activities and performance, promoting interagency coordination, and providing information channels to and from the president. In addition, they followed up on specific complaints about agency activity—thus creating the image of the staffer as *troubleshooter* or caseworker—and tried to be *mediators* of disputes between agencies.

Presidential objectives and strategy initially gave rise under Hoover to the location in the White House of an individual charged with executive branch outreach, and incipient market structuring emerged. Soon, environmental demand—the growth of the executive branch during the New Deal—became the driving force in the persistence of White House structuring. Due partly to environmental fluctuations, however, such outreach structures were even less stable than those for staffing, and there was relatively little differentiation. Under such conditions, presidents found it difficult to design structures that were congruent with decision settings.

The market structuring that emerged during the Hoover and early Roosevelt years was generally congruent with decision settings of considerable ambiguity. Other structures that FDR established to cope with the coordination problems produced by his New Deal initiatives were less congruent: they were largely hierarchical in decision settings characterized by considerable goal conflict. An effort to employ the newly created administrative assistant positions never really got off the ground as World War II intruded. During the war, market structuring again prevailed, presidential inspiration was sporadic, and the differentiation dynamic failed to produce structuring to address the competition among numerous structures handling overlapping tasks.

During the Truman administration, environmental imperatives (mainly postwar reconstruction) made executive branch outreach a high priority. The conflict and rapid change characteristic of the decision settings Truman faced required extensive mediation among agencies. Informal collegial-mediative structures surfaced in response. Formal hierarchical structuring emerged as well. Highlighted during this time was the importance of individuals: as we have seen, successful organizational governance depends on more than congruent structural design.

With Eisenhower, hierarchical structuring persisted, as the president emulated his two predecessors in designating specialists in executive branch relations. These efforts were not always congruent with conflictual decision settings that also seemed to demand efforts at mediation and adjudication. Once more, the definition of the problem that executive branch outreach was intended to address was "coordination," which made hierarchy seem reasonable and obscured the potential for controversy and uncertainty.

Kennedy retreated from the emphasis on hierarchy, a move that reflected both presidential choice and partisan learning looking back to Truman; Eisenhower's reporting structures, however, remained. Some collegial structuring as well as active presidential involvement replaced much of the Eisenhower approach. Yet the Kennedy administration likely relied too much on presidential inspiration without adequate structural support for follow-up and to address the full range of decision settings relevant to executive branch outreach.

Although retaining hierarchical reporting mechanisms, Johnson experimented with numerous structures of various types, responding in part to the environmental demand generated by the explosion of Great Society initiatives. A specialized domestic policy operation emerged and grew to incorporate collegial-mediative structuring for handling many interagency disputes—reminiscent of the Truman administration's responses to similarly challenging circumstances.

Overall, although the White House continued to rely on hierarchical reporting structures, structural instability remained the norm. This relative instability reflected both environmental volatility and presidential choice. Together, these influences made White House identification of fully congruent structures quite problematic.

HOOVER: LIAISON AMID AMBIGUITY

Most of the executive branch outreach activities in the Hoover administration can be classified as routine liaison, conducted through ad hoc market structures. At least formally, legislative liaison Walter Newton was also assigned to "take charge of the administrative offices of government for which the President is directly responsible, but which are not attached to any cabinet department."[3] In addition, Newton was to "generally assist in the usual White House work in coordination of the administrative work of all departments of the government."[4] For all the initial attention, however, Newton spent little time on any of these liaison tasks.

Other White House staffers were more active. For instance, a favorite Hoover device for promoting policy study and change was the White House conference or commission, with administrative assistants French Strother and George Hastings serving as the White House contacts.[5] At times, White House aides acted as agents for interjecting presidential direction into these formally collegial-consensual structures. Such activities involved them in frequent contacts with executive agencies.[6]

Nonetheless, market structuring was the dominant structural form. The Hoover administration confronted a setting of considerable ambiguity: not only were the plural professional staff and their responsibilities new, with few precedents for their operation, but these innovations also had to work in a political environment that became increasingly shot through with uncertainty and controversy over how to deal with a shattered economy. In such decision settings, market structuring was not only understandable but also generally congruent.[7]

ROOSEVELT: COPING WITH CHAOS

Market structuring continued into the Roosevelt years, but the volume of White House ties with the executive branch grew dramatically as the tasks and agencies of the federal government multiplied. Moreover, FDR experimented with several hybrid structures.

The emergence and evolution of governance structuring moved through three different phases, which reflected not only the changes in the executive branch and in the broader political environment but also the dynamics of presidential choice. The first phase, roughly from 1933 to 1936, was characterized mostly by market structuring, with sporadic presidential efforts at inspiration and initial experimentation with two hybrid structures. Mismatches quickly appeared between these structures and prevailing decision settings. During the second phase (1937–39), attempts were made to respond to the lack of congruence, and additional differentiation and hierarchical structuring emerged. In general, however, these changes had little impact, largely because they challenged turf-conscious agency officials. The arrival of the administrative assistants in 1939 marked the beginning of the final phase. Yet environmental factors (continued agency resistance, the wartime emergency, and additional expansion of the executive branch) and presidential management strategy conspired to produce mostly incongruent, not very effective structuring.

Phase One, 1933–36: Ad Hoc Ties

Liaison. At the outset, presidential secretary Louis Howe was assigned to deal with executive branch departments and agencies. Frequently, this involved simply keeping informed about what they were doing.[8] Howe relied on a range of executive branch officials for intelligence, as well as on Lorena Hickok, journalist and "roving reporter" for Harry Hopkins's relief operations, who tracked agency activities in the field as she traveled around the country.[9] Howe also set up a clipping service in the National Emergency Council (see below) to supplement his information channels.[10] In addition, he organized a committee to study government contracts[11] and for a time coordinated and closely monitored Subsistence Homestead projects and the Civilian Conservation Corps.[12]

Howe's health declined in 1934 and 1935, and Appointments Secretary Marvin McIntyre picked up many of his liaison responsibilities with executive departments.[13] Meanwhile, the president's military aide, Edwin M. ("Pa") Watson, unlike his predecessors, served as an actual link between the military services, the War Department, and the White House, sharing liaison responsibilities with Press Secretary Stephen Early. Those not officially in the White House also became more important. As he did throughout the administration, for example, FDR turned to Harry Hopkins—the "Generalissimo of the Needle Brigade"—for help in expediting executive branch activity and untangling red tape.[14]

In addition, President Roosevelt created two structures that were charged with agency liaison and whose directors can be treated as White House staffers. The Executive Council (EC), established in July 1933, consisted of the cabinet secretaries plus the heads of the emergency agencies. In December, the National Emergency Council (NEC) was formed to coordinate the work of the recovery agencies. Starting with ten members, it ultimately grew to have 33. Frank Walker (who left in mid-1934) and then Donald Richberg served as executive secretaries of the EC and executive directors of the NEC; the two bodies were consolidated in October 1934. The EC and NEC were hybrid structures that were intended to encourage coordination.[15] If the interaction of interested parties in a collegial-consensual structure (where they could share information and explore implementation options) did not produce common ground, presidential strategies could be imposed by the executive director.

These efforts had mixed success at best. Not surprisingly, many agency representatives resisted the hierarchical aspects of the councils, chafing at having to get approval for various actions.[16] At the same time, the more collegial features of the bodies were difficult for the White House to control. FDR complained, for example, that officials too often got involved in conflicts outside their jurisdictions.[17] Finally, the structures' uneven success in promoting coordination seems to have reflected Roosevelt's varying interest in imposing hierarchy or exercising leadership in the executive branch.[18] Thus, some observers distinguished between Walker's and Richberg's tenures on the councils:

> Mr. Walker enjoyed the full confidence of the President and was able to work effectively with the department heads. . . . The meetings of the Executive Council he looked upon as primarily means for the President to have personal contact with agency heads and not as an instrument for deciding major questions of policy. . . . [In contrast,] the publicity which [Richberg] received designating him "Assistant President" doubtless proved to be harmful in his relations with departmental heads.[19]

Richberg "assumed his duties to be those of an Assistant President [but this assumption] was not fulfilled in practice or in backing by the President."[20]

Troubleshooting. Also during this time, presidential staffers first became involved in troubleshooting, where market structuring also dominated. Howe served as a virtual caseworker for those with problems with the executive branch bureaucracy. He fielded complaints about, for example, the work hours in some Emergency Conservation work camps and the failure of the National Recovery Administration to develop an employment code for sleeping-car conductors.[21] Howe intervened as well in specific cases—for instance, working with the Veterans Administration in responding to the bonus march on Washington in May 1933.[22]

During Walker's tenure at the EC and NEC, he regarded the unit's primary function to be troubleshooting.[23] Similarly, Early followed up on various defense-related investigations, such as those on supply purchase problems,[24] and Watson handled complaints about military pay and pension problems.[25]

Mediation. The official White House staff was too small for much involvement in trying to settle the numerous conflicts that broke out in the larger and more complex executive branch. Still, at Early's suggestion, Watson reviewed all appeals of promotional decisions from army officers as part of an effort to insulate the president from external pressures.[26] Moreover, proto-aides occasionally got involved. Walker, for example, saw one of his tasks on the NEC as helping "in bringing together the interested parties to iron out conflicts."[27]

Conclusions. During this first part of Roosevelt's presidency, there was a mismatch between the prevailing governance structures and the decision setting. Throughout the period, there was significant goal controversy within the executive branch.[28] Agencies' overlapping tasks also meant continued technical conflict, which was exacerbated by turf struggles and personality clashes. None of the structures, including the Executive and National Emergency Councils, could authoritatively work even to quasi-resolve such conflict. Pressed White House staffers could do little more than ad hoc arbitration and reporting.

Although FDR on occasion tried to inspire executive branch officials to work toward his goals, he offered little sustained direction. As Raymond Moley acidly observed:

> To look on his policies as the result of a unified plan . . . was to believe that the accumulation of stuffed snakes, baseball pictures, school flags, old tennis shoes, and the like in a boy's bedroom were the design of an interior decorator.[29]

And after Howe, no official unmistakably spoke for FDR.[30]

Needed amid the prevailing uncertainty and conflict over both ends and means were more competitive and adversarial structures as well as more formal hierarchical structuring to provide direction and coordination. That structural mismatches prevailed can be attributed to both presidential choice and environmental factors. Certainly, FDR's preferences ran toward the less structured and more openly conflictual. At the same time, Roosevelt, much like Hoover, was operating in mostly uncharted waters in a context of seemingly irreducible controversy over appropriate responses, where a clear premium was placed on action over inaction. In addition, over time, factors in the immediate White House environment assumed marginal importance as executive branch officials struggled to protect the turf they had acquired initially.

Phase Two, 1937–39: Differentiation

If the first phase was characterized primarily by ad hoc and often chaotic relations between the White House and executive branch agencies, the second phase saw some effort at imposing additional hierarchical structuring, perhaps in response to the mismatch just identified. From the White House's perspective, however, more hierarchy accomplished relatively little.

Liaison. An effort to interject additional hierarchy into White House–agency relationships surfaced with the appearance of a new presidential aide, James Roosevelt, in early January 1937. Among his responsibilities was serving as liaison with the "little cabinet," the second-level representatives of the executive departments.[31] More important, after the bruising court packing defeat in Congress, the younger Roosevelt also became the liaison with independent and emergency agencies.[32] Called by at least one writer the "assistant President," he tried to meet with the heads of these agencies at least once a week, both to hear their concerns and to relay information from FDR.[33] Jimmy Roosevelt also attempted to "work out a plan to coordinate these agencies . . . and to help prevent duplication of work."[34]

At the time, some observers believed that these activities were significant. The president had expressed impatience at his lack of control over the "independent" agencies. Since Congress had refused to convert them wholesale to regular executive branch departments, FDR sought to use his son to induce them to behave more in accordance with the president's wishes. "[M]any of the new agencies are shivering in their respective boots. They know the Roosevelt finger is on them at last and are little comforted by the fact that it is being pointed by the son instead of the father."[35] Another journalist noted, however, that James Roosevelt's arrival merely

> regularize[d] the situation, with Jimmy reserving a half an hour a week for each agency and serving both as a funnel for the inner office and a conveyor of orders or advice in reverse. The problems he will handle will be mostly minor. Governor Eccles of the Federal Reserve, Harry Hopkins of WPA, . . . and other big shots will not be taking vital national policies to Jimmy.[36]

The latter commentator probably was closer to the truth. Indeed, some in the White House soon questioned the utility of James Roosevelt's efforts. By late September 1938, his assistant, James Rowe, suggested that they had been "going at the thing all wrong."[37] Jimmy Roosevelt left in October 1938, and Rowe took on most of his responsibilities with independent agencies.[38]

Troubleshooting and Mediation. In addition to his other duties, the younger Roosevelt handled complaints, investigated individual problems with agencies, and on occasion intervened in agency decision making.[39] In at least one instance, James Roosevelt helped mediate a dispute between the

Federal Power Commission and the Securities and Exchange Commission which had jurisdiction over utilities.[40]

Conclusions. Executive branch outreach during this second phase was not entirely successful. Directives from the White House were neither fully enforced nor considered legitimate by executive branch officials. For the most part, this reflected the operation of organizational dynamics in the immediate executive branch environment: agency officials strenuously objected to a seeming loss of direct access to the president and to a perceived decline in their (and their agencies') status and influence. Such hierarchical structuring was not necessarily incongruent with the decision setting; by this time, FDR had a relatively clear sense of his objectives and how they might be achieved. However, the president was unwilling to invest the considerable resources that would have been necessary to make this structure work.

Phase Three: Administrative Assistants and the War

Experimentation with White House–based structuring for executive branch outreach persisted during the final phase of the Roosevelt presidency. Market structuring generally prevailed, but numerous other structures also emerged. In the 1930s, the president had relied primarily on intelligence sources throughout the executive branch, supplemented by sporadic efforts at monitoring and intervention by White House staffers. With the appearance of the administrative assistants (AAs) in 1939 and then the explosion of war agencies and coordinating committees, FDR began bringing such people into the White House. At the same time, he gave many of them line assignments elsewhere in the executive branch (essentially reversing his earlier practice of using line officials for temporary staff work). By continually creating new coordinating, oversight, and mediation mechanisms and staffing them with more proximate, presumably more loyal aides, FDR was searching for ways to increase his own control over executive branch activities. Once more, mismatches between structures and decision settings appeared.

Liaison. Several of the AAs had duties that placed them in close contact with executive branch agencies, typically as participants in collegial structures. For example, although most of Lowell Mellett's responsibilities lay elsewhere, he chaired an interdepartmental committee of government housing officials.[41] Another AA, Lauchlin Currie, worked to promote cooperation among heads of agencies with economic responsibilities.[42]

Especially as the United States moved toward full involvement in the war, James Rowe and others began devoting much of their attention to defense-related issues. Rowe described his work as handling "minor matters not important enough to require conferences between the President and the heads of . . . agencies."[43]

As the war took up more and more of FDR's time, he relied far more on top-level staff to maintain liaison with executive branch agencies. Some specialization emerged between defense and domestic activities, though virtually all were affected by the war. Harry Hopkins's attention shifted in the 1940s to more war-related matters. He became a " 'fix-it-boy' on a global scale,"[44] working in a variety of collegial-competitive structures. In 1940, as a presidential assistant, he became executive secretary of the cabinet committee charged with administering lend-lease.[45] Later, he also chaired the Munitions Assignments Board and was a member of the War Mobilization Committee in the Office of War Mobilization (OWM).[46] In addition to trying to coordinate the work of executive branch agencies, Hopkins more generally served as "a channel of communication between the President and various agencies . . . notably the War Department . . . [and as] a buffer state: he kept problem-laden officials away from Roosevelt."[47]

Meanwhile, on the domestic side, the OWM (later the Office of War Mobilization and Reconversion)—the "supercoordinator of them all"[48]—was created in May 1943. Headed by former Supreme Court Justice James Byrnes, OWM was technically in the Executive Office, but Byrnes and his small staff operated out of the East Wing of the White House.[49] Formally in the White House Office and also charged with strengthening hierarchical White House control over domestic policy activities was Special Counsel Samuel Rosenman.[50]

Hopkins also found time to stay involved in domestic issues. Initially, he had "expected Byrnes to be his counterpart in domestic matters and hoped that they would cooperate as Roosevelt's major advisers."[51] Although at the outset Byrnes advised Hopkins to "keep the hell out of my business," by 1944 the *Report for the Business Executive* opined that it was Hopkins who was "a factor . . . in all domestic policy matters" and that Byrnes was far less influential.[52]

Troubleshooting. Several staffers also acted as troubleshooters. Rosenman, for example, fielded numerous complaints about poor agency performance and served as a virtual caseworker, especially on issues involving domestic policy and domestic war mobilization.[53] Lower-level aides typically responded to requests for troubleshooting from the president or more senior staff. In August 1941, for instance, Wayne Coy, at FDR's request, worked to expedite U.S. aid to the Soviet Union: "please, with my full authority, use a heavy hand—act as a burr under the saddle and get things moving! . . . Step on it!"[54]

Mediation. The explosion of executive branch agencies and activities, the unrelenting pressures of wartime, and FDR's growing preoccupation all contributed to considerable conflict within the executive branch. Not surprisingly, White House staffers became more involved in mediation.

Formally, Byrnes was Roosevelt's "deputy" for managing conflict among the war production and the war economics agencies, working within an adjudicative structure.[55] For the most part, his "OWM chose to deal with issues only if they could not be resolved at lower levels and interpreted its role narrowly as adjudicating controversies."[56]

As with much else during the Roosevelt years, this arrangement did not always work smoothly, and executive branch officials resisted some of Byrnes's efforts or avoided dealing with him altogether. In Byrnes's view, more than bureaucratic turf protection was involved. He complained (as Richberg had earlier) that Roosevelt did little to bolster his position. It was well known, for example, that the president rarely included Byrnes in discussions of relevant issues, which made "it impossible for me now to maintain unimpaired my own relationship with other agencies."[57]

Nor did Byrnes monopolize mediation activities in the executive branch. In 1943, for example, he joined Rosenman and Bernard Baruch in an informal collegial-mediative "Clearance Committee" that met with FDR weekly to help settle disputes among agencies.[58] Meanwhile, Hopkins served as an "umpire between the feuding dollar-a-year men and the New Dealers" in the defense agencies,[59] and Jonathan Daniels responded to "bureaucratic collisions" in the Department of Agriculture and the Tennessee Valley Authority, trying at FDR's request "to keep Lilienthal from getting Ickes mad."[60]

Conclusions. One can easily question the approach that produced the structuring of executive outreach during this final phase of the Roosevelt presidency. To be sure, goal and technical uncertainty pervaded executive branch activity, making market responses seem congruent initially. Frequently missing, though, was the systematic presidential leadership that also is prescribed under such cell 1 conditions (see Table 2 in Chapter 1). FDR often was too busy, too distracted, or too sick to focus on the seemingly narrower issue of executive branch direction. Nor, as Byrnes complained, did Roosevelt always give his agents enough backing to act on the president's behalf. When he did, the results could be strikingly different. For example, an admiring *Time* cover story in 1945 noted that Hopkins "always put the ostrich egg in the hen coop, . . . always raised the sights over the last highest production estimate."[61]

An even more important reason for the apparent mismatch between structuring and decision setting was the general absence of ties among the diverse structures. Richard Neustadt, for example, contended that competition among aides and war-imposed secrecy combined to isolate the president from needed information—the chief reason for the staff links between the White House and executive branch agencies in the first place.[62] This suggests a need for greater differentiation. In particular, more collegial-competitive structures that brought staffers with conflicting perspectives together might have been useful, perhaps with a senior aide such as Rosenman on hand to link such structures with the president.

In addition, as we have seen, the war "entangled bureaucratic jurisdictions even as it added scope and scale."[63] Yet never fully clear was where such disputes might be settled: Byrnes appeared to be weak, the Clearance Committee was overwhelmed by the demand for mediation, and responsibility for dispute resolution shifted unpredictably. Meanwhile, some observers complained that staffers such as Rosenman made matters worse: "When things are hopelessly entangled . . . [Rosenman] suggests the creation of other new agencies to divert attention from the tangled web in which the others at the moment may be enmeshed."[64] Clearly indicated was the need for more formal adjudicative structures, perhaps with senior White House staffers resolving disputes on the president's behalf.

These sorts of structural prescriptions, however, would not have been consistent with Roosevelt's strategies for executive branch outreach. At the same time, of course, environmental demands and expectations were overwhelming, and—like Hoover—Roosevelt had few if any relevant precedents. Finally, within the more immediate executive branch environment, organizational inertia and resistance remained problems as New Deal and war agencies struggled for resources and responsibilities and officials competed for the president's ear.

TRUMAN: ATTEMPTS AT RATIONALIZATION

The Truman administration sought to respond to both the seeming chaos of the Roosevelt White House and the complexities of the New Deal and wartime executive branch. It was assisted by dramatic environmental change: the end of World War II and some consequent lessening of the demands on government. Differentiation increased as a variety of governance structures emerged to link the White House and executive branch agencies. On the whole, the structures were congruent with their decision settings, and most Truman aides operated relatively easily within the overall hierarchy of the executive branch. Variable presidential and staff skill helps explain why some of the structures performed better than others.[65]

At the outset, the response to the disarray of the Roosevelt White House was to distinguish between "policy" and "operations." The former included policy formulation and was the chief responsibility of the special counsel's office (headed in turn by Samuel Rosenman, Clark Clifford, and Charles Murphy). "Operations"—which generally referred to the activities of executive branch agencies as they implemented existing policy—was handled by John Steelman, who was "The Assistant" to the president, and his staff. Despite this formal division, however, members of the two units became involved in many of the same activities, and most White House staffers participated in some form of executive branch outreach. Such aides tended to develop substantive policy specialties (detailed in Part II), which largely shaped their assignments for dealing with executive branch affairs.

Liaison

To some extent, Steelman's focus on labor conciliation distracted him from liaison.[66] His aides, however, maintained routine liaison with diverse agencies and sought to bring them under a White House–based hierarchy.[67] Yet the structures that developed were largely ad hoc and often short-lived, in part because the Steelman staff by no means monopolized White House contacts with executive branch agencies. Clark Clifford recalled that his job as special counsel included serving as liaison to cabinet departments and keeping in particularly close touch with the Justice Department.[68] In the process, he apparently rescued some executive branch officials from some of Steelman's less successful coordinating efforts. When "most of Steelman's coordinating ended in confusion," Clifford, with his "passion for orderliness and quiet," took over.[69] In addition, because of his national security interests, Clifford developed close relationships with top officials of the Navy, War, and State Departments.[70]

Other counsel staffers were active too. As special counsel, Charles Murphy and his aide David Lloyd, for example, received reports on the activities of the Displaced Persons Commission.[71] Stephen Spingarn was charged with coordinating the information the White House received on employee loyalty in the executive branch as well as with being a general "liaison officer between the White House and executive departments and agencies."[72]

Nor was staff liaison limited to members of the Steelman and special counsel units. Soon after Edwin Locke was appointed special assistant in June 1946, for instance, he began focusing on aviation. During his short time in the White House (he left in February 1947), he was a primary channel for reporting on Civil Aeronautics Board (CAB) actions and aviation issues.[73] The military aides remained the links with the War Department and the services.[74]

Troubleshooting

White House staffers continued to find themselves following up on individual complaints about agencies. Compared with previous administrations, there was somewhat more specialization within the White House, but few structures persisted.

Although aides in the special counsel's office handled some casework, Steelman's aides were far more involved. Perhaps because of his operational responsibilities, Steelman received diverse questions and complaints about agency activity (and inactivity) from members of Congress as well as from local, union, and party officials, which he and his assistants followed up with the appropriate agencies.[75]

Yet executive branch resistance to White House involvement was still easy to arouse, and other staffers were less discreet than Steelman in their activities. Early on, for example, Locke, apparently with Truman's approval, intervened in a Latin American air route case, which raised the ire of both the CAB and the aviation community.[76] Ultimately, the CAB "won the battle to subordinate the White House role in international decisions to that of approval and counsel on foreign policy matters. . . . Locke . . . is now merely an expediter."[77]

Meanwhile, as military aide, Harry Vaughan reportedly spent considerable time responding to requests and complaints from military personnel and veterans.[78] He described himself as an expediter; he told people who to contact in the executive branch and helped them gain access. Vaughan was frequently accused of improper activity, and columnists had a field day digging up dirt on the president's crony. Drew Pearson referred to Vaughan as "meddlesome Harry," who, for instance, interceded with the agriculture secretary to get grain quotas for distillers increased.[79]

Mediation

Numerous White House staffers also became involved in mediation. Vaughan, for example, tried to settle the disputes that inevitably developed among the 14 agencies that had responsibility for veterans' issues. Spingarn and Murphy in the counsel's office reported attempting interdepartmental "reconciling" from time to time.[80]

Yet most of the mediation efforts were undertaken by Steelman and his aides; within the unit there was some differentiation. With his background as a labor conciliator, Steelman was called in to mediate disputes among cabinet members, "practically always" at the officials' request.[81] Truman claimed that he made the final decision on how to resolve the dispute if the cabinet members could not resolve their conflict. "[Steelman] would give me the facts, and I would make the decision."[82] The president's approach initially appears to have involved adjudicative or adversarial structuring, with Steelman as an adviser to Truman, the final decision maker. Yet Truman's fuller description suggests that he saw himself moving decision making toward cell 5 (see Table 2 in Chapter 1):

It's been said that if you have two bureaus in disagreement in the same Cabinet member's office, sometimes the President can get an agreement, but if they are in different departments, such as Interior and Commerce, God himself couldn't get it settled. I wanted to get settlements by putting everything on the cabinet table and having the arguments in the cabinet room. But you can't get a settlement if the President doesn't have the facts. That was the purpose of having a conciliator—so the President would not have to put his foot down on the members of the Cabinet when it wasn't necessary. When the members knew the facts, they were willing to agree to what was right.[83]

In addition, Steelman and his aide Robert Turner used collegial-mediative structuring to resolve disputes. They would bring conflicting parties (from in and out of government) together to address, for example, the disposition of an experimental aluminum plant in South Carolina and controversies generated by shortages of railroad freight cars.[84]

The extent of Steelman's effectiveness at mediation is less clear, underscoring once more the significance of staff skill. David Stowe praised his superior's mediating skills.[85] In contrast, Koenig argued that Steelman failed at "shielding the President . . . from the interdepartmental brawls."[86] It seems that more than staff skill was involved. The president himself complicated matters by "hovering by. Inevitably he became ensnarled in the very difficulties and commitments he had originally sought to avoid."[87]

EISENHOWER: CONTINUED EXPERIMENTATION

The Eisenhower administration also relied on a variety of structures for executive branch outreach, but the stability of specific structures continued to be low. The White House no longer was extensively involved in mediation, and it experimented for a time with specialized structures for executive branch liaison. Formal hierarchical structures for intelligence gathering and monitoring of agency activity also emerged, replacing the more informal efforts of earlier presidents.

The most ambitious-seeming structures for executive branch liaison disappeared rather quickly. In part, this was because the notion of liaison was not taken very seriously from the start: the Executive Branch Liaison Office was an ill-disguised cover for White House "political" activities that senior staffers feared outsiders would perceive to be illegitimate, especially in the administration of a stridently "nonpolitical" president. At the same time, a variety of staffers with substantive policy assignments found themselves continually interacting with executive branch officials and performing a range of outreach tasks.

In contrast, the more modest, hierarchical mechanisms were more stable. At least from the White House perspective, such structuring no doubt seemed congruent. Not only did the president generally prefer orderly information flows and clear lines of authority, but his administration's limited policy agenda and the general perception of relatively little goal and technical uncertainty and controversy were consistent with routinized White House processes that emphasized reporting and coordination. Whether those perceptions were always accurate and the structuring fully congruent, however, can be questioned. The hierarchical mechanisms ran the risk of obscuring from the administration existing problems and controversies in the agencies. Also needed were structures in which ends and means might have been more fully probed and debated.

Liaison

Within the Eisenhower administration, the term "liaison" was allegedly "a forbidden word, because the White House never want[ed] to seem to exercise control over the individual responsibility of a Cabinet officer."[88] In reality, though, Eisenhower staffers, like their predecessors, maintained extensive links with executive branch agencies.

White House staff liaison with agencies remained decentralized and was handled in mostly ad hoc ways. As they had under Truman, liaison responsibilities in part reflected the substantive specialties of individual aides. For example, Special Counsel Gerald Morgan—who focused on legal matters—maintained contact with quasi-judicial agencies such as the Federal Trade and Interstate Commerce Commissions.[89]

Foreign and defense matters received special attention in the Eisenhower White House. At the outset, Charles Willis had responsibility for liaison with the State Department.[90] Later, Thomas Pike and then John Hamlin were appointed liaisons with the Defense Department.[91] In addition, one of both Paul Carroll's and then Andrew Goodpaster's duties as staff secretary was to serve as a channel of information to the president from the Departments of State and Defense and the intelligence agencies; Goodpaster was even called the "defense liaison officer."[92]

Other White House aides pursued across-the-board liaison tasks. Chief of Staff Sherman Adams, for example, met weekly with the undersecretaries of cabinet departments.[93] Similarly, early in the administration, Special Counsel Bernard Shanley and staffers such as Adams, Willis, and Wilton Persons (head of the White House legislative liaison unit) lunched frequently with independent agency officials. Later, legislative liaison staffer Homer Gruenther arranged similar staff lunches with department secretaries and lower-level appointees.[94] Such meetings operated as a hybrid collegial-consensual and hierarchical structure, allowing for both the interchange of information and White House guidance.

The Eisenhower White House also experimented, albeit halfheartedly, with creating differentiated structures for executive branch outreach. At the beginning of the administration, Val Peterson was hired to be a presidential liaison with cabinet departments and independent agencies.[95] When Peterson left in March 1953 to become administrator of the Federal Civil Defense Agency, his tasks were taken on by Undersecretary of Commerce Walter Williams and his aide, Stanley Rumbough. Although Williams, on detail to the White House, returned to the Commerce Department in late 1953, Rumbough stayed to help launch the Executive Branch Liaison Office under Charles Masterson (which, as Chapter 3 detailed, was in fact oriented toward public relations).

By late 1954, the president, increasingly frustrated with the decentralized White House liaison operation, asked Bryce Harlow (an Office of Congressional Relations [OCR] staffer and speechwriter) to take over Peterson's responsibilities.[96] Again, however, attention drifted away from liaison, and in early 1955, Howard Pyle was brought in to head the Executive Branch Liaison Office, which subsumed the Harlow operation; Masterson and Harlow formally became Pyle's assistants.[97] Despite the office's misleading name, there was little confusion about what Pyle's responsibilities would be. Adams told Press Secretary James Hagerty that, despite his actual assignment, Pyle should be introduced as the White House liaison to the executive branch.[98]

Yet the desire for specialists in agency relations persisted, and in June 1955, Fred Seaton assumed Pyle's responsibilities as liaison with executive branch agencies.[99] Seaton, who had been an assistant secretary of defense before joining the White House staff, took liaison more seriously than his predecessors had. He served as another channel to the Defense Department and monitored routine defense matters.[100] As a former publisher of the *Hastings* (Nebraska) *Daily Tribune,* Seaton also took special interest in agricultural issues.[101] Still, most of his energies were devoted elsewhere.[102] When Seaton left the White House in June 1956 to become interior secretary, experimentation with separate agency liaison structures ended.

More successful were efforts to use existing White House administrative units as vehicles for interjecting hierarchy into White House ties with executive branch agencies. One of the chief purposes of the staff secretariat (at least as envisioned by consultant Carter Burgess) was to "simplify and expedite . . . White House staff work with government agencies and departments."[103] Such work often had to do with routing correspondence to the appropriate agency and getting a timely reply that was acceptable to the White House.[104] The staff secretariat also prepared and monitored the "Suspense List," a daily compilation of items requested by the president or White House staff that were due from executive branch agencies.[105]

Beginning in July 1956 (about the time of Seaton's departure), another task of the staff secretary's office was the production of "Staff Notes." Designed to keep the president and senior White House aides up-to-date on ongoing departmental activities that had not yet been reported in the mass media, the notes served as a form of intelligence gathering. Goodpaster insisted that they were intended to provide "information reports [that were] separate from White House action processes; we have stressed to our contributors that these items are not to be used to obtain action approval or to accomplish end-runs.[106] The staffers who compiled "Staff Notes" were meant to be "bird dogs as well as editors."[107] Aides sought out negative information and often followed up on reports of problems.

The cabinet secretariat performed somewhat similar functions. For example, it also monitored and contributed to the "Suspense List." The unit sought in part to serve as a "radar set, constantly scanning what was going on" in the executive branch and elsewhere.[108]

Troubleshooting

Like their predecessors, Eisenhower aides also became involved in troubleshooting. On some occasions, this casework activity reflected the interests and past contacts of individual staffers. OCR aide Jack Martin, for instance, dealt with many requests from companies and individuals in Ohio, his home state.[109] Most of the time, though, the Eisenhower staff responded to specific incidents involving executive branch agencies that had come to White House attention. In 1955, for example, after considerable negative coverage, Press Secretary James Hagerty sought to persuade the Agriculture Department to retract its unfounded accusation that one of its economists belonged to two communist front organizations.[110]

Here, too, the administration's tendency to rely on specialists was apparent. In January 1956, Edward McCabe, a House staffer who had conducted investigations, came to the White House as associate special counsel. His initial task was to be "something of a coordinator of executive branch interests, in the face of Congressional investigations."[111] McCabe

> began working with the chief legal officers of the various departments, and . . . with the senior people of the Justice Department, and worked out a kind of informal *ad hoc* sort of committee, and stayed aware of where investigative activity was being centered.[112]

In addition, "Staff Notes" helped enhance the White House's ability to anticipate potential problems in executive branch activity, providing an "advance alert system."[113] For example, in 1957, McCabe alerted "Notes" staffer Albert Toner about problems with Rural Electrification Administration loan applications in the Department of Agriculture and asked Toner to pursue the matter with his contacts in Agriculture.[114]

Conclusions

The first stable structuring for executive branch outreach emerged during the Eisenhower years. At least one Eisenhower staffer—deputy cabinet secretary Bradley Patterson—has pointed to the possible risks of such hierarchical structuring:

> Perhaps [Eisenhower] didn't probe deep enough and far enough down into his own departments to know about the collision of alternatives long before an issue got to him. He tended to take what came to him at the top of the heap.[115]

Called for may have been the sorts of additional structures that challenged hierarchy's assumptions of consensus and certainty that would appear during the Kennedy years.

KENNEDY: WANING ATTENTION

Systematic attention to executive branch outreach decreased during the Kennedy administration.[116] Moreover, the outreach that did take place typically was at the president's direction. Although some stable structuring can be identified with the continuing activities of the cabinet secretary, reliance on hierarchy declined in emphasis, supplemented by more collegial structures.

That the Kennedy administration paid less attention to executive branch relations than did its predecessors should not be surprising. First, the environment had changed significantly: no longer facing the pressures of a rapidly expanding executive branch (as Roosevelt and Truman had), the Kennedy White House confronted the pent-up demand for legislation generated by eight years of a Republican president and six of divided government. Reinforcing the lower priority given to outreach was Kennedy's inexperience with and general lack of interest in issues of policy implementation and bureaucratic oversight. When the president did encounter resistance from executive branch officials, he stepped up the administration's troubleshooting activities.

The nature of White House structuring for the outreach that did take place—a decline in hierarchy, an increase in presidential direction—points to the influence of both organizational and presidential choice factors. Organizationally, partisan learning (looking back to Truman's less formal approach) may help account for the abandonment of some of the hierarchical structuring of the Eisenhower years as well as for the reassertion of the importance of the special counsel's office. Decreased emphasis on hierarchy and eventually active presidential involvement also reflected Kennedy's approach to management, which placed him at the center of White House staff activities.

The congruence of this kind of structuring is less clear. The approach of the Kennedy administration did not fully resolve the difficulty that Richard Neustadt identified in the Roosevelt White House and Bradley Patterson saw in Eisenhower's: the lack of capacity to unearth and respond to conflict at lower levels of the executive branch. To be sure, the emerging collegial structures, Kennedy's reliance on several White House aides to gather intelligence and ferret out problems, and the president's practice of speaking directly with lower-level officials had significant potential. Yet nearly exclusive reliance on presidential direction ("inspiration") to drive outreach activities—especially in an administration that paid relatively little systematic attention to the executive branch—was likely insufficient for reliably identifying and anticipating possible problems.

Liaison

Most involved in liaison activities was the cabinet secretary—first Frederick Dutton (who worked in the White House from February to November 1961) and then Timothy Reardon (who remained until the end of the administration).[117] Some of the hierarchical structuring of the Eisenhower years remained. Initially, Dutton requested that each department designate a "reporter," who would send him weekly (later biweekly) reports and who he sometimes used to follow up on actions decided on in cabinet meetings.[118] The cabinet secretary's office also cleared all major speeches or statements to be made by cabinet and subcabinet officials. In addition, twice weekly, each cabinet member was supposed to submit a report summarizing key decisions or projects that might be of interest to the president; the cabinet secretary then summarized the reports for Kennedy and followed up on the president's questions and comments.[119]

Again, the problems with relying on hierarchy surfaced. The departmental reports, for instance, were intended to flag agency problems. Kennedy wanted " 'personally composed, letting hair-down memoranda' with 'naked candor.' " Mostly, though, he received "fluff."[120]

The cabinet secretaries, however, supplemented the formal hierarchical structuring. Dutton claimed, for example, that he "got to know about two-thirds of the Cabinet members well enough that they informally would be candid with me, their grips [*sic*], their grievances, complaints."[121] He also monitored or participated in several more collegial structures, meeting frequently with the "little cabinet" to discuss issues that crossed agency lines, starting and tracking the progress of the subcabinet group on civil rights, and reporting to the president on the discussion at "the regular informal luncheon of the Cabinet."[122]

Troubleshooting

Compared with their predecessors, Kennedy staffers spent less time following up specific complaints about agency operations or decisions. As the administration proceeded, however, they paid increased attention to "digging out conflict" in executive branch agencies. Since the hierarchical structuring for reporting rarely unearthed such controversies, the president himself typically ordered specific inquiries. Cabinet secretaries Dutton and Reardon devoted considerable energy to pursuing presidential questions. Dutton, for example, reported to Kennedy on the requirements for Imperial of Canada to send ships to the People's Republic of China and the reactions of executive branch officials to it doing so.[123] Similarly, Reardon monitored agency progress in implementing the Area Redevelopment Program.[124] Without such presidential initiative, however, little happened.

JOHNSON: COMBINING APPROACHES

The volatility in structuring for executive branch outreach continued through the Johnson administration, which experimented with several of the approaches past presidents had used. White House involvement in mediation grew, and domestic policy aide Joseph Califano on occasion acted much like Truman staffer John Steelman. As in all the Democratic White Houses between 1929 and 1968, the special counsel's office played an active role, but under LBJ it became overshadowed by Califano and his staff. Meanwhile, the hierarchical reporting mechanisms introduced by Eisenhower remained, although White House turf struggles led the cabinet secretary to lose control over them. And much like the Kennedy White House, numerous staffers became involved in outreach, frequently at the president's request. Some market structuring reemerged.

Environmental, presidential choice, and organizational variables all help account for the general instability and the nature of White House structuring for outreach. External pressures and presidential policy objectives—the need to implement Johnson's ambitious domestic agenda, the turmoil produced by executive branch reorganization, mounting budget concerns—interacted to increase the salience of executive branch outreach and shaped White House responses. The need for accurate reporting of agency activities grew, as did demands for White House mediation. And once Congress had passed Johnson's Great Society proposals, policy staffers shifted their attention from the legislative arena to the executive branch.

The exact nature of the White House's structural responses, however, largely reflected presidential choice and organizational variables. Impatient for agency action, Johnson reached out to a variety of staffers to try to keep track of what was happening at the lower reaches of the executive branch. In addition to the hierarchical reporting mechanisms Eisenhower had relied on, Johnson, like his immediate predecessor, turned to a range of other aides, through a combination of adjudicative structures and presidential direction. Especially as the administration proceeded, however, LBJ had less and less time for guiding oversight; his staffers had other responsibilities, and reliance on hierarchical structuring increased. Given the persistent conflicts over goals and means in the executive branch—which worsened with growing resource scarcity—such structuring was incongruent with the prevailing decision setting.

At this point as well, organizational variables entered in. Unlike during the Eisenhower administration, senior staffers with clear commitments to the president's goals ultimately gained control of the reporting mechanism. This did not mean, however, that Johnson was necessarily better informed about problems in the executive branch; instead, his aides used the refined reporting system to buffer an increasingly distracted president and, on occasion, to pursue their own objectives.

Control of the hierarchical reporting structure, then, had become a political resource within the White House. Over the course of the Johnson administration, Califano and his staff took on numerous tasks. Indeed, some colleagues criticized Califano's "imperialism,"[125] although others emphasized his ability and noted that his "small empire" was built with presidential encouragement.[126] Whatever the interpretation, Califano and his aides succeeded in wresting authority over reporting from the cabinet secretary. Their efforts to identify problems and stake out turf also led to a diminished role in executive branch outreach for the special counsel's office and helped renew White House involvement in mediating executive branch disputes.

Liaison

As in the Eisenhower and Kennedy administrations, Johnson's cabinet secretaries—Horace Busby, Robert Kintner, and Charles Maguire[127]—tried to organize routine White House contact with executive branch departments and agencies. For example, they met regularly with the assistants to cabinet members and followed up on presidential requests made during cabinet meetings.[128] For a time, the cabinet secretaries also oversaw a hierarchical reporting and intelligence-gathering operation. In July 1965, the president ordered that agencies submit weekly reports of their activities to the White House.[129] The cabinet secretary received these reports (which became biweekly in 1967) and then summarized and analyzed them for Johnson.

Gradually, however, the cabinet secretary lost full control over the reporting system. As Vietnam occupied more and more of LBJ's time and energy, executive branch agencies began using the reports to get his attention. The volume of reports grew enormously (a problem exacerbated by the numerous reports staffers received that had to be shared with Johnson), and those in the White House felt inundated. In June 1967, Califano stepped in, initiating a White House review of "reporting procedures whereby Department and Agency principals communicate with the President and members of the staff."[130] Although cabinet secretary Maguire received the staff's summaries of recurring reports, it was Califano who reported the results to Johnson.[131] Finally, in October, Maguire informed the president that, in order to cut back on the load of agency information that LBJ had to read, Califano, Maguire, and James Gaither (a Califano staffer) had devised a daily summary sheet, to be prepared by Gaither and Maguire.[132] Even though the cabinet secretary continued to receive the agency reports, in December 1967, Special Counsel Larry Temple took over preparation of the daily summary form, thus becoming the "new Digest Czar."[133]

In addition, as in some previous administrations, there was considerable market structuring. In both 1964 and 1965, efforts were made to specify the aides responsible for "Cabinet level day-to-day contact" for particular agencies,[134] but there is little indication that these assignments were routinely followed. Even more active was Bill Moyers's "unofficial network of contacts in the departments, below the secretarial level, who were an invaluable source of information on agency activities and thinking."[135] And, like his predecessors, President Johnson assigned staffers specific liaison tasks, with partisan learning making aides in the special counsel's office especially likely to be called upon.[136]

More important, though, were those most systematically involved in domestic policy, who often had close ties with executive branch agencies. For instance, Douglass Cater, a specialist in health and education issues, was the official White House liaison with the Department of Health, Education, and Welfare (HEW) and at times functioned as a virtual advocate of the department and its programs.[137] Cater cultivated good relationships with HEW secretaries Anthony Celebrezze and John Gardner.[138] In 1967, Cater served as a channel between Gardner and Johnson, relaying the former's feelings that he was not " 'plugged in' on [LBJ's] thinking."[139]

After the burst of domestic policy formulation and lawmaking of the early Johnson years, implementation issues moved to the fore, and the Califano operation became more involved in executive branch liaison.[140] Califano and his aides designed their own hierarchical reporting structure to track the agencies' progress in getting Great Society programs in place and to promote coordination among programs and agencies.[141]

The activities of the Califano unit and those of Cater and Special Counsel Harry McPherson clearly overlapped, generating the potential for serious disputes over turf.[142] Cater, however, reported little conflict—especially when he was kept informed of the actions of the Califano staff.[143] Moreover, there were clear bounds to what Califano and his aides sought to accomplish in executive branch liaison. Califano recalled, for example, that "I doubt that I ever met, much less consulted or helped guide, more than one-third of [the] noncabinet agency and commission heads.[144]

Troubleshooting and Mediation

Much like Kennedy, Johnson frequently requested that staffers pursue reported problems in the executive branch.[145] Other times, staffers' specializations led to their involvement in casework. For example, Gaither (on Califano's staff), who focused on poverty issues, sought to coordinate executive branch responses to the demands by leaders of the Poor Peoples Campaign for information about agency activities, plans, and accomplishments.[146]

Similar to the other post-Truman administrations, the Johnson staff's involvement in mediation was mostly sporadic and ad hoc. Yet the flood of Great Society initiatives, the appearance of new cabinet departments such as Housing and Urban Development (HUD) and the Department of Transportation, and growing budget pressures triggered considerable controversy and countless turf battles in the executive branch in which the White House sometimes became embroiled. To address these growing problems, the president turned first to the cabinet secretary's office. One of Kintner's charges when he was hired was to "bring Great Society programs and their administrations into greater harmony. When interdepartmental disputes arise, he is supposed to settle them or bring them in manageable fashion before the President for his decision."[147] But there is little evidence to indicate that Kintner actually did this.

Soon, other efforts at systematic mediation surfaced. Given the Califano office's concern with policy implementation and its close ties to agencies, it began to function to an extent like Steelman's operation in the Truman White House. Staffers became part of a collegial-mediative structure, serving as "the locus for marathon coffee-consuming sessions dedicated to knocking heads together and untangling jurisdictions."[148] In general, bureaucratic disputes were "typically resolved by BOB [Bureau of the Budget] or the White House staff."[149] When agreement could not be reached, the president became the adjudicator. Califano, for example, brought disputes on budget issues between domestic agencies and the BOB to Johnson's attention, explaining the various positions and in at least some cases offering his own recommendations.[150]

CONCLUSIONS

By 1969, White House involvement in executive branch outreach had become institutionalized. Far less stable, however, were the ways in which that outreach was structured. None of the presidents examined here fully succeeded in fashioning outreach mechanisms that provided them with accurate and timely information about the problems and activities of executive branch agencies. Apparently needed as well were collegial-competitive and adversarial or adjudicative structures to alert the White House to disputes and uncertainties, to permit their exploration, and to provide possible guidance or conflict resolution. Instead, presidents relied on either their own direct involvement (as Truman, Kennedy, and Johnson all did to some extent) or hierarchical reporting mechanisms (as Bradley Patterson believed that Eisenhower too often did). Frequently, though, the press of events, the workload of presidents and their staffs, and the ongoing resistance of many executive branch officials to White House oversight combined to make such measures insufficient.

Nor did any of the presidents consistently use executive branch outreach by the White House staff to push agencies to work toward achieving administration goals. Although Harry Hopkins's activities under Roosevelt and Joseph Califano's efforts in the Johnson White House anticipated this, it was left to Richard Nixon to explicitly seek to use outreach as a means of achieving his objectives and to develop coherent strategies for doing so. And not until Ronald Reagan would the full impact of such an "administrative presidency" become apparent.[151]

6

Looking Beyond Washington

So far, much of the story of presidential outreach in the early modern era has been a tale of staff responsibility for tasks that still occupy White House aides. Yet other, now familiar duties of White House staffs were not as visible. This chapter spotlights two such cases. First, there was scant anticipation of what has become the Office of Public Liaison, an all-purpose center for outreach to constituency groups. Second, White House liaison to state and local officials was only sporadic.[1] In what follows, we examine the complex interplay between environmental and presidential choice variables that helps account for the generally minimal attention these tasks received and for their often unstable structuring.

OUTREACH TO CONSTITUENCY GROUPS

Not until Gerald Ford's administration did a distinct White House Office emerge for handling contacts with external groups.[2] To be sure, this unit had precursors in earlier White Houses, most notably the Minorities Office under Franklin Roosevelt and Harry Truman. By the end of the Johnson years, White House aides routinely established and maintained ties with a range of external groups. Still, little structuring became institutionalized during the period examined here. Constituency liaison was rarely a staff specialty, and market structuring typically dominated.

Although many groups came to expect staff channels into the White House, which ones received the most attention depended on both environmental and presidential choice factors. World War II and the Korean conflict raised the salience of veterans' liaison for a time. They also accelerated the demands of African Americans for fairer treatment, but until changes in the political environment and in presidential values and strategies combined to yield efforts at legislative reform, these demands produced low-visibility staff efforts at outreach. Presidential choice variables by themselves could be significant. Not surprisingly, for example, the Eisenhower administration focused more on business than on labor groups; Democratic White Houses throughout the period devoted at least some time and energy to maintaining ties with elements of the New Deal coalition.

Yet, except for the Minorities Office in the Roosevelt and Truman administrations, no White House staffer worked full time at interest-group outreach. Not only did this kind of structuring fail to reemerge, but group outreach itself was rarely seen as a task for specialists. Typically, presidential aides were assigned to be liaisons based on either their personal characteristics or their pre–White House ties. Thus, according to Johnson's press secretary George Christian, he and his White House colleagues

> joked among ourselves that Marvin Watson was the resident conservative, Ernie Goldstein the resident liberal, Cliff Alexander the resident Negro, Joe Califano the resident Italian, Larry Levinson the resident Jew, Mike Manatos the resident Greek, John Roche the resident intellectual, George Christian the resident Texan, Walt Rostow the resident hawk, Harry McPherson the resident dove, Tom Johnson the resident youth.[3]

Perhaps most important, even though group outreach efforts often were intended to elicit support for the president or for his policies and proposals, little was done "to orchestrate contacts in pursuit of administration goals."[4]

Not until the Nixon administration would White House staffers be assigned full time to group liaison and charged with attracting and harnessing group support for presidential political and policy goals. Finally, under Gerald Ford, these outreach tasks were placed formally in the Office of Public Liaison, a unit that in one form or another has remained in the White House ever since.

That staff attention to constituency outreach would both increase and become far more systematic seems almost inevitable. Beginning in the 1960s, with control over policy growing more centralized in the White House, clear channels to presidential staff became ever more important resources as the numbers of groups and interests proliferated and demands for access mounted.[5] At the same time, presidents' abilities to achieve their objectives grew increasingly dependent on their gaining and directing the electoral and lobbying support of such groups. Not only had parties become "less effective structures for establishing . . . broad-based coalitions of interest group support,"[6] but by the 1970s, a decentralizing Congress also had grown more difficult for presidents to work with. And, of course, once an Office of Public Liaison was established in the White House, groups came to expect such access no matter who was president.

Yet such factors are clearly only part of the story, for they fail to explain why administrations before Nixon paid so little systematic and sustained attention to group outreach. Another environmental factor—whether the same party controlled the White House and Congress—may be relevant. Nixon, for example, may well have believed that he needed to cultivate more group support to help him in his confrontations with an unfriendly Democratic Congress; certainly, his successor faced an even more hostile political environment. Probably more important, however, are presidential choice variables. Neither full-time specialists nor separate outreach structures would have been consistent with Kennedy's or Johnson's approach to organizing the White House; similarly, Dwight Eisenhower's efforts to distance his White House from visible involvement in "politics" likely militated against the creation of such experts in an otherwise highly differentiated staff organization. Nixon, in contrast, combined Eisenhower's organizational strategies with a clear emphasis on cultivating and using group support to help achieve political and policy objectives.

Because different kinds of interests received varying amounts of White House attention, the examination that follows focuses on how staffers dealt with two different kinds of groups. First, the discussion highlights the establishment and maintenance of White House ties with African Americans and groups involved in pushing for increased civil rights for racial minorities. Unlike other interests that also demanded and received entree to the White House (such as labor unions and farm groups), blacks were largely denied access elsewhere in government. They were not welcome, for example, in a Congress dominated by southern Democrats, and there were no constituency-based agencies to turn to in the executive branch (such as farm interests found in the Agriculture Department and business did in the Commerce Department and elsewhere).[7] As blacks' demands for change grew and as Democratic presidents especially came to appreciate the importance of the northern black vote, White House staff outreach to African Americans emerged.

Presidents, of course, also sought the support (or at least the lack of vocal opposition) of other interests. During this period, White House aides paid attention to a variety of groups and interests. The targets of staff outreach generally reflected presidential strategies and interests as well as environmental changes. Fairly typical of these constituency relations were White House ties with a second kind of group, economic interests.[8]

Outreach to African Americans

White House outreach to blacks between 1929 and 1968 was largely devoted to maintaining links with prominent black leaders and organizations and to monitoring and promoting the efforts of executive branch agencies to integrate their workforces and to end discrimination and segregation in the programs they administered. By the end of the Roosevelt years, these had become specialized tasks, performed by civil rights "experts" in the White House with ties to important civil rights constituencies. Much like executive branch outreach more generally, the extent of the activities in this area and the nature of the structural responses reflected both environmental change and presidential strategies and commitments, with organizational variables having more marginal effects. Yet unlike the executive branch outreach explored in Chapter 5, that involving blacks was driven more by White House efforts to respond to the demands of external groups and less by presidents' desires to track the progress of their own programs and objectives. Moreover, staff outreach to civil rights groups extended beyond seeking fairer treatment of blacks; it sought to provide direct links to presidents, secure electoral support from blacks, and, in many cases, contain black protest.

Although a handful of White House aides more or less specialized in outreach to blacks during most of this period, both the volume and the nature of the attention that blacks received varied. Environmental factors accounted for much of this volatility. World War II, for example, led to sweeping changes in U.S. society, economics, and politics. Initially, presidents sought to respond to the demands of blacks through almost furtive initiatives in the executive branch. Yet, as pressures for change mounted, these low-visibility efforts became less relevant. As administrations came to believe that they no longer needed to hide their ties with blacks, relatively isolated White House civil rights specialists also grew less necessary. Paying attention to the concerns and demands of blacks came to involve a broader range of presidential aides, and market structuring prevailed. By the end of the Johnson years, outreach to blacks had grown to be more like maintaining contact with other groups.

Hoover Through Truman: The Emergence of Specialization. As they would for many administrations, White House relations with blacks during the Hoover years presented a continuing problem. The minimal attention that blacks received largely reflected the contradictory desires of keeping black votes for the "Party of Lincoln" and making inroads among southern whites. The rift between the White House and blacks widened during the administration,[9] not least because the staff was perceived to be hostile toward blacks. Press Secretary George Akerson, for example, elicited considerable negative reaction for his vehement, overheated denunciation of a charge leveled during the 1928 campaign that Hoover had once danced with Mary Booze, a black Republican national committeewoman from Mississippi.[10]

For much of the Roosevelt administration, blacks received only marginally more attention, although several of those around the president maintained contact with the black community.[11] Perhaps the key link with black groups was Eleanor Roosevelt, who served as an access point in the White House and a frequent advocate for, among others, the NAACP and the National Sharecroppers Fund.[12] Walter White of the NAACP called her "the most reliable channel to the President" and alleged that Appointments Secretary Marvin McIntyre often did not pass communications on to FDR.[13]

Dramatic environmental change—U.S. involvement in World War II—both triggered and shaped the nature of an increase in White House outreach to blacks. During wartime, Roosevelt was most interested in quelling domestic controversy and in avoiding any situation that would distract resources and attention from responding to the external threat. In 1941, A. Phillip Randolph, head of the Pullman Porters Union, threatened to lead a march on Washington to protest segregation in the armed forces and the lack of jobs for blacks in the burgeoning wartime industries. In order to avoid the march, the president ordered the formation of black combat units and the promotion of black officers; he also created the Fair Employment Practices Commission (FEPC) to oversee compliance with an order that any employer receiving government contracts end discriminatory practices.[14]

In addition, Roosevelt launched what would become a staff specialization in civil rights. In early 1943, he directed White House staffer Jonathan Daniels and his assistant, Philleo Nash, to create a "network of interagency information exchange" in order to identify possible situations in which racial tensions might interfere with war production or lead to violence.[15] Because of the tremendous controversy surrounding racial issues both in and out of government, such efforts were shrouded in secrecy.

This civil rights specialization continued in the Truman White House. Although other staffers occasionally became involved in particular civil rights issues, a separate unit housing Nash and his superior David Niles (who had been an administrative assistant in the Roosevelt White House) handled most of the contacts with black organizations and executive branch agencies on civil rights matters.[16] The "Minorities Office"[17] was part of a loosely linked collegial-consensual structure in the White House as a whole. Nash and Niles pursued their tasks with little direction: the Minorities Office was generally an "isolated operation."[18] Niles and frequently Nash reported directly to the president, though both also had cooperative relations with members of the special counsel's office.[19]

These arrangements were mostly congruent with the prevailing decision setting. They reflected the general administration consensus on civil rights goals (nondiscrimination; avoidance of conflict with Congress members, southern Democrats, and black leaders), the uneasy compromises reached on strategies (which emphasized low-visibility activities and gradualism), and the relatively low salience of the issue in the Truman White House.

Over the course of the Truman years, the range of staff tasks expanded. In addition to using various executive branch officials as intelligence sources, Nash and Niles also monitored, pushed for, and evaluated agency progress in ending discriminatory practices; served as liaisons with civil rights groups; and followed up on particular complaints.[20]

In addition, Nash monitored and handled correspondence related to the operations and activities of the Fair Employment Practices Commission until it was disbanded in June 1946.[21] Nash and Niles also were actively involved in helping to form, monitoring the progress of, and shaping the reports of the three civil rights committees of the Truman administration: the President's Civil Rights Committee, the President's Committee on Contract Compliance, and the Committee on Equality of Treatment and Opportunity in the Armed Services.[22]

The greater White House activity in civil rights under Truman probably reflected environmental, presidential choice, and, to a lesser extent, organizational variables. Most important was the higher and more variegated external demand for presidential response. With the end of the war, most blacks' and other civil rights supporters' attention shifted from primary concern with discrimination in the military to its presence in voting, housing, education, and other areas. Moreover, with the promise of employment in wartime industries, black migration to northern cities had jumped during the war. Once in the north, they also became voters, a fact lost on neither the big city bosses nor many elected officials.[23] At the same time, influential organizations such as the Urban League and the NAACP had grown dramatically during the war. Meanwhile, violent attacks on returning servicemen focused additional attention on the plight of blacks in the United States.[24]

For his part, Truman was willing to make at least some sort of response. Unlike Roosevelt, he agreed to the formation of the President's Committee on Civil Rights; in February 1948, Truman sent Congress a special message on civil rights that called for laws against lynching and poll taxes; and in 1949, he issued the executive order that integrated the armed forces. Finally, Nash and Niles continued in the White House, where they served to buffer the president and other staffers from some of the external pressures,[25] while also providing intelligence about such demands.

Eisenhower: Declining Emphasis. Relatively little of this concern with civil rights continued into the Eisenhower administration. In the new president's view, having an assistant for minority issues "would only accentuate the differences between minorities and majorities, rather than serving to bring them together on the common basis of American citizens."[26] Although the task remained in the White House, little structuring remained, and no staffer worked anywhere near full time on civil rights issues.

Maxwell Rabb (an assistant to Sherman Adams) was the White House contact for racial minorities.[27] Rabb explained, however, that he got the job by default: "nobody else dared take it on."[28] Wilton Persons, for example, did not want his congressional liaison staff "tainted" with such activities.[29] Still, Rabb insisted that his outreach work with minorities was a "sideline."[30]

Most of the activities Rabb did undertake involved troubleshooting. For example, he tried to minimize the damage generated by Rep. Adam Clayton Powell's public charges that administration officials were dragging their feet in desegregating schools on military bases. Rabb met with Powell and drafted Eisenhower's public response promising immediate action—which Powell immediately "hailed . . . as a 'Magna Carta for Minorities.' "[31] Following the shooting of Emmett Till (a 14-year-old black who had been accused of whistling at a white woman in a Mississippi store) in 1955 and a decline in the president's Gallup poll ratings among African Americans, Rabb organized sessions with black executive branch officials, much like the meetings Nash and Daniels arranged during World War II, to provide an "early warning system for administration problems with minorities."[32] After Rabb left the White House in May 1958, Rocco Siciliano (whose main responsibility was personnel) became the staffer for minority outreach.[33] Mostly, Siciliano kept in touch with black leaders and listened to their grievances.

Also intermittently (and reluctantly) involved in outreach to the African American community was the first black professional to work in the White House, E. Frederic Morrow, the administrative officer for special projects.[34] According to Morrow, he "made it very clear" to President Eisenhower

> that I did not want to be the expert on the Negro in the White House. . . . [O]nce I got bogged down in being an expert on the Negro, I would never be anything else, and I would not have the respect from my colleagues that I would have as a bona fide staff member.[35]

Still, he did a considerable amount of speaking to black groups, making more than 300 addresses during his tenure in the White House.[36] Increasingly, blacks identified Morrow as a channel into the White House.[37] Morrow grew more active after Rabb left[38]—for example, working to convince Eisenhower to meet with black leaders, preparing the president for and monitoring those meetings when they finally started, and meeting himself with representatives of black groups.[39] Morrow also became involved behind the scenes: "Whenever a tough race question pops up in the United

States, Fred gets into it on his own, and tries to do something about it. Ordinarily, no one in the White House would know that he had a hand in it."[40]

That so much less outreach activity could be observed in the Eisenhower White House underscores both the lack of persistence of these tasks and the changing values of key environmental, presidential choice, and organizational variables. First, since much of the push for change in the civil rights arena was being channeled through the courts, there were somewhat fewer pressures for systematic executive action. Moreover, by the 1950s, the electoral calculations had become different for a Republican president: "During the Eisenhower administration, the whole Republican party seemed to be embarrassed by the civil rights question."[41] Meanwhile, beginning in 1955, Eisenhower faced a Democratic Congress largely controlled by conservative southern committee chairs who were openly hostile to civil rights initiatives and quick to criticize a Republican administration.

Such environmental influences were reinforced by the president's own apparent preferences for doing relatively little. In Morrow's view, at least, Eisenhower "didn't give a tinker's dam. [The need for change] didn't touch him; it just didn't dawn on him."[42] Similarly, Burk contends that Eisenhower "could never bring himself to recognize that civil rights represented a cause on which delay, compromise, and accommodation with the racial segregationists was neither morally right nor politically possible in the long run."[43]

Kennedy: A Short-lived Renewal. With the Kennedy administration came an increase in both the volume and the scope of staff civil rights activity, much of which was reminiscent of the Truman White House, as partisan learning would lead one to expect. As in previous White Houses, relatively few staffers dealt with civil rights issues; over the course of the administration, attention to civil rights concerns, especially those in the executive branch, waned.

Most active in the Kennedy White House were Cabinet Secretary Frederick Dutton, Assistant Special Counsel Lee White, and special assistants Frank Reeves and Harris Wofford.[44] At the outset, Dutton offered the president advice on how to organize the administration's civil rights activities in the executive branch.[45] The cabinet secretary's call for a special assistant to coordinate activities was at least partially met: Harris Wofford spent much of his time monitoring and promoting agency civil rights efforts, assisted by Dutton and Frank Reeves.[46] In addition, Wofford made speeches to civil rights groups, kept in close touch with the NAACP and black leaders, advised Kennedy on meeting with black groups, and urged the president to make statements on civil rights, noting that "Negro leaders feel sorely the absence of any such statement."[47] When Wofford moved to the Peace

Corps in May 1962, Lee White inherited most of these responsibilities. Meanwhile, throughout the administration, Reeves sought to "provid[e] an ear within the White House and the White House staff for the Negro organizations and others who wanted to feel at least that their problems and complaints were receiving consideration."[48]

At the outset, two different structures emerged for overseeing executive branch civil rights activities. First was an ad hoc weekly meeting of "the key administrative men on civil rights to share information and discuss strategy," which Wofford initiated. Among the participants were Wofford, Burke Marshall of the Justice Department, Berl Bernhard of the Civil Rights Commission, Louis Martin from the Democratic National Committee, and John Feild, director of the President's Committee on Equal Employment Opportunity.[49] This collegial-consensual structure was designed to coordinate executive branch nondiscrimination efforts; it worked, with the staff assistance of an attorney detailed from the Civil Rights Commission, to collect a wide range of information on agency activities.

The second, and probably more important, structure was the Subcabinet Committee on Civil Rights. Authorized by the president in early 1961 (at Dutton's suggestion), the committee was to "discuss ways of improving federal services in the civil rights area."[50] Wofford had more ambitious objectives: the Committee was "an open conspiracy . . . to invoke the full power of the executive branch against racial discrimination in all parts of American public life."[51] The committee—whose members were agency-designated representatives at the assistant secretary level—took up topics such as government contracting, the recruitment of blacks to government service, and ways of increasing black voter registration in the South.[52]

The group was intended to place agency civil rights activities within a hierarchical structure directed from the White House, much as the Truman Minorities Office had attempted. It sought not only to promote new strategies for pursuing civil rights objectives but also to alert the White House to particular agency problems and to provide a channel through which the progress of various agencies and programs could be tracked and encouraged.[53] One of the group's first requests was for reports from all departments and agencies on the "degree and location of areas of discrimination" within their jurisdictions and on their capacities to respond.[54] At first, Dutton oversaw the operation of the group, selecting the agencies to be represented on the committee, convening the first meeting, approving its agenda and reports to the president, receiving and reacting to the various departmental reports the group solicited, and serving as a channel to Kennedy.[55] Wofford, however, chaired the group; he and Reeves attended most meetings and were the initial White House recipients of agency reports.[56]

When White replaced Wofford as chair, he used the group mainly for reporting purposes and to evaluate particular proposals for changing government employment practices.[57] The reduced activity under White likely reflected the other demands on his time and the development of a division of the Civil Rights Commission to staff the subcabinet group. Probably more important, spinning such activity out of the White House was also designed to keep the president from being too closely and continuously linked with civil rights activities.

In addition, White House civil rights staffers engaged in more general liaison and intelligence gathering.[58] Both Wofford and White were the White House contacts for the Civil Rights Commission. On occasion, this task involved more than simple liaison. Both men sometimes found themselves mediating between the commission and the Justice Department. According to Wofford—a supporter of the commission—Justice did not treat the commission as the independent agency its members believed it was: Burke Marshall and Attorney General Robert F. Kennedy "viewed the Civil Rights Commission as sort of cluttering up the field and jumping in where it would cause more harm than good."[59]

Much like Niles and Nash, Kennedy staffers also frequently went beyond serving as liaisons and tried to more actively shape executive branch activity. Dutton and Reeves, for instance, drafted the executive order desegregating government facilities and employee organizations.[60] Wofford, with input from Dutton, Special Counsel Theodore Sorensen, Assistant Special Counsel Richard Goodwin, and Burke Marshall at Justice, drafted the March 1961 executive order creating the President's Committee on Equal Employment Opportunity, which combined the existing presidential committees on government contracts and government employment policy.[61]

These aides also pushed Kennedy to become more visibly active in civil rights issues. Wofford recalled that one of the tasks of the subcabinet group was to "persuade the President to do more in this area than he might otherwise have done."[62] Dutton, Wofford, and White, among others, worked to persuade Kennedy to finally make the "one stroke of a pen" needed to end discrimination in federal housing, a step JFK did not take until Thanksgiving eve 1962.[63]

In general, although other White House staffers occasionally joined them, particular Kennedy aides were actively involved in overseeing and promoting civil rights in the executive branch and in maintaining links with blacks.[64] Not only did staff efforts decrease over time, but with the possible exception of Reeves, no one spent most of his time on civil rights–related activities as Truman aide Philleo Nash had.[65]

In addition, most of the activities took place at some remove from the Oval Office. Wofford noted, for example, that "[Kennedy] didn't particularly want to hear about [civil rights] because he was busy."[66] Moreover, the civil rights experts on the White House staff typically did not participate in discussions of possible presidential actions in the field: JFK's "key decisions, anything that was really cutting in civil rights, were made alone with Bob Kennedy, and you really didn't know what happened."[67]

Once again, environmental, presidential choice, and organizational variables help explain these dynamics. Public and congressional opposition to the development and enforcement of aggressive civil rights policies remained. Following his razor-thin margin of victory and confronting a Congress dominated by the Conservative Coalition, the president "was not eager to expend needed political capital" in pursuing such policies.[68] Such influences led Kennedy—as they had Truman and Eisenhower before him—to pursue a strategy of seeking incremental change through low-visibility alterations in executive branch practices. The White House approach was "minimum civil rights legislation, maximum executive action."[69] At least at the outset, this suggested some presence by White House staffers in executive branch activities.

Yet Kennedy was also the president that cynics joked was "long on profile and short on courage" when it came to civil rights.[70] Wofford was more generous:

> [The president never] talked through the issues or looked ahead and set long-term priorities in civil rights. He certainly wanted to do enough so that the civil rights constituency was not too unhappy and beyond that he wanted to make substantial headway against what he considered the nonsense of racial discrimination.[71]

Still, at various points, Dutton, Wofford, and Reeves all complained about the speed with which Kennedy was willing to move in civil rights.[72] Although Wofford and Reeves agreed that Kennedy had given them "a mandate to do anything [they] could get away with,"[73] it should not be surprising that, without their initiative, White House involvement in civil rights–related activities diminished.

Furthermore, the perceived nature of the civil rights problem had changed somewhat by late 1962. The administration belatedly began to recognize the need for a legislative strategy,[74] and in February 1963 Kennedy asked Congress to enact civil rights legislation.

Johnson: Shifting Attention to Other Arenas. The Johnson administration paid less attention to civil rights activities in the executive branch: the action was in Congress and, increasingly, in the streets as riots broke out around the United States. What staff specialization there was appeared at lower levels of the White House hierarchy and finally disappeared; the volume and the range of activities contracted.

Early in the administration, Cabinet Secretary Horace Busby offered Johnson advice on how to deal with issues likely to be important to the black community, typically with an eye toward the implications for the growing competition between Johnson and Robert Kennedy. For example, Busby advised Appointments Secretary Jack Valenti that a representative from the White House should be sent to the funeral of a black educator killed in Georgia: "Almost surely, the Attorney General will be there or be represented."[75]

For brief periods, as they had under Kennedy, members of the special counsel's staff devoted much of their time to civil rights activities. Lee White continued to work on civil rights and remained in touch with black groups.[76] In 1964–65, Associate Special Counsel Hobart Taylor monitored the Plans for Progress program and served as executive vice chair of the President's Committee on Equal Opportunity. His replacement, Clifford Alexander, handled inquiries about civil rights that came to the special counsel's office and kept in contact with the black community.[77] After White left the staff in early 1966, Special Counsel Harry McPherson inherited his civil rights duties.

Clearly, the environment had changed during the Johnson years, reducing the salience and significance of less visible executive branch activities while producing more sweeping legislative actions and seeking to quell racial violence. Nor was President Johnson very interested in this particular form of executive branch outreach. For instance, when McPherson conveyed to LBJ Hobart Taylor's concern that the Plans for Progress program was weakening and that it would benefit from some presidential attention to the participating business executives, Johnson responded: "leave Plans for Progress up to the Vice President and tell Taylor to quit promoting me on this."[78] Far more appropriate (and comfortable) for LBJ was to treat African Americans in much the same way as he treated any of the other interests clamoring for the president's attention: he would "recruit allies who represented identifiable constituencies and could deliver votes."[79] Johnson's successors followed his lead.

Outreach to Economic Interests

Between 1929 and 1969, White Houses paid less regular attention to maintaining systematic liaison with economic groups than they did to forging links with African Americans. This hardly meant, of course, that they considered economic interests to be less important. Rather, both business and labor had other places in the executive branch and the political parties to turn to with their demands, and most administrations had officials with longer-term ties to such interests.

The nature and intensity of White House outreach in this area varied with the party controlling the White House, the objectives of particular presidents, and external demands. Never was outreach so salient, however, that it led to fully specialized staffers or to more than ad hoc structuring. In the absence of either consistent presidential objectives and strategies or clear environmental expectations of such relations, market structuring seems roughly congruent with the prevailing decision settings.

Although Herbert Hoover met routinely (indeed, almost obsessively as the depression worsened) with business leaders, his staff was not significantly involved in such contact. During the Roosevelt years, more systematic efforts were made to establish staff linkages with identifiable groups and interests. Early in the administration, relations were more exclusive, emphasizing those constituencies with particular significance to the Roosevelt White House. Labor was especially important, as a key element of the "New Deal Coalition" that FDR sought to forge. Indeed, Truman staffer John Steelman later charged that "labor had access to the backdoor" in the Roosevelt White House, and business did not.[80]

After 1939, at least one administrative assistant was designated the labor liaison.[81] First was Daniel Tobin, Teamster Union president and, since 1936, the chair of the labor division of the national Democratic Campaign Committee.[82] Tobin took credit for

> establishing negotiations with the representatives of the American Federation of Labor [which was in a dispute with the CIO], with the result that at this time [August 1940] there is a better feeling obtaining and most of the misunderstandings have been eliminated.[83]

Tobin resigned in August 1940 to return to his job as Democratic National Committee (DNC) labor representative for the 1940 campaign, and James Rowe and later Wayne Coy took on most of his responsibilities.[84] Toward the end of the administration, David Niles, head of the new Minorities Office, also served as a liaison for labor groups.[85]

Business, in contrast, had far less systematic contact with the Roosevelt White House prior to World War II. With the so-called second New Deal, what contact there was was often hostile.[86] But as the United States began preparing for war, the business community became more important to the administration and relations improved. In 1942, for example, administrative assistant Lauchlin Currie reported that at a dinner forum with 90 business executives, "the same group I have been meeting with for the past two years, . . . the atmosphere was better than it has been in the past. There was little griping at Government and the New Deal was not even mentioned."[87]

Environmental factors continued to shape White House relations with economic groups after the war. Postwar labor problems and the difficulties of moving from a wartime to a peacetime economy likely account in large part for the extensive attention the Truman White House paid to labor-management issues. In October 1945, John Steelman came to the White

House to concentrate on labor matters; when John Snyder moved from the Office of War Mobilization and Reconversion (OWMR) to Treasury in June 1946, Steelman replaced him. Finally, later that year, the remains of OWMR were moved into the White House under Steelman's direction.[88]

Although Steelman and his staff performed a variety of tasks, Steelman himself spent most of his time keeping in contact with labor leaders and some business executives and working to mediate particular labor disputes.[89] According to Steelman staffer David Stowe, there was some division of labor: Steelman "dealt mostly with the management and with the AF of L and all of the dealings with the CIO seemed to gravitate to my office."[90] Meanwhile, Steelman aides Harold Enarson and Milton Kayle worked with labor groups as Congress considered restrictive labor legislation.[91]

Charles Jackson and John T. Gibson were the Steelman staffers with the most extensive links in the business community.[92] Much of their time was spent working with the Advertising Council, a nonprofit public-service organization involving major advertising firms that produced public-service spots for the government.[93] Jackson and Gibson worked within a collegial-consensual structure to coordinate the council's free advertising services with the various agencies that used them, helping to plan ad campaigns and linking advertising firms with specific agencies.[94]

For all this activity, however, Steelman and his aides hardly had a monopoly on contacts with labor and business groups. Like his predecessor Sam Rosenman, Special Counsel Clark Clifford on occasion talked with labor leaders.[95] David Lloyd of the counsel staff dealt with the "more progressive elements in the business community"[96] as well as with a variety of labor groups as part of his job as liaison with "liberal" and "progressive" groups.[97]

In the Eisenhower White House, group ties generally weakened. Still, some links with labor remained. Maxwell Rabb was the key White House contact for labor groups as well as an occasional troubleshooter in labor-management disputes.[98] Yet other staffers were also involved. Gabriel Hauge, for example, met with labor leaders in the course of his economic advising responsibilities.[99]

Not surprisingly for a Republican administration, most sentiments were with business, not labor. Indeed, Appointments Secretary Bernard Shanley was "roundly criticized" for allowing a group of labor leaders from the textile industry in to see the president.[100] Even though National Security Assistant Robert Cutler argued early on that "the emphasis on business leaders seeing the President should cease,"[101] the administration "appointed business representatives in huge numbers to government regulatory boards and commissions . . . and expanded the number and role of industry advisory committees."[102] Business executives often met with Eisenhower and were invited to his stag dinners. Hauge also met with business representatives, and Howard Pyle spent considerable time speaking to business groups as part of his "public-relations" activities.

The White House continued to house liaison staffers for the Ad Council. James Lambie spent nearly half his time in this capacity, allocating council services among government agencies and arbitrating competing claims.[103] Lambie also arranged the annual Ad Council meetings and organized presidential briefings for advertising and business leaders.[104]

In addition, the administration engaged in limited experiments with a "governing party" approach to group liaison, seeking to build support for some of its programmatic goals.[105] Clarence Randall's foreign economic policy operation (see Chapter 9), for example, worked directly with a range of business organizations in developing a legislative package to encourage foreign investment.[106] Meanwhile, given the administration's interest in agricultural policy, legislative liaison staffers Jack Z. Anderson, Bryce Harlow, and Jack Martin, as well as Special Counsel Bernard Shanley, were in regular contact with representatives of farm groups.[107]

Closest perhaps to more recent White House efforts to cultivate programmatic support from groups was the administration's attempt to mobilize business backing for the 1959 budget. Concerned about the significant Democratic gains in the 1958 congressional elections, Eisenhower initiated a "massive appeal" to generate opposition to "spendthrift legislation" and to promote support for anti-inflationary measures and a balanced budget.[108] Orchestrated by Cabinet Secretary Robert Gray, White House aides held a series of lunch meetings with the heads of large national business organizations: "Our only criteria [sic] in enlisting national groups was 'Is their mailing list long enough to be worthwhile?' "[109] Significantly, no labor organizations were contacted. "For some reason, they considered 'an amount' of continuing inflation to be in the best interests of the workingman [sic]."[110]

In the Kennedy White House, outreach to economic interests was less important than it had been under Eisenhower. To a considerable extent, this reflected Kennedy's "marginal interest" in business and labor relations.[111] Yet, when his administration did engage in liaison with economic interests, it typically focused on generating support for specific presidential programs. Howard Petersen (special assistant for international trade policy) and his staff, for example, worked to mobilize business support for the president's trade program, including winning their backing for the passage of the Trade Expansion Act of 1962 (as Chapter 9 explores further).

More generally, White House responsibility for economic outreach was broadly diffused, and little in the way of structuring emerged. In mid-1962, for example, Theodore Sorensen proposed ways for cabinet members to work to improve the administration's relations with business.[112] At the same time, Deputy National Security Assistant Carl Kaysen, Associate Special

Counsel Myer Feldman, and Special Assistant Ralph Dungan kept in contact with labor leaders and relayed their concerns and complaints to the president.[113] Cabinet Secretaries Dutton and Reardon were technically the White House liaisons to the Ad Council, but they spent even less time at the task than their predecessors had.

Economic ties strengthened to some degree under Johnson, reinforced by growing economic problems that both led the president to seek the support of business and labor leaders and pushed them to press for access to the Oval Office. Once more, however, little specialization appeared, and market structuring continued.

Various Johnson aides established ties with labor leaders. Lee White continued his contacts from the Kennedy administration, and Bill Moyers, Lawrence O'Brien, Joseph Califano, Marvin Watson, and Douglass Cater all dealt on occasion with the AFL-CIO.[114] In fact, so many staffers interacted with labor leaders that in 1966 President Johnson requested that "those involved in labor liaison make a conscious attempt to notify the other staff assistants of the contacts" and that they keep the president "informed of very important labor contacts or labor criticism."[115] LBJ himself further complicated matters, however, by naming Cabinet Secretary Robert Kintner and White House aide Milton Semer contacts with the Teamsters.[116] By 1967, still other White House aides had also become involved in labor liaison. Former press secretary George Reedy, for example, assumed some responsibility for labor liaison when he returned to the White House in 1968.[117]

Meanwhile, other aides kept in contact with business leaders. Among Appointments Secretary Marvin Watson's responsibilities was maintaining ties with industries and business associations.[118] Similarly, Special Counsel Harry McPherson was in touch with a range of business groups and executives and developed "talking points" for Johnson's meetings with business leaders.[119] When Robert Kintner, a former NBC executive, joined the staff, he brought with him a range of contacts throughout the business community.[120] And, reflecting their substantive policy responsibilities, counsel staffers Myer Feldman, DeVier Pierson, and Harry McPherson kept in contact with farm groups.[121] Again, the Ad Council received minimal attention from a series of White House staffers, including cabinet secretaries Busby, Kintner, and Maguire.

For a time, Johnson aide Joseph Califano and his aides occasionally intervened in labor-management disputes, much as Steelman's staffers had. Their activities ended abruptly in 1966 during an airline machinists' strike—the president announced a wage settlement that the union then rejected.[122] Even after that, however, the Califano office kept Johnson updated on labor unrest.[123]

Thus, by the end of the Johnson years, White House aides routinely established and maintained ties with a range of external constituencies. Presidential interest in and environmental demand for such activity, however, waxed and waned, and little stable structuring emerged.

OUTREACH TO STATE AND LOCAL GOVERNMENT OFFICIALS

Like outreach to constituency groups, liaison with subnational government officials is a quite visible White House outreach activity today.[124] Yet intergovernmental outreach was not lodged in the White House until the 1950s, where it survived only through the Kennedy and early Johnson administrations, failing to become a permanent feature there until the early 1970s. When intergovernmental outreach was in the White House, market structuring typically prevailed.

Both the instability and the ad hoc structuring can be explained by presidential choice and environmental factors. Rarely were relations with subnational governments a high priority for presidents in this period.

On occasion, however, presidents turned to state and local officials for programmatic and political support. Well before the time examined here, for instance, Theodore Roosevelt started the Governors' Conference: in 1908, he summoned the nation's governors to the White House to enlist their help in persuading Congress to pass the president's natural resources legislation.[125] The second Roosevelt was "actively involved" in the 1933 establishment of the U.S. Conference of Mayors, which FDR hoped would not only back his programs but also help sustain the urban portion of his New Deal coalition.[126] Later, LBJ would seek the backing of big-city mayors for many of his Great Society initiatives. Yet such presidential attention to intergovernmental affairs was at best sporadic and only sometimes involved White House staffers. Much like White House outreach to nongovernmental constituency groups, little systematic effort was devoted to mobilizing the support of subnational officials. Given uncertain, changing goals and means, market structuring seems congruent with the volatile decision settings.

Probably even more important in explaining the lack of continuing White House involvement in intergovernmental liaison and the fluid structuring, however, are environmental factors. Executive branch agencies jealously protected their own ties with state and local officials and frequently protested what they considered to be White House "interference." Meanwhile, pressure for channels to the president from subnational officials was low during much of the period. From the end of the depression until the mid-1960s, few state and local officials saw much reason for ongoing relations with the federal government, little of which was significant enough for presidential involvement. Only in the 1960s was there the "massive breakthrough in domestic legislation directed at states [and] local governments."[127] Such legislation, in turn, increased the importance of the national government as a source of badly needed resources, as a potential threat to the decision autonomy of state and local officials, and as the locus for bedeviling interagency coordination problems. Once enacted, Great Society programs almost immediately entangled presidents in the "intergovernmental thicket."[128]

At the same time, organizations of state and local officials were becoming reenergized. By the end of the 1960s, all the important organizations representing subnational officials (e.g., the Conference of Mayors, the National Governors Conference, the National League of Cities) had offices in Washington and became increasingly active in lobbying Congress, working with executive branch agencies, and demanding at least some channels into the White House.

By the end of the decade, changes in state and local governments added to the pressures on the White House for liaison. For much of the early modern era, state governments were the backwaters of U.S. politics, the "fallen arches" of the federal system. Charges that state officials were corrupt and incompetent abounded; problems were exacerbated in the South by segregation, blatant racism, and the ever-present threat of violence. Most states, run by rural-dominated legislatures and governors who were "good-time Charlies," did little to assist their increasingly troubled cities. These problems provided the rationale both for increased national involvement in the federal system and for presidents to distance themselves from state and local officials. Yet, as Washington slowly stepped up its activity, many states were being transformed—in large part due to court-ordered reapportionment and, in the South, national civil rights legislation. Whatever the impetus, the "new breed" of state and local officials began demanding increased attention in Washington and came to be viewed as more reliable and viable partners.

Precursors of White House Structuring

Maintaining ties with subnational officials received little focused attention during the Hoover, Roosevelt, and Truman years. For a brief period in the Roosevelt administration, Administrative Assistant James McReynolds was assigned the task of "coordinat[ing] Federal programs involving intergovernmental relations."[129] Although there are no surviving records of McReynolds's activities, the liaison effort apparently was short-lived:

> partly because the administration did not back the efforts of the coordinators and partly because of the almost unlimited ingenuity of department and agency administrators in finding means of resisting any

attempt to develop uniform policies and procedures and to coordinate programs.[130]

Eisenhower: Emerging Specialization

The Eisenhower White House was the first to devote sustained effort to staying in touch with elected officials at other levels of the federal system. Not until well into the administration, however, was any aide made explicitly responsible for intergovernmental outreach. Instead, staff members who had been governors undertook such efforts informally. Former Nebraska governor Val Peterson, for example, was formally assigned to serve as liaison with executive branch agencies but soon found himself approached by his former peers.[131] Similarly, Chief of Staff Sherman Adams, an ex–New Hampshire governor, dealt regularly with governors and on occasion with municipal officials, serving mostly as an information channel between them and other administration officials.[132]

Although other White House aides also engaged sporadically in intergovernmental activities,[133] no staffer assumed specific responsibility for or devoted much time to intergovernmental outreach until the mid-1950s. Some specialization emerged in February 1955 when Howard Pyle, a recently defeated Arizona governor, took over the Executive Branch Liaison Office (a position Peterson had held for only two months in 1953). Peterson's job description was reconstructed to include intergovernmental liaison, and Pyle assumed responsibility for handling federal-state relations and for dealing with departments whose programs affected the states.[134] Within a few months, Pyle was named deputy assistant for intergovernmental relations.[135] But, as Chapter 3 noted, Pyle actually spent most of his time working to enhance the administration's image among party officials and in the country as a whole.[136]

In October 1955, Adams brought Meyer Kestnbaum, the president of Hart, Schaeffner and Marx clothiers, to the White House as an unpaid consultant to "organize the work of federal-state relations."[137] More specifically, Kestnbaum was charged with implementing the recommendations of both the presidential commission on intergovernmental relations that he had headed and the recently disbanded Hoover Commission.[138] Kestnbaum was directed to look for ways to return some power to the state and local levels.[139] Ultimately, however, at least according to Sherman Adams, these efforts "came to naught" because of the president's general lack of interest.[140]

In May 1958, Robert Merriam took over Pyle's responsibilities for intergovernmental liaison (as well as a range of other tasks).[141] Unlike his predecessor, Merriam devoted significant time to his state-local responsibilities. For example, he "kept in touch with all the major organizations of state and local officials—the Governors' conference, the American Municipal Association, county officials, etc.,"[142] and he "constantly kept groups of governors coming to talk with the President."[143] Merriam also was a member of the Federal-State Joint Action Committee, oversaw its transition to the Advisory Commission on Intergovernmental Relations (ACIR), and served as the first White House liaison to the ACIR.[144]

Other members of Pyle's and later Merriam's staff spent time on intergovernmental tasks too. Under Pyle, Charles Masterson handled relationships with officials from states that were federal grant recipients.[145] First Jack Stambaugh and later Douglas Price and Warren Warrington did staff work for and monitored the activities of the Joint Action Committee.[146] In addition, Stambaugh served for a time as the White House member of a cabinet committee charged with transferring federal functions to the states.[147]

For all the White House activity, however, few representatives of groups of state and local officials believed that they had much "effect on the federal system." Nonetheless, Jean Appleby reported that White House involvement worked to raise "the awareness of federal officials who had not been very concerned with intergovernmental relations."[148]

Kennedy: Waning Attention

Intergovernmental relations remained a staff responsibility in the Kennedy White House. Yet, although specific staffers continued to handle intergovernmental outreach, they neither monopolized relations with state and local officials nor devoted all their energies to the task. Meanwhile, turf struggles broke out between the White House and executive branch agencies.[149]

Initially, intergovernmental liaison was part of Cabinet Secretary Dutton's job assignment.[150] For example, he sought to develop "working relationships between White House operations and the Democratic governors of key states"[151] and brought potential problems to the president's attention.[152] Dutton also organized a series of White House regional conferences held in 12 cities to permit state and local officials and other citizens to share their concerns with selected cabinet members.[153]

After Dutton left the White House in late November 1961, Brooks Hays joined the staff and took on the intergovernmental liaison task, reporting to Myer Feldman in Special Counsel Theodore Sorensen's office.[154] Hays spent a great deal of time traveling, meeting not only with state and local officials but also with a range of business, rural development, and church groups.[155] He also chaired a governors' committee on improving state-national planning for capital improvements, which produced a presidential directive to federal agencies to improve their coordinating activities.[156] Hays reported spending considerable time, along with his executive assistant Warren Cikins, working with the ACIR.[157] For the most part, though, Hays seems to have acted much like Pyle—most of his efforts were devoted to improving the administration's "image" among a variety of groups and interests.

In addition, another Sorensen staffer, Lee White, followed up on the conferences Dutton had organized.[158] White also helped organize a proposed White House conference on urban problems, which never materialized because of concerns that it threatened to embroil the administration in a visible discussion over civil rights.[159]

Johnson: Moving Out of the White House

Market structuring of White House intergovernmental liaison continued during the first full year of the Johnson administration. Brooks Hays left the White House in February 1964; although he continued as a consultant until mid-1966, much of his time was devoted to church-state issues.[160] Until early 1965, Hobart Taylor handled most White House correspondence with governors and other state and local officials.[161] White served as White House representative on the ACIR, and Ralph Dungan occasionally handled complaints from local officials.[162]

This arrangement proved inadequate as environmental demands for attention mounted. Appointments Secretary Jack Valenti wrote to the president, for example, that the handling of correspondence with subnational officials "needs a more effective eye and judgment paying attention to it."[163] Part of the response was to assign new staff member Marvin Watson the responsibility of handling "Federal-state relations."[164] For the most part, though, Watson focused on the partisan political aspects of these relations.[165] He was decidedly *not* the "special assistant for intergovernmental relations."

Instead, at about the same time, Johnson moved the chief responsibility for local government liaison to Vice President Humphrey's office, in large part because Humphrey was a former mayor (of Minneapolis).[166] The president also appointed former Tennessee governor Buford Ellington as director of the Office of Emergency Planning (OEP) in the Executive Office; chief among Ellington's responsibilities was to be "general liaison with state governments."[167] When Ellington resigned in early 1966, he was replaced by C. Farris Bryant, who had been governor of Florida; Bryant, in turn, was replaced in early 1968 by former Texas governor Price Daniel.[168] Bryant saw his chief task as being an "advocate for governors with the President and with the executive branch bureaucracy."[169] This arrangement was formalized by Executive Order 11426 issued in 1968, which named the director of the Office of Emergency Preparedness the presidential assistant for federal-state relations.[170]

After 1965, no staffer in the Johnson White House had ongoing responsibility for intergovernmental liaison. Although several aides became involved sporadically,[171] intergovernmental relations generally returned to the status it had held in pre-Eisenhower White Houses. It would not return to the White House Office until Nixon's second term. Faced with louder and increasingly well-articulated demands from state and local officials for greater national responsiveness, a visible White House role in intergovernmental liaison no doubt struck those in Nixon's administration as a reasonable answer. Strategic concerns, of course, were hardly irrelevant. The Republican Nixon sought enhanced subnational participation as part of his New Federalism initiatives, and, as was the case with outreach to constituency groups, he pursued that involvement far more systematically than had any of his predecessors.

CONCLUSIONS

Between 1929 and 1968 the White House sought to develop and maintain staff links with groups and government officials outside Washington. Such relations were useful for learning about conditions throughout the country, tracking presidential approval, soliciting support for administration initiatives, and providing at least symbolic access to the president. By the end of the Johnson years, the White House had routinized ties with a range of external constituency groups. Outreach to state and local officials, however, was more sporadic. Despite these differences, in neither arena did presidential aides devote consistent or systematic attention to mobilizing external interests in support of presidential objectives; nor did stable structuring emerge. Such ongoing efforts—although anticipated—would not appear until Richard Nixon assumed the presidency.

PART II
Policy Processing

7
Domestic and Economic Policy

One of the key features of the modern presidency is the expectation that presidents will exercise leadership in domestic and economic policy—formulating programs, sending initiatives to Congress and pushing for their adoption, providing direction for the executive branch, working to coordinate the efforts of the vast federal bureaucracy and of state and local officials, and responding to the concerns of numerous and diverse constituencies. Many of these tasks—especially during the early modern presidency—involved outreach and were explored in Part I. This chapter focuses on the policy formulation activities associated with the "domestic presidency,"[1] which encompasses both traditional domestic policy and nonforeign economic policy.[2]

A rudimentary capacity for White House involvement in domestic and economic policy deliberation appeared during the Hoover administration, largely as a result of Hoover's policy agenda. Continuation of similar capability, especially in economic policy, was virtually guaranteed by the onset of the depression, but Roosevelt showed less interest in a White House response than had Hoover. Not until Truman, who was faced with the massive problems of postwar reconversion, did the White House become a focal point for substantive policy. With Truman as well came the first extensive White House governance structuring for domestic and economic policy making. Yet responsibility for domestic policy was not placed in a separate, relatively specialized unit in the White House Office until the Johnson administration, setting a general pattern that has guided Johnson's successors.[3]

Although domestic policy involvement was structured in similar and often congruent ways during the period, stability generally was low. Meanwhile, White House staffers were far less involved in economic policy and

143

focused mainly on implementation rather than formulation. Structuring was mostly hierarchical, congruent with the demands of coordination when policy goals and strategies presumably have been agreed upon. Nonetheless, stability of these structures was also rather low.

The most obvious factors contributing to the emergence of these structures are environmental: the period 1929 to 1969 saw external demands on the presidency proliferate. Heightened expectations on the part of both the public and Congress, coupled with an explosion of new programs and agencies, increasingly focused responsibility on the presidency for policy leadership and for guidance of policy implementation. These forces clearly compelled some form of presidential response, but they alone did not necessitate changes in the White House Office.

To explain those, one must examine the political and organizational properties of the executive branch as they interacted with presidential choice factors. Most broadly, presidents differed in their preferred levels of policy activism and the desired nature of that activity. Eisenhower was largely content to consolidate and refine the domestic policies of his predecessors, leading him to seize the initiative mostly in the implementation arena. In contrast, Presidents Hoover, Roosevelt, Kennedy, and Johnson pressed innovative agendas. To the extent that certain activities become especially important to presidents, one might expect presidents to charge personal staffers to monitor those tasks if not take them on themselves.

Still, presidential choice alone does not fully explain why some activities appeared in the White House rather than elsewhere in the executive branch. Necessary to consider as well are the attributes of "domestic policy." Presidential policy strategies and responses to the environment develop within a complex and fragmented organizational context. There was no clear locus of domestic policy responsibility within the executive branch, as there was for economic policy. Indeed, domestic policy itself is really a residual category, a receptacle for a wide variety of issues and programs that do not clearly fit elsewhere or necessarily relate to one another. As a result, presidents confront a multiplicity of agencies and their associated constituencies. Yet presidents also are expected to formulate coherent legislative programs and to furnish consistent guidance to the executive branch.

This leaves presidents with relatively few strategic options. One option, which is often recommended but seldom followed, would be the comprehensive reorganization of executive agencies in an effort to clarify their missions and better direct bureaucratic efforts to areas of interdependence—as both Johnson and Nixon sought quixotically to do. The most serious problem with this approach, apart from the obvious question of political feasibility, is conceptual. If domestic policy is really more a "garbage can" than a set of clearly delimited and logically interrelated concerns, no purely structural strategy can be expected to untangle the issues or work notably better than any other. This contrasts sharply with what is typically labeled economic policy, which is more amenable to location within a few specialized institutions, largely because it has been defined as a relatively coherent policy area.

In domestic policy, early modern presidents fell back on a strategy of drawing many issues into the White House because they lacked clear alternatives. When presidential priorities dictated exceptional concern for a particular issue, the White House provided at least a temporary home. At the same time, the fragmentation and poor definition of the domestic policy sphere encouraged the development of staff capacity for coordinating and tracking policy-related activities throughout the executive branch and the intergovernmental system. This was reinforced by external expectations of presidential leadership. The White House may well have seemed the most reasonable site, since the staff was responsible only to the president and was, at least in principle, most sensitive to his political and policy objectives.

Such an arrangement was not always satisfactory, of course. Increasing White House involvement sometimes generated demands for still more intervention. Among the consequences were an overloaded staff, undue visibility given to certain issues, and heightened agency influence over "policy" as the White House became enmeshed in "operations."[4] Staff structures and responsibilities grew more specialized and differentiation increased, reflecting the fragmentation and, on occasion, the parochialism of both the executive branch and domestic policy constituencies.[5]

The final factor in accounting for the emergence of domestic policy structuring is most clearly organizational. Over time, the growth and specialization of the White House policy staff became self-sustaining, to an extent. The continuing presence of a staff required that aides be given tasks to perform. This, in turn, produced a need for supervision, coordination, and task assignment within the White House. These developments triggered the by now familiar differentiation dynamic in which organizational growth and specialization fostered the development of additional structures and tasks—and often promoted further growth and complexity. Moreover, as staff involvement in policy persisted, competitors in the executive branch, most notably the Bureau of the Budget (BOB), became less influential and ultimately less active participants. This created still more opportunities for the White House staff.

As White House involvement in the tasks of the domestic presidency became institutionalized, a small number of staff structures recurred. Hoover located staffers in a hierarchical chain as liaisons between the administration and various citizen commissions designed not only to generate policy ideas but also to oversee implementation. This structuring was largely congruent with the decision setting: typically, Hoover had clear policy objectives in mind and appointed external bodies to explore various means of achieving them, with guidance from the White House. Such structuring would reemerge in the Kennedy and Johnson administrations, but it would not represent the primary response.

Structuring in the Truman White House pointed to the second organizational response in the domestic and economic policy arena: differentiated White House structures for linking the White House with executive branch agencies. For the most part, the structuring during the Truman administration was congruent with prevailing decision settings. Collegial-consensual and collegial-competitive structures permitted the airing and comparison of policy alternatives when goals, technologies, or both were in question. Collegial-mediative structuring emerged to settle disputes, often supplemented by adjudicative structures. Meanwhile, the hierarchy that emerged within the special counsel's office and the Steelman unit and that linked the White House and the executive branch permitted activities to be guided and monitored once ends and means had been specified. Kennedy and Johnson both employed the counsel's office in similar ways, but Eisenhower did not.

Despite the recurrence of similar structuring for domestic and economic policy throughout the early modern era, even more striking is the failure of such structures to stabilize across administrations. Each administration produced its own version of one or both organizational responses, locating similar governance structures in different White House units and varying their tasks.

During the Eisenhower administration, with low levels of activity in domestic policy formulation, most of Truman's structuring vanished, and little replaced it. Kennedy, however, reestablished the counsel's office as the center of policy activity, combining loose internal hierarchy with adjudication. The unit proved to be a platform for activists who plunged into issues fraught with both controversy and uncertainty; it did not, however, provide a stable forum for policy deliberation and coordination.

Partisan learning was clearly present: Democrats, in the tradition of FDR, tended strongly toward locating policy responsibility in the counsel's office. Yet even that pattern was altered during the Johnson administration. Under Johnson, the counsel's office lost its preeminence, staffers with domestic policy responsibilities multiplied, and a separate domestic policy operation surfaced. Several often competing structures emerged. Despite conditions favorable to a differentiation dynamic, however, structures linking and integrating the various centers of domestic policy formulation largely failed to appear.

Among the explanations for this instability is the nature of domestic policy. Conceptually, as contended above, domestic policy is hard to define. As a result, no particular set of structures will seem in the abstract to be best suited for handling domestic policy. In addition, the domestic policy arena includes a multiplicity of actors and constituencies, with varying levels of influence, skill, and legitimacy.

This expectation of structural instability is reinforced when one considers presidential involvement. Two features stand out. First, presidential interest in domestic policy overall was at best sporadic. Within administrations, such events as the onset of war and the launch of *Sputnik* put domestic issues on the back burner; attention varied too with the electoral cycle,[6] as well as with the level of presidential enthusiasm. LBJ, for example, moved from intense interest and involvement to almost total indifference.[7] Much of the time he was most interested in policy innovation and legislative adoption, but on occasion he monitored executive branch operations closely.[8]

Second, even when presidential interest was high, preferred presidential management strategies varied significantly. As scholars have frequently remarked, this can be seen in the sharp contrast between the Eisenhower and Kennedy presidencies.[9] Furthermore, approaches shifted even within administrations. During the Eisenhower and Johnson years, for example, concern for White House organization and reorganization was itself a continuing theme. And virtually all the presidents in this period found virtue in at least occasionally changing staff assignments and priorities or assigning the same task to several aides.[10]

Nonetheless, certain patterns appeared early and persisted. Foreign policy (which Chapter 8 examines in greater detail) was handled through channels distinct from those structuring domestic policy during virtually the entire period and was not a primary White House concern until World War II. Meanwhile, primary responsibility for economic policy remained in the cabinet departments, independent agencies, the BOB, and, after 1946, the Council of Economic Advisers.

In addition, in the White House as a whole, functional differentiation was proceeding. Much of this was taking place at the margins of domestic policy, in such areas as legislative liaison, press relations, and constituency liaison. Staffers who performed these tasks were initially near the center of domestic policy activities in the White House; gradually, however, they moved toward the periphery as their responsibilities became more narrowly defined (as happened with, for example, legislative liaison under Eisenhower and press relations under Kennedy).

Organizational variables are especially helpful in explaining these continuities. First, presidents and their advisers tried to cope with the ambiguity of domestic policy in part by decomposing the complex of problems into a set of more easily addressed tasks.[11] Those activities most amenable to clear definition were hived off and sometimes moved out of the White House altogether. Second, once structures did emerge, expectations and the force of precedent attached to them, increasing the likelihood that they would be replicated in succeeding administrations. Meanwhile, even in policy areas that were less clearly delimited, most White Houses devoted at least some attention to dividing tasks—experimenting with, for instance, specialists in policy formulation and policy implementation, aides who maintained contact with particular agencies, and subject matter experts. Here, structural fluidity was far greater.

STRUCTURING FOR DOMESTIC POLICY

Most treatments of the policy process distinguish among at least three stages: formulation, adoption, and implementation. Although these stages are rarely clear-cut empirically, they can prove useful analytically when trying to untangle White House dynamics. This section concentrates on general domestic policy; the following section examines structures for nonforeign economic policy. The emphasis is on policy formulation, since previous chapters discussed both adoption and implementation (Chapters 2 and 5, respectively). Because White House staffers developed specialties in domestic and economic policy during this period, however, their involvement in the latter stages of the policy process is touched on in passing.[12]

Policy formulation refers primarily to the development of administration proposals to submit to Congress. By the end of the Johnson years, the number of White House aides with domestic policy responsibilities grew, and these staffers began to shape policy as well as coordinate the policy development process. With the partial exception of the Eisenhower administration, the White House became the central arena for policy formulation, and the BOB in particular lost its preeminence. Staff specialization emerged, especially after FDR, although boundaries were rarely sharp or inviolable. Even as annual programming became more routinized, administrations throughout the period sought ideas from outside government. The two approaches to staff structuring—liaison with extragovernmental actors and flexible, collegial structures within a hierarchy—recurred, but their location in each White House, their participants, and their relationships to major actors such as the BOB varied from one administration to the next.

Hoover

Herbert Hoover entered office intent on pursuing domestic reform. Full of ideas himself, he nonetheless relied on conferences, committees, and commissions to recommend or legitimize contemplated action. By mid-1932, 30 conferences and commissions (e.g., the Conference on Child Health and Protection, the Commission on the Conservation and Administration of the Public Domain) had submitted recommendations. Critics complained loudly that the "tentacles of the commission octopus will be seen swarming out from the White House to the Capitol."[13]

French Strother and George Hastings on the White House staff played supporting roles. They helped organize and served as liaisons for the conferences and commissions[14] and also did research for the president's own analyses, thus providing an essentially hierarchical link between the White House and the "tentacles" of the network of commissions.[15] In addition, Hoover was the first president to turn to the Bureau of the Budget, created in 1921, for policy analysis.[16]

Roosevelt

During the Roosevelt years, the presidency became even more of a focal point for domestic policy innovation. Until World War II, however, the White House staff continued in a supporting role. In the 1930s, program initiatives came from a variety of presidential operatives who were placed throughout the executive branch but worked closely with FDR—including such prominent figures as Raymond Moley and Rexford Tugwell during the first New Deal and Tommy Corcoran and Ben Cohen during the second. With the growth of the White House staff after 1939, the new administrative assistants began to be "magnets for ideas."[17] Throughout, too, Eleanor Roosevelt pushed her husband to address the needs of the poor and minorities.[18]

With the war, some White House staffers became much more influential, though they shared power with others in the Executive Office. Special Counsel Samuel Rosenman, for example, oversaw domestic program development.[19] But the real power still lay outside the immediate White House staff. Most notably, as head of the Office of Economic Stabilization and then the Office of War Mobilization and the Office of War Mobilization and Reconversion (OWMR), James Byrnes was in many ways FDR's "chief assistant for domestic matters."[20]

Truman

Responsibility for postwar demobilization and reconversion returned to the White House during the Truman years as John Steelman, director of the phased-out OWMR, joined the White House staff. Although the Steelman unit was ostensibly oriented toward overseeing implementation rather than formulating policy, the two proved impossible to fully disentangle. Formally a hierarchy, the Steelman staff also operated in both collegial-mediative and adversarial structures. In the first part of the Truman administration, however, tensions between the Steelman unit and Special Counsel Clark Clifford created a need for additional mediative structuring within the White House. When Clifford was succeeded by Charles Murphy, such structural differentiation evolved informally, linking the Steelman and Murphy staffs.

Throughout the administration, policy formulation continued to be the responsibility of the special counsel. The counsel and a small staff assembled proposals from throughout the executive branch and fashioned them into the president's legislative program; the staff also drafted legislation and the accompanying presidential messages to Congress. The counsel's office did more than simply collate agency proposals, however. Rosenman is credited with developing many of the ideas associated with the Fair Deal.[21] More generally, the office's direction of speech and message writing involved it directly in policy formulation and deliberation.[22] The latter involved a collegial-consensual structure in which writing teams interacted closely with the president. White House Press Secretaries Charles Ross and Joseph Short also participated in policy discussions, often in formal staff meetings that tended to be collegial-consensual in nature.[23]

In addition, the BOB became much more active. Aides from the White House and the BOB participated in another collegial-consensual structure, with the BOB supplying expertise and counsel staffers handling uncertainty about or, occasionally, controversy over administration goals. The new Legislative Reference Service in the BOB (established in 1947) worked closely with the White House, soliciting input for the president's program from executive branch agencies, analyzing the ideas for consistency with presidential objectives, and coordinating the preparation of draft sections for the president's budget and economic reports and the State of the Union address.[24] The BOB tended to perform "critical objective analysis," with the special counsel's office adding a "political twist" for the president.[25]

Under Murphy, the counsel's office became structured internally as a formal hierarchy with clear deadlines and responsibilities, though it typically functioned rather collegially. Murphy also expanded the unit to include five professionals who had fairly well defined tasks.[26] David Bell, for example, worked most closely with the BOB and tended to specialize in housing, conservation, and natural resources; Stephen Spingarn handled civil rights and civil liberties issues.[27] Although Clifford was involved in a variety of foreign policy issues (such as the recognition of Israel and development of the Truman Doctrine),[28] under Murphy the counsel's office concentrated almost exclusively on domestic affairs.

Eisenhower

Systematization and specialization continued in the Eisenhower White House, although the specific structures developed under Truman disappeared. Still, given Ike's less ambitious policy goals, far less attention was paid to domestic policy formulation. Meanwhile, the locus of activity shifted away from the counsel's office, which began to handle strictly legal matters for the president.[29] As it did during the Truman years, the BOB solicited and assessed agency proposals for the president's legislative program; however, it was less central to policy exploration and deliberation, most of which took place in the departments, subject to White House approval.[30]

Chief of Staff Sherman Adams oversaw domestic policy development but rarely became involved in policy substance: he was a "coordinator and facilitator."[31] On presidential initiatives such as interstate highway construction, however, Adams was a key participant. He saw to it that Eisenhower was involved in policy deliberation and debate; the president received substantive advice from departmental officials, ad hoc cabinet committees, and a range of White House aides. Staff specialization continued, although there was little stable structuring. For example, various aides concentrated on economic and agricultural policy, public works, and natural resources. Staffers primarily tracked policy problems and assessed agency proposals for addressing them; each aide was assigned agencies with which to maintain contact on "matters of Congressional significance."[32] In addition, Press Secretary James Hagerty frequently was included in policy debates, though he lamented his lack of influence on domestic spending.[33] The overall result was a basic hierarchy that organized the assembly of information and permitted structural fluidity in the face of diverse decision settings.

Kennedy

After the languor of the Eisenhower years, the Kennedy White House seized the initiative for formulating policy. As in the Roosevelt and Truman White Houses, the chief responsibility again was lodged in the counsel's office, under Theodore Sorensen. The press secretary (Pierre Salinger) no longer was a key participant in policy deliberation.[34] The BOB initially receded in importance, with the Legislative Reference Service primarily clearing minor bills.[35] The two BOB directors, however, were personal advisers to the president; David Bell met weekly with Sorensen to exchange information on domestic and fiscal policy.[36] In a development that harked back to Hoover, task forces put in place during the campaign and transition generated a variety of policy proposals at the outset of the administration. Sorensen melded these into the 1961 legislative program. In subsequent years, the BOB resumed its task of soliciting and coordinating departmental proposals as part of the annual programming process.[37]

During the Kennedy years, too, White House aides functioned less as liaisons with executive branch agencies and more as policy initiators. They also drew in ideas from outside government, culling proposals from ad hoc task forces and informal contacts in the business, cultural, and academic communities. Some policy specialization persisted, but priorities and assignments shifted frequently.[38] Associate Special Counsel Myer Feldman, for instance, handled oil, coal, and fuel policy, transportation, agriculture, communications, and consumer affairs.[39] Assistant Special Counsel Lee White was responsible primarily for natural resources, housing, urban affairs, civil rights, public works, veterans affairs, small business, and Indian affairs.[40] For his part, Sorensen was involved across a wide range of issues, advising the president on domestic and, after the Bay of Pigs, foreign policy and drafting and coordinating substantive policy speeches and messages. As matters became more controversial or more salient, they typically moved up the shallow internal hierarchy in the counsel's office to Sorensen,[41] who often adjudicated disputes.

Not all policy innovations came from the White House, however. The Council of Economic Advisers (CEA) took the lead in formulating proposals to reduce poverty and improve transportation, and CEA chair Walter Heller and his staff pushed hard for community action demonstration projects.[42]

Johnson

Domestic policy initiative remained in the White House during the Johnson years, but the counsel's office again lost its preeminent position. Sorensen left soon after LBJ took office; although his successors (Myer Feldman, Lee White, and Harry McPherson) actively participated in domestic policy formulation, policy became the primary responsibility, first, of presidential assistant Bill Moyers and then, more significantly, of a domestic policy unit headed by Joseph Califano.

During the early Johnson years, the main catalysts for domestic program initiatives were so-called external task forces whose members came from outside government. At the outset, Moyers managed task force operations, placing a White House staffer on each and directing legislative program development—a structural throwback to Hoover, though more likely modeled on JFK. When Califano arrived in July 1965, he took on these responsibilities and shifted emphasis to interagency task forces, effectively reinstating a main element of the second basic structural approach in which White House staffers drew policy ideas from the executive branch. He also placed the task forces on an annual cycle and integrated them into the routine for developing the president's legislative program and the annual budget. Task force recommendations supplemented ideas submitted by individual departments and agencies; all proposals were reviewed by senior White House staffers and officials from the BOB and CEA and discussed with relevant agency heads before being presented to the president.[43]

Califano slowly built his staff to five professionals and relied on the now-familiar internal hierarchy with a capacity to adapt structurally to controversy and uncertainty. Again, some specialization emerged. For example, Larry Levinson—Califano's "first violin"[44]—worked generally on preparing the legislative program, but he also concentrated on veterans and consumer affairs, law enforcement, and transportation.[45] Besides overseeing the task force operation and serving as the "system manager" for legislative programming,[46] James Gaither specialized in education, health, poverty, and job training;[47] Matthew Nimetz's emphases were criminal justice, urban, environment, and transportation matters.[48] By 1967, Califano aides were making substantive contributions rather than simply struggling to assemble the ideas of others. Fred Bohen, for example, helped develop the Housing Act of 1968, with its 10-year program to build 26 million public housing units.[49]

Although Califano has been called the "chief of staff for the legislative program"[50] and his office was considered the primary arena for domestic policy formulation, others in the White House were significant participants as well. The counsel's office remained near the center of activity. Until they left, White and Feldman continued the work they had done in the Kennedy administration. Although McPherson did not dominate policy as Sorensen had, he did participate in decisions on civil rights, housing, and urban affairs,[51] and he helped draft the Omnibus Crime Act of 1968.[52] Moreover, as the top writer, McPherson had a "hand in virtually every presidential utterance on major policy."[53] In addition to handling many legal matters, Associate Special Counsel DeVier Pierson worked on agriculture, communications, and natural resources policy.[54]

Another presidential assistant, Douglass Cater, was the White House specialist in education and health and also worked on communications and conservation policy. Cater helped draft, for example, the Elementary and Secondary Education Act and Medicare legislation. Press secretaries again participated in policy formulation, though to a lesser extent than in the pre-Kennedy period. Bill Moyers struggled to remain involved in policy deliberation but found his time increasingly taken up by press office business. His successor, George Christian, sat in on most important discussions but was a less active participant.[55]

The BOB increased in importance over the course of the Johnson administration as resource constraints grew with rising U.S. commitments in Vietnam. Califano aide James Gaither reported growing coordination between the staff and the BOB in developing the legislative program and in linking task force recommendations and proposed program initiatives to the budget process.[56] Still, former BOB official Harold Seidman complained bitterly that the White House failed to treat the bureau "as an institution. [It] used individual Budget Bureau staff as leg men to do the pick and shovel work."[57] Hyde and Wayne concluded that the BOB was a significant actor, but "its voice was only one among many."[58]

The early modern era, then, saw domestic policy formulation become more centralized in the White House Office and staff specialization and structural differentiation mount. Still, although administrations relied on roughly similar organizational approaches, governance structuring for the most part was unstable.

STRUCTURING FOR ECONOMIC POLICY

Economic policy did not fit the patterns just sketched. White House aides were generally less significant players than in domestic policy.[59] Only rarely did staffers work solely on economic policy issues or have a grounding in economics. The complexity and uncertainty that often characterized the policy environment—and the presence, after 1946, of the Council of Economic Advisers—further reduced the influence of White House aides. Although staffers tracked decision making and frequently represented presidential interests and viewpoints, they seldom participated in policy formulation. Instead, they served as coordinators and on occasion became involved in implementation. Dominant structuring was hierarchical, but it was rarely stable within or across presidencies.

During the Hoover and much of the Roosevelt administrations, the White House was the arena in which economic policies were fashioned, but there was little staff capacity. Instead, presidents relied on executive branch officials and advisers from outside government. After 1939, Administrative Assistants Lauchlin Currie and Dan Tobin provided at least some assistance. Currie, an economist, served as liaison with the Federal Reserve, Federal Deposit Insurance Corporation, Securities and Exchange Commission, and lending agencies;[60] fielded complaints from labor;[61] and advised the president on monetary and fiscal policy. Tobin, a labor leader, for a short time advised on labor policy and served as a contact with organized labor.[62] With the war, Rosenman added battling inflation to his domestic policy tasks,[63] but the ad hoc war mobilization agencies carried much of the load.

The attempted division between "operations" and "policy" in the Truman White House also appeared in economic policy. Steelman's staffers became heavily involved in operational matters, reflecting environmental demands: first, the challenges of reconversion and, later, mobilization for the Korean War.[64] The special counsel's staff tracked and participated in discussions of labor legislation.[65]

Steelman also was the White House liaison with the newly created Council of Economic Advisers. This was not a particularly successful arrangement. The first chairman, Edwin Nourse, resented not having direct access to the president (who was suspicious of the congressionally man-dated CEA) and resisted Steelman's rather clumsy efforts to redraft the council's first economic report.[66] Gradually, the special counsel's office en-tered the relationship. Nourse's replacement, Leon Keyserling, worked closely and cooperatively with Clifford and Murphy.[67] Murphy assistant David Bell sat in on CEA meetings on the economic report, interjecting the president's points of view but rarely arguing with members; Bell and Mur-phy accompanied CEA members when they met with Truman.[68]

In general, Truman staffers participated actively in discussions of eco-nomic policy and in drafting major reports and statements. By the end of the administration, informal collegial-competitive–mediative structuring had emerged. Aides in both Steelman's and Murphy's offices met fre-quently with one another and consulted with Keyserling; Murphy coordi-nated and oversaw the entire process.[69] Again, one sees the working of the differentiation dynamic, as the emergence of formal structures virtually compelled a parallel development of informal structures to link them.

The CEA became more influential during the Eisenhower years. White House staffers played a supporting role, serving mainly as coordinators and liaisons. The president assigned an aide (Gabriel Hauge, then Donald Paarlberg) to concentrate on economic policy; later in the administration, other staffers were appointed to work on foreign economic policy (see Chapter 9). In effect, this replaced Truman's informal collegial structuring with hierarchy, signaling that the locus of decision making had largely moved out of the White House.

The economic adviser was consulted on a variety of economic policy questions;[70] he also served as the White House contact for departments on issues of economic policy and trade, handled tariff problems, and worked closely with the CEA chair. Most of the president's economic advice, how-ever, came from the treasury secretary and the CEA chair.[71] Labor disputes also were largely kept out of the White House,[72] though Cabinet Secretary Maxwell Rabb was an occasional troubleshooter.[73] The special counsel's of-fice worked on labor legislation,[74] and Hauge kept the president informed on potential labor problems.[75]

The Kennedy and Johnson administrations saw the "halcyon days" of the CEA.[76] It was largely responsible for the Kennedy tax cut and for push-ing JFK toward acceptance of the "new economics," which advocated a more active role for the federal government in the economy.[77] The troika—the chair of the CEA, the director of the BOB, and the secretary of the treasury—began meeting regularly during this time, with the CEA clearly the dominant participant.

As in the Eisenhower administration, the White House served as a source of coordination, but not generally as a site of decision making. The division between domestic and foreign economic policy responsibilities remained, with Sorensen handling the former and Carl Kaysen of the National Security Council staff the latter. Sorensen, for example, attended troika meetings with JFK and assembled advice on wage-price issues;[78] he was CEA chair Walter Heller's channel to the president.[79] Feldman, the associate special counsel, oversaw trade and tariff matters.

Hierarchical structuring persisted in the Johnson White House, as staffers remained largely coordinators. Moyers and Califano took on Sorensen's role of synthesizing policy options and advice. Heller spoke highly of all three: "[They were] utterly superb in putting things together for the President and bringing them to the President, not prejudicially, not angled the way they wanted them."[80] Califano was more active, reflecting in part his explicit assignment to link the president's legislative program with economic policy. He monitored the deliberations of the troika and quadriad (the troika plus the chair of the Federal Reserve Board)—communicating LBJ's views but not setting the agenda[81]—and received frequent reports from the BOB director, CEA chair, and commerce and treasury secretaries.[82] Redford and McCulley credit Califano, for example, with orchestrating a compromise among executive branch officials in a dispute over suspending the investment tax credit.[83] As in domestic policy, the development of policy specialization on the staff tended to encourage policy activism on the part of the specialists.

Furthermore, Califano and his staff became more involved in operational activities than had any staff since Truman's. For instance, they intervened in labor disputes, at least until the 1966 airline machinists' strike in which the president announced a wage settlement that the union then rejected.[84] Even after that, staffers kept LBJ updated on labor unrest.[85] Califano's office also worked to implement the administration's voluntary wage-price guidelines. At first, Califano himself was heavily involved in monitoring wage and price changes and in identifying "jawboning" opportunities, working with the CEA and an ad hoc interagency committee. By mid-1966, he added a staff member to perform these tasks, although Califano and the chair of the CEA continued to pay close attention.[86] For all the concern, though, no systematic process for applying guideposts ever was established.[87]

CONCLUSIONS

From the administration of Herbert Hoover through that of Lyndon Johnson, the formulation, adoption, and implementation of domestic policy clearly came to be tasks of the White House. The relevant staff grew, and differentiated structures and substantive specialization began to appear. At the same time, domestic policy as such was not handled in the kind of relatively stable structures that emerged in other, more clearly defined areas. In several respects, these developments may be seen as a legacy, informing and influencing the approaches of the administrations that followed.

By the final two years of the Johnson administration, Califano and his aides had established a distinct domestic policy operation within the White House, although they never claimed an exclusive franchise over all domestic policy discussion. The Califano staff may be seen as a clear forerunner of Richard Nixon's Domestic Council, thus marking the beginning of the institutionalization of a domestic policy staff in the White House. Presidents Ford, Carter, Reagan, Bush, and Clinton all have had some kind of distinct domestic policy operation. However, the problems posed by the ill-definition of domestic policy have persisted. Both within and across administrations, domestic policy units have varied considerably in their structuring, activities, and status within the White House. More than almost any other area, the fluidity of domestic policy structures offers evidence that the presidency can be, in Margaret Wyszomirski's words, a "discontinuous institution."[88] Domestic policy continues to present presidents with problems of organizational design.

Meanwhile, as we have seen, other units in the White House have grown more distinct. As their missions have become more clearly defined, and as they have come to be considered legitimate actors, they have been able to protect their core functions from other possible claimants. At the same time, as boundaries have sharpened in cases such as press relations, their involvement in policy has receded.

In contrast, domestic policy units typically have been unable to develop clear and stable missions. In partial consequence, their staffers have not been as successful in defining and protecting their turfs. For example, constituency-oriented units have flourished in recent staffs. Such offices may engage in some policy advocacy to satisfy constituency groups, but they tend to direct most of their efforts toward maintaining channels of communication and providing symbolic reassurance. Similarly, White House structures for "communications"—with which Eisenhower and Johnson experimented (see Chapter 3)—offer advice on policy substance but concentrate on "packaging" and "selling" presidential policies.

Underlying any concern with domestic policy structuring in the White House is the issue of presidential capacity in domestic policy. It seems apparent that presidents face a vexing puzzle. On the one hand, presidents have greater leeway than they do in other spheres to organize domestic policy activities as they desire. On the other hand, it is not at all clear that any of their efforts have notably increased presidential ability to address difficult policy problems. And the failure to settle on an accepted approach (or even a range of workable models) may well have hindered domestic policy staffs in the inevitable White House battles over turf and influence.

Perhaps presidents face inherent limits on their capacity to address issues of domestic policy. Certainly, environmental forces such as fractious constituencies and fragmented interests within government—which both compel presidents to draw domestic policy issues to the White House and hamper their efforts to organize in response—are unlikely to disappear.

Arguably as important, however, is the notion of domestic policy itself. As we have suggested, its ambiguity has both helped push a range of issues into the White House and militated against the development of stable structural responses. The acceptance of the idea of a distinct domestic policy staff has almost forced presidents into thinking of domestic policy as a unitary entity. They, in turn, have often been frustrated in their efforts to design acceptable staff mechanisms for addressing domestic policy issues.

Analysts may be subject to similar difficulties as we try to explore and identify the determinants of presidential domestic policy capacity. We too may be guilty of seeking to impose order on complex and messy realities in a less than completely constructive way.

More fine-grained conceptualizations may provide an alternative. Kennedy's and Johnson's reliance on task forces, Gerald Ford's later use of the Economic Policy Board, Ronald Reagan's first-term experiment with cabinet councils, and Bill Clinton's appointment of task forces in health and welfare policy suggest that structures may be developed for more focused purposes. Such actions are consistent with the problem-contingency perspective on designing structures that are congruent with relevant decision settings.

The account of White House structuring for domestic policy is thus a story that is even now unfinished and perhaps only barely begun. Presidents beginning with Johnson can be seen as addressing the conceptual confusion that has proved so frustrating in the past, but the pattern of organizational experimentation and dissatisfaction continues. It is not apparent that the story will—or should—have a conclusion. The White House involvement in domestic policy and the diverse approaches to handling it that characterized the Hoover through Johnson administrations seem likely to persist.

8
National Security Policy

One of the framers' justifications for a single executive was that the president could represent the United States with a single voice in dealings with other countries. Chief executives, of course, have long relied on others for advice in foreign and defense policy. Not until the early modern era, however, as the United States became more enmeshed in global affairs, did presidents turn to staffers in the White House Office for assistance in national security policy.[1]

Although a military presence in the White House dates back to the time of George Washington,[2] this hardly meant that White House military aides were equipped to advise presidents on matters of national security. Instead, the military aide's duties were "those of a major domo, in charge of arrangements for musicals, dinners, receptions, and other such functions."[3] The counterpart position of naval aide, which first appeared under Theodore Roosevelt, was scarcely an improvement. Clark Clifford, who entered the White House in 1945 as assistant naval aide, described the task

> as being similar to a "potted palm" because one of its most important requirements, then and now, was to stand quietly in the background at social and ceremonial events, on the alert for some unescorted woman who needed to be helped to her seat, or to assist some lost guest in search of the White House washrooms.[4]

A more serious national security presence did not emerge in the White House office until environmental change of the most dramatic kind—World War II—compelled it. Then, as new wartime governance structures proliferated across the executive branch, liaison between them and the president became an urgent requirement. Franklin Roosevelt initially improvised such structuring, assigning Adm. William Leahy to mediate between the president and the Joint Chiefs and tapping Harry Hopkins as the key presidential representative for a variety of diplomatic assignments.

Beginning with Harry Truman, presidents sought not only to institutionalize liaison but to create collegial-competitive structures, mostly revolving around the National Security Council (NSC), for policy deliberation. Such structures arose and persisted because they were largely congruent with their decision settings and because the Cold War made them a continued necessity. However, presidential choice significantly influenced how they were designed and operated. Additionally, most presidents of this period experimented with supplementary structures of varying kinds.

Truman, like FDR, originally relied on simple structures revolving around prominent individuals—Leahy and Clark Clifford, primarily. But by his second term, Truman had acquiesced in Congress's decision to create the NSC and had improvised his own relatively complex structural response, a staff headed by Averell Harriman. Like Roosevelt, though, Truman created mainly temporary expedients. Indeed, the Harriman operation addressed the liaison problem only tangentially, although it did fashion its own niche in national security planning and ultimately moved intact outside the White House.

Dwight Eisenhower divided the NSC apparatus into two distinct components, each with separate White House staff liaison to the president. He used the NSC itself as a collegial-competitive planning structure, complemented by the Operations Coordinating Board, a collegial-consensual structure designed to monitor the implementation of NSC decisions. Although each of these structures was congruent with some features of the national security decision setting, their task definitions depended on the assumption that one could in practice clearly separate "policy" from "administration." In fact, this proved to be quite difficult. Eisenhower supplemented this relatively elaborate structuring with an array of other advising arrangements as well as an innovative staff secretariat, a small hierarchy that was congruent with a setting of relative certainty.

John Kennedy, impressed by the coordination problems and alleged decisional difficulties of the Eisenhower approach, dismantled most of it. The NSC remained a primary locus of policy deliberation, however, and JFK initially tried to separate policy (or goals) from administration (or technology) in his design of the NSC machinery. After the Bay of Pigs, he moved to integrate the two. Kennedy supplemented the NSC with a loosely structured set of largely ad hoc arrangements best described as a hierarchy with the capacity for collegial-competitive decision making.

Johnson did little to change the system he inherited. In a broad sense, these arrangements—featuring a strong national security assistant supervising collegial-competitive decision making—were congruent with the requirements of the decision setting. Over most of the early modern presidency, the White House incorporated some version of the same general approach to governance, but the stability of many specific structures was low. However, in a policy environment perhaps less diverse but at least as volatile as that of domestic policy, neither the elaborate Eisenhower system nor the less formal Kennedy-Johnson approach performed fully satisfactorily.

Although the environment was the engine driving national security responsibility into the White House and keeping it there, considerable room remained for individual presidents' objectives and strategies to shape governance. The earliest presidents of this era were placed in a reactive posture by the onset of preparations for World War II and then the Cold War and Korean conflict. Yet even they shaped governance structures in line with basic predispositions evident elsewhere in their administrations. FDR, for instance, created diverse, overlapping, shifting structures inside and outside the White House, promoting multiple advocacy (collegial-competitive governance), sometimes at the expense of order and continuity; thereby he created an opportunity, even a need, for a person like Harry Hopkins to try to master the situation. Harry Truman, though largely improvising, still sought in his employment of Harriman to tentatively approach some kind of regularization of governance structuring.

With Dwight Eisenhower one sees perhaps the strongest influence of presidential choice factors. Eisenhower was, in the eyes of his admirers, the ultimate organizer, a man who believed in process above almost all else. In national security as elsewhere in his administration, Eisenhower sought to design governance structures that would match the demands of the surrounding decision settings, and structural differentiation increased. Ike's strong belief in formal structuring, grounded in a commitment to collegial processes that were embedded in presidential hierarchy, powerfully shaped the way his administration addressed issues of governance.

John Kennedy's sense of organizational strategy was entirely different in detail from Eisenhower's, though the ultimate goal was not. Kennedy sought to create collegial governance through the minimizing of formal structuring and the ad hoc employment of informal interaction coupled with team spirit and a healthy involvement by the chief executive. Kennedy's approach encouraged the development of both informal structuring and a "culture" that encouraged the advocacy of diverse viewpoints. Kennedy also found himself consciously innovating, but without either a strong sense of strategic purpose or much success.

In contrast, Lyndon Johnson's approach to national security governance was surprisingly passive. A president whose usual concern for orderly structuring was high, LBJ was content to employ the tools given him by his predecessor. Here, in an inherited presidency, one sees the strongest contribution of organizational factors. First because he was preoccupied elsewhere, and then perhaps out of a sense that things had gone too far to change, Johnson eschewed innovation that directly involved the White House staff.[5]

ROOSEVELT: NATIONAL SECURITY ENTERS THE WHITE HOUSE

Franklin Roosevelt's military aide, Edwin "Pa" Watson, was an influential White House figure primarily because he served simultaneously as appointments secretary for six years (see Chapter 10). But only the arrival of war brought significant defense policy expertise into the White House, and only then because, absent relevant structures elsewhere, there was no place else to put it.

Harry Hopkins, former administrator of the Works Progress Administration and former secretary of commerce, was appointed special assistant to the president in early 1941 for the announced purpose of advising on the lend-lease program. That modest-sounding charge immediately enmeshed Hopkins in a web of relationships involving shipping, production, and diplomacy, leading him to be called "Roosevelt's own personal Foreign Office."[6] The United States' entry into the war, however, greatly expanded Hopkins's responsibilities.

Hopkins became heavily involved in war production issues, relying on Administrative Assistant Isador Lubin, who was Hopkins's representative on the War Production Board and reported to Hopkins on a variety of other matters, ranging from British shipping losses to U.S. public opinion regarding the war.[7] But the influence of Hopkins, who literally lived in the White House during the war, was not limited to matters of materiel. As the war progressed, he became a key liaison with Churchill and Stalin, advising on and participating in virtually all major diplomatic events during the war.[8]

Hopkins became an invaluable linchpin, holding together FDR's chaotic wartime decision and implementation processes, partly because he knew more about what was going on in different places than anyone else, and partly because of his closeness to the president. Although his particular job would be impossible to replicate—the shifting multiplicity of conflicts and uncertainties inherent in the war effort did not lend themselves to stable governance structuring—Hopkins nonetheless set a precedent for a powerful foreign affairs presence in the White House, with a broad mandate to advise and to intervene in decisions throughout the executive branch.

Nor were Hopkins and Lubin the only White House staffers committed to foreign and military matters during the Roosevelt years. Two other administrative assistants, William McReynolds and then Wayne Coy, held the part-time post of liaison officer for emergency management. The liaison officer was conceived as head of the Office of Emergency Management (OEM), which was created in mid-1940 "to serve as liaison between the President and the defense agencies and as a framework for creation of stronger organizations than were then authorized by law."[9] Although it had the potential for considerable power, the OEM never became more than a shell for war agencies not specifically authorized by legislation. Little coordination was attempted through it, and the liaison officer effectively had no authority.[10] Meanwhile, as will be discussed below, Adm. William D. Leahy was far more influential than a typical naval aide.

Roosevelt's organizational improvisations were enough to win the war, though they left serious unresolved issues for his successors. The precedent of having a strong White House foreign and defense policy capacity was initially ignored, but making and coordinating policy in the Cold War era ultimately compelled subsequent presidents to—one way or another—roughly reinvent the role of Harry Hopkins.

TRUMAN: IMPROVISATIONAL GOVERNANCE

Hopkins resigned for health reasons in July 1945, leaving the new president, Harry Truman, with few in the White House able to advise on national security policy. In one sense, this was not a problem, for the efforts of such larger-than-life figures as George Kennan, George C. Marshall, James Forrestal, James Byrnes, and Dean Acheson were available to Truman as he sought to position the United States for its postwar responsibilities. Yet, as brilliant as these men were, they worked in and through their departments, lacking guaranteed access to the president. The controversies of the time clearly required governance structures congruent with decision settings in which there was serious debate over both the goals of U.S. policy and the proper approaches to their attainment.

William Leahy: Chief of Staff to the Commander in Chief

In fact, one such structure already existed, revolving around Adm. William D. Leahy. In mid-1942, Leahy had been given the novel position of chief of staff to the commander in chief. In this job, Leahy presided over meetings of the Joint Chiefs of Staff (then only a de facto body) and acted as a liaison for the individual chiefs with President Roosevelt. Leahy understood this go-between role to be the key element of the job, since each service head—General Marshall, Admiral King, and General Arnold—felt a need to communicate daily with FDR, who did not have time to see each of them that often.[11] Leahy's task, then, was to preside over a Joint Chiefs of Staff (JCS) that attempted to operate in a collegial-consensual manner but that frequently discovered itself in need of a higher authority to adjudicate matters of controversy. When that happened, Leahy was the link to the president, with whom he met every day.[12]

A structure such as the JCS would be expected to work well as long as a basic consensus on overriding war goals prevailed, as it did. Truman therefore continued to rely on Leahy, meeting with him each day, and trusting him for advice on matters of international relations that went beyond the purely military.[13] Leahy served until 1949, when legislation created the chairman of the JCS, rendering his job unnecessary.

What Truman needed even more in the postwar confusion, however, was a comparable method for providing foreign policy advice of the broadest scope. This was the vacuum into which Clark Clifford stepped.

Clark Clifford

Clifford came to the White House in September 1945 as assistant naval aide, brought on board by his friend from Missouri, Naval Aide J. K. Vardaman.[14] Underoccupied by his assigned duties, Clifford, a lawyer, began to assist Special Counsel Samuel Rosenman, beginning with researching and drafting a presidential message on universal military training. Soon Clifford's work with Rosenman became his primary White House task, continuing when he succeeded Vardaman as naval aide in April 1946. So successful was Clifford that in July 1946, following Rosenman's resignation, Clifford replaced him as special counsel. In this position, Clifford became one of Truman's closest advisers, a generalist whose potential interests spanned virtually the whole range of policy and political issues. In 1946, such an adviser was bound to be drawn to foreign policy.

Clifford's first major foreign policy assignment arose when Truman, in the process of reconsidering the policy of attempting to cooperate with the Soviet Union, asked him to summarize all agreements with the United States that the Soviets had broken.[15] Clifford enlisted the assistance of George Elsey, a young naval officer who had worked in the White House Map Room during the war; he became Clifford's only assistant. At Elsey's suggestion, the project was expanded to be a survey of the views of top U.S. foreign and defense officials concerning the Soviet Union and proper responses to the growing threat the USSR was seen to represent. The Clifford-Elsey Report, as it became known, was not made public, since the president feared the consequences should the Soviets learn of it. Although its importance in shaping Cold War strategy is debatable, it clearly established Clark Clifford as the main White House contact for the foreign policy establishment.

Clifford's involvement in national security policy was always informal, and it failed to develop well-defined structural aspects. Clifford drafted major foreign policy speeches[16] and was a key author (with Elsey) of the 1947 and 1949 National Security Acts, which created the Department of Defense, the National Security Council, and the position of chairman of the Joint Chiefs of Staff. As Elsey told it, the very idea of a National Security Council is traceable to Clifford's dismay at the disarray of foreign policy decision making at the close of the war.[17] Moreover, Clifford became embroiled in the infighting over running the new decision system. For instance, he worked to protect the NSC and its careerist executive secretaries, Sidney Souers and James Lay, from attempts by Secretary of Defense James Forrestal to dominate the NSC machinery.[18]

In some respects, Clifford's activities as a broker and adviser anticipated the job of the national security assistant more closely than Hopkins's did.[19] But Clifford, as special counsel, could not be a full-time foreign policy specialist. Elsey, Clifford's assistant until August 1949, when he was made an administrative assistant in his own right, was closer to being such a specialist. He served as a White House point of contact for executive branch officials[20] and became involved in most White House dealings over mid-level matters of foreign policy. However, he never attained anything like Clifford's status as an adviser. Thus, when Clifford left the White House in January 1950, he left a partial void in top-level foreign affairs advising.[21]

Clifford's successor as special counsel, Charles Murphy, lacked Clifford's background and interest in national security policy. So, in January 1950, Truman tried to compensate by appointing Sidney Souers, the retiring executive secretary of the NSC, as a White House consultant. Although Souers was helpful in dealing with Congress over China policy,[22] he in no way replaced Clifford. Other advisers and structures were needed.

Robert L. Dennison

Harry Truman's best-known armed services aide, Gen. Harry Vaughan, was not a policy adviser as much as a personal confidant and political presence in the White House. But Truman did receive important policy assistance from his second naval aide, Capt. (later Rear Adm.) Robert L. Dennison. Dennison, who came to the White House in January 1948, worked not only with the Defense Department but also with the Bureau of the Budget (BOB) on defense and maritime issues. This led BOB director Roger Jones to refer to him as a "substantive military aide,"[23] a policy adviser in fact, despite his formal status. Dennison's advice ranged over matters of military strategy and personnel policy and even included a stint as personal representative of the president in the Philippines.[24]

Dennison augmented Clifford's efforts both by providing a link to Defense that complemented the special counsel's stronger ties to State and by offering a military perspective at a time when the military aspects of foreign policy loomed exceedingly large. Like Clifford's, his work was virtually required by the policy environment of the time, and it evolved out of an initially more modest White House job thanks to the talent of the individual and the demands of the situation. In neither case did Truman consciously seek to create governance arrangements; rather, he took advantage of available talent and energy. Not everything, however, could be handled that way.

W. Averell Harriman

After Clifford left in 1950, the problem of coordinating foreign and defense policy became acute. Partially in response, Truman made W. Averell Harriman a special assistant with the general mandate of overseeing foreign policy implementation and "the integration of the various interests of the Departments and agencies concerned with the development of Government-wide policies related to our international responsibilities."[25] One specific reason for Harriman's recall from Europe, where he was monitoring the implementation of the Marshall Plan, was Secretary of State Dean Acheson's hope that Harriman could help him in his difficult relations with Defense Secretary Louis Johnson.[26] Acheson also sensed the vacuum that Clifford's departure had left in the White House and hoped that Harriman could fill it.[27]

His flexible mandate enabled Harriman to define his position broadly enough that he could later refer to it as the "pre-Kissinger, Kissinger job."[28] Harriman had a small staff, but much of his work consisted of advising the president and other policy makers and engaging personally in diplomacy.[29] In fact, he operated quite differently from Kissinger, tending to be a conduit to Truman for the views of the policy community—including the NSC (on which he sat) and especially the State Department[30]—rather than a competitor. Once Secretary Johnson departed, Harriman focused on "bringing urgent matters to the surface,"[31] though the hope that he would be able to improve the implementation of NSC decisions was not fulfilled.

Like Leahy, Harriman found himself in a setting where fundamental goals were generally agreed to, but the means of achieving them were uncertain and sometimes controversial. Harriman's basically collegial-consensual approach was, like Clifford's, mostly congruent. Moreover, when goals and implementation strategies had been agreed upon, Harriman also became the agent in a hierarchy headed by his principal, the president. Then he was

Truman's "enforcer to make sure that orders were followed and that policy was not disturbed by rivalry and needless bickering."[32]

When, in October 1951, Congress consolidated economic and military aid programs under the Mutual Security Administration—whose organization the Harriman staff had a large hand in planning—Harriman was named to head it. He took his staff with him. Aide Lincoln Gordon recalled: "We didn't change our office locations; we just changed our titles and our stationery."[33]

Perhaps surprisingly, Harriman did not become an element of the developing NSC apparatus. At the time of his appointment, Harriman was unhappy that he had not been asked to replace Souers as the president's personal representative to the NSC.[34] Although his work fit without serious friction into Truman's foreign policy decision system, he never became a strong link between the NSC, especially the NSC staff, and the White House. As the Korean War forced Truman to rely on the NSC more than he had initially wished, the requirement for such a link—a representative of the president with at least some discretion over matters of process—became clearer.[35] It would be left to Truman's successor, however, to forge it.

EISENHOWER: A HEAVY DOSE OF GOVERNANCE

Alert to the need for more effective use of the NSC, Dwight Eisenhower quickly took several actions to change both the structure of the council and its connection to the White House. From the standpoint of White House governance, two such steps were of considerable interest. First, Eisenhower created the position of special assistant for national security affairs, placing liaison with the NSC and its staff organs formally in the White House and adding an influential presidential representative to the deliberations in and around the council and its Planning Board. Second, in October 1953, Eisenhower established the Operations Coordinating Board (OCB) to see to the implementation of NSC policies, assigning a member of the White House staff to be the president's representative to that body.[36] With this reorganization, Eisenhower and his advisers consciously redefined the nature of the governance challenges in the national security policy area and developed structures congruent with their understanding of the prevailing decision setting.

Beyond revising governance arrangements involving the NSC, Eisenhower also experimented with elevating the relative importance of arms control in the national security policy arena, appointing the first special assistant in charge of disarmament. The difficulties encountered by that assistant, Harold Stassen, would illuminate the larger challenges of governing in the national security realm. Finally, Eisenhower created the position of staff secretary and appointed to it experienced military officers who were influential in the day-to-day management of foreign affairs.

The National Security Assistant and the Planning Board

Robert Cutler was sworn in as the first White House national security assistant (NSA) in January 1953. He was given responsibility for preparing the NSC agenda (subject to presidential approval), and he chaired the Planning Board, a senior staff organ, while generally supervising the NSC staff.[37] He also was charged with overseeing policy implementation, bringing problems that could not be handled through ordinary NSC processes to the attention of the president.[38]

In chairing the Planning Board, Cutler's role was explicitly conceived as coordinating, in Eisenhower's name, within a collegial-competitive structure for high-level policy deliberation that produced documents for NSC discussion and decision. Cutler did not view his job as that of a policy maker, as some of his successors were prone to do, but rather as one "concerned primarily to ensure that the paper is adequate and that it satisfactorily reflects the views of the members of the Planning Board representing the various agencies."[39] It was understood that since the Planning Board had to deal with national security goals and priorities, agency views would frequently differ. Moreover, the Planning Board's attention was to focus on goals; the Operations Coordinating Board was created to see to matters of implementation—the means of attaining the goals.

Cutler, who served two terms as NSA (his first lasting until April 1955, then again from January 1957 to July 1958), operated carefully, seeking to avoid appearing to be an independent policy force.[40] Indeed, the harshest criticism of Cutler from his colleagues—who tended to admire him—was that he was too ready to take matters of controversy to the president rather than hammering out a decision himself.[41] Cutler's successors, Frederick Dearborn and Gordon Gray, were likewise restrained.[42]

If there was an overriding critique of the Eisenhower NSC arrangement, it was not that any particular NSA did a poor job but that the decision process tended to be too consensus oriented. White House aide C. D. Jackson, for instance, complained that Cutler's insistence on detailed accords among the participants in preparing planning documents "resulted in a group of planners who did little else but indulge in fierce semantic battles, resulting in watered down gobbledegook conclusions."[43] Approximately the same conclusion—that superficial agreement was secured at the cost of papering over issues of genuine controversy—was reached in 1960 by the Senate's Jackson Subcommittee in its study of national security decision making.[44]

Conventional wisdom has tended to blame an overly "formalistic" approach to governance for the problem of watered down, overly consensual policy planning.[45] However, this criticism may reflect a misunderstanding of the operation of governance structures.[46] A collegial-competitive governance structure need not force consensus—it is often working best when it produces options and defines disagreements. Still, there may be incentives in any particular setting to redefine the problem as one in which the reaching of a consensus decision is desirable. The NSC structure, it must be remembered, was part of a hierarchy, with the president at the apex. To the extent that the analysis and planning the NSC produced were insufficiently hard-edged, the ultimate problem—and the remedy, if any—came from the top. Had Eisenhower wished to discourage a tendency toward vague consensus, it would not have been impossible for him to do so.[47]

The Operations Coordinating Board

The OCB, like the Planning Board, was a committee composed of representatives of the departments and agencies involved in national security policy and chaired by the undersecretary of state. Its creation formalized the separation of planning from operations, that is, of goals from technologies. The premise upon which OCB was built was that the NSC planning process would provide the framework of goals within which implementation would take place.[48] This meant that OCB's decision setting for the most part was assumed to be one of uncertainty about technology in the context of consensus on goals (cell 2 of Table 2). Collegial-consensual governance structuring would be congruent with such a setting. In cases in which consensus might fail in the face of, for instance, departmental disagreement about technologies, some provision for adjudication of disputes (cell 8) also would be indicated. OCB was structured consistently with such a diagnosis and prescription. To the extent that it struggled—as it did—one may question the basic assumptions about goals and means.

OCB was set up to be independent of the Planning Board and the NSA. The latter was invited to attend OCB meetings, but he was not a member or otherwise formally associated with it. Since the OCB was an advisory body with no direct power of action, a link to the White House was essential. This was provided by a special assistant. The first incumbent, C. D. Jackson, was already on the staff as special assistant for Cold War planning; working with the OCB was only part of his overall responsibility.[49] Jackson's successor, Nelson Rockefeller, also served part time with the OCB.[50]

Unlike the Planning Board, the OCB did not always work from a formal agenda, nor did it rely as heavily on staff papers. Formal meetings were preceded by informal luncheons, during which the collegial-consensual nature of the OCB was most apparent:

the luncheons served as a forum in which OCB members consulted informally with other high-ranking government officials on a wide spectrum of concerns related to the Board's activities. Agreements were reached during the luncheon on some matters. Others were referred to an appropriate OCB working group for study and recommendations. Still others were referred to relevant agencies for decision outside the OCB framework.[51]

Formal meetings, which did have an agenda, tended to be devoted to discussing "operation plans" prepared by working groups. Here, the OCB more closely resembled the Planning Board, including the tendency to generate consensual, uncontroversial products. As the outcomes of intendedly collegial-consensual structuring, such documents were less vulnerable to criticism.

Nevertheless, dissatisfaction with the coordination of national security operations was sufficient to lead Rockefeller in the spring of 1956 to recommend that the OCB be given command authority and that the NSA chair it.[52] Rockefeller's main concern was what he saw as an absence of links between policy and operations. He sought, in effect, to integrate these within a more powerful, more hierarchical (though still collegial—the NSA would chair but not command the OCB) metastructure, with the special assistant for Cold War planning, representing the president, at the top. The special assistant would bridge the gap between planning and operations and provide a means for settling disagreements.[53]

The congruence of such a remedy depended on the assumption that goals, at least, could be determined outside the OCB itself, presumably in the NSC—the same basic assumption that already animated the board's structuring. In an insightful commentary on this proposal, William Jackson, Rockefeller's successor and vice-chair of the OCB, criticized that very premise. The problem of "coordination," he suggested, was tied to

the extreme difficulty or virtual impossibility of making a clear distinction, in practice, between policy and operations. . . . Situations . . . are brought into OCB and other interdepartmental mechanisms for discussion and possible resolution under the assumption that these are within the scope of "coordination of operations" although they really represent situations in which a policy decision has to be made. One of the basic difficulties with the OCB has been that its role in these cases which involve policy conflicts has not been defined.[54]

The logic of an analysis such as Jackson's pointed toward the integration of the OCB with the NSC and its Planning Board rather than simply their "coordination." Yet Secretary of State John Foster Dulles, among others, resisted Jackson's idea that the OCB be involved at all in implementation, contending that that was the responsibility of departments.[55]

Nevertheless, in February 1957, there was a move in the direction of integration: the OCB was shifted into the broader structure of the NSC, and the NSA (Cutler) was made the OCB's vice-chair. William Jackson's position was abolished, but, on Cutler's recommendation, a new position of special assistant for security operations coordination was created. This assistant—Frederick Dearborn until his death in early 1958, then Karl Harr—was given a general mandate to function as a liaison between the OCB and the Planning Board as well as with the rest of the national security establishment.[56]

Even this degree of integration proved insufficient, however. So, in January 1960, NSA Gordon Gray was named chair of the OCB, with Harr continuing as vice-chair. This not only strengthened the link between the OCB and the rest of the NSC but also gave the president a stronger presence on the OCB and eliminated a situation that had been bothersome to many: the fact that the State Department representative as chair of the OCB was, in effect, trying to be both a neutral arbitrator and a protagonist.[57] Gray concluded his term with a report to the president in which he claimed that "in the eyes of the highest officers of the departments that do business through the Board, it has become an increasingly effective mechanism."[58]

Harold Stassen, "Secretary for Peace"

Harold Stassen began the Eisenhower administration as director of mutual security, assuming the job Averell Harriman had under Truman. He moved to the White House in March 1955, in part, according to Sherman Adams, because Dulles had grown "quite out of patience with the manner and approach" of Stassen as an administrator.[59] In the White House, Stassen took on an arms-control portfolio and was initially given the title of special assistant and cabinet rank, leading some to dub him "Secretary for Peace." Stassen assembled a staff of about 50, raising suspicion on the part of some White House colleagues that he was building an empire.[60]

The foreign policy climate of the 1950s probably doomed Stassen's efforts. Even if progress were possible in principle, Stassen and Dulles disagreed so fundamentally on the issues that the former's influence was bound to be limited. Ambrose has argued, however, that the real problem between the two involved jurisdiction, with Dulles insisting that all disarmament proposals be cleared through State and that Stassen report to Eisenhower through Dulles.[61] Finally, Dulles prevailed. In March 1957, Eisenhower announced that Stassen would report to the president through Dulles and that Stassen would no longer attend cabinet meetings. Less than a year later, after Stassen had failed to convince the president to accept a Soviet offer of a moratorium on nuclear testing, Eisenhower asked Stassen to resign his position and accept another job in the administration.[62] Stassen chose instead to leave government.[63]

The explanation of Stassen's demise is straightforward. Arms control was an arena of intense disagreement over national goals (not all of Eisenhower's advisers took the possibility of real progress seriously) as well as tactics. Under the circumstances, it was predictable that no satisfactory governance structuring would emerge. It was thus equally predictable that a special assistant with a relatively general mandate and no particularly close relationship to the president would be no match for a turf-minded secretary of state and his allies.

Stassen was not replaced. The effort at policy development and coordination from the White House that his position represented not only was far from successful but also reflected the general instability of structuring for national security policy during the years 1932 to 1960. There would be neither a "new Hopkins" nor a "Secretary for Peace." Even the position that seemed to be an exception under Eisenhower, the national security assistant, would change substantially when Eisenhower left. Like domestic policy, national security policy was proving difficult to govern.

The Staff Secretaries: Carroll and Goodpaster

Eisenhower's penchant for structural innovation was brought to bear on the day-to-day workings of foreign and defense policy through the creation of the job of staff secretary. The primary purpose of this position was the screening and coordination of all documents coming into the White House (see Chapter 11), including those pertaining to foreign and defense policy.

Eisenhower's first staff secretary, Paul Carroll, was an army general who quite naturally took a special interest in national security matters. Carroll and his assistant, Arthur Minnich, developed a division of labor so that Minnich largely handled the domestic side of the staff secretary's work and Carroll specialized in foreign and defense materials.[64] Carroll, who had briefly been responsible for liaison with the military before becoming staff secretary, also gave Eisenhower his morning intelligence briefing, assembling materials from the CIA and the Departments of State and Defense.[65] Carroll staffed all meetings with the president on national security matters (preparing background materials and often attending the meetings) and served as liaison with other national security staffers, such as C. D. Jackson.

When Carroll died suddenly in the fall of 1954, he was replaced by another army officer, Andrew Goodpaster. Goodpaster achieved considerable stature not only as an administrator but also as an adviser. Neither he nor

Carroll suffered serious interference from Sherman Adams or others on the White House staff, and their access to the president stands as one of the better-known refutations of the notion that absolutely everything that got to Ike had to go through Adams first. Their relationships with the national security assistants also seem to have been virtually free of friction. Gordon Gray, for instance, related with enthusiasm how easily he worked with Goodpaster and how highly he esteemed the staff secretary.[66]

A simple hierarchy—congruent with a decision setting largely characterized by agreed-upon goals and certain technology, and run by competent and well-respected individuals—the staff secretariat was an unmitigated success.[67] Nor can one discount the atmosphere at the top levels of the Eisenhower White House. As Minnich stated, the system worked in large part through informal relations: "personal relations were easy . . . because just about every one of us had very high respect for the ability of others, and the commonness of purpose that we all had."[68]

Nonetheless, the staff secretariat would not survive the change in administration. The new president would have entirely different ideas about the governance of national security policy.

KENNEDY: SIMPLIFICATION AND INFORMALITY

John Kennedy, whose background was in Congress, did not believe in extensive governance structuring. In this he was reinforced by the legacy of the Democratic Party, which looked back to the improvisations of FDR as a golden age and firmly viewed Eisenhower's approach as an instance of hardening of the governmental arteries. At the outset, Kennedy abolished the Planning Board,[69] the Operations Coordinating Board, and the staff secretariat, arguing, as Special Counsel Theodore Sorensen related, that all this amounted to "needless paperwork and machinery."[70] Instead, JFK proposed to rely on a lean staff of generalists whom journalist Charles Bartlett effusively described as "a team of Phi Beta Kappa'd Hopkinses."[71]

Beyond his own organizational predilections, Kennedy was influenced by the views of others, including Democratic elders such as Truman White House veteran Richard Neustadt.[72] The most important influence, however, was the work of the Senate Subcommittee on National Policy Machinery (better known as the Jackson Subcommittee after its chairman, Democrat Henry Jackson of Washington). In 1960, this committee produced a negative appraisal of the Eisenhower national security governance system and strongly recommended that President-elect Kennedy avoid "over-institutionalization," use the NSC as an "intimate forum" for policy discussion, and keep the NSC staff small.[73] Despite advice from Eisenhower that he avoid reorganization until he was more familiar with the existing machinery, JFK followed his instincts, his advisers, and the Jackson Committee's preferred approach.[74]

The result was less complex, more flexible, less dependable, perhaps more creative governance, with greater freedom and authority residing with fewer top officials. The role of the national security assistant metamorphosed, in Kevin Mulcahy's terms, into that of a counselor.[75] The position of deputy assistant for national security became more important, and the small, flexible NSC staff worked at the heart of what came to be called a "little State Department."

Beyond his reorganization of the NSC machinery, Kennedy engaged in two other governance experiments. In the first, he virtually recreated the role that Admiral Leahy had played under Truman. Confronted by mounting military-political challenges as well as a need for additional planning capability, Kennedy named Gen. Maxwell Taylor to be military representative of the president. Taylor served in this capacity for a little over a year and was not replaced. An even clearer example of this tendency toward instability was Kennedy's second experiment, the appointment of Chester Bowles to be special representative and adviser to the president on foreign policy. Finally, whatever the governance structuring at any given time, Kennedy insisted on strong personal involvement in national security policy making and management, and on including a variety of key advisers.

The National Security Assistant: McGeorge Bundy

The job given to McGeorge Bundy, Kennedy's first and only NSA, was characterized by his predecessor, Gordon Gray, as essentially that of the Eisenhower NSA plus the national security tasks of the staff secretary.[76] Thus, Bundy was to be both the president's representative to the NSC (and head of its staff) and manager of the foreign and defense policy paper flow.

One element of the Eisenhower NSA's job that was expressly not included in Bundy's assignment was interdepartmental coordination. Not only was the OCB abolished, but the president explicitly instructed Bundy to leave coordination to the departments, with State expected to take the lead; the NSA and the NSC staff were warned not to compete with the departments.[77] The intended effect was to move the White House and the NSC staff out of the coordinating business and for them to focus instead on policy substance and process.

A consequence of this arrangement was the reemergence of a version of the policy-administration dichotomy that had so troubled Eisenhower's staff. The problem Kennedy encountered was the State Department's inability or unwillingness to coordinate as aggressively as the president wanted, with the result that matters of policy, embedded in issues of implementation, were not always handled as JFK would have liked. Therefore, the responsibility for overseeing implementation (and its policy implications) in the area of foreign (though not so much defense) policy soon devolved onto Bundy's staff.[78] The failure of the mainline institutions of national security in the Bay of Pigs invasion at the outset of the administration further accentuated the need for an aggressive White House policy presence such as Bundy.[79] The merger of responsibility for monitoring and coordinating policy making and implementation toward which the Eisenhower administration had been tending was thus at least partially accomplished, albeit informally, by Kennedy and Bundy.

In addition, Bundy had a relationship with the president that was qualitatively different from that of his predecessors. He was "part of his [JFK's] *personal* staff,"[80] a policy adviser, sometimes an advocate within the councils of the administration, and often a spokesman for the administration to the outside world. This last task was especially important, for Kennedy did not draw a strict line between politics and national security and thus did not exclude his "political" advisers from that policy area. Among others, Theodore Sorensen, Arthur Schlesinger, Richard Goodwin, and, above all, Robert Kennedy, were prominent in the flow of advice and counsel around the president. To be effective, Bundy also needed to be close to John Kennedy.

Although the job grew, the position of NSA had become sufficiently institutionalized—and sufficiently vital to the policy process—that its fundamental responsibilities did not change under Bundy. These tasks were to see that the president was informed of major options and points of view prior to making a decision and that his decisions were executed. Bundy defined the job this way:

> I and a small group of other staff officers try to handle the preparation of papers and meetings and other matters which require the President's own attention. We try when the President has made the decision or indicated the course of action which he prefers, to ensure that that decision is coordinated throughout the many departments of the government which are concerned with national security affairs.[81]

In the administration's first year, Bundy and his deputy, Walt Rostow, worked out a rough division of labor. Bundy handled "the institutional side of national security,"[82] and Rostow focused more on long-range planning; Bundy was more involved in European matters, and Rostow and a small staff specialized in developing areas (other than Latin America).[83] This system worked to the satisfaction of the principals until Rostow's departure for the State Department in late 1961. He was replaced by Carl Kaysen, whose special interest lay more in the area of foreign trade. Rostow's attention to long-range policy was not really replaced.

In addition, before and after Rostow's leaving, the planning process was supplemented by the creation of task forces, which generally included White House staff representation.[84] Less central to the Kennedy approach than it had been to Eisenhower's was the meeting of the NSC itself. Instead, the NSA and his staff spent much of their time preparing specialized briefings for the president. The staff, divided into four geographical areas to parallel the organization of the State Department, met daily. Its work expanded into the "implementation" side of the policy process, just as Bundy's had. According to Bromley Smith:

> One major change gradually developed which greatly increased the responsibilities of the NSC staff. Bundy took over the management of the president's day-to-day foreign policy and national security business. This activity had been handled for President Eisenhower by the White House Staff Secretary.[85]

Aware that the lack of collegial-competitive structuring that was congruent with the requirements of long-term planning led to that task being neglected, Bundy tried sporadically to institute additional mechanisms to address the problem. For instance, he established an interdepartmental standing group to monitor the NSC and deal with issues given to it by the NSC. This had little impact and soon fell into disuse. In 1963, he revived it, with himself as chair, but again it faded away, replaced to an extent by ad hoc committees. Similarly, an effort to keep alive the Executive Committee, the group that had produced the U.S. strategy during the Cuban missile crisis, quickly failed.[86] Although these structures were roughly congruent with the decision settings, Bundy was too preoccupied elsewhere to sustain a focus on planning. Meanwhile, the president's tendency to concentrate on short-term events did nothing to create a sense of urgency about long-range thinking.

Estimates of the success of the Kennedy system vary. Maxwell Taylor, who observed it from the inside, was critical, lamenting the loss of the Planning Board and the OCB but concluding that Kennedy's people improved their performance over time.[87] Others, such as Joseph Bock, admitted that the system's informality sometimes led to misunderstandings and oversights but gave it high marks in large part because of the atmosphere of collegiality JFK encouraged, Bundy's skill, and the president's active role in the process.[88]

It is hard to appraise the performance of the NSC staff apart from the broader organizational context in which it was embedded. Kennedy, seemingly indifferent to governance structuring, nevertheless managed to pack considerable innovation into his relatively brief presidency. Partly, it seems, he was motivated by a sense that his arrangements worked only imperfectly.

But he also simply wanted to have good people close to him. One such person was Gen. Maxwell Taylor.

The Military Representative of the President

Maxwell Taylor was brought to the White House in the aftermath of the Bay of Pigs fiasco as a consultant and chair of what came to be called the Cuba Study Group. Bent on making Taylor a full-time aide, Kennedy initially considered reestablishing Admiral Leahy's position of chief of staff to the commander in chief but decided against it, since it would overlap the duties of the chairman of the JCS.[89] Instead, Kennedy created the job of military representative, whose description included advising the president on military matters, intelligence, and Cold War planning, with particular concern for Berlin and Southeast Asia. Although partisan learning is evident in this near emulation of Roosevelt and Truman, Taylor's job also resembled some of what General Goodpaster had done in the Eisenhower White House, though Taylor did not perform any routine administrative duties. Taylor had no command authority, and he was expected not to interpose himself between Kennedy and the Joint Chiefs, Bundy, or the director of the CIA.[90]

Taylor's central duty, Cold War planning, turned out to be largely counterinsurgency planning. He established a special working group in this area and advised the president in this and other areas of defense policy. As Taylor characterized it, "My task seemed to be one of anticipating problems of the President in the areas of my responsibility and of being ready to help the President when they came before him."[91] Kennedy, according to Taylor, was both busy and disorganized, so briefing papers submitted in advance generally had no effect.[92] Face-to-face briefing proved more satisfactory.

Taylor's tour in the White House was at least a moderate success, as he saw it. Initial turf difficulties with Bundy were worked out satisfactorily through communication and some informal structuring, such as sending aides to each other's staff meetings.[93] However, Taylor's position never really became settled in the White House. He served for about 14 months, from July 1961 to September 1962, before moving to the Joint Chiefs as chairman. Subsequently, he continued his role in Vietnam policy making as ambassador to Saigon. Like so many national security advisers with vague mandates, he was not replaced in the White House.

Chester Bowles: Special Representative and Adviser

Chester Bowles, former congressman and governor of Connecticut, was one of the country's most visible and respected liberal politicians. His involvement in the Kennedy administration, especially in foreign affairs, was crucial to maintaining liberal Democratic support for a president whose own commitment to liberalism was suspect in many quarters. Thus, when turmoil at the State Department, where he was undersecretary, forced his ouster through "reorganization," Bowles was offered a position as a "roving ambassador" as a way to keep him on the Kennedy team.[94] When Bowles turned this down, the issue of where to place him became acute. The solution, engineered principally by Theodore Sorensen, was to put Bowles on the White House staff with the elaborate title of the president's special representative and adviser on Asian, African, and Latin American affairs.[95]

Bowles's assignment was to advise the president personally on the politics of the developing world. Bowles had forebodings about the job:

> When I met the President at the White House . . . I expressed my frank skepticism about what it all meant; my ability to make a useful contribution, I said, would largely depend on the closeness of my personal relationship with him. . . . I was concerned by the lack of personal rapport between us. . . . I was not, I said, the tough, terse, yes-or-no type he apparently found it easiest to work with, and there was nothing I could do to become one.[96]

After just under a year, Bowles essentially concluded that his reservations had proved correct, his policy influence was small, and he would have to leave the administration.[97] Kennedy provided an honorable way out by appointing Bowles ambassador to India.

JOHNSON: CONTINUITY AND CONTROVERSY

Lyndon Johnson meant his administration to be dedicated to domestic, not foreign, policy. Fate, of course, did not permit this. But LBJ, who was greatly given to improvisation in his White House arrangements in the domestic, economic, and political realms, did little of it in the area of national security. Rather, he relied on the structures and many of the personnel his predecessor left behind. Under Johnson, the organizational weaknesses that Kennedy had partially compensated for with his own involvement became more glaring, especially in the harsh light of failing policy in Vietnam.

The National Security Assistant

McGeorge Bundy continued for over two years as NSA after Kennedy's assassination. He finally left the White House in February 1966, although he returned thereafter as a consultant. He was succeeded by Walt Rostow, his former deputy.

Bundy's job under Johnson was similar to what it had been under Kennedy, but his position in the White House hierarchy was somewhat lower. The NSA's access to the president grew more difficult, and his memos often went to other aides instead of directly to Johnson.[98] Nevertheless, Bundy normally met with LBJ each morning, and the working relationship between the two was satisfactory.

Walt Rostow, whose selection as Bundy's replacement inspired some controversy within the administration,[99] continued in Bundy's basic pattern, although his access to LBJ was less likely to be obstructed.[100] The major features of the job remained overseeing operation of the NSC and its staff (this was more important under Johnson, who valued NSC meetings more than Kennedy had), working with advisers and advisory boards, serving as liaison with departments and agencies, preparing and presenting briefings and background research, and occasionally dealing with everyone from members of Congress to foreign diplomats to the media.[101]

With Rostow's accession to the job of NSA, Johnson moved Bundy's deputy, Robert Komer, to a new position of special assistant in charge of coordinating development programs in Vietnam. This is notable mainly for being the only change in the White House Office that was clearly motivated by the growing conflict in Vietnam.

Moyers's "Back Door"

As doubts about the wisdom of the administration's Vietnam policy grew, it was inevitable that some among LBJ's "political" advisers would develop both views and contacts that would involve them in national security policy. One of those aides, Press Secretary Bill Moyers, became involved more than marginally, cultivating a network of mid-level contacts throughout the executive branch and, it is alleged, sometimes providing access to the president for persons and views in disfavor with the "hawkish" NSA. Journalists such as David Halberstam[102] and Patrick Anderson[103] have stressed the importance of Moyers's network as a source of alternative views. Anderson, for instance, quotes one "second-level official" as saying:

It was early in 1965 that I became aware of Moyers' role as an advocate of peace in Vietnam—a guy who saw this as a conflict that could not be resolved militarily, one that would eventually have to be negotiated. And this was at a time when negotiations were anathema to people like [Secretary of State] Rusk. Working with Moyers, you could conspire to outflank some of the more difficult customers at the top.[104]

For all this effort, it is not clear that Moyers provided the president with much in the way of information or opinion that he would not otherwise have received.[105] In any case, Moyers left the administration in early 1967, his attempts to change the course of the war having failed.

Skill, Strategy, and Governance

The most common appraisal of the Johnson experience in national security policy is that his advisory arrangements failed him.[106] Why this was the case for Johnson more than for Kennedy stems in part from the interaction among the governance structures and presidential strategy and skill. LBJ was less adept than Kennedy at employing a loosely structured arrangement of advisers and decision makers to produce the kind of comprehensive and thoughtful analysis a president needs. Johnson valued governance structuring more than Kennedy had—as evidenced by LBJ's employment of the NSC and his regular Tuesday lunches with top foreign policy advisers. Moreover, his informal interventions in the policy process tended to be more consistent and productive than Kennedy's. Johnson, then, might well have been better served by more complex, routinized structures—something more like the Eisenhower system—than those he inherited. However, he did not act to establish such structures, perhaps in part because he felt that he had never quite mastered the details of national security policy making. Still, such retrospective evaluations are suspect, since we judge the structuring on the basis of knowledge of the outcomes. Moreover, Johnson's policies in Vietnam—arguably a continuation of Kennedy's—were intensely controversial at the time, placing far greater than normal pressure on national security governance structures. At some point, controversies over ends and means became so intense, so intertwined with one another, that the governance problem simply had no stable solution. It is tempting to blame leaders for such difficulties, but it is not always wise. In Johnson's case, the apparent lack of congruence arose from turbulence in the environment more than from the structures themselves.[107]

CONCLUSIONS

In Herbert Hoover's time, there was no need for the White House staff to provide advice on national security policy or liaison with the State and War Departments. By Franklin Roosevelt's third term, such needs had become clear, and the president struggled to meet them. Significant environmental change—first World War II, then the Cold War (including the surrogate conflicts in Korea and Vietnam)—generally shaped the nature of White House national security arrangements. The need to mobilize the armed services as well as to take unprecedented control of the economy during World War II dictated the broad outlines of the jobs to be done by such aides as

William Leahy and Harry Hopkins. The necessity of discovering and pursuing a U.S. strategic role in the dangerous postwar world called for structures that could facilitate policy planning as well as coordination among the diverse bureaucracies involved. Although the Cold War provided a more stable context for Harry Truman's successors, the environment (or interpretations of it) continued to suggest specific responses—from C. D. Jackson's concern with "psychological warfare" to Maxwell Taylor's work on counterinsurgency to Bill Moyers's efforts to provide channels of advocacy for Vietnam "doves."

Presidential choice variables also contributed significantly to White House structuring for national security policy. In contrast, organizational factors are less critical in the explanation of national security governance than in any other area, except perhaps domestic policy. Controversy over both means and ends so frequently engulfed this policy area that no particular kind of structure would have offered a likely long-term solution. The appearance and disappearance of not only advisers but also the structures they created or worked in is testimony to the existence of such difficulties.

Nevertheless, some organizational order emerged during the period under study, both within and across administrations. Within administrations, Eisenhower's experience suggests that a president with clear objectives can create relative stability with relatively satisfactory results. Across administrations, at least some structuring—involving the NSA—achieved relative stability. Dating perhaps from Hopkins or Harriman, but certainly at least from Cutler, the NSA's efforts at facilitating collegial-competitive decision making through the NSC machinery became a constant that endures to this day. Presidents may differ in how they use their NSAs, but the basic job is always similar, and no president would seriously consider eliminating the position.

Not surprisingly, we would attribute the stability of this NSA structuring to its congruence with the general decision setting. This is hardly a novel analysis in the national security area, where calls for "multiple advocacy" and the avoidance of "groupthink"—essentially what we mean when we refer to collegial-competitive governance—have become standard fare. Nonetheless, the success of the structures that pivot around the NSA lends additional weight to the claim that, even in the most turbulent of policy environments, even in an arena where presidential choices and skills have diverged so sharply, more congruent governance structures can be recognized and are likely to survive.

9

Specialized Policy Structures

One way in which early modern presidents sought to cope with burgeoning policy demands was through the creation of specialized policy structures in the White House. These structures typically were staffed by subject-matter experts who were charged with developing and overseeing the adoption of specific initiatives or with coordinating and monitoring executive branch activities in particular policy areas.

This chapter examines several of these more or less ad hoc structures that waxed and waned as environmental influences shifted or presidential agendas changed.[1] Rather than surveying all such structures that emerged during the early modern era, we examine a purposive sample of specialized policy units. Three dichotomous variables guided the sampling: (1) whether the explanation for the *emergence* of structuring was primarily environmental pressure or presidential choice, (2) whether the structuring was *stable* (i.e., whether it survived more than one administration), and (3) whether the structuring *succeeded* in meeting its goals.

Table 3 arrays the units from which the sample was drawn along these three dimensions. The clustering suggests several generalizations. First, environmental influences were principally responsible for the emergence of more than half the units, but presidential choice still primarily influenced the appearance of several more. Second, instability was common. Only two of these specialized policy structures survived more than one administration: science advising and consumer affairs. The latter, of course, is one of the more marginal White House activities; beginning with Nixon, consumer aides have moved in and out of the White House.[2] Somewhat similarly, White House–based structuring for foreign economic policy tended to come and go; by the end of the Johnson administration, however, these issues (like domestic economic policy) were largely dealt with outside the

Table 3. Specialized Policy Structures: Emergence, Stability, and Success

Policy Structure	Reason for Emergence		Stable?*	Successful?**
	Environmental Demand	Presidential Choice		
Science	DDE–LBJ		Yes	Yes, DDE and JFK; no, LBJ
Consumer affairs	JFK, LBJ		Yes	No
Foreign economic policy	FDR–LBJ	FDR–LBJ	?	Yes, Dodge and Randall, DDE; Peterson, JFK No, LBJ
Aviation	DDE		No	Yes
D.C. affairs	JFK		No	No
Public works		DDE	No	No
Arts		JFK	No	Yes
Mental retardation		JFK	No	Yes

*Structuring is considered stable if it survived more than one administration.
**Structuring is considered successful if it achieved its stated goals.

White House. Finally, roughly half the units can be judged successful in meeting their stated goals, some of which were explicitly short term and some of which clearly implied that the tasks would evolve beyond the White House Office.

In the discussion that follows, we focus on five specialized policy structures: those for public works planning; mental retardation; science policy; advising on Washington, D.C., affairs; and foreign economic policy. The first two units were largely the result of presidential initiative, the next two emerged mainly because of environmental influences, and the last surfaced due to both factors. Only science advising was relatively stable, though foreign economic policy structures of some kind appeared in the White House through much of the early modern era. Finally, structuring for the mental retardation unit was largely successful, as was that for science and for foreign economic policy—at least on occasion.

FOREIGN ECONOMIC POLICY

In the late 1920s and the 1930s, the political and economic environment, dominated by the domestic impact of the Great Depression, did not compel special attention to be paid to foreign economic policy.[3] Neither Herbert Hoover nor Franklin Roosevelt placed such matters high on his list of priorities. It took a major environmental change—the threat and then the reality of war—to highlight issues of foreign economic policy.

The war forced only a few foreign economic issues to the fore—mainly the lend-lease of military equipment and the provision of economic aid to such beleaguered combatants as Britain, China, and the Soviet Union. Advice and coordination on these matters drifted, largely unplanned, into the White House along with preparations for World War II. Thus environmental change interacted with presidential strategy—the addition of six administrative assistant positions in 1939—in producing White House structuring that had not been precisely planned by anyone.

After the war, the movement of the economy from a military to a peacetime one required continued White House attention to issues of postwar relief and trade on a more limited basis. It was not until 1950 that the issue of the balance of trade loomed large enough to catch Harry Truman's attention and led him to create a special-project unit in the White House to analyze the issue. The problems of trade came into the White House at this time for the same reason that many other matters have drifted there: responsibility across the rest of the government was diffused, and the president saw a need for focus and coordination.

With the administration of Dwight Eisenhower came the first attempt to pay sustained attention to the design and operation of governance structures in the foreign economic policy area. Joseph Dodge, author of a study calling for more coordination, was appointed special assistant and charged with implementing the report through the Council on Foreign Economic Policy. His successor, Clarence Randall, was already a trade adviser in the White House. Finally, Eisenhower created an ongoing role for a foreign aid adviser. In characteristic Eisenhower fashion, multiple formal governance arrangements had sprung up, enhancing White House capacity and, by triggering the differentiation dynamic, requiring the devotion of additional resources to coordinating the coordinators.

These efforts reflected both Eisenhower's policy priorities and his preferred organizational strategies. As in other areas of his administration, structuring for foreign economic policy coordination and advising was successful and generally congruent with prevailing decision settings. Eisenhower's strategic preference for formal, collegial governance structures had most of its usual consequences here: effective information exchange and policy deliberation, limited by the inherent political problems associated with governance of the executive branch, and purchased at the price of structural complexity that sometimes created a need for both extra negotiation and additional governance structuring.

As one would expect, John Kennedy hewed more to Roosevelt's and Truman's approaches to handling foreign economic policy. Most of the structures of the Eisenhower administration were unceremoniously abandoned and replaced with temporary, rather ad hoc governance arrangements. Although JFK eliminated the special assistants for foreign economic policy and economic affairs, he did continue White House involvement in foreign aid, appointing George McGovern as director of the agricultural aid program, by now called Food for Peace.

Moreover, Kennedy, like his predecessor, established special units. JFK's other initiative—the creation of a temporary White House staff office to mount a large-scale lobbying effort for the Trade Expansion Act of 1962—was prompted primarily by a policy priority of the administration. The idea of a special-purpose lobbying and public-opinion unit in the White House was novel, and it worked successfully, finally leading to the creation of the office of the special representative for foreign trade, which moved advising on trade issues into the Executive Office of the President (EOP).

The only promise of institutionalized foreign economic policy advice under Kennedy lay in the deputy national security assistant's emphasis on the area. Lyndon Johnson elaborated on the arrangement by creating the position of special assistant with responsibility for economic development in Vietnam, while continuing the focus of the deputy NSA on foreign aid. Here, it seems clear that environmental change—the increasing salience of developing countries in general and of Vietnam in particular—dictated the organizational adaptation. Otherwise, Johnson made less effort than Kennedy to place foreign economics in the White House.

Thus, the history of White House structuring for dealing with foreign economic issues over a 30-year period is essentially one of improvisation, partial attention, and structural instability. Only one president sustained a focus in this area strong enough to result in relatively stable structuring, and his work did not survive his time in office. Otherwise, the story is mostly one of fluctuating environmental demands for coordination competing only somewhat successfully for the attention of presidents whose priorities lay elsewhere. Further, as with domestic policy and foreign policy more generally, organizational factors explain relatively little.

Roosevelt: Tentative Beginnings

The early years of the New Deal were a time of intense preoccupation with domestic economic issues, a period of economic nationalism so pervasive that foreign economic policy seldom occupied center stage.[4] As the environment shifted in 1940 with war looming, the priorities of the administration necessarily changed, as issues such as lend-lease and other aid to the struggling allies in Europe and Asia jumped to the fore. The work of Harry Hopkins and Isador Lubin (summarized in Chapter 8) responded to these challenges. More squarely in the area of foreign trade and aid was the role of another of FDR's original administrative assistants, Lauchlin Currie. Currie's White House position, created in response to the wartime emergency, stands as the first important instance of a foreign economic adviser attached to the president's staff.[5] In its ad hoc nature and its relative independence from White House governance structures, the job would set a pattern for many of Currie's successors.

At first, Currie, the first economist ever to serve on the White House staff, was assigned mainly to monitoring the domestic economy and "clearing programs and proposals with interested agencies."[6] By 1941, Currie began to be primarily concerned with international matters, especially issues affecting China, in which he took a special interest. Currie's involvement in foreign economic matters was such that in July 1943 he was detailed from the White House to the Foreign Economic Administration as deputy administrator, first focusing on administrative matters, then becoming principally occupied with lend-lease.[7] Upon his return to the White House in January 1945, he was immediately sent to Switzerland to negotiate a trade agreement.[8]

Truman: Reconversion and a Special Project

Currie's position did not survive the change in administrations. Despite the absence of direct involvement by the White House staff in foreign economic policy during Truman's first years, however, considerable work in this area was going on at the Office of War Mobilization and Reconversion (OWMR). In 1947, when elements of the OWMR were transferred into the White House, economist Robert Turner became the closest thing to a successor to Currie.

Turner's work dealt with trade and tariff issues, the distribution of relief to Europe, and even the question of raising tolls at the Panama Canal.[9] For the most part, Turner's job is better characterized as overseeing policy implementation than as providing policy advice. He frequently was charged with creating ad hoc collegial-competitive structures to handle assignments such as working out a compromise among the Departments of Army, State, and Navy on a "letter of understanding" concerning the sale of German textiles in the United States.[10]

As the problems of reconversion receded, however, foreign economic issues declined in visibility and importance. Meanwhile, the nature of environmental demands shifted, and administration interest grew in the policy questions raised by mounting imbalances between U.S. imports and exports. In March 1950, Truman persuaded Gordon Gray, a former assistant secretary of the army (who would later serve Eisenhower as national security assistant), to become a temporary White House aide. Gray's job description was to "assist the President in mobilizing and coordinating staff work within the various agencies of the Government looking toward a careful analysis of the various factors bearing on the present disparity between exports and imports."[11] In particular, Gray was expected to systematically solicit the views of parties outside the government, and he was given a modest staff of seven professionals (three university professors, four detailees from various departments), as well as a budget for numerous consultants.[12] In essence, Gray and his aides were charged with assembling an extensive collegial-consensual governance structure.

Another environmental jolt, the outbreak of the Korean War, seriously interfered with these plans. Meetings with local leaders were canceled, though small "area teams" of one business leader and one economist from each of eight regions were brought to Washington.[13] These were augmented by mail solicitations of information and opinion. The Gray Project, as it was called, thus had to rely to an unanticipated extent on within-government sources, both for inputs and for review of the draft report.[14]

Despite these limitations, the Gray Project was able to put together a comprehensive study of policies and procedures that was sent on to an advisory board headed by Nelson Rockefeller. The collegial-consensual structure at the core of the project was generally congruent with the prevailing decision setting: it primarily probed the means of trade policy (which could best be characterized as "uncertain," in contrast to the ends, which were generally agreed upon) through a combination of expertise and inputs from interested parties.

Eisenhower: Structuring Governance

The Gray Project was one of the first White House "special projects." Special-project structuring within the White House became a favorite strategy of Dwight Eisenhower's, in part because it enabled him to take fullest advantage of business executives who were sometimes available only on a temporary or part-time basis. A congressional special-project appropriation typically provided a staff and other resources that could magnify the impact of particular advisers and permit those advisers to concentrate their efforts on a relatively narrow range of issues. Nowhere was this clearer than in the field of foreign economic policy.

Joseph Dodge. The first Eisenhower staffer charged with handling foreign economic policy was Joseph Dodge. A Detroit bank executive, Dodge initially joined the administration as budget director. When he left that job in 1954, he agreed to author a study on executive branch organization for foreign economic policy, which he submitted in August 1954.[15] The study was well received, resulting in Dodge's being asked in December 1954 to become a White House special assistant for foreign economic policy and implement the study's recommendations.[16]

Dodge's principal contribution was to set up and chair the Council on Foreign Economic Policy (CFEP). The council included in its membership the secretaries of state, treasury, agriculture, and commerce; the director of the International Cooperation Administration (foreign aid); a member of the Council of Economic Advisers; and the White House assistants for economic policy (Gabriel Hauge) and national security (Robert Cutler). As its composition suggests, the aim of the CFEP was to coordinate foreign economic policy across the government. At a minimum, it was expected to serve as a buffer for the president. As Dodge saw the CFEP's task, it was to keep "one Cabinet member from going to the Chief alone and getting a ruling on something that sounds plausible without presentation of another viewpoint."[17]

Like so much of the rest of Eisenhower's governance, the CFEP generally operated as a collegial-competitive structure, allowing bureaucratic stakeholders with policy disagreements to both guard their own turf and contribute to a full airing of alternatives. However, depending on the issues at hand, the CFEP also could operate as an adversarial or adjudicative structure, establishing a forum for advocacy and decision. Consistent with the need for restoration of order in an area of interagency competition, the CFEP was considered a success by Dodge, who took pride in achieving compromise without appeals to higher levels in the administration hierarchy.[18]

At the same time, although a collegial-competitive structure typically is an excellent device for "multiple advocacy," its acceptance of the legitimacy of continuing controversy is apt to render it less than effective at tasks such as long-range planning. Thus, NSA William Jackson expressed impatience with the CFEP's coordination function, wishing that the council would "tackle the stratospheric questions, like what to do about the world burden of defense in a nuclear age."[19]

In addition to his work with the CFEP, Dodge and his staff (which never numbered more than three professionals) were part of collegial-consensual structuring that emerged to coordinate their activities with those of others in the White House—as the differentiation dynamic would lead one to expect. Dodge and his aides were particularly adept at working in concert with Gabriel Hauge, the president's economic adviser, whose responsibilities in such areas as tariffs and trade clearly overlapped Dodge's. Hauge and Dodge understood the latter to be primarily in the "policy" field, while the former oversaw "administration." Such a distinction, whose artificial nature had been troublesome in the national security field, held up better in this case.[20]

Clarence Randall. A second major White House player in the foreign economic policy arena was Clarence Randall. The chairman of the Board of Inland Steel, Randall originally came to the White House to chair a commission of 17 that was charged with studying the substance of foreign economic policy. In early 1954, the Randall Commission Report, which advocated free trade, was presented to Eisenhower and Hauge, who embraced it enthusiastically.[21] Randall was asked to stay on as a part-time special consultant, largely to prepare and advance a legislative program implementing the commission's recommendations. He was given a small staff—a staff director and three clerks—funded as a special project.

Soon Randall's mandate expanded. In April 1954, Hauge assigned him the task of policy coordination among agencies involved in foreign trade—this coming before the creation of the CFEP. Specifically, Randall was to coordinate on negotiations such as the General Agreement on Tariffs and Trade.[22] Randall also began participating in a White House staff working group on economic policy.[23] This collegial-consensual structure was congruent with a decision setting marked by general agreement on policy goals and some uncertainty about the means for achieving them.

In other cases, Randall's presence triggered struggles over organizational turf. For example, he could not abide Harold Stassen, at that time still foreign aid chief.[24] In June 1954, Stassen was named the president's personal representative on all economic matters, foreign and domestic. Randall was livid and persuaded Sherman Adams and Gabriel Hauge to modify Stassen's mandate, limiting it to the issue of developing antirecession policy.[25]

When the CFEP was organized and Dodge joined the White House to chair it, Randall began to focus on working with Congress on foreign trade policy. His work also included travel abroad and follow-up at home. After a trip to Turkey in January 1956, Randall again showed his affinity for informal governance arrangements by convening an interdepartmental group to report on the trip, then continued to meet with it over time.[26]

When Dodge resigned in mid-1956, Randall accepted the position of chair of the CFEP, venturing back into the role of coordinator, despite the fact that this work had proved frustrating to him earlier.[27] At the helm of the CFEP, Randall tried to become more a part of ordinary White House governance than Dodge had been. Unlike Dodge, he attended regular White House staff meetings, hoping to cultivate contacts on the staff and develop a better understanding of what was happening in the administration in order to improve the operation of the CFEP.[28] Randall worked easily within the larger White House hierarchy, coordinating his continuing legislative initiatives through Adams. Meanwhile, he continued to participate frequently in ad hoc governance activities, mostly interdepartmental meetings on specific problems.[29]

Clarence Francis. Among those with whom Randall developed a constructive relationship was the final White House specialist in foreign economic
policy, Clarence Francis. The retired chairman of the board at General
Foods, Francis joined the Eisenhower administration in March 1954 at
Sherman Adams's behest. His initial task was to put together an interagency committee that ultimately drafted Public Law 480, the Agricultural
Trade and Development Act.[30] Francis then took on the task of implementing PL-480, coordinating the disposal of the country's agricultural surplus.
He too acquired a small staff and a special projects appropriation.[31]

Francis's work mainly involved expediting PL-480 contracts. In this he was
aided by two collegial-consensual structures—the Interagency Committee on
Agricultural Surplus Disposal and a citizens' advisory committee. Neither was
fully congruent with the decision setting, in which there was frequently controversy. At the outset, Francis bumped up against economic adviser Don
Paarlberg (Hauge's successor) in 1959, when the Food for Peace foreign aid
program was first implemented, with Paarlberg as coordinator.[32] Discussions
between the two, however, were enough to resolve the differences.[33] More serious were the policy disputes that were a continuing element of the work. Especially difficult to handle was the resistance of Secretary of State John Foster
Dulles to anything that smacked of aid to U.S. enemies or interference in the
traditional markets of its friends.[34] The difficulty was exacerbated by an environmental factor—the rising productivity of U.S. farms.[35]

Despite these sorts of problems, the work of economic advisers Francis,
Dodge, and Randall overall testifies to the effectiveness of Eisenhower's approach to White House governance. His successor would embrace quite different organizational strategies. Perhaps surprisingly, however, in the area
of foreign economic policy, this would not lead to the abandonment of the
special-projects model.

Kennedy: More Special Projects

John Kennedy abolished the positions of special assistant for foreign economic policy (Randall), special consultant for surplus food disposal (Francis), and special assistant for economic affairs (Paarlberg). Yet he virtually
replaced the latter when the position of deputy special counsel occupied by
Myer Feldman became substantially that of an economic adviser. Kennedy
also continued the White House staff's work in supervising the Food for
Peace program. Moreover, he created a separate unit for passing important
trade legislation and increased the involvement in foreign economic issues
of the National Security Council (NSC) staff.

Food for Peace. Kennedy's decision to locate Food for Peace in the White
House was driven less by the program's needs or organizational inertia than

by electoral politics. George McGovern, who was appointed special assistant and director of Food for Peace, was a recently defeated Democratic Senate candidate from South Dakota with intentions of running again. The creation of a White House special project for him mainly reflected Kennedy's political purposes. According to McGovern:

> President Kennedy's commitment to the Food for Peace idea was genuine, but he didn't have to establish a special office for it in the White House. He did so largely as a favor to me, to keep me in a visible and favorable position for another campaign in South Dakota.[36]

Kennedy defined McGovern's job broadly to encompass not only supervising Food for Peace but also coordinating all activities involving the movement of agricultural produce overseas. In effect, this merged most of Francis's and Paarlberg's responsibilities in this area.[37]

McGovern claimed that the office had a positive impact, cutting red tape (e.g., mediating between the Departments of State and Agriculture to expedite food agreements) and publicizing Food for Peace domestically.[38] The record also shows, however, that a great deal of attention had to be devoted to turf battles, as McGovern constantly fended off efforts by both State and Agriculture to take over his program, attempts by the Bureau of the Budget (BOB) to move his operation outside the White House, and even an effort by Vice President Johnson to commandeer some of his office space.[39]

McGovern left the White House to launch his Senate campaign in the spring of 1962. In August, Richard W. Reuter, an assistant director under McGovern, became director. Under Reuter the staff expanded, but the responsibilities of the office remained essentially what they had become under McGovern: legislative liaison, expediting policy implementation, and public relations.[40] The Food for Peace office continued as a White House unit well into the Johnson administration. By late 1965, however, Reuter and his aides were finally absorbed into the State Department, as an element of the Agency for International Development (AID).

Howard Petersen and the Trade Expansion Act. The Trade Expansion Act of 1962 was a centerpiece of the Kennedy economic program. Its intent was to broaden the president's authority in international trade negotiations, with an eye toward helping the United States compete with the more collectivist economies of Europe. To secure support for the bill—among the public, in the business community, and especially in Congress—Kennedy created another special-project unit headed by a Republican banker from Philadelphia, Howard Petersen.[41]

Petersen and his staff of five to six professionals were unusual for a special-project group in that they were of necessity linked with other elements of the White House staff. In particular, given the nature of the job, it was important that the Petersen group work with Larry O'Brien's congressional relations staff. This relationship proved highly satisfactory.[42]

Nevertheless, in the recollection of Petersen's deputy Myer Rashish, the Petersen unit was "surprisingly" left alone by most other White House aides.[43] Deputy special counsel and economic adviser Myer Feldman, the other seemingly key staff ally, kept Petersen's operation at arm's length. According to Rashish, this was because Feldman "viewed the whole thing with some bemusement in the sense that he thought we were really shooting for the moon and might get a minor star in the process."[44] Feldman's boss, Special Counsel Theodore Sorensen, actively supported Petersen's efforts.[45]

The Petersen staff was organized in a manner typical of most special-projects groups. The staff was highly specialized, with a deputy, a congressional liaison specialist, a liaison with industry, a public-relations specialist, a writer, a TV and radio specialist, and, at various times, people who focused on liaison with interest groups. Also typical, however, was the fact that the reliance on detailees led to turnover and some lack of focus on the part of part-timers.[46] The staff's hierarchical structure was congruent with its decision setting, since both the goals and the technologies involved were well understood.[47] In addition, a collegial-consensual structure—an interagency steering committee at the undersecretary level—guided the group's efforts in putting together the legislative package. This was a congruent response to the need to probe for useful tactics.

Petersen's project was a success. The Trade Expansion Act passed Congress in late 1962. Having won his victory, Petersen resigned in November 1962. His successor was Christian Herter, who assumed the new designation of special representative for foreign trade and presided over implementation of the act. Herter's time as a White House staffer was limited—in July 1963, his office was removed from the White House budget and located in the EOP.

Kennedy compensated in part for the loss of expertise by eliminating the advisory structures that Eisenhower had created in foreign economic policy and relying on the NSC staff. Economist Walt Rostow, the first deputy national security adviser, was best known for his writing on economic development, and he naturally took an interest in these matters during his brief (a little less than a year) tenure. He was succeeded by Carl Kaysen, who was principally responsible for foreign trade policy and was actually paid out of special-projects funds.

Johnson: No Projects, Some Advice

Lyndon Johnson declined to employ the special-projects model to create units relevant to foreign economic concerns in the White House. Nor, more generally, did he rely much on the White House staff for specialized foreign economic policy advice or coordination. Other than Reuter's Food for Peace operations and the involvement of the deputy assistant for national security and the deputy special counsel (Feldman), Johnson inherited nothing from Kennedy. Initially, he did little to add to White House capability. Indeed, when Feldman left the White House and Reuter moved to the EOP, the cupboard was nearly bare. In the Johnson White House, foreign economic advice became even less central than it had been under Kennedy, and far less so than under Eisenhower.

The deputy NSA continued to hold responsibility for advising on trade and related issues. Otherwise, there was little other White House involvement in foreign economic policy until Ernest Goldstein joined the staff in September 1967. Goldstein, however, had little in the way of a fixed assignment, and his only firm job at the outset was working with regulatory agencies.[48] But he "began to pick up things that other people wanted to get rid of or that were free for assumption."[49]

Goldstein first became involved with the Cabinet Commission on Balance of Payments, a body composed of departmental and agency representatives. As White House representative on the commission, Goldstein became interested in a variety of issues, including generating new ideas for exports, working with the AID concerning extra-U.S. expenditures, and dealing with airlines over fare structures.[50]

Goldstein's entry into foreign economic matters initially created turf problems, since Deputy NSA Ed Fried already specialized in the area. When NSA Rostow acted to protect Fried's prerogatives, Joseph Califano was called on to referee the matter, working out a division of labor in which Goldstein received those issues Fried did not want, with the exception of balance of payments, which Goldstein kept over Rostow's objections.[51] When Goldstein later acquired the job of liaison with the Treasury Department, he and Rostow negotiated an arrangement whereby foreign economic material went first to Rostow, who kept Goldstein informed.[52] Still, Goldstein did not become a major White House actor in foreign economic policy. Limited to a marginal role, he turned to other matters, including domestic economics, seeking without great success a central policy role.

Further Evolution of Foreign Economic Policy Advising

By the end of the Johnson administration, structuring for foreign economic policy had largely left the White House. Nonetheless, some of the initiatives of early modern presidencies reappeared. In January 1971, for example, Richard Nixon established the Council on International Economic Policy (CIEP). This structure was analogous to Eisenhower's CFEP, but Nixon's version was formally a part of the Executive Office, and fully half of the CIEP's members were EOP staffers.[53] Like the CFEP, the CIEP did not survive the change to a Democratic administration. Instead, Jimmy Carter—also acting as partisan learning would lead one to expect—relied on NSC staffers as his "principal operators" in the sphere of foreign economic policy.[54]

SCIENCE ADVISING

In foreign economic policy, both the environment and presidential choice were important in accounting for the emergence of White House structuring. Structures for science advising, in contrast, provide a good illustration of the overwhelming importance of the environment—especially the presence and consequent waning of perceived crises—in producing a White House response. The shock of the Soviet launching of *Sputnik I* in October 1957 prompted Eisenhower to create the post of special assistant to the president for science and technology. Eisenhower also upgraded the Science Advisory Committee, which was housed in the Office of Defense Mobilization (in the Executive Office), to the President's Science Advisory Committee (PSAC); the PSAC was lodged in the White House and chaired by the science adviser.[55]

Although science advising has become a normal feature of the White House, between the 1940s and the late 1960s, structuring was less than stable, and science advising moved from the Executive Office to the White House and back again. Meanwhile, its location in the general White House hierarchy fluctuated, its policy influence rose and then fell, and the science adviser's direct access to the president diminished. Under Eisenhower and Kennedy, structures for science advising were generally congruent with prevailing decision settings, but they were less so under Johnson.

Critical to understanding these shifting fortunes were environmental influences. In addition to being the catalyst for the creation of the science adviser position and for moving the support staff into the White House, *Sputnik* also served as the "fast trigger" that shot space technology to the top of the president's policy agenda.[56] After NASA was established, growing concerns about an alleged "missile gap" between the USSR and the United States (which reached fever pitch during the 1960 presidential campaign) kept the salience of science advising high.

By the early 1960s, however, these issues dropped in importance, and the necessity for such a high-visibility, high-priority response lessened. The science adviser moved down in the White House hierarchy, and his staff was shifted to the EOP. At about the same time, questions began surfacing both in and out of government about the need for exploring more than the "scientific" aspects of national security. Relevant as well, many argued, were political, diplomatic, economic, and military issues.[57] As the 1960s wore on, these questions grew into more general criticism and distrust of science and technology, providing another environmentally grounded reason for putting the science staff under the direction of generalist White House aides.

Meanwhile, without a clear crisis in national security, the nature of the science advising task itself changed. The attention of the science staff and the PSAC turned more to nonsecurity issues, in which science aides seemingly had less of a monopoly on expertise and staffers throughout the executive branch had both stakes and legitimacy.[58] In such a setting, science appeared to be just another competing interest, providing one more powerful rationale for placing an intermediary between the science adviser and the president.

Yet in some ways, science advising at the presidential level also became a victim of its own success. As the federal government turned its attention to science and technology in the late 1950s and early 1960s, science units multiplied throughout the executive branch. Not only did the need for a White House science office decline in importance, but these decentralized offices became rivals that competed with presidential science staffers for resources and credibility.[59]

Interaction between environmental factors and presidential needs and objectives also became important. The task of the science advisers during the 1960s was almost inevitably problematic. On the one hand, they advised the president and, as members of the administration, were expected to support and defend his decisions; on the other, the broader scientific community—emboldened by growing federal involvement in funding research and development and the presence of a channel to the president—expected the adviser to serve as an advocate. Especially as budgets tightened and LBJ grew more embattled, these demands began to pull in opposite directions: "Vietnam turned out to be a no-win situation for the science adviser. The critics wanted him to help them with Johnson, and Johnson expected the adviser to 'deliver' his constituency on the issue that counted most."[60] The result seems preordained: the science adviser became less influential and occupied a lower position in the White House hierarchy.

This decline in influence was reinforced by an organizational factor: once the science adviser was named head of the Office of Science and Technology, he took on many tasks that took him away from the president. "He was expected to testify before Congress . . . , negotiate with BOB, deal with other executive professionals, and work with (and against) the agencies."[61] Together, these institutional responsibilities for dealing with the environment constituted yet another centrifugal force on the relationship between the president and the science adviser.

At the same time, a second organizational factor helped to further reduce the influence of the science adviser. Individual White House staffers tried to protect their policy turfs throughout the period. Conflict increased notably during the Johnson years, probably in large part due to the generalized White House suspicion of staffers and units that performed outreach tasks and thus appeared to represent "special" interests.

Finally, distinctly presidential factors contribute to the explanation of the fall from grace of science advising. Presidents differed, first, in their understanding of the role and importance of science in public policy making. Katz maintains that Eisenhower opposed much government intervention in science and technology and took an "anti-expansionist approach to science and technology policy in the White House."[62] Yet the president plainly believed that scientists provided crucial input into national security policies. Indeed, science adviser James Killian reported being

> troubled by [Eisenhower's] almost exaggerated confidence in the judgment of the scientists that he had called upon to help him. He somehow came to have the feeling that this group of scientists were endowed with an objectivity that he couldn't expect to find in the other contacts that he had in government.[63]

Kennedy accorded science much the same priority, although the science adviser lost his "uniqueness," since the president relied on "many idea initiators."[64]

President Johnson, however, understood science differently—less as an end in itself and more as one of many tools that might be used to achieve his political and policy goals.[65] Science advising, then, became less central, one specialty among many, and it may have seemed desirable to move the science adviser further down in the White House hierarchy. This drop in influence likely was reinforced by the rise of domestic policy concerns noted earlier: the connections between basic research and applied technologies grew far more obscure, and the apparent benefits to be derived from "science" declined.[66] Influence continued to fall as the president's general distrust of academics (with whom he identified scientists) curdled into outright hostility.

The influence of the science staff also depended at least marginally on the quality of the personal relationship between the president and his science adviser. Both Killian and George Kistiakowsky, for example, reported having trusting relationships with President Eisenhower.[67] Many have described Jerome Wiesner as having a close and constructive relationship with John Kennedy, as "one more of a number of bright and informed men" surrounding the president.[68] President Johnson and Donald Hornig, in contrast, had a much more formal and impersonal relationship. Hornig attributed the distance in large part to LBJ's obvious discomfort with academics.[69]

Precursors of a White House Presence

As in so many other arenas, a presidential capacity in science first appeared under Franklin Roosevelt. In 1933, FDR formed a Science Advisory Board, though he dissolved it in 1935 amid concerns about costs and the alleged dangers of "centralized control" of science.[70] An environmentally induced influence—worry about the adequacy of presidential advising on scientific and medical research relevant to possible U.S. involvement in the spreading European war—led the president to establish the Office of Scientific Research and Development in the Office of Emergency Management in June 1941. Following the war, "the office was eventually absorbed within the National Military Establishment (the forerunner of the Defense Department)."[71]

Then, in 1946, President Truman established the President's Scientific Research Board, which John Steelman (the assistant to the president) chaired. The board did little beyond issue a 1947 report with "recommendations on Federal organization for science, administration of resources, training and utilization of scientific manpower and medical resources."[72] Steelman also was the White House liaison for the Interdepartmental Committee on Science, which coordinated programs across agencies.[73]

Again war, this time in Korea, served as the catalyst for the next advisory mechanism.[74] In 1951, Truman issued an executive order establishing the Scientific Advisory Committee (SAC) in the Office of Defense Mobilization in the Executive Office. The Committee's purpose was

> to advise the President, the National Security Council, and other agencies in matters related to scientific and technological developments of significance to national security and on the utilization of scientific resources to assure their availability in the event of mobilization.[75]

Eisenhower: The Move to the White House

Although the SAC continued under Eisenhower, as environmental pressures declined, it never became a very visible or significant actor.[76] Things changed with the *Sputnik*-induced installation of a White House science adviser and the creation of the President's Science Advisory Committee in November 1957.

Under both Eisenhower and Kennedy, the science adviser was a senior official with direct access to the president. The adviser's counsel was sought primarily on a range of military and national security issues. Meanwhile, according to David Beckler, staff director of both the SAC and the PSAC, moving into the White House increased the body's "prestige" and "visibility" as well as its general level of activity.[77]

Two science advisers served Dwight Eisenhower—first James Killian, president of MIT, and then George Kistiakowsky, a Harvard chemistry professor, who replaced Killian in mid-July 1957. Each met routinely with the president, typically with either Staff Secretary Andrew Goodpaster or his assistant John Eisenhower also in attendance.[78] Kistiakowsky remembered that, although he saw the president alone only "every month or so," he did not press for such meetings: "I found that I could communicate very effectively otherwise in . . . group occasions or channeling my information through General Goodpaster."[79]

Killian, Kistiakowsky, and their staffs spent most of their time on defense-related issues.[80] For example, they commented on the defense budget and on proposed weapon systems as well as advised the president on bomb and missile testing and on test ban negotiations.[81]

Much of Eisenhower's science advisers' time was spent working with a variety of committees throughout the executive branch.[82] Probably most important was the PSAC. Because there was some concern in the scientific community that too much power might be centralized in the White House science adviser, the PSAC was formally independent of him, appointing its own chair and meeting directly with the president. Perhaps not surprisingly, however, the committee elected both Killian and Kistiakowsky as chairs. The advisers set up PSAC panels and subcommittees, collegial-consensual structures designed to address issues about which the president requested advice; these were largely congruent with a decision setting characterized by presidentially specified goals and technical uncertainty.[83] Most of the subjects were related to national security, ranging from arms control to matters involving interservice rivalries to reviews of the U.S. missile program and nuclear-propelled aircraft.[84] According to Killian, the PSAC and many of its ad hoc panels also operated as adjudicative structures, providing "judicial review" for particular projects.[85]

Beginning in March 1959, the science adviser became responsible for chairing the Federal Council for Science and Technology, a less congruent structure. The council brought together officials from federal agencies with large research and development programs.[86] Kistiakowsky recalled that he spent considerable time with the council but that "it failed dismally. It remained a gathering of individuals who represented frequently opposing agency positions and were just unable, unwilling . . . to think on a national, federal level."[87] Apparently conceived as a collegial-competitive structure, it lacked a decision rule to resolve the disputes that frequently arose among participants with their own goals and means. More congruent with such a decision setting might have been a collegial-mediative or an adjudicative structure, with the science adviser, backed by the president, as the mediator or adjudicator.

Although the science unit was largely self-contained, it did have links with other parts of the White House. Probably most important was science staffers' involvement in speech drafting, which in the Eisenhower administration typically involved collegial-consensual policy discussion.[88] In some instances, science aides seemed to threaten the turfs of their White House colleagues. Although Kistiakowsky was unsure "whether Adams ever liked the idea of having a science adviser because he was so jealous of his privileges," he did get along well with Adams's successor, Wilton Persons, and with Staff Secretary Andrew Goodpaster.[89]

Relationships could also be difficult elsewhere in the executive branch. Killian was especially careful in his contacts with departments and agencies: "So as not to fall into the problems of Stassen or Rockefeller, I made sure to inform Cabinet officials when discussing material of interest" with the president.[90] Even so, the first presidential science adviser recalled that Secretary of Defense Neil McElroy viewed Killian's appointment "with some alarm . . . interpret[ing it] to mean that I was to serve as the President's lieutenant, to have responsibility for the missile program."[91] Despite Killian's good working relations with McElroy's deputy Donald Quarles and with Robert Lovett, McElroy's successor, the science adviser sensed that "throughout my experience in Washington there was a feeling on the part of many people in the Department of Defense that I was a person to be watched and one who might be troublesome to the Department."[92] More bluntly, Kistiakowsky characterized some Pentagon officials as "intolerable."[93] At least in his view, much of the difficulty with other executive branch officials came from Eisenhower's charge to work for a comprehensive test ban, which the Defense Department opposed and for which the State Department offered "only weak support."[94] Nor did structures for resolving such matters emerge, as the hypothesized differentiation dynamic might have led one to expect.

Kennedy: Changing Responsibilities

During the Kennedy years, much of the work done by both the science unit and the PSAC continued to focus on the military uses of science and the foreign policy implications of particular governmental decisions on science research and development and education.[95] Kennedy science adviser Jerome Wiesner monitored the space program and space-related issues such as regulation of communications satellites, subject to the oversight of Special Counsel Theodore Sorensen.[96] This was more than just a routine reporting relationship; it was a rather potent use of White House hierarchy. According to Katz, Wiesner was excluded from the final formulation of plans for the *Apollo* mission because he, unlike Sorensen, did not favor sending human beings to the moon.[97]

In addition, Wiesner, like his two predecessors, regularly attended NSC meetings and chaired both the PSAC and the Federal Council for Science and Technology.[98] He also became central to a collegial-mediative structure that extended into the executive branch. For example, when the United States resumed atmospheric testing of nuclear weapons in 1962, Wiesner "mediated a behind-the-scenes dispute on the matter between the Public Health Service . . . and the AEC [Atomic Energy Commission] and Defense . . . , balancing the potential risks to health against potential risks to military security in light of what the Russians were thought to have achieved in their tests."[99] The science adviser generally had direct access to the president,[100] and until the creation of the Office of Science and Technology (see below), he supervised a staff only slightly larger than Kistiakowsky's.[101]

The trend toward greater involvement in "domestic" science issues persisted.[102] In Kistiakowsky's view, this shift was accentuated by organizational factors: NSA McGeorge Bundy and Secretary of Defense Robert McNamara dominated the national security policy arena, reducing Wiesner's influence on foreign policy matters.[103] Relatedly, Hart contends that the tension that developed between Bundy and Wiesner made it more difficult for the latter to gain access to JFK.[104] Whatever the reason, Wiesner became more heavily involved in domestic matters. He chaired an interdepartmental energy study, monitored pesticides problems, and oversaw PSAC work on air traffic control and biological alternatives to persistent pesticides.[105] Wiesner also participated more heavily than his predecessors in activities that focused less on policy substance and more on constituency outreach—for instance, serving as White House liaison with scientific groups and working to recruit more scientists to government service.

The most tangible change in science advising, however, came in 1962 with Reorganization Plan 2, which, among other things, moved the science unit out of the White House again and into a new Office of Science and Technology (OST) in the Executive Office. Richard Neustadt had recommended such a shift during the transition, arguing that it would give the science advisory unit greater stability and continuity.[106] Wiesner became director of the OST in June 1962 and also continued as the president's science adviser, with a formal home in the White House Office. Rather soon after these changes, the size of the science staff approximately doubled.[107] The reorganization essentially made the science staff responsible to two masters, enabling the OST to advise Congress but also attenuating its White House links.[108]

Johnson: Increasing Conflict, Declining Influence

Wiesner resigned in early November 1963; Kennedy named his replacement, but Donald Hornig did not take over until after the assassination. Although Hornig stayed until virtually the end of the Johnson administration (resigning in December 1968), he was not a close personal adviser to the president, as his predecessors had been. During this period, science advising focused increasingly on domestic concerns and became enmeshed in more conflict.

Formally, Hornig's job was much like Wiesner's: he directed the OST, was the president's science adviser, and chaired the PSAC and Federal Council.[109] Yet the nature of Hornig's work changed dramatically. He was little involved in national security issues and only somewhat more active in space-related activities, with Vice President Hubert Humphrey taking over as chair of the National Aeronautic and Space Council.[110] Increasingly, the subjects the science adviser handled involved domestic policy concerns such as health, energy, air pollution, and water problems.[111]

At the same time, Hornig moved further down in the White House hierarchy, losing most direct access to the president, to whom he was "a virtual stranger."[112] Instead, Hornig typically reported to domestic policy staffer Joseph Califano and worked to build coalitions with White House aides such as Douglass Cater on health and education, Califano on energy, and Bill Moyers on the environment.[113]

Hornig also spent more time on constituency outreach activities, frequently acting as an advocate for the scientific community.[114] This, in turn, increased the suspicion with which science advising was looked at by other White House aides, especially as budgets tightened.[115] Still, Lambright found that Hornig was particularly influential in encouraging funding for basic research, in which role he was seen as a legitimate spokesperson; he was less successful in other areas, in part because of competition from other interested parties.[116]

Further Evolution of Science Advising

The science staff's declining policy influence and limited access to the president continued into the Nixon administration, culminating in the abolition of both the science adviser's White House sinecure and the OST in 1973. President Ford and his successors, however, returned to an arrangement similar to that under Johnson: a science adviser who typically reports to the president through senior White House staffers and who heads the Office of Science and Technology Policy in the EOP. Much like structuring for foreign economic policy, that for science advising became institutionalized in the Executive Office.

WASHINGTON, D.C., AFFAIRS

Even without an apparent crisis like that which brought science advising into the White House Office, environmental demand for government action may produce a White House response. The appointment of a White House aide to handle the problems of Washington, D.C., was such an instance. In 1962, the growing social, economic, and political problems in the District of Columbia led President Kennedy to designate a national capital adviser.

Unlike the previous case, however, this was neither a stable nor a notably successful response, thanks to a variety of environmental, organizational, and presidential choice factors. As the 1960s progressed, the political and social environment changed dramatically: violence broke out in Washington and other U.S. cities, and resources grew scarcer as Vietnam heated up and opposition to the urban initiatives of the Great Society era mounted. The staffers handling D.C. affairs confronted not only the tangled problems of the capital but also rising competition from White House colleagues whose responsibilities overlapped. Moreover, an increasingly embattled Lyndon Johnson neither had the time for nor wanted the notoriety of a special focus on the District of Columbia. By 1968, the D.C. affairs portfolio was absorbed into Joseph Califano's domestic policy operation.

Demands that the White House pay more attention to conditions in the District of Columbia did not begin during the Kennedy years. In 1959, a congressional Joint Committee on Washington Metropolitan Problems recommended the addition of a White House staffer whose sole responsibility would be to focus on politics and problems in the nation's capital.[117] After the Eisenhower administration did not respond, both the Federal City Council and the *Washington Star* urged President Kennedy to do so. Initially, though, the task fell to White House aides with other primary responsibilities—Lee White in the special counsel's office and the cabinet secretaries (first Frederick Dutton and then Timothy Reardon).[118]

By mid-1962, Attorney General Robert Kennedy joined in the chorus that was urging the creation of a separate adviser—in large part because the hostile, southern-dominated District of Columbia committees in Congress refused to respond to Washington's growing problems.[119] President Kennedy announced his intention to make such an appointment in July 1962, and Charles Horsky took over in September.[120]

Horsky was a former president of the Washington Housing Association and chair of the District Commissioners Planning Advisory Council. In general, he attempted to create and involve himself in informal collegial-mediative structures designed to help resolve local conflicts and to ease D.C. officials' dealings with executive branch agencies. For example, Horsky helped create a board of directors to address issues of juvenile delinquency, and he assisted in the negotiations leading to the creation of the United Planning Organization, an umbrella agency for human resources planning.[121] As part of the White House hierarchy, Horsky also was positioned to keep the president and key members of Congress informed of local problems and activities.[122]

Horsky stayed in the White House until February 1966. He was not replaced until early 1967, when Stephen Pollak became the national capital adviser. Pollak stayed only about ten months and then left to become an assistant attorney general. During his time in the White House, Pollak's work increasingly overlapped that of other domestic policy staffers. He and Douglass Cater, for example, reported to the president on the Washington, D.C., school system, and he and Califano aide Fred Bohen shared responsibility for preparing legislation and drafting messages concerning the District of Columbia.[123] Meanwhile, Pollak himself became involved in other activities, serving, for instance, as a White House liaison with state and local officials around the country when urban violence broke out.[124]

When Pollak left the White House, his D.C. responsibilities were picked up by various members of Califano's staff. By this point in the administration, the Califano unit was sufficiently developed in capacity so that a separate adviser for the District of Columbia, which was facing many of the same problems confronting other urban areas, became redundant. Moreover, a staffer for D.C. affairs ran the risk of infringing on the powerful Califano's turf. Nor, by this time, was the president himself interested in focusing attention on the troubled capital.

THE PRESIDENT AS PATRON: PUBLIC WORKS PLANNING AND MENTAL RETARDATION

As the first three cases suggest, much of what administrations do reflects environmental demands and expectations. At the same time, the interests and objectives of the chief executive should not be ignored. Some of these presidential concerns provided the rationale for specialized policy offices in the White House. This final section examines two such cases: the public works planning unit in the Eisenhower White House, and Kennedy's creation of an office to handle federal policy on mental retardation.

Only the latter achieved some degree of success, helping to get legislation passed in Congress. Given an overloaded White House staff and a sizable presidential policy agenda, it probably made sense to rely—much as both Eisenhower and Kennedy did in foreign economic policy—on subject-matter specialists to draft and lobby for desired initiatives. When it came time to implement policy or to oversee the actions of executive branch agencies, however, such structures became distinctly less effective as they ran afoul of entrenched agency interests and typically uninterested presidents. Moreover, neither of these specialized offices survived a change in administrations.

This instability was reinforced by organizational and environmental factors similar to those that pushed science advising down in the White House hierarchy. With both mental retardation and public works, more generalist White House staffers steadfastly resisted units that represented apparently "special" interests. These specialized White House offices also triggered the opposition of executive branch agencies on whose turf they allegedly trod, and a BOB anxious for budgetary discipline and greater managerial coherence frequently insisted on their dismantling.

In these two cases, too, unlike that of foreign economic policy, neither clear environmental pressures nor strong, well-mobilized constituencies necessitated an ongoing White House response. Without significant presidential commitment, these special-projects units fell victim to the organizational factors arrayed against them.

Eisenhower and Public Works Planning

The first example of structuring dependent on presidential patronage was the Eisenhower administration's public works planning unit. The office was created in August 1955, and John Stewart Bragdon (an adviser on public works to the Council of Economic Advisers) was named its first head. Initially, according to Bragdon, Eisenhower directed him to "determine the needs of public works throughout the U.S., organize and stimulate advance planning and long-range planning, and secure better coordination in the field of water resources."[125] The public works planning unit was relatively small, staffed by three or four professionals through much of its existence. Bragdon was named to the Civil Aeronautics Board in 1960, and an assistant, Floyd Peterson, was named acting special assistant for public works planning. BOB director Maurice Stans recommended liquidation of the office in 1960,[126] and President Kennedy took his advice.[127]

From the start, the public works unit faced considerable opposition from other parts of the executive branch and accomplished relatively little. Bragdon complained, for example, that "although I have on several occasions asked [BOB] to inform me of cases needing coordination [in the area of water resources and public works planning] this has not been done except for brief periods and random instances."[128] In any event, the agencies involved routinely refused to cooperate with the unit's attempts to "coordinate" their activities. The BOB also joined Treasury in blocking Bragdon's efforts to develop a contingency plan for public works construction during recessions.[129] Similarly, when public works staffers studied the interstate highway system at the president's direction, they confronted "agency jealousy and resistance, Congressional unwillingness to change procedures for allocating projects, and top [White House staff] unwillingness to take the time to understand the proposals for change."[130] In particular, Bragdon and his aides faced opposition to their proposal to introduce tolls on at least part of the system.[131]

Nor did Bragdon get along well with his White House colleagues. In handwritten drafts of a memoir of his White House years, for example, Bragdon labeled

> Adams [a] Little Napoleon, Seaton Politician "Nothing But," Merriam young politician on the make, Morgan another sub politician–hatchet boy, Pyle Politician Ultra-Conservative, Jack Martin shrewd No. 1 Boy, Persons "slick" = smooth correct.[132]

The nature of the public works policy arena during this time also added to the unit's difficulties. It was characterized by controversy over both goals (e.g., should public works be used as a tool to combat recessions?) and technologies (e.g., should the interstate system include tollroads?). In such a setting, with resistant agency officials and indifferent senior White House aides, an isolated public works office with authority only to coordinate could scarcely be expected to have much of an effect. Needed instead was more adversarial or adjudicative structuring, which would have permitted Bragdon to impose some presidential notions about desired executive branch activities. There is little evidence, however, that Eisenhower, once he created the unit, gave it much guidance or paid much attention to it. Under those circumstances, a collegial-competitive structure might have brought together some of the disagreeing parties, with White House officials perhaps providing mediation among competing agencies. Even so, without significant presidential or senior White House staff commitment, such mechanisms likely would have been largely ignored by key players.

Kennedy and Mental Retardation

Although Kennedy quickly eliminated the public works planning office when he became president, he established other specialized policy structures in the White House. In October 1961, at the urging of his sister Eunice Kennedy Shriver, the president announced the formation of a President's Panel on Mental Retardation, charged with evaluating current programs and making recommendations for improving research, treatment, and education.[133] Deputy Special Counsel Myer Feldman worked with Shriver in putting together the proposal for the panel, helped appoint its members, oversaw its activities, and sought agency comments on the final report.[134]

Despite opposition from the Department of Health, Education, and Welfare (HEW)—where many of the relevant programs were lodged—and the BOB,[135] in December 1962 Kennedy created the position of special assistant to the president for mental retardation to carry out the panel's recommendations.[136] Dr. Stafford L. Warren (a former chancellor at UCLA) was named special assistant, but he did not begin working full time until May

1963. Dr. Bertram Brown of the National Institute of Mental Health (NIMH) helped Warren set up his office, but Dr. Patrick Doyle soon moved from the Public Health Service in HEW to serve as Warren's deputy. Over the next several months, the office grew to include five other professional staffers.[137]

Much, but by no means all, of the staff's activity was directed toward passing legislation. Warren spent most of his time on outreach, trying to raise consciousness about the challenges of mental retardation: "he just did a lot of infiltrating, and proselytizing and advocating."[138] Even so, Warren's colleagues joked about their need to monitor his activities. Doyle recalled that "one of the most delightful things about Dr. Warren was that he was unencumbered by political insight."[139]

Meanwhile, Doyle probably undertook the widest range of tasks, assisted by others in the office. In addition to writing and giving speeches, he worked with the unit's advisory group and oversaw the operation of the office. Doyle also had the main responsibility for setting up a White House conference on mental retardation and spent an estimated quarter of his time working to get legislation passed in Congress. Finally, Doyle worked with various executive branch departments (mostly HEW, but also the Departments of Defense, Labor, and the Interior), encouraging them to follow up on the panel's recommendations.[140]

The office was structured hierarchically, with White House staffer Feldman, Eunice Shriver, and Sargent Shriver monitoring its operations. The three received weekly memos that summarized the unit's activities.[141] In addition, Feldman attended events sponsored by organizations dealing with retardation, discussed HEW legislative proposals and budget requests for programs involving the retarded with department and BOB officials and the Shrivers, and worked in Congress to get various proposals passed.[142] Although Feldman worked relatively closely with Warren's staff, Eunice Shriver recalled that all her activity involved Feldman: "It was all Mike. And he was terrific."[143] The two Shrivers were themselves quite active; they lobbied Congress and sought to encourage the clergy to become more involved in counseling on mental retardation and mental illness.[144] At least as important, they ran interference for the mental retardation office within the White House, easing access to the president and helping smooth relations with uninterested White House aides.[145]

Except for these links, the unit was fairly isolated from the rest of the White House. Although Doyle reported working frequently with the congressional liaison office,[146] Office of Congressional Relations (OCR) aides Mike Manatos and Larry O'Brien accorded mental retardation legislation "low priority." Other staffers were even less helpful. Appointments Secretary Kenneth O'Donnell, for example, "didn't . . . help in the least."[147] "He had no concept of professionalism at all" and, from the perspective of a mental retardation office staffer, failed to appreciate the possible political payoffs from focusing on mental retardation.[148] In general,

> the big problem was that mental retardation with the people right around Kennedy had a low priority. Sometimes you had the feeling that they were very condescending because Eunice was involved, and that they were going along because of this not because they had any real substantive interest.[149]

Meanwhile, outside the White House, "a lot of agency people . . . had to be dragged along by the napes of their necks."[150] The American Medical Association sharply resisted much of the retardation legislation.[151] And Eunice Shriver's agreement with the National Association for Retarded Children (NARC) that NIMH should not receive additional funding or authority because of its poor past performance drove a wedge between the White House and the agency. This "estrangement" increased when the Hospital Improvement Program and the National Clearinghouse for Mental Retardation were not placed in NIMH.[152]

Nor was President Kennedy particularly interested in the work of the mental retardation office. Indeed, Warren met with JFK only twice to discuss mental retardation.[153] According to Doyle, the president largely responded to his sister's intense concern with the issue.[154]

By October 1963, most of the mental retardation legislative package had passed, and the necessity of the White House unit became an issue. HEW Secretary Wilbur Cohen argued that his department should take over implementation of the legislation and the office's other tasks, in order to avoid "conflicting lines of responsibility."[155] Then came the assassination, and "the flavor went out of the chewing gum for the whole retardation effort."[156]

Lyndon Johnson created the President's Committee on Mental Retardation but placed it and the remaining White House mental retardation activities in HEW.[157] Without a presidential patron and with intense opposition from a key executive branch agency, the unit disappeared from the White House.

CONCLUSIONS

Beginning with Franklin Roosevelt, early modern presidents relied on specialized White House structures to address a range of policy concerns. Typically staffed with subject-matter experts, these structures were charged with developing and overseeing the adoption of initiatives or with coordinating and monitoring executive branch activities in particular policy areas. In some cases, the specialized units reflected idiosyncratic presidential interests. Other times, perceived crises underscored an apparent need for highly visible organizational responses. On still other occasions, external demand for governmental action and the absence of any reasonable response mechanism led to the creation of new White House staff units. Yet, as we have seen, the existence of such structures was frequently precarious: they were vulnerable to White House turf battles, environmental opposition, and declining presidential support.

Still, such structuring persists. President Clinton, for example, has relied on so-called war room operations for formulating health care and welfare reform proposals and for seeking congressional approval of the North American Free Trade Agreement. These collegial-consensual or collegial-competitive structures bring together White House staffers and subject-matter and political experts from in and out of government. Pushed by external pressures and reinforced by presidential efforts to demonstrate concern and responsiveness, Clinton and some of his predecessors have also created units to address policy problems such as AIDS, drug abuse, and government red tape. Although the cases examined in this chapter would lead one to predict that such efforts would produce some success, the cases also underscore their limited stability and suggest caution regarding their probable effectiveness.

PART III
Coordination and Supervision

10
Writing and Scheduling

The White House staff has grown in large part as a consequence of presidents' needs to extend their reach into both the national government and the political society that surrounds it. Part I examined the growth of White House capacity for direct outreach and negotiation with numerous political constituencies, and Part II focused on White House staff interactions with a variety of policy communities. In Part III we look at structuring for White House tasks that cut across these distinctions. This chapter explores the ways in which White House staffers were employed to link the president as an individual with the surrounding political and policy environments. Within the White House Office, this involved aides in two tasks: writing the president's words and scheduling the president's time.

These two tasks shared important elements. On the one hand, each involved a great deal of routine activity whose bearing on policy and politics was relatively remote. On the other hand, both writing and scheduling entail work that is politically charged, often policy relevant, and subject to environmental challenges and turbulence.

SPEECH AND MESSAGE WRITING

The importance of public speeches and messages to the modern presidency has long been recognized. More than 50 years ago, Thomas Dewey observed, in a classic overstatement, that "the man who writes the president's speeches runs the country."[1] Dewey's contemporary, Secretary of State Dean Acheson, noted more sourly that speechwriting was "often where policy is made, regardless of where it is supposed to be made."[2] These comments capture the most important feature of presidential writing: although technically routine and frequently having little or no substantive importance, writing can be the occasion for discovering and crystallizing policy content. When presidents must speak, they need to have something to say. If policy is unclear in advance of a speech, it often must be clarified in the writing process.

Warren Harding employed the first White House writer, Judson Welliver. Herbert Hoover, however, adhered to the tradition of presidents doing most of their own writing, although he did employ an administrative assistant for less important, ceremonial remarks. Hoover structured his own writing in a collegial fashion that anticipated the approach of his successors.

Structuring for staff writing first emerged under Franklin Roosevelt and remained relatively stable through the Kennedy administration. During this time, Dewey and Acheson pointed to the policy relevance of the writing process. Writing provided an opportunity for interaction among the president and top advisers, along with a deadline by which policy had to be articulated. The need to state policy often amounted to a mandate that policy be established, or at least clarified.[3]

In addition, these administrations generally structured the writing task collegially, which was congruent with prevailing decision settings. The Roosevelt, Truman, and Eisenhower administrations typically relied on collegial-consensual structuring. Writing was viewed as an exercise in building and clarifying shared values; it involved tapping a reasonably broad circle of writers and editors in order to ensure the best product. Hints of policy conflict appeared during Truman's early years and during the Kennedy administration. In both cases, the response was more collegial-competitive structuring, with representation of diverse stakeholders. Ultimately, of course, hierarchy obtruded, since presidents were active participants.[4]

However, since not all writing had policy relevance and most "minor" speeches involved little uncertainty or controversy, additional structural differentiation was possible.[5] Dwight Eisenhower, in the tradition of fellow Republicans Harding and Hoover, responded by naming writing specialists for these less substantive speeches. Similarly, Eisenhower placed the primary responsibility for writing "major" speeches in the hands of specialists,[6] although these writers also participated in the collegial-consensual structures. In general, writing specialists were placed at lower levels of the overall White House hierarchy. The general stability in structuring for writing ended under Lyndon Johnson. LBJ returned in part to the Eisenhower model by expanding the minor writing function into a small staff that supplemented the policy generalists who wrote major speeches. However, in the absence of workable collegial structuring, problems related to defining "major" and "minor" and coordinating generalists and specialists plagued the Johnson system. Underscored was the need for additional governance structuring, but the differentiation dynamic stalled, and such structures never emerged.

The emergence of governance structures for presidential writing during the early modern era can be attributed primarily to the extraordinary demands the environment placed on modern presidents for speeches and all sorts of other messages and utterances. Although the number of nationally broadcast speeches presidents make each year has not changed significantly since the Truman administration,[7] the number of policy statements to major groups, foreign appearances, and public appearances outside of Washington (all of which normally require at least the delivery of remarks) has risen sharply. Lyndon Johnson, for example, made an average of 49 "public appearances" in the United States during each year of his administration, compared with 13 for Harry Truman, 19 and 11 for the two Eisenhower terms, and 32 for John Kennedy.[8]

This increased demand is usually explained by changes in the fundamentals of U.S. politics. Samuel Kernell's suggestion that the political environment has changed from "institutionalized pluralism" to "individualized pluralism" captures these dynamics well.[9] The growth in the power and popularity of television and greater ease of travel, for instance, contribute in one way or another to making presidents increasingly reliant on direct access to the public, as does the decline of political parties as effective intermediaries. Likewise, the increase in the number and complexity of the problems and constituencies that presidents must address contributes to the pressure for more presidential communication.

The slow shift toward individualized pluralism beginning in the 1960s is consistent with the efforts in the Johnson White House to gain control over its burgeoning writing responsibilities. Looking to specialized writers for assistance also seems reasonable when so many of the demands for presidential writing were for minor speeches or ceremonial, nonpolicy remarks—what Bill Moyers once dismissed as "Rose Garden rubbish."[10]

This increased demand for speeches and messages required presidents to make strategic choices. The decision to take advantage of the potential audience for presidential remarks is itself such a choice, and not all presidents have responded with wholehearted enthusiasm.[11] But none has wholly resisted. Similarly, all presidents since Roosevelt have chosen to delegate at least most of their writing to others, and all have followed FDR's precedent of having the bulk of their remarks written within the White House Office. Still, as noted, different presidents made different strategic choices about the particulars of organization. Eisenhower's and Johnson's moves toward both increasing capacity and professionalizing writing by introducing writing specialists are the most notable examples.

Of course, an administration's organizational decisions tend to reflect more than conscious presidential choice. Organizational precedent, or inertia, also must be considered. Over the early modern presidency, only two basic approaches to structuring presidential writing emerged. This may be explained in part by new presidents' attempts to simplify some of their organizational choices by simply following precedent and incorporating large elements of their predecessors' organization. Indeed, it is rather striking that there is such stability, even across parties. Moreover, partisan learning is also evident, at least in the propensity of Democrats to prefer less formal systems than those used by Eisenhower (and his Republican successors).

In addition, the appearance of specialized writing staffs is consistent with a pattern of increasing specialization and consequent structural differentiation within the White House as a whole. At the same time, change within any given administration is bound to be inhibited by the oft-noted tendency of participants to protect their organizational turf. This likely reinforced the shift to specialized writers anticipated by Eisenhower and Johnson, and it helps explain the resistance of policy staffers in the Johnson White House to the perceived influence of professional writers.

Hoover: Hierarchical Structure, Collegial Process

Herbert Hoover was the last president to write most of his own speeches. Even so, he received substantial help from others. His administrative assistant—French Strother, then George Hastings—wrote mostly routine speeches and messages involving little or no policy substance. Strother, at least, occasionally worked on longer speeches.[12] In addition, Strother and Hastings did research for speeches, suggested speech topics, and transmitted speech ideas from elsewhere in government.[13]

Theodore Joslin, Hoover's second press secretary, provided virtually the only firsthand description of writing in the Hoover White House.[14] The president wrote with others present—among them, cabinet members and White House aides Walter Newton, Strother, and Joslin. The onlookers did not write but rather listened while the president dictated, made suggestions, and assisted with the physical production of drafts. Hoover was willing to take advice, but the final decisions on content and style were his. Hoover's approach thus embedded a strong element of collegial-consensual decision making within a structure that nonetheless emphasized the position of the president at the top of the White House hierarchy.

FDR: Collegiality and Top Adviser Involvement

Franklin Roosevelt, like all his successors, delegated the primary responsibility for writing to others. The first truly staff-driven structures for writing emerged during his administration.

Writing was a major activity throughout the Roosevelt years. Although others did much of the actual writing, the president was never far from the process. "The work that was put in on these speeches was prodigious, for Roosevelt with his acute sense of history knew that . . . his ultimate measurement would depend on the reconciliation of what he said with what he did."[15]

From the outset of the administration, the bulk of the writing was done by top advisers. At the beginning, the key speechwriters were the most prominent members of the "brain(s) trust"—especially Raymond Moley, who was the chief writer through the end of 1933, and Rexford Tugwell.[16] However, Moley left at the end of 1933, and Tugwell's influence waned at the same time.

The key writers on the second team were Ben Cohen and Tommy Corcoran, who combined speechwriting with legislative drafting and lobbying. From 1934 to 1936, Corcoran and Cohen were involved in virtually all major speeches. Even so, in 1933 and 1934, numerous others also drafted speeches, among them Felix Frankfurter, National Recovery Administration Director Hugh Johnson, and Roosevelt's son James; Moley often acted as a "screen" for major speech drafts.[17] The 1936 arrival of Justice Samuel Rosenman of the New York Supreme Court as an unofficial staffer led to a third phase, during which the key writers were Rosenman and Stanley High.[18]

High, a journalist, became attached to the White House in the campaign year of 1936 but left the next year. With his departure, Rosenman, Corcoran, and Cohen became the "regular speechwriting team" until the 1940 convention.[19] Rosenman established himself in a central position: by 1937, all speeches, messages, and press statements had to be cleared through him.

The final FDR team—Rosenman, Harry Hopkins, and playwright Robert Sherwood, with assistance from Archibald MacLeish—formed in 1940.[20]

Although Roosevelt nearly always involved his writers, he sometimes dictated a first draft himself and controlled the content through aggressive editing. Despite the plethora of writers, Stephen Hess observed that FDR's style was virtually constant.[21] Indeed, Rosenman contended: "One reason that [FDR] changed the make-up of his speech-writing team from time to time was that he found that the views of this or that person were becoming too sharply different from his own basic convictions."[22]

FDR's much discussed penchant for placing his assistants in competition with one another seldom extended to writing. Instead, writing under Roosevelt was essentially a team enterprise carried out through a collegial-consensual structure.[23] Writing was frequently accomplished through face-to-face collaboration, with the president himself an off-and-on participant in the group.[24] Roosevelt's personal secretary, Grace Tully, provided a detailed description of the typical process, which tended to begin with a memo or a speech draft from a department head or other relevant adviser. Roosevelt would then annotate or redraft the material before handing it over to the writing team. Then began a process of rewriting. After a draft was produced, a

> trial reading then would take place before such an audience as Hopkins, Sherwood and Rosenman and a free-for-all of suggestions, insertions, deletions and so forth would then be invited. . . . The average number of drafts was probably five or six, but I [Tully] recall as many as twelve on one or two occasions.[25]

An elaborate, more broadly consultative routine was developed for the preparation of the president's annual message to Congress, which became the State of the Union message in 1942. It was originally the product of the normal speechwriting process, but by the mid-1940s, preparation of this speech involved systematic inputs solicited from the Bureau of the Budget (BOB) and the major cabinet departments.[26] This process would become even more comprehensive in subsequent administrations.

Stephen Hess referred to writing in the Roosevelt White House as a "mechanism for forcing decisions."[27] An occasion for a speech or message often required that policy choices be made so that policy could be articulated. The collegial-consensual structure FDR created for this purpose did not produce broad consultation or the kind of extensive "staffing" that would characterize later presidencies. But it did keep the process close to the president, clearly under his ultimate control.

Truman: Continued Collegial Structuring

In the Truman White House, writing bore many resemblances to that function in the Roosevelt administration. There were many writers over the course of the administration, structuring was generally collegial-consensual, and the president was closely involved.

Immediately following FDR's death, Rosenman continued as a key writer, joined by several members of the new Truman team.[28] When Clark Clifford succeeded Rosenman in early 1946, Clifford immediately became the leading writer. Also important at this time were George Elsey (Clifford's only official assistant), Rosenman (who continued to contribute, at least during Clifford's incumbency), Administrative Assistant Charles Murphy, and White House staffers David Bell and David Lloyd. Press Secretary Charles Ross also participated, but only as a reviewer.[29] When Murphy succeeded Clifford as special counsel, Bell and Lloyd became the key members of the writing team, and Murphy assumed Clifford's role as head of the operation.

Through all the personnel changes, the process remained collegial, and a number of others participated. For example, Press Secretary Joseph Short participated regularly in speech conferences, as did John Steelman, Matt Connelly, and Correspondence Secretary Bill Hassett. Substantive policy specialists joined in when their expertise was required. Staffers from the BOB were especially likely to become involved and participated regularly in the preparation of the State of the Union address.[30]

During the early years, policy conflict arose on occasion, and collegial-competitive structuring emerged. Especially likely to clash were Special Counsel Clifford, leader of a "liberal" White House faction, and the more conservative John Steelman.[31] Even so, over the course of the administration, what Richard Neustadt called "collective drafting" in a collegial-consensual structure became more and more routine, especially during Murphy's tenure as special counsel.[32]

The special counsels understood their job to be partly one of liaison with and conduit for the rest of the administration. Murphy observed, "We had a regular operating practice to permit any department with a legitimate interest in the subject of a message to have a staff person participate in the work on that message. Sometimes this got to be quite cumbersome, but it was always done."[33]

The president sometimes joined these sessions or had Clifford or Murphy deliver a penultimate draft for his solo inspection.[34] Yet Truman's only certain participation, besides initial discussions at the very outset, was to preside over the "freezing session," where top advisers from in and out of the White House made final changes. "The President would go through the speech line by line and word by word. . . . Additionally, there was a thorough discussion of the substantive problems involved in the speech."[35]

The Truman administration produced a highly formalized procedure for producing the three major speeches and messages that were written on an annual basis: the State of the Union, the Economic Report, and the Budget Message. Murphy explained the process:

We developed a system whereby the Bureau of the Budget would request the departments to send in . . . their recommendations for legislation, indicating which portions they thought should be part of the president's program and which should be part of the departmental programs. The departments were asked to draft these recommendations in three versions: one for the budget, one for the Economic Report, and one for the State of the Union message. When they came in, the bureau would take the budget version, the Council of Economic Advisers would take the Economic Report, and the White House staff would take the State of the Union version. Then we would talk with each other and with the president about what we were going to do with all of the recommendations.[36]

Throughout the Truman years, the writing process was one of policy definition and discussion. Most of the key participants were primarily oriented toward policy substance; they were not writing specialists.[37] Structuring was collegial from the start, largely consensual, but competitive when the occasion required. As had been the case under Roosevelt, writing under Truman was intimately linked to the making, not just the marketing, of policy.

Eisenhower: Continuity and Exception

The Eisenhower administration stands as a modest exception during the early modern period, for his writers were not top-level staffers. Instead, they were specialized speechwriting aides, not the general-purpose advisers preferred by Democratic presidents Roosevelt, Truman, and Kennedy. Nevertheless, writing under Eisenhower shared important characteristics with the FDR approach: it was highly collegial, with much emphasis on garnering diverse inputs into speech drafts, and the president was closely involved.[38]

Several individuals held the job of administrative assistant in charge of "messages." The first was Emmet Hughes, a journalist who had worked in the campaign as a speechwriter. He left the White House in October 1953 and was succeeded by Bryce Harlow, a former congressional staffer who had been doing legislative liaison work for the president. In December 1954, Harlow moved to liaison duties with executive departments. His replacement was Kevin McCann, on leave from the presidency of Defiance College. When McCann left in February 1957, he was succeeded by Harlow, then Arthur Larson, and finally Malcolm Moos. The latter administrative assistants were each assisted by a junior staffer. What is notable about this group of aides is that, in contrast to such advisers as Rosenman, Clifford, and Sorensen, none was a powerful policy shaper within the administration.

Despite the presence of writing specialists, senior aides routinely participated in writing, though not in the relatively freewheeling manner of the Democratic administrations of the period. White House economic adviser Gabriel Hauge, for example, drafted all or part of most speeches that dealt with economic topics until his departure in September 1959. Aide Clarence Randall did some writing in the field of foreign economic policy, as did Appointments Secretary Bernard Shanley on domestic issues.[39] The chief of staff (Sherman Adams, then Wilton Persons) coordinated the process. Unlike earlier administrations, however, a writing specialist integrated the work of these top aides, and a careful clearance system involved many other staffers in editing and contributing substantive expertise.

Eisenhower's involvement in writing appears to have been somewhat variable. Roderick Hart, for instance, insists that the president typically "would not involve himself in the early stages of speechwriting" and edited "only after the hard intellectual work had been done."[40] Harlow partially contradicts this view: at least for the State of the Union, the process began with a conversation with Eisenhower.[41] Moreover, several record that Ike sometimes intervened early and continually. Stephen Ambrose, for instance, describes the preparation of the Chance for Peace speech of 1953 in which the president monitored "every word of the many drafts, often providing them with imagery and telling phrases."[42] By all accounts, Eisenhower was an aggressive editor.

Apart from the actual speech preparation process, Eisenhower did not interact with his writers on as close a basis as did Roosevelt, Truman, or Kennedy. Of the administrative assistants, only McCann was anything like an intimate, having written for Eisenhower before he became a presidential candidate.[43] Still, Harlow recalled agreeing to take the writing job only after Sherman Adams assured him that he could spend time with the president and learn how he expressed himself; this resulted in Harlow's being included in meetings of the cabinet, legislative leaders, and the National Security Council (NSC), and in presidential travel.[44]

Writing in the Eisenhower administration was definitely a policy-forcing and -clarifying activity. The elaborate structures of initiative and clearance were created with that in mind. In that respect, the Eisenhower system greatly resembled its predecessors and its immediate successor.

Kennedy: Reviving the Democrats' Pattern

John Kennedy was no doubt influenced in the handling of writing, as in other administrative choices, by the Truman experience. JFK worked closely with his special counsel, Theodore Sorensen, formulating speech themes and reading and editing drafts. Typically, the president called in top advisers for a discussion of the substance of a speech.[45] Sorensen then prepared the first draft, which Kennedy and substantive policy specialists who had been present at the first meeting commented on. "Finally, when there was agreement on content and emphasis, JFK would go to work on the text with his own pencil."[46] Kennedy's personal involvement in the writing process thus at least equaled that of Truman, though it fell somewhat short of Roosevelt.

Although Sorensen was the primary writer of substantive speeches and messages, many others also participated. President Kennedy sometimes read drafts to Press Secretary Pierre Salinger, National Security Assistant

McGeorge Bundy, and Appointments Secretary Kenneth O'Donnell for their comments and criticisms.[47] Staff from such agencies as the NSC and BOB also participated regularly.[48] The process of preparing major speeches and messages, especially the annual State of the Union, greatly resembled the Truman system, with Sorensen at the center, coordinating the efforts of department and White House staff as well as the BOB.[49]

Richard Goodwin was, during his relatively brief White House tenure (through November 1961), the number two speechwriter. He too could influence policy through writing: for instance, he headed a White House review of U.S. hemispheric policy, then wrote the Kennedy speech that embodied his ideas in the Alliance for Progress. However, Goodwin chafed at the limitations of this second-banana role, and his involvement in writing elicited some jealousy from Sorensen, which generally kept Goodwin farther away from policy issues than he would have liked.[50]

Sorensen was clearly the pivotal figure in writing, an adviser who shaped policy as well as presidential rhetoric. At the same time, the presence of substantive policy experts with access to the collegial writing structures meant that many could have at least some influence on expressions of policy. Indeed, since even offhand mention of, for instance, the arts or mental retardation in a presidential speech or message could raise public and governmental expectations, advocates such as Eunice Shriver actively lobbied Kennedy's advisers to include mention of specific issues. Shriver, an advocate of mental health reform, often approached Deputy Special Counsel Myer Feldman with her concerns, with the result, she reported, that "they'd put it in all the time."[51]

LBJ: The Beginnings of Change

In its early years, Lyndon Johnson's administration was heavily influenced by the Kennedy experience, in writing as in other things. Although there was no equivalent to Sorensen, most writing was handled by senior aides who also were involved in the substance of policy making, among them presidential assistants Bill Moyers and Richard Goodwin, National Security Assistant Walt Rostow, and Special Counsel Harry McPherson.[52] Writing assignments, as well as some of the actual drafting, were the responsibility in 1964–65 of Special Assistant Jack Valenti. Writing was handled in a collegial-competitive structure,[53] with the process serving as a focal point for the airing out of some of the administration's internal policy conflicts. Johnson—often highly knowledgeable about policy issues—was actively involved in writing, from the initial provision of detailed guidelines to the final editing.[54]

LBJ, a president who was intensely but sporadically concerned with the organization of the White House, produced one significant innovation in structuring speech and message writing: the development of a permanent staff of five to seven writers who handled the more routine, less politically sensitive assignments. This was a noticeable jump from its only precedent: Eisenhower's employment of a single junior writer in addition to the top writing aide. Even so, LBJ's writers, generally a talented group, never supplanted the top White House staffers as principal authors of the more important speeches, though their significance did grow somewhat in the later years of the administration. Johnson dealt directly only with the senior staff.

However well these arrangements may have worked early in the Johnson administration, they fared far less well as the years passed. As early as 1964, and certainly by 1966, a perception had grown in and out of the administration that writing was in disarray, a consequence of intensifying policy disagreement in the White House and the country as a whole, and of the confusion resulting from the lack of an orderly system for assigning and supervising writing.[55] By late 1965, Valenti had lost his coordinating role, although nobody fully replaced him.[56]

In 1965, President Johnson responded by bringing Robert Kintner, a broadcast executive, into the White House, partly to help organize the writing effort. Kintner and his assistant Charles Maguire succeeded to a degree, trying to bring both the specialized staff and the top advisers into a hierarchical structure for coordinating writing.[57] They also instituted a minor reorganization, merging the specialized speechwriting staff with a separate unit that handled special messages.[58] In addition, writer Robert Hardesty was transferred to the congressional liaison unit, charged mainly with writing material for speeches by friendly members of Congress.[59] Kintner, however, never exercised full control over writing. This was mainly due to the continuing semi-independent influence of top policy staff over writing. McPherson and his assistant John Roche met regularly with the specialized writers. All speeches were sent initially to Roche and then to McPherson for editing and revision.[60]

In mid-1967, Kintner left the White House. Charles Maguire attempted to take over his job but was less successful, due largely, in his opinion, to resistance from the senior staff.[61] In the view of one member of the writing staff, Peter Benchley, "chaos" erupted.[62] McPherson was then named chief speechwriter and tried to restore order, but with little success. Communication between McPherson and other top aides and the specialized writing staff became even more problematic. Benchley relates that McPherson "was not an effective intermediary between the writers and the President. Consequently, we often wrote speeches on our own ignorant presumption of what the President should, or wanted to, say."[63] In effect, the insistence by senior staff members on relative autonomy in their writing activities seriously undermined efforts aimed at creating orderly governance structuring.

Thus, the writing structures relied on by presidents from FDR through JFK broke down during the Johnson administration. Johnson and his aides searched for alternative arrangements but never found either the right structures or the necessary stability to produce fully satisfactory results. The top staff who coordinated or participated in writing never really found a way to constrain themselves to collegial-competitive structures within the general White House hierarchy, with the result that insufficiently structured competition caused confusion and anxiety. The specialized writing staff, although carefully structured, was too far down in the hierarchy to have much effect on the turmoil at the top and was, in any case, structured as a collegial-consensual operation, with little provision for representation of diverse policy interests. The differentiation that produced this complex structuring also generated a need for additional differentiation, which was not forthcoming.

The creation of a staff of writers below the top policy levels in the White House nonetheless represented an innovation that would last. Every president following Johnson has relied on a separate writing office, placed several levels down in the White House hierarchy and staffed by writing "specialists" who frequently have little if any policy expertise.[64]

Conclusions

During the early modern period, writing and policy deliberation tended to be rather closely linked. Writing often took place in collegial structures where diverse interests and specialties were represented and varying viewpoints explored. Closure could be reached because of deadlines for delivering speeches or preparing messages and because these structures were embedded in a hierarchy guided by vigilant presidents. Such structuring often was congruent with the uncertain and controversial decision settings these administrations faced. This might well have increased the probability of producing both "good" policy and a suitable link between the making and the articulation of policy.

There were, of course, no guarantees. Many of the policy pronouncements made during this period can be (and were) questioned. Some interests were not represented or were ignored, and presidents did not always closely monitor or become informed by the deliberative process.

Even so, the change that came with the Johnson administration—the emergence of full-blown professional writing staffs located several steps away from the president and other top advisers—is perhaps troubling. The introduction of this hierarchical element increased the likelihood of an unfortunate separation between policy making and policy explanation. In the Johnson case, there is evidence that this occurred, to the extent that the speech staff became involved in the drafting of speeches whose policy content incorporated significant uncertainties or controversies. And it was a precursor of the growing disjunction between writing and policy deliberation that has been observed in more recent presidencies.

The Venerable Tradition of the Appointments Secretary. Presidential secretaries long have interposed themselves between their presidents and those who would approach them. In the earliest days, when secretaries mainly handled stenography and correspondence, the screening and disposition of the mail served to place these aides in a strategic spot between the president and the public. Moreover, as guardians of the presidential office, these early secretaries bore responsibility for controlling the flow of presidential visitors.

The first secretary to serve as a noteworthy roadblock to access to the president was Abraham Lincoln's aide John "The Impassable Mr." Nicolay.[65] However, the model for the contemporary appointments secretary was fashioned by George B. Cortelyou, secretary to William McKinley. Cortelyou thoroughly supervised McKinley's daily schedule, providing the president each morning with a typed list of those who would be seen that day, along with the business to be transacted and other relevant information.[66] Cortelyou's successor, William "Stonewall" Loeb, Jr., secretary to Theodore Roosevelt, continued in this vein. Not only was Loeb widely renowned—and sometimes resented—for his ability to protect his chief from unwanted visitors, but he also took the lead in planning Roosevelt's travel schedule.[67] Loeb's centrality in the White House was underscored by the fact that he had the only telephone in the White House in those days before extensions.

The control of scheduling by strong individual staffers emphasizes the nature of the work. The job of managing appointments has two main aspects. One is the essentially routine activity of implementing the daily schedule. Although this places demands on the secretary's judgment and tact, the decision setting still can be characterized by goal consensus and technical certainty. Congruent structuring in such a setting is hierarchy—in this case, a simple one linking president and aide.

The second aspect of the appointments position is deciding what the schedule will be or, in the absence of a firm schedule, improvising one. This delicate matter of estimating the president's personal and policy priorities ultimately can be handled satisfactorily only by the president. But a sympathetic and experienced political adviser can help, both in counseling the president and in fielding the plethora of requests for the president's time and attention. Uncertainty or controversy over both ends and means may characterize such a setting. The consequences of seeing, or refusing to see, particular people can generally be estimated, but not always with certainty and only by a shrewd political operator; similarly, divining presidential purposes is an art dependent on wisdom and experience. The secretary and the president must be as closely attuned as possible. Additionally, when there is consensus on presidential objectives but uncertainty or controversy over the means of attaining them, collegial structures that include other White House staff aides may offer useful assistance to the appointments secretary.

The first early modern White House, Hoover's, did not structure the scheduling work in a manner congruent with this sort of decision setting; instead, market structuring prevailed. Under Roosevelt, however, congruent structuring emerged: a simple hierarchy linking the president and the appointments secretary and more informal collegial structures involving the secretary and other White House staffers. Such structuring mostly persisted through subsequent administrations, with variations reflecting the skills of particular appointments secretaries, their positions in the overall White House hierarchy, and growing environmental demands on the president.

Hoover: Division and Confusion

In Herbert Hoover's secretariat, the aide closest to the president was "personal secretary" Lawrence Richey, who also was the nearest thing to Hoover's chief of staff. In addition, Richey functioned in many respects as Hoover's appointments secretary. He was, for instance, responsible for the president's daily calendar, and he handled the mail.[68] Richey's general oversight of White House administrative matters anticipated a role that all appointments secretaries would continue to play. In part because of the breadth of Richey's responsibilities, however, he ended up sharing some of the appointments secretary's duties with Press Secretary George Akerson.

Akerson, like Richey a long-time Hoover aide and Richey's foremost rival on the staff, was primarily responsible for controlling journalists' access to the president, thus coming in for the inevitable heat generated by Hoover's reluctance to be interviewed. Members of Congress, likewise, tended to blame Akerson for the president's unavailability to them.[69] Adding further to at least the perception of Akerson as an appointments secretary was the fact that he was frequently charged with showing visitors into the presidential office.[70] In addition, Akerson scheduled Hoover's speeches and oversaw his travel itineraries.[71]

The main result of this overlapping responsibility, accompanied by rivalry between Akerson and Richey, was confusion. Those wishing to see the president were often unsure which secretary to see in order to get access.[72] It is no surprise that the arrangement also produced some dubious judgments. Horace Albright, director of the National Park Service under Hoover, recalled, "Lots of people had the feeling during that Administration that they couldn't get past those secretaries, and that they didn't use very good judgment in the people they turned down and the people they let in."[73]

Within two years Akerson was gone, having lost his battles with Richey, who was always closer to Hoover personally. When Akerson left the White House, journalists and others, including administration officials, hoped for more sympathy and better access, but they were disappointed. When Theodore Joslin took over, "it wasn't any time at all until he was just as bad as George Akerson. If anything, worse."[74] Joslin and Richey continued to share responsibilities, although relations between the two were considerably less tense than those between Richey and Akerson.[75] Indeed, if Joslin and Richey can be accused of generating internal problems, it is because they made too little effort to expose the president to conflicting views.[76]

Hoover's problems clearly resulted from his own strategic decision to allow ambiguity and competition to characterize the appointments function in his White House. Even Hoover's seeming devotion to the canons of the management science of his day failed to lead him to respect such principles as strict division of labor when he assembled his secretariat.[77]

Neither the division of labor nor the hierarchical ties in the Hoover White House were very clear, resulting as one would expect in some confusion and inefficiency. Instead, Hoover's arrangements were vulnerable to competition among his staffers. Richey and Akerson clashed over policy—especially over how much to expose Hoover to the press and public (see Chapter 3)—and were rivals for the attention of the president. Replacing Akerson with Joslin helped. But the problem that then arose—too little presidential exposure to conflicting information and ideas—was exacerbated by the overly protective secretaries' doubtful judgments. The diminution of conflict need not have precluded the kind of frank advice that could have helped the president transcend some of his own limitations. Hoover, however, did not get or seek such assistance.

Roosevelt: Defining the Job

Upon his inauguration, Franklin Roosevelt immediately designated Marvin McIntyre, who had first served FDR in the vice presidential campaign of 1920, to be appointments secretary. In designating a single aide to be responsible for this area, Roosevelt neatly solved the main problems that had bedeviled Hoover.

McIntyre virtually defined the job of the appointments secretary in the modern presidency. First and foremost, he managed the president's daily schedule, exercising a soundness of judgment that won him the respect of his White House colleagues.[78] Decisions regarding whom the president should and should not see are both the staple of the appointments secretary's work and the element most apt to be controversial. McIntyre was more successful than many of his successors in avoiding allegations that he denied access unwisely or for his own political reasons. In this he was aided by Roosevelt's personal secretary, Marguerite "Missy" LeHand, who, like McIntyre, controlled a door to FDR's office. LeHand was known to admit persons whom McIntyre would not approve, thus providing a useful safety valve without provoking any serious confrontations. LeHand and McIntyre informally forged a collegial relationship that added helpful flexibility to the basic hierarchy in its dealings with competing claims on the president's time.

McIntyre also inherited from Richey the task of general administrative supervisor in the White House, though the bulk of the routine administrative work was shouldered by the chief clerk. But when, for instance, Roosevelt wanted a cabinet meeting, he asked McIntyre to call it. Again, LeHand was a valuable colleague, managing the president's immediate office.[79]

Also like Richey, McIntyre was an intimate colleague of the president. He, along with the other secretaries, met with FDR in the president's bedroom each morning to go over, among other things, the presidential schedule. Unlike his forerunner, McIntyre cultivated cordial relations with the rest of the staff. Despite reports of tension early in the administration, the Roosevelt secretariat worked closely and collegially, bound by mutual admiration as well as strong ties of loyalty to the president. They were not, by any stretch, policy advisers. However, McIntyre, a veteran Washington operator, had extensive connections in the political community, was involved in congressional patronage, and provided political intelligence and advice. Indeed, Samuel Rosenman remembered him as "one of the few men who would frankly speak his mind to the 'Boss,' even though what he had to say was thoroughly unpleasant."[80]

When McIntyre temporarily left the White House for health reasons in early 1939, he was replaced by Gen. Edwin "Pa" Watson, FDR's military aide.[81] Already a virtual member of the secretariat, Watson fit into the job with virtually no friction. The amiable Watson's status as "one of the boys" can be seen between the lines of a letter Steve Early wrote to McIntyre in the summer of 1939, wryly criticizing Watson's propensity for wearing ribbon-bedecked uniforms at official functions, and noting:

> As for being an expert "bouncer" and keeping the Boss on schedule, Pa was very impressive at the beginning. However, he is slipping rapidly. Had he been on the job as you were during the long years from March 4, 1933, I doubt whether the President would be leaving the White House for the office much before the time for him to meet himself going back to the Mansion after the day's chores have been done. . . . However, he is the best we have in a pinch and we work with him, overlooking his omissions with tolerance and understanding.[82]

More seriously, Watson did come in for some criticism regarding political bias, or selective gatekeeping. Although not the active partisan political operator that McIntyre had been, Watson was well known to be one of FDR's more conservative aides. Some saw Watson as using his position to influence the president. For instance, Richard Neustadt recounts that Watson "helped shape the decision to dump Henry Wallace by making sure a steady stream of Wallace's opponents got in to see the president all through the spring of 1944."[83]

Nonetheless, Roosevelt's appointments secretaries successfully defined and performed a job that would become one of the clearest examples of institutionalization in the White House. Their closeness to the president—especially at the morning staff meetings—served to harmonize their judgments with FDR's preferences and to give the secretaries legitimacy when they played the necessary role of traffic controller for the Oval Office. Moreover, the degree of sympathetic discretion exercised by LeHand and her successor, Grace Tully, took the edge off any cumulative resentment that might have built up. Roosevelt's approach worked well enough to be a model to his successors. The problems that Harry Truman would encounter showed that there is more to success than having congruent governance structuring.

Truman: Institutionalization and Problems

Harry Truman named Matthew J. Connelly to the position of appointments secretary. Like his predecessors, Matt Connelly was a longtime associate of the president, having worked for the Truman Committee in the Senate, then as Vice President Truman's executive secretary. Connelly's duties greatly resembled those of McIntyre and Watson. He scheduled Truman's appointments as well as his outside engagements and speeches,[84] and he monitored the flow of paper to the president and controlled incoming phone calls.[85] In addition, Connelly oversaw routine White House administrative matters.[86]

Connelly also was a presidential intimate. Along with such aides as Donald Dawson, George Schoeneman, and Harry Vaughan, Connelly was one of the "people Truman liked to have around. They were comfortable. They were fun."[87] In addition, the appointments secretary was a regular at Truman's staff meetings and attended pre-press conference briefings.[88] At staff meetings, Connelly generally opened the discussion, going over the president's daily agenda and upcoming commitments and leading discussions of possible speech opportunities for Truman.[89] Connelly's duties also included helping to edit the president's speeches.

Connelly's performance of the appointments secretary's job was, for the most part, well regarded by his colleagues. Richard Neustadt, for instance, recalled that Connelly allowed top staffers access to Truman, though he might delay it on occasion.[90] Over other would-be visitors Connelly exercised considerable discretion "within limit—but his greater power was over timing of the visits of those powerful folk who couldn't be denied access."[91] As was the case under FDR, the appointments secretary also could be gotten around, since he controlled only one of the doors to the Oval Office. Perhaps the most admiring judgment on Connelly was pronounced by the president in a speech to a group of Masons:

> I brought [Connelly] along to the White House to keep the door for me. He does a remarkable job. He can make every one of you Masons believe that he is a Mason, and he can make a Knight of Columbus believe that he is a Knight of Columbus.[92]

Like Watson before him, Connelly was identified as one of the White House conservatives, and he drew fire for allowing this to affect his judgments.[93] In addition, as a Truman crony, he could be accused of jealousy. Connelly's particular bête noir was Special Counsel Clark Clifford. In Drew Pearson's telling, Connelly was one of "the little band of mediocrities around the President [who] just do not want brainier men than they are close to him" and who helped force Clifford out of the White House.[94] Clifford himself remembers that Truman associates such as Connelly and Vaughan held him in low esteem, though he dismisses this as part of the normal White House "struggle for power and recognition by the president."[95]

Also in the pattern of his predecessors, Connelly was heavily involved in partisan politics. His work included attending to patronage matters involving members of Congress.[96] To relieve some of this burden, he hired aides Joseph Feeney and Charles Maylon to work under him as special-purpose congressional liaison workers (see Chapter 2). Beyond that, Connelly was

> contact man for the politicians from all over the states. . . . I handled all the politics in the White House except for Truman . . . we maintained a liaison with the National Committee, to see about political things—working together is part of the game.[97]

In the end, it was Connelly's political connections that brought about his disgrace. Shortly after he and Truman left office, Connelly was convicted in a tax-fixing case and served time in a federal prison. Nonetheless, Truman "never wavered in his loyalty."[98]

Eisenhower: Variable Performances

Dwight Eisenhower's eight years in office saw three men fill the job of appointments secretary. Thomas Stephens was the first and the last, serving from inauguration through January 1955, then returning in March 1958 to finish out Eisenhower's second term. In between, Bernard Shanley served a term—briefly interrupted by his virtual dismissal—from February 1955 through November 1957. Robert Gray filled in between Shanley's departure and the return of

Stephens. Structuring remained mostly stable, and the tasks of these secretaries were quite similar to those of Connelly and his predecessors. The outcomes, however, clearly differed.

An Irish-born New York lawyer who had been Eisenhower's appointments secretary during the 1952 campaign, Tom Stephens brought to the White House the same kind of political savvy and connections that had characterized his predecessors. Although he was not as personally close to Eisenhower as Connelly had been to Truman, he was a respected adviser, especially in the realm of partisan politics.

Stephens's duties as appointments secretary were for the most part the ones that had become conventional. His most visible task was to supervise the president's daily schedule and to monitor the comings and goings in the Oval Office.[99] He was active as a liaison between the administration and the political community, including Congress and the Republican National Committee. He also participated in scheduling the president's speeches and, like his predecessor, was regularly involved in editing them.[100]

In the relatively complex organization of the Eisenhower White House, Stephens's job intersected the work of both the chief of staff and the staff secretary, creating at least the potential for some conflict and confusion. However, the staff secretary was able to relieve the appointments secretary of some of the administrative responsibilities shouldered by his predecessors. Stephens and staff secretaries Paul Carroll and Andrew Goodpaster worked collegially, with the staff secretaries occasionally providing backup for the appointments secretary and Stephens participating occasionally in monitoring and controlling the flow of paper to the president. Stephens's collegial relationship with Sherman Adams was similarly good, allowing Adams, Stephens's nominal boss, to have a strong voice in scheduling without undermining Stephens's routine authority.

A further collegial component was a personal secretary who occasionally exercised her own initiative. Ann Whitman would sometimes allow herself

> to be used as a conduit through whom certain officials got papers directly to the president, who might not have seen them if they had gone through the processes of the staff. One of the three interior doors to the Oval Office opened from her office. If she felt that the president would approve, she sometimes let people in to see him on short notice when no appointment had been scheduled.[101]

In 1969, when Richard Nixon's Chief of Staff H. R. Haldeman sought to solidify his own control of communication with the president, he moved personal secretary Rose Mary Woods down the hall, thus precluding what he called the "Ann Whitman end run."[102]

In early 1955, Stephens left the staff, ostensibly to practice law in New York, but principally to do political spadework for the 1956 presidential campaign.[103] He was replaced by Bernard Shanley, then White House special counsel. Like Stephens, Shanley had come to the White House from the 1952 presidential campaign. The job of appointments secretary changed little if at all under Shanley's stewardship. White House satisfaction with the work performed, however, dropped sharply.

Far more than Stephens, Shanley ran into problems over his political judgments about who should see the president. Soon after he took the job, for instance, Shanley was, in his words, "roundly criticized" by Republican partisans for letting labor leaders from the textile industry see Eisenhower.[104] Later, according to Ann Whitman, Postmaster General Arthur Summerfield told her "that Bern Shanley had three times refused to let him see the President during negotiations about his Post Office budget."[105]

When Eisenhower suffered his temporarily disabling heart attack in late September 1955, it provided an occasion for Sherman Adams to try to move Shanley out of his job. The relationship between the two was cool, in large part due to Adams's unwillingness to delegate to Shanley as much authority as the latter desired.[106] Although efforts were made to find Shanley another satisfactory staff job, he finally resigned on November 9, 1955. Shanley, however, repaired to Eisenhower, who overruled Adams and ordered Shanley back on the job as of the end of December.[107] Shanley finally left the White House almost two years later, in November 1957, to embark on an unsuccessful run for the governorship of New Jersey.

Shanley's problems as appointments secretary seem not to have been attributable to governance structuring so much as to the lack of fit between the job and the ambitions and attitudes of its incumbent. Collegial-consensual governance requires a common acceptance of the ground rules of collegiality, a condition particularly difficult to sustain when the colleagues in question are hierarchical superior and subordinate. When Shanley was replaced by Robert Gray, and then by the returning Tom Stephens, the controversy essentially disappeared.

Kennedy: A Return to Truman

Following the by now time-honored tradition of picking a longtime political associate to handle appointments, John Kennedy chose Kenneth O'Donnell for the job. O'Donnell was a crony of JFK's from his earliest political days and a charter member of the "Irish Mafia" that surrounded Kennedy in the White House. He was closer personally to the president than any of his predecessors had been and at least as influential. O'Donnell carried out the accustomed political tasks of the appointments secretary while broadening the job and adding a new dimension of policy influence.

O'Donnell's position was defined in essentially the same way that Matt

Connelly's had been. Since Kennedy abolished the White House staff secretariat, O'Donnell was responsible for overseeing White House administrative matters in addition to the usual tasks of scheduling the president's day and monitoring the Oval Office. Because JFK had abolished the job of chief of staff, O'Donnell also exercised considerable control over the flow of paper into the Oval Office. O'Donnell's partisan political contacts were extensive, allowing him to play an influential liaison role that also recalled Connelly.

O'Donnell's closeness to the president involved him as well in a wider range of activities than most of his predecessors. For instance, O'Donnell was initially very active in patronage matters, with patronage officer Dorothy Davies reporting principally to him. In addition, he took on the job of administrative officer for special projects—a separate position under Eisenhower—and in that capacity involved himself enthusiastically in opposition to the projects on the arts and mental retardation.[108] He also functioned in some capacity as a correspondence secretary.[109]

O'Donnell's real importance in the Kennedy White House, however, derived less from his formal responsibilities than from his closeness to the president. Press Secretary Pierre Salinger, for instance, observed that O'Donnell had greater access to Kennedy than any other staffer and had the "absolute confidence" of the president; "O'Donnell had the greatest influence in shaping the President's most important decisions."[110]

O'Donnell assumed a job that had been more narrowly defined under Eisenhower but had still proved challenging enough. With the consolidation of all of Connelly's former work plus O'Donnell's extra interests, the job became too big for one person. In response, O'Donnell extended the hierarchy to include a handful of his own aides. In addition to Davies in the personnel area, O'Donnell assigned a staffer to help him with administrative tasks. William Hartigan served in this capacity for the first eight months of the administration, taking charge of office assignments, the White House budget, and other general administrative matters, including serving as liaison with the White House career staff.[111] In May 1961, O'Donnell added John McNally to take care of such things as receiving gifts sent to the White House and dealing with White House visitors. When Hartigan left, McNally took on his administrative duties.

O'Donnell, like all appointments secretaries, was seen by some as an obstacle in their path to the president. But he worked hard to avoid being perceived as biased in his decisions, routinely checking with other staff members regarding the appropriateness of a visitor.[112] Top officials, including Salinger, McGeorge Bundy, Ted Sorensen, and Larry O'Brien, could gain access for "quick, informal visits" without appointments.[113] And, true to White House tradition, Kennedy's personal secretary, Evelyn Lincoln, managed to get people in without O'Donnell's sanction.

Johnson: Very Different Texans

When Lyndon Johnson assumed the presidency, his appointments secretary and office manager, Walter Jenkins, was generally regarded as the nearest thing to a chief of staff in the Johnson White House. When Jenkins resigned in the face of alleged sexual impropriety in October 1964, aides Jack Valenti and Bill Moyers shared Jenkins's duties for the duration of the presidential campaign. Valenti for a time retained overall responsibility for the appointments job, in addition to his other duties and interests. But the day-to-day work of the appointments secretary went to Marvin Watson, who joined the White House staff in February 1965. Watson held the position until January 1968, when it passed to his assistant, James R. Jones.

Walter Jenkins's relationship to Lyndon Johnson rivaled that of O'Donnell's to Kennedy, and his responsibilities were even more extensive. Jenkins's service to LBJ went back to Johnson's days in the House of Representatives. Jenkins performed the by now familiar roles of gatekeeper, monitor of the paper flow to the Oval Office, schedule planner, and top administrative officer of the White House. O'Donnell's abbreviated hierarchy reappeared; Jenkins had one assistant, Richard Nelson.[114] Like O'Donnell, Jenkins was heavily involved in patronage matters and served as a confidant to the president. He also was the designated White House liaison to the Democratic Party organization.[115] Stephen Hess described Jenkins's first-among-equals position in the LBJ White House:

> At first the President's staff had a semblance of hierarchy because of the presence of Walter Jenkins, who had served Johnson since 1939 and who functioned loosely, if not in title, as the White House Chief of Staff. Jenkins's age was closer to the President's, which also fortified his claim to authority over the younger assistants.[116]

Jenkins's sudden departure in the middle of a presidential campaign not only produced some immediate disarray but also caused longer-term problems, since his stature within the White House could not be fully replicated. Indeed, Hess suggested that the loss of Jenkins helped transform the staff into what Eric Goldman perceived as "a shifting band of individuals and groups moving in mutual suspicion around the commanding, demanding figure of Lyndon Johnson."[117]

For the duration of the campaign, Valenti and Moyers took on Jenkins's responsibilities, with help from O'Donnell, who remained in the White House until after the election. After the election, Valenti continued to oversee long-range scheduling but passed the day-to-day work of the appointments secretary, including routine scheduling and much of the administrative responsibility, to newly hired special assistant Marvin Watson, a longtime Johnson acquaintance and Texas political ally.[118] Soon Watson was performing virtually all the normal duties of the appointments secretary. Watson also assumed some of the political responsibility typical of the appointments job, taking on liaison with the Democratic National Committee and other such duties from O'Donnell, who worked mostly as a political specialist under Johnson.[119]

With Watson came Jim Jones, who assisted Watson with the routine appointments chores and also did political work, especially with Congress. In addition, Jones assumed much of the administrative responsibility that had occupied O'Donnell's aides, Hartigan and McNally. Watson's staff later grew with the addition of Douglas Nobles and David Bunn.[120]

Likewise in the tradition of O'Donnell, Watson soon became heavily involved in patronage and the political clearance of appointees. He was the linchpin of the "surrogate" appointments operation described in Chapter 4. Thus, Watson effectively gathered to himself most of the conventional responsibilities of the appointments secretary, including White House administrative tasks.

Although he acquired considerable influence, Watson never quite became another Jenkins. Special Counsel Larry Temple, who worked closely with Watson and then Jones, observed that Watson was closer to being a chief of staff than anyone else in the White House; at the same time, Temple noted that none of the special assistants had to go through Watson to get to LBJ, and a great deal of business bypassed Watson entirely.[121] Still, other aides resented Watson's influence.[122] Their allegations tended not to be ideological in content (though Watson was perceived as relatively conservative) but were aimed at his perceived narrowness and lack of perspective.[123] Nevertheless, Temple argued that Watson did not attempt to screen LBJ's appointments for ideology, that Johnson was quite accessible, and that in any case the president wielded ultimate control over the scheduling of appointments.[124]

Marvin Watson was appointed postmaster general in April 1968. Even before that, he relinquished his job as appointments secretary to his assistant, Jim Jones. Jones made no major changes in the routines established by Watson, and he was by no means the major White House player that his predecessor had been.

Conclusions

Thus, the position of appointments secretary and structuring for presidential scheduling provide impressive examples of institutionalization in the White House. The core duties of the job were essentially similar across all administrations from Roosevelt to Johnson, as were the incumbents of the office. With few exceptions, appointments secretaries were political veterans who were close—professionally if not personally—to the president. They were qualified to make difficult political judgments, likely to have the president's confidence when they did, and able to consult directly with the president when necessary.

In the main, they regarded themselves as extensions of the president's purposes and judgment. Their evident restraint in using their positions for their own partisan or ideological purposes is rather remarkable. Meanwhile, beginning with FDR, these responsibilities were handled in both hierarchical and collegial structures.

One additional pattern is clearly evident: the gradual growth of the appointments secretary's responsibility and, with it, the development of a small staff in the office. This was only partially a product of entrepreneuring on the part of the secretaries themselves. More clearly, the task expanded because the demands of political liaison and buffering for the president grew in an increasingly complex environment (as did, for instance, the jobs of legislative liaison and speechwriting). Meanwhile, the capacity of the political parties to absorb some of these pressures was gradually declining.

A final observation, though it can hardly be called a "pattern," is that in the more formally structured Eisenhower White House, the range of responsibilities of the appointments secretary did not grow in comparison with the range in the preceding administration. In fact, it shrank. One might imagine, therefore, a possible partisan difference, or perhaps one stemming from the degree of formal organization in the White House.

CONCLUSIONS

In the organization of both writing and scheduling, the early modern presidencies provide hints of what their successors would bring. In the area of writing, the gap between writing and policy that became evident in the Johnson administration did not prove to be a serious issue under Nixon. The writers during the Nixon years generally enjoyed a clear connection to policy deliberations and often played the role of advocates. Yet in all subsequent administrations, the detachment of writers from policy discussions would reappear as a serious organizational issue in the White House.

Scheduling under Nixon superficially followed the Eisenhower pattern of lodging overall responsibility in the chief of staff. Rather than the collaborative approach that Sherman Adams took toward appointments secretaries, however, H. R. Haldeman used his position as chief of staff to exert aggressive control over scheduling, virtually absorbing the most important duties of an appointments secretary. Haldeman's use of this tool to gain influence within the White House has been widely criticized in the subsequent debate over the danger and the necessity of a strong chief of staff.

11
Governing the White House Staff

The emergence of a plural White House staff, in the form of Hoover's secretariat, came in response to a perceived need to expand the reach of the presidency into the surrounding environment. This development, however, also added to the president's burden, since the staff itself now had to be governed.[1] Subsequent presidents increased the capability and complexity of the staff, and in doing so magnified the governance challenges they faced.

This chapter examines the various arrangements for governing the White House staff as a whole that appeared during the early modern era. In explaining structuring for staff governance, we are especially attentive to presidential preference because, in this area more than any other, presidents have had relative freedom to design structures according to their personal managerial strategies and philosophies, even though the need for such structuring often was dictated by environmental pressures and growing organizational complexity. Our analysis of these efforts therefore focuses more directly than earlier chapters on the frequently observed consequences of presidential strategy and style. The discussion is also more directly relevant to the ongoing debate over how best to organize the White House.

From the president's perspective, governing the White House Office involves ensuring that aides operate in ways that are consistent with presidential objectives and interests and coordinate their own activities. The Hoover and early Roosevelt administrations provide evidence for the congruence of simple, flexible structuring with these political and administrative demands. Although basically hierarchical, FDR's version easily accommodated collegial-consensual deliberation. The Hoover administration, lacking this capacity for collegial interaction, illustrates how failure to devise congruent structures can seriously handicap a presidency.

The clearest lesson to be drawn from the Hoover experience is the need for some sort of structuring for staff governance. Hoover's plural staff simply did not function as a collective entity. If a president wishes to forge a small band of assistants into an extension of presidential reach, some collegial-consensual structuring appears to be necessary, in addition to the general White House hierarchy. Such collegial-consensual structures allow aides to communicate with the president and encourage them to communicate with one another. The latter is especially important, both because staff members' work invariably overlaps and because communication can help overcome the problems of suspicion and jealousy that have always plagued courtiers. These difficulties were endemic during the Hoover years.

In a White House that places the president at the hub of the "wheel" of staff organization, the president must be personally involved; typically, this entails some arrangements for regular meetings with staff. A presidency featuring a strong chief of staff does not require such direct presidential involvement, but such a chief of staff most likely will have to play surrogate president, meeting with White House aides on a regular basis.

Certainly, one can imagine alternatives to such sessions. Paper, for instance, can substitute for personal contact. In the early modern era, however, all presidents after Hoover relied heavily on face-to-face contact for staff governance, but their approaches to designing and operating such governance structures varied considerably.

Especially during the Truman and Eisenhower years, the greatly enhanced demands on the presidency resulted in experimentation with significantly different solutions to essentially the same problem. Truman chose to expand on his predecessor's collegial-consensual structuring. Eisenhower, by contrast, relied on differentiation, producing an interlocking set of structures that for the most part were more strongly hierarchical than Truman's. Central to many of these new structures was the office of chief of staff. Presidential strategy is the clear explanation for the difference in these approaches to balancing the need for collegiality (e.g., in political decision making) with an equally compelling need for hierarchy (e.g., for coordination). Both approaches were congruent with significant elements of their decision settings, and both generally have been judged successful.

The Kennedy administration provides an unusual instance of partisan learning, a reversion to a model that was in some ways simpler than that of Truman. Kennedy sought to govern the White House by relying on a relatively flat hierarchy, with the president at the top; this, of course, is the "spokes-of-the-wheel" approach. Problems arising from the lack of a strong collegial-consensual linking of staffers to one another became evident during Kennedy's term and grew even clearer under his successor. Throughout his presidency, Lyndon Johnson sporadically searched for alternative structures, a quest that ultimately yielded little more than frustration.

THE SECRETARIAT: EARLY APPROACHES TO STAFF GOVERNANCE

In examining the Hoover and Roosevelt administrations, we pay particular attention to the composition and governance of the small core staff, or secretariat. The intimate size of these two presidents' staffs rendered distinctions between "formal" and "informal" governance unnecessary. By the end of the Roosevelt years, they would become more relevant: as the staff expanded and became more differentiated, the problem of governing a complex organization grew increasingly challenging.

Hoover: Coping with a Plural Staff

Herbert Hoover did not feel compelled to publicly explain his decision to expand the professional White House staff from the traditional single secretary to a staff of four—three secretaries and an administrative assistant. As we noted earlier, the move drew considerable criticism, with an *American Mercury* correspondent complaining that the "Big Executive" in the White House now needed a "whole machine-gun squad" to accomplish the work of one secretary.[2]

Prior to Hoover, the secretary to the president typically was more concerned with the personal and political aspects of the president's work (e.g., public and press contact, political strategy, scheduling) than with policy or executive branch liaison. Hoover, however, did not closely observe such precedent. In keeping with tradition, Lawrence Richey was primarily a personal secretary and master of political intelligence, George Akerson (and his replacement, Theodore Joslin) was a press secretary with appointments duties, and French Strother (the one administrative assistant) wrote speeches. Walter Newton's duties, however, included administrative liaison and oversight along with congressional relations; Strother (and his successor, George Hastings) devoted considerable time to working with Hoover's several policy advisory commissions.

The secretariat was hardly a ringing success. Richey came under incessant fire, principally for spying on others inside and outside of government, including his fellow secretaries. He and Akerson struggled mightily against each other. Akerson soon lost credibility, but his failings were nearly forgotten in the wave of criticism that engulfed Joslin. Newton was never seen as effective in either his legislative or his administrative roles. Meanwhile, Strother and Hastings orbited on the perimeter of power—and of usefulness. Little in the way of formal or informal governance structuring emerged. Hoover's reach was not greatly amplified; if anything, his failings were.

Even though Hoover neither resolved the problems of overlap inherent in a plural staff nor chose the most suitable aides,[4] the idea of a secretariat was clearly desirable, even necessary, for a presidency with activist aspirations. Until the Great Depression came to dominate the domestic politics of his administration, Hoover—in some respects a descendant of progressive Republicanism—aspired to be a policy innovator. Rather than responding to any notable change in the political environment, then, the development of a plural White House staff was dictated principally by the president's political strategy and policy ambitions.[5]

Roosevelt: The Emergence of Structuring

One need not make a case for Franklin Roosevelt as an activist, so it is not surprising that he continued plural staffing of the White House. This was compatible with FDR's political and policy goals, and, unlike his predecessor, Roosevelt was genuinely comfortable in such a setting. Roosevelt's initial secretariat mirrored Hoover's only in the designation of a press secretary, Stephen Early. Louis Howe was an all-around adviser who concentrated on political tasks but also engaged in various kinds of administrative oversight. The last of FDR's three secretaries, Marvin McIntyre, became appointments secretary.[6] Again, the secretariat was a hybrid of the personal-political and the policy-oversight realms, with emphasis on the former.

The death of Louis Howe did not end the secretariat's involvement in administrative oversight. Within a few months he was succeeded by James Roosevelt, who concentrated more of his effort in this area than Howe had.[7] James Rowe, who succeeded Jimmy Roosevelt and performed the same basic duties, was given the title of administrative assistant (AA)—one of the three original AAs appointed in July 1939. The tasks of the press and appointments secretaries continued as before—indeed, as we have seen, they became permanent elements of the institutional White House. The concern of the president's secretaries during this period with such things as liaison and administrative monitoring was not the product of negligence or happenstance. It clearly grew from and reinforced the Brownlow Committee's perception that the president needed help in coping with the growing federal government. With the arrival of the Brownlow-mandated AAs in mid-1939, the tendency of the secretariat to expand in this direction largely halted.[8] Rowe's designation as an AA reflected the administration's sense that secretaries were not to be policy assistants. The only new secretarial duty created after that point was that of correspondence secretary in early 1944.[9]

Unlike Hoover's aides, Roosevelt's staff generally worked in harmony with both their boss and one another. Camaraderie among them was high.[10] FDR began his days by meeting with his aides, thus giving them not only a degree of coordination and direction that Hoover's staff had lacked but also a chance to become informed about one another's work and to air any grievances they might have. In this area, Roosevelt, whose approach to management has been criticized as haphazard by nearly all but his most ardent admirers, clearly had hit on a device that worked. Moreover, as in speechwriting, FDR approached this aspect of governance without stimulating competition among his aides.

Roosevelt's morning meetings, which took place in the president's bedroom and lasted about half an hour, provided an opportunity for discussion of matters of policy and governance as well as routine assignments and the daily schedule.[11] The warmth and informality of these meetings also fostered a milieu in which staffers could speak freely. Marvin McIntyre in particular was known for his rare ability to tell Roosevelt hard truths that others were reluctant to articulate.

When the White House staff grew abruptly in 1939 and thereafter, Roosevelt, by now preoccupied with impending war, did not incorporate his new aides into any orderly system. As Richard Neustadt put it: "to run a staff in Roosevelt's style imposes heavy burdens. He himself dropped some of them during the war."[12] The AAs tended to hover on the fringes of White House governance, a tendency consistent with their frequent assignment to tasks of a specialized nature that were rather far removed from the immediate purview of the president.[13] Even the longtime secretaries fell out of the presidential orbit somewhat. Jonathan Daniels recalled asking his boss, Marvin McIntyre, a question about reporting to FDR in October 1942, only to be told,

> "Hell, you see the President as much as I do." I must have shown my surprise because he said, "Of course, I see him seven or eight times a day, but I never get a chance to talk to him any more and am hardly ever with him without somebody else. That is the reason I have to do a lot of these things I do without consulting him."[14]

Nonetheless, Roosevelt met with at least some of his senior staff for the remainder of the administration. Although these staff meetings were most often collegial-consensual (within the context of the overall White House hierarchy), they could become effectively hierarchical, collegial-mediative, or adjudicative, depending on the issues at hand. Roosevelt could efficiently give marching orders, encourage brainstorming, or settle disagreements as the situation required. At least for the inner circle of staff involved, this flexible governance tool was congruent with its setting and clearly successful.

TRUMAN: RESPONDING TO MOUNTING RESPONSIBILITIES

The Truman White House was the last one in which the distinction between "secretaries" as a group and other White House aides was much noted. Truman's secretariat consisted of the by then conventional elements: a press secretary (initially Charles Ross), an appointments secretary (Matthew Connelly), and a correspondence secretary (Bill Hassett for most of Truman's presidency, then Beth Short). Their work continued in the vein of FDR's last secretaries, emphasizing the personal and political dimensions of the president's job but with relatively little involvement in the work of policy formulation or implementation. The secretaries were distinguishable from the administrative assistants, who tended to be subject-matter specialists and reported to Truman through either the special counsel, especially during Charles Murphy's tenure, or the assistant to the president, John Steelman.[15]

Organizational inertia and a need for continuity in the crisis of Roosevelt's death rather than presidential governance strategy largely dictated these arrangements. Nevertheless, Truman was quite comfortable with them.

Staff Meetings

Like Roosevelt, Truman's preferred device for coordination of his staff was the daily staff meeting. Initially, Truman followed FDR's practice of limiting participation to the secretaries and their assistants, but soon the military aides began to attend, as did top advisers such as John Steelman and Clark Clifford. By early 1947, some administrative assistants such as Donald Dawson, Charles Murphy, and David Stowe had begun to attend as well.[16] In part, Truman's broadening of participation was in response to requests from several aides, including military aide Harry Vaughan and then Naval Aide Clifford.[17]

Early in the administration, these staff meetings were controversial. Attendees were accused of constituting a "kitchen cabinet" or a gathering of presidential "cronies." For a short time in the spring of 1946, the sessions were even discontinued, but they were soon reinstated when aides complained that they found it hard to know what was going on in the White House.[18] At this point, Truman's decision to resume broad-based staff meetings can be seen as a strategic choice, grounded partly in his need to manage sometimes difficult office politics and partly in a growing realization that the meetings served his broader purposes.

Truman's staff meetings, like Roosevelt's, provided a chance for discussion of routine matters, such as the daily schedule, as well as policy questions. Given their composition, they tended to be considerably more policy oriented than FDR's morning talks. The format of the sessions became routine, as described by press secretary Charles Ross in 1949.[19] Ross would begin, followed by Steelman (who did "not bother the President with anything unnecessary" and spoke "tersely"), Murphy, Dawson, and Connelly. Then Special Counsel Clifford would present "varied items," many of which concerned foreign affairs and the work of the State Department, but also "other things, legislation and matters that seem outside his bailiwick and that, at times, seem to intrude on the work of others." Finally, Hassett, the military aides, and executive clerk William Hopkins would hold forth.

Hopkins, a longtime White House careerist, believed that the meetings were highly successful, since they "conserved the President's time and . . . tended to keep all the staff better advised as to what their colleagues were doing and tended at least to keep everybody moving in the same direction."[20] Others agreed. Clifford aide George Elsey, for instance, fondly recalled the "free and easy atmosphere,"[21] and Administrative Assistant David Stowe credited the staff meetings with facilitating coordination.[22] Even the evident animosity toward Clifford that Ross confided in his diary probably was diffused somewhat by the opportunity for others to become informed of the special counsel's activities and to question him directly. Later, when Charles Murphy replaced Clifford, such tension largely dissipated.

Truman's staff meetings had the same flexible governance properties as Roosevelt's. However, Truman's strategy of broadening participation changed their tone and focus. The larger and more diverse group limited opportunities for informal brainstorming, but it created more chances both for adjudication of policy disputes and for collegial-competitive argumentation. Not only did the meetings help keep the staff informed, but they also allowed the president to remain at the center of staff activity and communication.

This was a system consistent with President Truman's conception of his job and congruent with the basic requirements of staff management. For a different chief executive, however, an approach that was so time- and energy-consuming would be far less appealing.

Informal Structures

The Truman White House grew well beyond the size of its predecessor, primarily due to the inloading of the remnants of the Office of War Mobilization and Reconversion, along with erstwhile OWMR Director John Steelman. Steelman and his aides occupied the East Wing of the White House, and the rest of the staff—those with jobs tracing to FDR's administration—inhabited the West Wing. With the rise of the ambitious and controversial Clark Clifford to prominence in the West Wing, the potential for rivalry and staff conflict was high. The daily staff meeting assumed great importance in such a setting, but it was not enough to deal with all the tensions that inevitably surfaced.

In part, Clifford and Steelman clashed because of Clifford's aggressiveness, Steelman's limitations, or both, depending on which observers one believes. The basic problem, however, was more likely the putative separation of "policy" and "operations" that distinguished their jobs (the former Clifford's responsibility, the latter Steelman's). Such a distinction seldom works out in reality, and the two men did not always succeed in making sense of it. Clifford began early in his tenure, for example, to serve as liaison with cabinet officers who were unhappy with Steelman's performance in that role.[23] Their difficulties were aggravated by ideological differences between the moderately conservative Steelman and the liberal Clifford.[24]

When such tensions appeared, the most effective antidote often was provided by informal relations among their assistants. Steelman aide David Stowe recalled that he, Clifford staffer George Elsey, and Administrative Assistant (and sometimes informal Clifford assistant) Charles Murphy fruitfully coordinated their work, trying to avoid conflict. Murphy's involvement, which included dropping in on Steelman's staff meetings, was especially important.[25] When Murphy replaced Clifford in early 1950, he continued to be cooperative. This pleased Steelman, who was bothered by conflict among staff members and saw his own staff as a "ball team."[26] In fact, Murphy noted that Steelman, rather than being territorial, had a tendency "to let his business drift my way."[27] In addition, Steelman's and Murphy's staffs had many members who had been at the Bureau of the Budget before coming to the White House. These aides found it quite easy to work smoothly together.[28]

EISENHOWER: EXPERIMENTING WITH STAFF GOVERNANCE

The positions of press and appointments secretaries continued under Dwight Eisenhower, but that of correspondence secretary did not. The term "secretariat" came to have renewed, if different, significance due to the creation of the staff and cabinet secretariats. Although the staff secretary and the appointments secretary worked closely together, the notion of all the White House secretaries constituting a single secretariat disappeared. Instead, Eisenhower created the position of chief of staff and augmented that with the staff secretariat, each in its own way responsible for staff management and coordination.

The continuation of the press and appointments jobs indicates not only a certain organizational inertia but also the success of the incumbents in those positions before and during the Eisenhower years. Presidential strategy, however, was clearly responsible for both the downgrading of the correspondence secretary's job and the development of the new positions and offices.

As the number of top policy staffers grew and structural differentiation increased, the problems of governing the White House multiplied as well. Eisenhower experimented with a variety of approaches, including staff meetings. Over time, however, he evidently concluded that the role of staff meetings, and that of the president in White House governance, should be much more limited than it had been under his predecessors.

Staff Meetings

From the beginning of the administration, Eisenhower met weekly with senior staff, prior to press conferences. These meetings were part of an elaborate pre-press conference briefing process and focused on preparation for reporters' questions. Thus, they did not reliably perform the overall coordinating and informing functions that staff meetings had for Roosevelt and Truman.[29]

Regular staff meetings of the sort that Roosevelt and Truman had used became the province of Chief of Staff Sherman Adams rather than the president. Initially, Adams called and chaired daily morning meetings, with Eisenhower in attendance only on Mondays.[30] As many as 25 top staff members typically attended. Despite the numbers, the sessions were not stiff, choreographed affairs. Special Counsel Bernard Shanley recalled one meeting, at which he presided in Adams's absence, as "a good free for all" and another as a "bitter" discussion.[31]

As the administration progressed, the frequency of meetings dropped, as did the likelihood of Eisenhower's presence. By the end of the first term, staff meetings were held only two or three times a week;[32] soon afterward, the sessions took place more or less weekly, with normal attendance at about 30. Adams continued as the regular chair, and Eisenhower did not usually participate. In early 1959, Wilton Persons, who had replaced Adams, instituted a regular Monday meeting involving only eight top staff members, again without the president.[33]

The Eisenhower experience points to several conclusions. First, it is possible to effectively employ a top staffer as a surrogate for the president, as long as it is generally understood that this aide clearly speaks for the boss. Adams's staff meetings appear to have accomplished many of the purposes that Truman's did, despite Eisenhower's far more limited participation. Second, the declining frequency of staff meetings over time suggests that, for a staff as large and complex as Eisenhower's, such sessions are not likely to be as central to orderly governance as they are under the more intimate and fluid circumstances of a White House like Truman's. Finally, Persons's attempt to initiate smaller staff meetings is evidence that, for some purposes at least, it is possible for such structures to become so large as to be unwieldy.

An additional reservation must be advanced as well—one that applies to the Eisenhower White House in several areas. Extensive staffing prior to presidential involvement has many virtues, including full consideration of options and the opportunity for coordination. Yet it can easily lead to trade-offs and compromises that effectively round off the sharp edges of policy debate before the president has had a chance to participate. For a president like Eisenhower, who was not generally interested in radically changing policy, this may have been acceptable. But it held little promise of leading him beyond the limits of such an approach to policy making, if that had been desirable.

Chief of Staff

Even by Truman's time, the White House staff had grown to the point where simply coordinating its various elements had become a challenge. The size of the White House staff was, in Samuel Kernell's phrase, "no longer limited by the president's span of control."[34] Eisenhower's more formally structured and hierarchical approach to governance had an answer to this challenge: the position of chief of staff. Sherman Adams, the former New Hampshire governor and campaign chief of staff whom Eisenhower appointed to the job, described the position:

> Eisenhower simply expected me to manage a staff that would boil down, simplify and expedite the urgent business that had to be brought to his personal attention and keep as much work of secondary importance as possible off his desk.[35]

Adams was responsible for coordinating all staff activities other than those involving foreign affairs, a job of such wide-ranging responsibility that the press readily dubbed him "the assistant president." Adams had principal responsibility for patronage and personnel, and he oversaw other White House functions such as scheduling, press, writing, and congressional liaison.[36] In general, he controlled staff members' access to the president.[37] Still, Adams stressed that he was a manager rather than a policy maker and that he was not given delegated presidential authority, although his broadly defined "duties and responsibilities were implied rather than stated."[38]

For the most part, Adams's characterization is accurate. Obviously, anyone standing at the nexus of presidential authority and activity as he did was bound to have influence over policy, but he seldom pushed an agenda or aspired to control policy outcomes. He was essentially a process manager and, as Stephen Hess put it, Eisenhower's "personal 'son of a bitch.' "[39] Adams's task was to facilitate and coordinate the myriad governance structures of the Eisenhower White House and to strive for enhanced efficiency in White House operations. He was well positioned for the job, at the top of a relatively hierarchical White House organization. Even so, as we have repeatedly observed, the Eisenhower system was far more diverse and flexible than the caricatured "military model" its detractors envisioned. Indeed, given his governance duties, Adams could scarcely have afforded to be simply the rigid martinet he was sometimes portrayed as being.[40]

Adams resigned in late 1958, the victim of personal and official entanglement in the affairs of Bernard Goldfine, a businessman who got into trouble with two federal agencies. His place was taken by legislative aide Wilton Persons, whose style was far more relaxed than that of the laconic, humorless Adams. The Eisenhower system was by then firmly in place, so the difference in tone brought by Persons made only a marginal difference in White House governance.

Staff Secretariat

As it became clear in the 1940s that a large and complex White House staff would be a permanent element of the modern presidency, scholars and practitioners of administration began to consider the problem of organizing it. One of the earliest suggestions was a staff secretary, envisioned as a non-political careerist whose prime duty would be to monitor and coordinate the flow of paper throughout the White House. The first such recommendation came from the first Hoover Commission, and it was actively discussed in the Truman White House.[41] However, Truman, who typically resisted formal organizational schemes, declined to implement this one. Nor did he need to. William Hopkins recalled that "the flow of paper in the White House office under President Truman was probably the best I have experienced."[42]

Eisenhower did not employ a staff secretary immediately, but the idea was pressed on him early by management consultant Carter Burgess.[43] Presumably, it was on the president's mind when, on two occasions recalled by Andrew Goodpaster, he grew frustrated with staff slipups. After the second, he fumed to an aide: "I said just a week ago I was not going to be my own Sergeant Major and I'm not. I'm going to have a Staff Secretary and [Brig. Gen. Paul] Carroll, you are it."[44] Along with assistant Arthur Minnich, Carroll set up the first staff secretariat in the fall of 1953.

Although political appointees operated the staff secretariat rather than the careerists the Hoover Commission recommended, its workings had little to do with politics or policy. The basic duty of the office was to review all papers intended for the president and route them to the right people, as well as to co-ordinate the dissemination of papers coming out of the presidential office.[45] The staff secretariat became, in the words of Wilton Persons, "the one office in the White House that knows the most about what is going on and where it is taking place."[46] In its early years, the staff secretariat also attempted to monitor executive agencies, but it fell short of Eisenhower's expectations, leading to the creation of the cabinet secretariat in the fall of 1954.[47]

When Carroll died in September 1954, he was succeeded by Goodpaster, a fellow army officer. Goodpaster served for the rest of Eisenhower's presidency; Minnich continued as assistant until August 1960, when he was replaced by James Lambie.[48] This continuity facilitated the efficiency and dependability for which the staff secretariat had become known.

The staff secretariat, a simple hierarchy, was clearly an effective organizational response to the growing volume and complexity of routine White House business. In effect, it abstracted the hierarchical element of Truman's flexible staff arrangements, orienting itself toward those aspects of the White House decision setting with which a hierarchy was congruent.

Informal Structuring

The formally structured Eisenhower White House, led for most of its time by the formal-minded Sherman Adams, did not develop many informal governance structures of the sort found under Truman. Relatively informal structures did emerge for handling such tasks as speechwriting and policy deliberation, but informal structuring tended to be limited in scope.

KENNEDY: THE PRESIDENT AS HUB

In one sense, the story of formal staff structures in John Kennedy's White House is a simple one: there were virtually none. Since Kennedy organized the White House in a manner reminiscent of Truman, this raises the question of how communication and coordination were accomplished, if indeed they were. The answer is that Kennedy accomplished at least the minimum necessary in these areas through a strategy of holding frequent ad hoc meetings with individuals or small groups. Kennedy disliked formal group sessions and therefore avoided them as much as possible.[49]

To supplement Kennedy's mostly bilateral approach to staff coordination, staff members also interacted in ad hoc sessions with some frequency. As journalist Joseph Kraft noted, however, coordination was not a primary concern among a staff whose

> relationship (despite the talk of the Irish Mafia and the Harvard clique) is neither partnership nor feud, but a kind of disengagement, rein-

forced by separateness of function and personality. Formal papers are at a minimum, but all staff members are encouraged to bring to the President all official problems.[50]

Aide Harris Wofford agreed, contending that there "was not a great sense of clearing everything and having everybody there; there was a great sense around the White House of sort of 'do your thing.' "[51] The critical bilateral relationships and relative structurelessness were undergirded by a high degree of staff loyalty to Kennedy. Walt Rostow noted that

> Once someone was taken in to be a part of that wheel he stuck. The tie wasn't made casually. . . . Kennedy made a fairly quick judgment as to whether he would take somebody in or not; but once he decided, then that relationship was reliable.[52]

Although transition adviser Clark Clifford suggested to Kennedy that he maintain the staff secretariat, JFK resisted.[53] He did retain the title of staff secretary, which went to Ralph Dungan, but the president rejected the orderly, hierarchical structuring as inconsistent with the free-flowing approach he preferred. Although both Dungan and Appointments Secretary Kenneth O'Donnell did some monitoring of the paper flow, they did not control it like Goodpaster and Minnich.

Kennedy's approach was clearly the result of a strategic choice that was not fully made in emulation of Truman or anyone else. Most observers report that, on a day-to-day basis, the arrangements worked. They depended heavily, of course, on the willingness of the president to sustain extensive bilateral communication as well as the staff's ability to coordinate informally. Whether Kennedy could have sustained this over four or eight years seems a reasonable question,[54] as does whether one-to-one staff coordination should be regarded as the best expenditure of a president's time. Nonetheless, for the duration of the administration, Kennedy's governance arrangements mostly achieved their goals.

JFK's approach clearly did not always lead to the kind of consultation that fully aired out the relevant considerations or action alternatives. Similarly, Kraft has questioned whether such a system could lend itself to the creation of programs, as opposed to immediate responses to events.[55] Still, the arrangements fit Kennedy's main purposes; he was a pragmatic problem solver, not a planner.

Informal Structures

Since Kennedy's staff was a throwback to the Truman model, one would expect informal governance structures to be important within it. Indeed, informal structuring grew. One example is the ad hoc meetings of staff members that became so routine that they substituted in part for general staff meetings. At times, these stabilized into more formal collegial-consensual governance structures. For instance, as Chapter 6 detailed, Cabinet Secretary Fred Dutton and civil rights advisers Harris Wofford and Frank Reeves cooperated routinely on civil rights matters, working with the departments as well as other aides in the subcabinet group on civil rights. Cooperation between Richard Goodwin and Arthur Schlesinger on Latin American policy provides another example, though of a more transient and informal sort.

Such structuring, like its Eisenhower counterparts, was not primarily intended to handle conflict. More closely analogous to the circumstances of the Truman era was the perceived split on the Kennedy staff between the "Irish mafia" and the "Harvard intellectuals." Especially at the beginning of the administration, this schism was anticipated to play a major role in the politics of the Kennedy White House.

Things did not quite work out as predicted, however. In fact, most observers have noted that in the loosely organized, mostly collegial Kennedy White House, these factions were not as important as many expected they would be.[56] Nonetheless, there was enough concern about such divisions that Dutton saw himself and staff secretary Ralph Dungan as intended by the Kennedy brothers to constitute a "third group" not tied to either faction. Dutton commented, "I thought my charge was to stay between them. I think I was less effective in terms of the White House staff and maybe less effective in my own self-interest by trying to honestly observe this third group rule."[57] Dutton (though not Dungan) rather quickly became a marginal White House player, a problem he attributed to his belonging to neither "group." The informal, Murphy-like role he envisioned simply proved unnecessary.

JOHNSON: THE CHALLENGES OF INFORMALITY

Overall, Lyndon Johnson had little more faith in staff meetings than his predecessor had. Although LBJ met in the morning with a few top aides in a manner reminiscent of FDR, infrequently held general staff meetings, sometimes met with a few senior aides, and occasionally suggested that somebody else call a staff meeting, his preferred approach was to gain information and give assignments in bilateral meetings with staffers.[58] Johnson abolished even the title of staff secretary. Overall, the Johnson administration's experience paralleled its pattern in other areas of governance: sporadic attention by the president to organizational matters, occasional entrepreneuring by staff members, but little follow-through and no real progress toward solving the recurring problems of governing a dynamic but contentious and unwieldy organization.

The first example of regularized staff meetings occurred in early 1965, when Bill Moyers, at the president's request, began to hold regular gatherings that did not include LBJ. Over time, however, "such efforts tended to dissipate toward meetings of a few who needed to coordinate their efforts."[59] Concern about leaks from the sessions also limited the president's enthusiasm for them.

In May 1966, with Moyers now the press secretary, new Cabinet Secretary Robert Kintner, pursuing his mandate to better organize the White House and at LBJ's specific request, began calling regular meetings.[60] At the initial gathering, 18 aides were invited and attendance was good, including Vice President Humphrey. In the first few sessions, a range of topics was discussed, including management issues (e.g., the volume of the president's night reading) and policy (e.g., economic aid to Vietnam). Those in attendance welcomed the forums; in fact, the sessions' success sparked a flood of requests from other staffers for inclusion. By January 1967, the list of invitees swelled to 35.[61] The meetings had become unwieldy and less useful than before, prompting Kintner to ask LBJ whether he wanted to continue assembling groups of that size[62] and to institute a series of sessions with a smaller group of top staff.[63]

Kintner's resignation from the White House in June 1967 ended the practice of regular, general-purpose staff meetings. Senior aides finally settled on holding meetings of relatively narrowly defined groups in order to provide some degree of functional coordination and permit airing of grievances:

> Jones held Friday afternoon meetings of a small group to plan presidential appearances. Sanders, who had succeeded O'Brien, held weekly meetings of congressional liaison staff. McPherson, or his aide Maguire, held weekly meetings of the writers' group. Califano arranged meetings on the legislative program for the next session. At the president's request occasional meetings with him of people in particular work areas were called by the area chiefs—Sanders, Maguire, etc. Yet the meetings of all the chief assistants for sharing of knowledge had been abandoned, except for an occasional call by the president to achieve coordination of staff activity in a particular area.[64]

Although such sessions proved useful, they generally failed to respond to the need for more systematic coordination across White House tasks.

In addition, many staff members believed that sessions with the president were too infrequent. As Moyers expressed in a mid-1966 memo to Johnson, "I find a great desire on the part of these people [staff] to serve you better, which depends upon their knowing more of your thinking."[65] LBJ sent the memo to Marvin Watson for follow-up, but evidently little happened.

Johnson's struggles suggest that a primarily bilateral approach to dealing with staff members has significant costs and limitations, even if the main purposes are simply information gathering and minimal coordination. LBJ himself realized this, encouraging first Moyers and then Kintner to improve matters through staff meetings. But Johnson, for the most part, withheld his own participation. That plus staff changes and the president's vacillating interest ensured that such practices would be ephemeral.

Largely missing was a stable forum for substantive discussions. In a policy environment characterized by goal controversy and frequent uncertainty about implementation, collegial-competitive governance structuring that embraced relevant participants was often needed but only sometimes available.

Informal Structures

The most important informal structuring that emerged during the Johnson years was the development of the functionally defined groups that began to meet regularly in the latter years of the administration. Although staffers had diverse points of view, no other stable informal structures developed to mediate or coordinate among them. Again, the differentiation dynamic failed to operate, but there was a great deal of ad hoc collaboration:

> Flexibility was the salient feature of Johnson's White House operation. Pivotal points of integration were fixed by the nature of the tasks to be performed. These often developed in an ad hoc way. . . . Whether brought about by assignment by the president or the initiative of staff members, a consequence sometimes was overlaying and crisscrossing of individual tasks. . . . This made collaboration across loose boundary lines imperative. The collaboration was in the main improvised in response to immediate pressures.[66]

In a very different environment, the Johnson White House had in some ways returned to the approaches that developed during the latter years of the Roosevelt administration.

CONCLUSIONS

The obvious importance of presidential choice factors in structuring staff governance has led to the tendency to regard the White House Office as almost purely a reflection of presidential style.[67] In all the early modern administrations, except perhaps those of Hoover and Johnson, there was an evident fit between the president's governance strategies and his general preferences concerning working relationships with his staff. Even the two seeming exceptions have explanations. In the instance of Hoover, the problem evidently was his lack of attention to the need for some minimal governance strategy, even for a tiny staff. In Johnson's case, the inherent difficulty of grafting his own approach to that of JFK, coupled with LBJ's fleeting attention to governance strategy, led to a relatively high level of ongoing dissatisfaction with staff governance. Moreover, in both cases, learning and responding were complicated by overload from a distinctly hostile environment.

The environment itself also was a crucial factor in the evolution of White House staff governance, as the complexity of political and policy issues and the decay of political parties compelled presidents to find organizational ways of coping with the office. As presidents sought to respond to the heightened demands on the modern presidency, they greatly diversified and enlarged the White House staff. Among the early modern presidents, only Kennedy stands as an exception to this generalization. And if we regard the Kennedy-Johnson administration as one entity, even that apparent anomaly disappears.

Moreover, this staff growth—an organizational factor in its own right—shaped and complicated presidential responses. Quite clearly, staff expansion rendered inadequate arrangements that had served well at earlier times. Roosevelt's Brownlow Committee was the first to identify staff inadequacy as a problem and to propose adding personnel and tasks as solutions. The growth of the staff under Truman followed a similar pattern, eliciting such responses as larger staff meetings. Such ad hoc structuring not only did not fit Eisenhower's preferences but arguably was inadequate for a staff operation of the scope Eisenhower planned. Notably, at least one of Eisenhower's major innovations—the staff secretariat—had been discussed seriously by Truman's people.

Kennedy again stands as an exception. Still, one wonders whether some formalization (similar to, for instance, Ford's or Carter's eventual appointment of a chief of staff) might not have occurred as JFK realized that being the hub of the wheel is taxing and that he too would need help. Indeed, that is somewhat the story of the Johnson White House, although LBJ could never give staff governance enough sustained attention to develop and implement a clear alternative strategy; in any event, he was reluctant to accord too much power to any single aide.

Kennedy aside, in the other early modern White Houses, one can detect hints of organizational factors that would soon produce institutionalization and some degree of stability. Most clearly, the position of chief of staff under Eisenhower foreshadowed a response that, in various specific versions, would become a feature of all administrations from Richard Nixon's through Bill Clinton's. Although these later presidents have had diverse strategic preferences, there appears to be, if not a growing consensus on White House governance, at least a reduction in the range of options that receive serious consideration.

Epilogue

Our analysis of governance structures began with the expectation that, in the inherently political setting of an organization like the White House Office, simple hierarchy would not always be the structural form that emerged. In its stead would be several different kinds of structures such as those described in Table 1 (see Chapter 1). This expectation was emphatically borne out in our examination of the developing White House staff.

Indeed, once the White House had grown beyond the early Hoover prototype, collegial structures of various kinds became the most common and arguably the most important ways of organizing White House governance. From Roosevelt's speechwriting teams through Truman's staff meetings, Eisenhower's working group on economic policy, Kennedy's structure for promoting civil rights programs within the executive branch, and Johnson's functionally defined staff groups, collegial-consensual structures performed a wide variety of critical governance tasks. Some collegial-consensual structures, such as those associated with the press office, became institutionalized in the White House.

Also evident were collegial-mediative arrangements such as the structure that developed around Charles Murphy's staff as a go-between linking Clark Clifford's and John Steelman's operations in the Truman White House. Collegial-mediative structures linking the White House with elements of its environment (e.g., congressional liaison) were apparent. Likewise in evidence were collegial-competitive structures such as Eisenhower's National Security Council Planning Board and Robert Kintner's staff meetings during LBJ's presidency.

Adjudicative structures were common as well, and they were an especially important means of regularizing presidential participation in the work of the staff. Admiral Leahy's involvement of Roosevelt in disputes among the Joint Chiefs during World War II was a prototype, but adjudicative structuring was not limited to foreign policy decision making. For example, an informal adjudicative structure emerged around the appointments process under Kennedy, linking Dan Fenn's staff with the "Irish mafia"; another adjudicative structure involved Johnson in the Califano staff's oversight of executive agencies.

Adversarial structures, requiring the judgment of a neutral party, were rare in the decidedly nonneutral setting of the White House. However, in the staff meetings conducted for Eisenhower by process manager Sherman Adams, we see at least a close approximation. There, under some circumstances, Adams acted as a relatively detached arbiter of competing ideas or claims.

Finally, market structuring appeared, for example, in scheduling under Hoover, constituency group liaison and public relations from FDR forward, and executive branch oversight during the Hoover administration and the later Roosevelt years.

This is not to deny that hierarchy existed. Indeed, the emergence of hierarchical structuring in the Hoover and Roosevelt secretariats, the staff secretariats under Eisenhower, and some aspects of the congressional liaison and executive outreach operations from Eisenhower onward provided the White House with fundamental support systems. Meanwhile, policy staffs, such as Murphy's under Truman and Sorensen's under Kennedy, required at least nominal hierarchical structuring, even though their work did not always follow that pattern. Special-projects staffs were without exception hierarchically structured. Hierarchy, though hardly the dominant mode of White House governance, was far from unimportant. And of course, *all* staff operations took place within the larger hierarchy of the White House Office and thus were subject to presidential direction.

Somewhat to our surprise, we also observed a number of multipurpose structures. These are governance structures that, without substantially changing their membership or all their operating procedures, worked as more than one type of structure, coping with more than one type of decision setting. Their emergence emphasizes that governance structures are neither static nor necessarily limited to one kind of decision setting or purpose. Examples of multipurpose structuring include Eisenhower's National Security Council Operations Coordinating Board, which could operate as either a collegial-consensual or an adjudicative structure, depending on the issue before it; the Council on Foreign Economic Policy under Eisenhower, which could be collegial-competitive, adversarial, or adjudicative; and collegial writing structures such as those serving Roosevelt and Truman, which could be collegial-consensual or collegial-competitive as required.

To some extent, these instances of multipurpose structuring reflect the ambiguity that is inherent in defining structural types. The boundaries separating the types identified in Table 1 are necessarily somewhat vague. One thus would expect both difficult calls as to structural form and some structures that could be different types at different times.

Yet these multipurpose structures also point to a substantive lesson. Given sufficiently strong interpersonal resources—constructive staff relationships, flexibility in the tasks aides performed, and a shared sense of purpose, for instance—along with generally representative participation, governance structures can be adaptable. It is not necessary to imagine organizations in every instance multiplying their governance structures in order to meet each recurrent challenge from the environment or each presidential objective.

ACCOUNTING FOR THE DEVELOPMENT OF STRUCTURES BY TYPE OF TASK

Chapter 1 suggested that the three clusters of explanatory factors we have discussed—environmental, presidential choice, and organizational—would vary in their helpfulness in accounting for governance structures, depending on the types of task being examined (outreach, policy processing, or coordination and supervision). We proposed: (1) environmental factors would be most important in explaining structuring for outreach, (2) organizational variables would be more important in explaining structuring for policy processing and especially important in accounting for coordinative and supervisory structures, and (3) presidential choice factors would influence the effects of and be affected by both environmental and organizational factors. Our findings generally support these initial propositions and permit the third to be usefully clarified.

Environment

Environmental change clearly was a major factor in accounting for overall growth in the structural complexity of White House governance during the early modern era of the presidency. In all our accounts of White House structuring, environmental factors were present. Their significance, however, varied systematically.

As expected, environmental factors loomed most important for the structuring of outreach tasks. Our explanations of the efforts made in such areas as congressional liaison, executive branch outreach, and relations with the public and with specific constituency groups repeatedly identified the environment in which the White House Office was embedded as the primary force producing structural emergence and differentiation. The external forces evident in these areas virtually compelled presidential attention and thus provoked some White House response.

In contrast, when structures for policy processing are considered, the environment was important but less dominant. The principal executive branch loci for advancing policy claims and formulating policy were, for the most part, outside the White House Office itself during this era. As a consequence, White House involvement was less central, more often focusing on coordination and monitoring than on serving as a central forum for policy deliberation. Moreover, environmental turbulence sometimes worked against the emergence of other than market structures, as the case of domestic policy illustrates. Nonetheless, since policy generally was made in response to White House perceptions of environmental conditions, the environment was repeatedly cited in analyzing governance in this area.

When one turns to structuring for managing the White House, the contribution of environmental factors receded even more. Here, the broad environmental influences such as the proliferation of policy challenges and interest groups the presidency confronted had an indirect effect, causing the White House to grow and thus creating the need for organizational responses. But the particular governance approaches the various presidents chose rarely were affected directly by identifiable environmental factors.

Presidential Choice

The results also allow us to modify and improve the third proposition above: presidential choice variables were most important in explaining structuring for coordination and supervision, somewhat less significant in accounting for policy structuring, and least important in influencing structuring for outreach. The overall importance of presidential choice in responding to each of the three kinds of tasks varied inversely with the weight assigned to environmental factors. However, since the White House Office was in a certain sense an extension of the president, presidential factors never dropped to insignificance, or even near it.

Although the environment arguably compelled the emergence of governance structures to handle outreach, presidential strategy was influential in determining the exact timing of emergence as well as the specific forms of these structures. The difference between Truman's congressional relations efforts and the far more differentiated staff of Eisenhower, for instance, cannot be attributed to any noticeable change in the relevant environment. Rather, the quite dissimilar organizational strategies of the two presidents largely account for the difference. The same can be seen in other areas, such as outreach to particular groups. In these cases, not only strategic preferences but also the variable priority presidents placed on such concerns shaped their responses. Presidential choice thus surfaced as a shaper of specific responses to environmentally driven demands. This, of course, conforms to the basic logic of the problem-contingency approach to explaining organizational governance and is consistent with the third proposition above.

The same logic holds for policy processing, but the weighting changes. For instance, the diverse efforts of presidents in the area of domestic policy making clearly reflected not only presidents' different policy goals and strategic preferences but also the intensity of each president's interest in domestic policy making. Likewise in foreign policy, the sharpest contrast—between Eisenhower's system and Kennedy's—stemmed not so much from any significant change in the international or domestic environments between 1953 and 1961 as from the distinctive approaches to governance adopted by the two presidents. Indeed, Johnson's relative neglect of governance in this area stemmed in part from his initial intention to concentrate on domestic rather than foreign policy. Environmental and presidential factors still interacted strongly, but the latitude available to presidents to shape governance was discernibly greater.

In the area of internal White House supervision and coordination, the environment receded into the background, and presidential choice became clearly dominant. The sharp contrasts evident among most of the administrations of this era, beginning with that between Hoover and Roosevelt, resulted mainly from the very different approaches to governance each president took. Here, the logic of the personal contingency perspective offers the most compelling explanation of the particular forms of governance that developed.

Organization

The impact of organizational factors differed across the three types of tasks as well, though perhaps less systematically than the other two clusters of variables and less systematically than we expected. Moreover, the particular organizational factors that were most important varied across the clusters of governance tasks.

The most noticeable organizational effect in the handling of outreach was the structural stability achieved within and around units handling, for example, the press, congressional liaison, and patronage. These connections with the environment, once congruently structured, became firmly embedded in the expectations of outside actors and in the structuring of the White House Office. At the same time, organizational inertia alone could rarely overcome external opposition to White House involvement, as in the case of executive branch outreach. Meanwhile, once outreach structures became stabilized within the White House, aides often resisted perceived efforts to challenge their turfs, such as the opposition of press staff to differentiated public-relations structures.

In contrast, structuring for policy processing was rarely stable. In fact, contrary to our expectations, organizational factors played a distinctly minor role in shaping White House structures for governing the policy process. The only such factor consistently in evidence was "office politics," as White House rivals struggled for influence and access to the president. But even these internal struggles were as much environmental as organizational in origin, since the aims of the internal combatants typically reflected those of actors outside the White House.

Organizational factors weighed more heavily in explaining the structures associated with the coordination and supervision of White House operations. Partisan learning was clearly in evidence, especially in Kennedy's dismantling of the elaborate structures of the Eisenhower White House in an effort to return to the relative informality of the Truman era. The differentiation dynamic appeared more frequently, producing the emergence of such structures as staff meetings and the staff secretariat. Perhaps surprisingly, however, there was not a great deal of stability in these structures. Only the relatively simple structuring of the office of the appointments secretary and of hierarchical reporting mechanisms for linking the White House and executive branch agencies persisted through the Johnson administration.

Implications

The above discussion highlights two points. First, as expected, environmental variables were the most important in explaining the development of governance structures for outreach, and of secondary but still strong significance with respect to policy processing; they receded farther into the background in accounting for structuring for coordination and supervision. Second, the importance of presidential choice formed almost a mirror image of the impact of the environment on White House structuring: of secondary importance in outreach, primary importance in policy processing, and dominant in coordination and supervision.

We can suggest at least one explanation for this pattern. Outreach tasks and structures were the most permeable to the environment. Presidents must continually pay attention to external actors such as Congress, the press, interest groups, and the public, but if they are to govern, they cannot fully attend to these actors themselves. External demands thus pushed presidents to respond with structures that were congruent with meeting these needs. It is noteworthy that the first presidents to attend seriously to governance structuring—Hoover and Roosevelt—devoted most of their staff resources (until 1939, at any rate) to outreach.

Policy processing is an element of White House work that is, on the whole, less vulnerable to direct external pressure. Although presidents do not really control whether they will respond to Congress or to their political coalitions, they do have relatively greater influence over their targets and priorities in all phases of the policy process. In short, the White House is less permeable in these areas, and environmental demands are not necessarily as immediately compelling. Instead, a greater amount of latitude is available for presidential choice.

By the same token, the White House is least permeable when it comes to coordination and supervision. These tasks do not, for the most part, greatly concern external actors as long as they are somehow competently performed, which renders them mostly invisible from the outside. As a result, presidential discretion over the inner governance of the White House is maximal.

GOVERNANCE STRUCTURES AND CONGRUENCE

These explanatory variables do not fully determine the specific structural forms that emerged and endured in the White House. Also important to consider, we argued, is the extent of goal and technical uncertainty, controversy, or consensus (certainty) that characterizes the relevant decision setting. Table 2 contained both predictions of and prescriptions for the structures that would be congruent with particular decision settings.

Analysis of structural congruence in the present context is necessarily impressionistic, due to two significant limitations. First, our interpretation of the status of goals and technologies in any particular area over any given period was based on our general knowledge of the situation, not on any formal measurement. Our estimate of the degree of consensus over goals or the certainty of technology was not made independent of our knowledge of the structures that actually developed and their fate. If one is concerned that analysts might be tempted to find what they are looking for, then this sort of measurement clearly must be taken as suggestive, not definitive.

Second, our characterization of governance structures, although far from arbitrary, is of necessity subjective. As pointed out earlier, the lines between different types of structures can be blurry. Although we have taken as much care as possible in identifying structural types, such identification leaves room for disagreement. Finally, the emergence of multipurpose structures also reminds us that in governance there is no single best way to organize for all purposes; even when one specifies the relevant contingencies, there may be more than one structure that is potentially congruent with the decision setting.

The Empirical Propositions

The expectation that organizations will, over time, tend to create and keep congruent governance structures can be examined straightforwardly. We can analyze the data by enumerating the various structures that did emerge, noting whether we consider them congruent or incongruent with their decision settings, and then determining whether they were stable. To simplify the analysis, we look only at the *major* structural developments uncovered in the earlier chapters. For convenience, we identify structures according to the White House unit in which they were located or the task with which they were involved. Still, it must be recalled that it is the governance structure, *not* the unit or task, that is the object of attention. Moreover, some of the entries in Tables 4 and 5 refer to multiple structures (as in the case, for instance, of congressional liaison).

Table 4 displays evidence relevant to the relationship between emergence and congruence. The 18 major governance structures have been judged congruent with their decision settings (high congruence), "mixed" (some congruence), or incongruent (no congruence) for each applicable administration. As the table shows, the proposition that organizations tend to create structures congruent with their decision settings receives considerable support.

To test the proposition that congruent structures are more likely to be stable, we took the structures that were determined to be highly congruent with their decision settings and identified those that, by some reasonable definition, endured. We set a relatively low standard for stability: persistence of a structure across at least two consecutive administrations. In determining structural stability, we required not only that some sort of structuring exist across successive administrations but also that the specific structures persist.

The findings here are clear (see Table 5). Thirteen of the seventeen highly congruent structures achieved stability. Only three—outreach to minorities, domestic policy, and the staff secretariat—clearly did not.[1] Congruence did not guarantee survival, but congruent structures tended strongly toward stability. At the same time, such stability does not imply permanence: only seven of the fourteen stable structures endured through the Johnson administration (see Table 4).

The fact that congruent structures tend toward stability does not, of course, necessarily distinguish them from less congruent structures. We therefore examined the stability of those structures that were determined to have only some or no congruence. Again, the relationship is strong (see Table 5). Structures that were not fully congruent clearly tended toward insta-

Table 4. Congruence of Governance Structures

Governance Structure	Congruence		
	High	Some	None
Congressional liaison	DDE–LBJ		
Press	HCH–LBJ		
Public relations	FDR–HST, JFK–LBJ	DDE	
Patronage	FDR–DDE	JFK–LBJ	
Civil service liaison	FDR–HST, JFK–LBJ	DDE	
Executive outreach		HST–DDE	JFK–LBJ
Executive outreach: hierarchical reporting	DDE–LBJ		
Outreach to minorities	FDR–HST, JFK		
Domestic policy	HCH, HST	FDR, DDE–JFK	LBJ
National security	HST–DDE	FDR, JFK–LBJ	
National security: NSA structuring	DDE–LBJ		
Foreign economic policy	DDE–JFK		
Science advice	DDE–JFK	LBJ	
Writing	FDR–JFK	LBJ	
Scheduling	FDR–LBJ		HCH
Secretariat	HCH–HST		
Staff secretariat	DDE		
Staff meetings	FDR–DDE	LBJ	

bility. Only two of the ten less-than-congruent structures—domestic policy and executive outreach—achieved stability, and neither of these lasted over more than two administrations.

The Normative Proposition

We also suggested that Table 2 might be used evaluatively as well as empirically. As we have just seen, there is some evidence of cumulative learning across administrations: most of the congruent structures were at least minimally stable, and most of the other structures were not. Few structures, however, became permanent. If we are correct in contending that there are

Table 5. Stability of Governance Structures

Governance Structure	Stability?	
	Highly Congruent	Less Congruent
Congressional liaison	Yes	—
Press	Yes	—
Public relations	Yes	No
Patronage	Yes	No
Civil service liaison	Yes	No
Executive outreach		Yes
Executive outreach: hierarchical reporting	Yes	
Outreach to minorities	No	
Domestic policy	No	Yes
National security	Yes	No
National security: NSA structuring	Yes	
Foreign economic policy	?	
Science advice	Yes	No
Writing	Yes	No
Scheduling	Yes	No
Secretariat	Yes	
Staff secretariat	No	
Staff meetings	Yes	No

some general principles that could fruitfully guide the design of governance structures, they either were not thoroughly learned during the early modern era or, more likely, were not passed on. One can blame partisan learning in substantial part for this: some lessons that might have been drawn from Eisenhower's successes likely were lost amid partisan claims that Eisenhower's system had failed.

One could also argue, of course, that these notions of structural congruence are simply incorrect or unhelpful to presidents: structures were unstable because they did not work. Yet several times in the earlier chapters, we argued that the absence of congruent structuring helped account for performance failures. Examples include such areas as staff management (Hoover), executive branch liaison (Roosevelt), patronage (early Truman), civil service liaison (early Eisenhower), Chester Bowles's foreign policy advisory activities (Kennedy), and relations between the press office and public-relations specialists across several administrations. We certainly would not contend that congruent governance structuring guarantees success. After all, there are examples of similar governance structures that performed rather differently—congressional liaison under Kennedy and Johnson, for instance. Likewise, some different structures performed similarly, such as Truman's and Eisenhower's management of paper flow. Nonetheless, our analysis pointed to enough instances to support the contention that the absence of congruent structuring may significantly impede White House governance.[2]

ACCOUNTING FOR MULTIPLE GOVERNANCE STRUCTURES

Finally, we return to the propositions about structural differentiation from Chapter 1. In general, we find support for them, but expectations of a differentiation dynamic were overstated.

First, we contended that differentiation (that is, structural elaboration) would increase as environmentally induced uncertainty or controversy increased. There is strong support for such a relationship. During the early modern period, the development of new problems for the presidency created enormous uncertainty, which likely helped lead to the emergence and multiplication of White House staff structures. One need only mention the wars—hot and cold—the decline of the political parties, changing norms concerning relations with Congress, the explosion of the number of programs in the executive branch, and proliferation of the news media during this period. The Eisenhower White House, for example, experimented with numerous structures for handling national security policy and for linking those mechanisms.

Controversy also was frequently present in the White House environment. The diversity of interests and interest groups—including foreign governments and members of Congress—that the president had to attend to grew along with the size of the federal government and its increased involvement in numerous policy areas. White House governance structures in several policy arenas not only coped with such forces but also came to incorporate them; for instance, domestic policy staffs began to include specialists on a wide range of specific policy areas, some of whom were advocates for particular groups or points of view. The structural diversification of the congressional liaison staff likewise reflected the need to deal with an increasingly variegated as well as less disciplined Congress.

Second, we proposed that differentiation would increase over the course of a president's term. This proposition is supported in four of the six early modern presidencies. Structural differentiation increased markedly during both the Roosevelt and Truman administrations, and modestly during Eisenhower's and Johnson's terms. Differentiation did not increase during the Hoover administration and rose only slightly during the Kennedy years. Overall, this constitutes moderate support for the proposition. It should also be noted that Chapter 11 suggested that had the Kennedy administration run its full course, increased differentiation might well have occurred. In Hoover's case, it can be acknowledged that it would have been surprising indeed if the president had been successful in extracting additional funding from an increasingly hostile Congress for his novel experiment in staffing. But he apparently never even considered such a step.

The third proposition suggested that differentiation would increase across administrations. This proposition is generally supported. The complexity of governance structuring grew with every new administration except that of Kennedy.[3] With the transition to Johnson, the trend resumed and, of course, accelerated under Nixon. In light of the mounting challenges from the environment over the 40–year period, this increased differentiation is anything but a surprise.

The final proposition referred to a differentiation dynamic: as differentiation increases, governance issues become more salient and governance mechanisms proliferate. In its original form, the proposition did not predict that this dynamic would always or automatically occur, but rather suggested its possibility. On the basis of empirical evidence, we can point to a recurrent phenomenon, one that we observed several times. Many of our examples, unsurprisingly, appeared in the area of staff management, including the use of staff meetings and the creation under Eisenhower of the staff secretariat. Yet the differentiation dynamic appeared in other arenas as well. FDR, for instance, relied on a collegial-mediative staff structure as well as his own involvement in an adjudicative structure as he strove to exert White House control over patronage. In nonforeign economic policy during the Truman administration, informal collegial-mediative and collegial-competitive structuring emerged to link White House staffers with each other and with the Bureau of the Budget and the new Council of Economic Advisers in the Executive Office.

At the same time, in numerous cases, the differentiation dynamic did not appear when one might have expected it to. No structures emerged to integrate the activities of Herbert Hoover's secretaries or to address the persistent conflicts among press and public-relations staffers. Most strikingly, the dynamic frequently did not operate in the Johnson White House, in areas ranging from personnel to domestic policy to speechwriting and staff governance. This, in turn, may underscore the dangers associated with intense but sporadic presidential interest in staff structuring, especially under conditions of mounting goal and technical controversy.

CONCLUSIONS

Overall, the detailed account of the evolution of White House staff structuring supported many, but by no means all, of our theoretical expectations. The concept of governance structure provides a useful means of identifying some of the key aspects of a highly political organization like the

White House Office. Moreover, the general logic of the problem-contingency perspective worked well in accounting for most of the emergence of governance structures in the White House. Presidential responses to the demands of prevailing decision settings explained much of the governance structuring we discovered across all three major White House tasks. However, the relative contributions of environmental and presidential choice factors to the explanations varied systematically according to the permeability of the White House with regard to each type of task. And, against this background, organizational variables behaved less predictably and, overall, explained less than we expected. Nonetheless, they appeared to be important often enough that an explanation of the emergence, nature, and stability of staff structuring cannot be complete without them.

In addition, our expectations about the emergence of congruent governance structures generally were fulfilled, although the links between congruent structuring and stability were weaker than anticipated. Finally, with the exception of the differentiation dynamic, our propositions about structural differentiation received solid support.

If there was a significant surprise, it was that the White House Office showed less overall structural stability than we had expected, even where structuring was clearly congruent with prevailing decision settings. Nonetheless, it is clear that the White House had a continuing organizational existence across administrations: it decidedly was *not* wholly reinvented after each change of president. Indeed, later White Houses most likely show more structural continuity than those we examined. Still, during the early modern era of the presidency, presidential choice variables—the factors least conducive to structural stability—accounted for somewhat more than we had anticipated. Whether that is true of later White Houses will require further investigation.

We do not conclude, as books on this subject are wont to do, with advice to presidents on the best way to organize the White House. Indeed, our approach is predicated on the idea that there is no one best way, but there may be some useful principles. If there is a practical contribution of this research, it is to begin to define, and to lend some empirical credibility to, those principles of organizational governance.

Notes

INTRODUCTION

1. For elaboration, see John Hart, *The Presidential Branch* (New York: Pergamon Press, 1987), ch. 2.

2. A Washington Correspondent, "The Secretariat," *American Mercury* (December 1929): 385; emphasis in the original.

3. Much of what is referred to as "White House operations" actually is located elsewhere, mainly in the Old Executive Office Building. The most prestigious location, of course, is the West Wing of the White House—close to the president and thus to the perceived "action."

4. This is consistent with Gary King's recommendations for presidency scholars in "The Methodology of Presidential Research," in *Researching the Presidency: Vital Questions, New Approaches,* ed. George C. Edwards III, John H. Kessel, and Bert A. Rockman (Pittsburgh: University of Pittsburgh Press, 1993).

5. See, e.g., several of the selections in George C. Edwards III and Stephen J. Wayne, *Studying the Presidency* (Knoxville: University of Tennessee Press, 1983); Terry M. Moe, "Presidents, Institutions, and Theory," in Edwards, Kessel, and Rockman, *Researching the Presidency;* Joseph A. Pika, "Moving beyond the Oval Office: Problems in Studying the Presidency," *Congress and the Presidency* 9 (Winter 1981–82): 17–36.

6. We should at the outset lay out our own assumptions about theory development. Clearly, any theory can be evaluated according to several criteria—among them, its contribution to understanding a political phenomenon or particular political dynamics, its apparent "progressivity" in adding to cumulative knowledge or understanding, its prescriptive utility, and its parsimony. Although all such criteria are important, at any given stage of theoretical development there may be critical contradictions among them. In particular, understanding and parsimony may often be at odds, especially relatively early in the theory-building process. We contend that, although rigorous and systematic conceptual work that guides empirical anal-

ysis clearly is needed in the analysis of staff structuring, parsimony is currently neither the only nor the most important evaluative criterion. Cf. Karen M. Hult, "Advising the President," in Edwards, Kessel, and Rockman, *Researching the Presidency,* 138ff.; Moe, however, disagrees (ibid., 380). Moreover, if parsimony is "a judgment, or even assumption, about the world," then we see presidential staffing and the contexts presidents confront as relatively complex and uncertain. See Gary King, Robert O. Keohane, and Sidney Verba, *Designing Social Inquiry: Scientific Inference in Qualitative Research* (Princeton, N.J.: Princeton University Press, 1994), 20 and passim.

7. For elaboration, see Karen M. Hult and Charles Walcott, "Studying the White House: Some Observations and a Brief Argument," *Presidency Research* 11 (Spring 1989): 5-17.

8. See, e.g., Stephen Hess, *Organizing the Presidency,* 2d ed. (Washington, D.C.: Brookings Institution, 1988); Samuel Kernell, "The Creed and Reality of Modern White House Management," in *Chief of Staff: Twenty-Five Years of Managing the Presidency,* ed. Samuel Kernell and Samuel Popkin (Berkeley: University of California Press, 1986); Bradley H. Patterson, Jr., *The Ring of Power: The White House Staff and Its Expanding Role in Government* (New York: Basic Books, 1988); James P. Pfiffner, *The Strategic Presidency: Hitting the Ground Running* (Chicago: Dorsey Press, 1988).

9. See, e.g., Phillip G. Henderson, *Managing the Presidency: The Eisenhower Legacy—From Kennedy to Reagan* (Boulder, Colo.: Westview Press, 1988); John P. Burke and Fred I. Greenstein, in collaboration with Larry Berman and Richard Immerman, *How Presidents Test Reality: Decisions on Vietnam, 1954 and 1965* (New York: Russell Sage Foundation, 1989). The latter do, however, compare Eisenhower's "formalism" with LBJ's approach to decision making.

10. For example, see James David Barber, *Presidential Character: Predicting Performance in the White House,* 4th ed. (Englewood Cliffs, N.J.: Prentice Hall, 1992).

11. For instance, Tower Commission, *The Tower Commission Report* (New York: Bantam Books, Times Books, 1987); Colin Campbell, "The White House and Presidency under the 'Let's Deal' President," in *The Bush Presidency: First Appraisals,* ed. Colin Campbell and Bert A. Rockman (Chatham, N.J.: Chatham House, 1991); Charles Kolb, *White House Daze: The Unmaking of Domestic Policy in the Bush Years* (New York: Free Press, 1994); Bob Woodward, *The Agenda: Inside the Clinton Administration* (New York: Simon and Schuster, 1994).

12. For example, see Alexander George, *Presidential Decision-Making in Foreign Policy* (Boulder, Colo.: Westview Press, 1980); Richard Tanner Johnson, *Managing the White House* (New York: Harper and Row, 1974).

13. Exceptions include Hart, *The Presidential Branch,* and Patterson, *Ring of Power.*

14. Samuel Kernell, "The Evolution of the White House Staff," in *Can the Government Govern?* ed. John E. Chubb and Paul E. Peterson (Washington, D.C.: Brookings Institution, 1989); Moe, "Presidents, Institutions, and Theory"; Terry M. Moe, "The Politicized Presidency," in *The New Direction in American Politics,* ed. John E. Chubb and Paul E. Peterson (Washington, D.C.: Brookings Institution, 1985).

15. Moe, "Presidents, Institutions, and Theory."

16. Formally, the White House Office came into being in September 1939, as a unit in the newly created Executive Office of the President. Here, the White House Office is also used as a shorthand reference to the professional aides appointed by Presidents Hoover and Roosevelt (before 1939) to work officially as White House staffers or "secretaries." By our count, Hoover had up to four such aides during his administration; by 1939, FDR had four assistants as well.

17. In contrast to the White House Office, much more is known about the operation and evolution of other parts of the Executive Office of the President. On the National Security Council staff, see, e.g., William P. Bundy, "The National Security Process," *International Security* 7 (1982–83): 94–109; I. M. Destler, "National Security II: The Rise of the Assistant," in *The Illusion of Presidential Government,* ed. Hugh Heclo and Lester M. Salamon (Boulder, Colo.: Westview Press, 1981); Stanley L. Falk, "The National Security Council under Truman, Eisenhower, and Kennedy," *Political Science Quarterly* 79 (1964): 403–34; Carnes Lord, *The Presidency and the Management of National Security* (New York: Free Press, 1988); Anna Nelson, "National Security I: Inventing a Process (1945–60)," in Heclo and Salamon, *Illusion of Presidential Government.* On the Council of Economic Advisers, see, e.g., David Naveh, "The Political Role of Economic Advisers: The Case of the U.S. President's Council of Economic Advisers, 1946–76," *Presidential Studies Quarterly* 11 (1981): 492–510; Herbert Stein, *Presidential Economics* (New York: Simon and Schuster, 1984). On the role of the Bureau of the Budget (now the Office of Management and Budget), see, e.g., James F. C. Hyde and Stephen J. Wayne, "White House–OMB Relations," in *The Presidency: Studies in Public Policy,* ed. Steven A. Shull and Lance T. LeLoup (Brunswick, Ohio: King's Court Communications, 1979).

18. John P. Burke, *The Institutional Presidency* (Baltimore: Johns Hopkins University Press, 1992), 200–201, n. 14.

19. Thomas Cronin was perhaps the first scholar to raise the issue of staff size per se as a policy question, and he provided some rather startling figures describing staff growth. Thomas E. Cronin, "The Swelling of the Presidency: Can Anyone Reverse the Tide?" in *American Government: Readings and Cases,* 8th ed., ed. Peter Woll (Boston: Little, Brown, 1984); see especially the table on p. 347. Since then, other scholars, using such sources as the *Statistical Abstract of the United States* and the federal budget, have produced comparable but always slightly different numbers. The differences reflect problems of data and definition in the counting of "staff." Probably the most useful of these tabulations—in part because the figures greatly resemble most other counts, and in part because administration means rather than selected years are reported—has been provided by Gary King and Lyn Ragsdale, *The Elusive Executive: Discovering Statistical Patterns in the Presidency* (Washington, D.C.: Congressional Quarterly, 1988), 205.

Several things are noteworthy about the King and Ragsdale figures, including the pattern of steady growth up through Ford, the subsequent decline (although there are counting issues with respect to Reagan), and the lack of any apparent growth from Coolidge to Hoover. The latter points to a limitation of these figures. Since we know that the staff—as we use the term—grew to four under Hoover, their number of 37 has an unclear meaning. What it counts, of course, is all White House employees—the majority of whom were stenographers, drivers, and the like. Although these numbers may roughly correlate with growth in professional staff, and thus in White House capacity for policy and outreach, they do not directly measure it. To do that, one needs a more direct estimate of professional staffing.

20. Neustadt to Kenneth Hechler, 15 October 1981, Neustadt Papers, Box 6, Truman Presidential Library.

21. Ibid.

22. Note that these estimates are slightly higher than Neustadt's comparable numbers in his book *Presidential Power: The Politics of Leadership from FDR to Carter* (New York: Wiley, 1980), 193. There, he estimates Truman at 12, Kennedy and Johnson at 17.

23. Ibid. Similarly, the figures in King and Ragsdale, *Elusive Executive,* 205, indicate that the average number of full-time White House employees grew from 304 under Johnson to 478 and 563 in Nixon's first and second terms, respectively.

24. Neustadt to Hechler, 15 October 1981.

25. Cronin, "Swelling of the Presidency."

26. See, e.g., Moe, "Politicized Presidency," 235–72; Richard P. Nathan, *The Administrative Presidency* (New York: Wiley, 1983); Elizabeth Sanders, "The Presidency and the Bureaucratic State," in *The Presidency and the Political System,* 3d ed., ed. Michael Nelson (Washington, D.C.: Congressional Quarterly, 1990).

CHAPTER 1. ANALYTICAL FRAMEWORK

1. Such a view is grounded in the work of, for example, Max Weber and Luther Gulick and L. Urwick. See Max Weber, "Bureaucracy," in *Max Weber: Essays in Sociology,* ed. Hans Girth and C. Wright Mills (New York: Oxford University Press, 1946); Luther Gulick and L. Urwick, *Papers on the Science of Administration* (New York: Institute of Public Administration, Columbia University, 1937).

2. For an elaboration, see Karen M. Hult and Charles Walcott, *Governing Public Organizations: Politics, Structures, and Institutional Design* (Pacific Grove, Calif.: Brooks/Cole, 1990), 16–19. The image of organizations as control systems has had a continuing influence on the theory and practice of management in the private sector. See the emphasis this view receives in, for example, Bengt Abrahamsson, *Bureaucracy or Participation: The Logic of Organization* (Beverly Hills, Calif.: Sage, 1977); Gregory K. Dow, "Configurational and Coactivational Views of Organizational Structure," *Academy of Management Review* 13 (Winter 1988): 53–64. The perspective also has "provided important ideological support for the essentially authoritarian structures of modern public and private management." Hult and Walcott, *Governing Public Organizations,* 19).

3. See, e.g., Samuel Kernell, "The Creed and Reality of Modern White House Management," in *Chief of Staff: Twenty-Five Years of Managing the Presidency,* ed. Samuel Kernell and Samuel Popkin (Berkeley: University of California Press, 1986).

4. See, e.g., Bronston T. Mayes and Robert W. Allen, "Toward a Definition of Organizational Politics," *Academy of Management Review* 2 (October 1977): 672–78; Jeffrey Pfeffer, *Power in Organizations* (Marshfield, Mass.: Pittman, 1981). In

the political science literature, see Graham T. Allison, *Essence of Decision* (Boston: Little, Brown, 1971), especially ch. 5.

5. Terry M. Moe, "The Politicized Presidency," in *The New Direction in American Politics*, ed. John E. Chubb and Paul E. Peterson (Washington, D.C.: Brookings Institution, 1985).

6. This understanding of organizational politics and its implications for studying organizations is discussed more fully in Hult and Walcott, *Governing Public Organizations*, and Karen M. Hult and Charles Walcott, "Organizational Design as Public Policy," *Policy Studies Journal* 17 (Spring 1989): 469-94. For an earlier application to the White House staff, see, e.g., Charles Walcott and Karen M. Hult, "Organizing the White House: Structure, Environment, and Organizational Governance," *American Journal of Political Science* 31 (February 1987): 109-25.

7. Routinization reduces the amount of time, energy, and attention individuals in an organization need to devote to problem solving. These are crucial considerations, given the typical scarcity of such resources. Routinization also increases the predictability of organizational activities, which tends to be desired by organizational members and external constituents and overseers alike.

8. See Hult and Walcott, *Governing Public Organizations*, ch. 2, for an elaboration of this argument.

9. Our emphasis is consistent with Terry Moe's recommendation that presidency scholars "take a more restrictive view of what they want to explain" and focus on "structures in particular." Terry M. Moe, "Presidents, Institutions, and Theory," in *Researching the Presidency: Vital Questions, New Approaches*, ed. George C. Edwards III, John H. Kessel, and Bert A. Rockman (Pittsburgh: University of Pittsburgh Press, 1993), 354.

10. Hult and Walcott, *Governing Public Organizations*, 34.

11. "Formal" structures are those that are specified in writing (e.g., in an organizational chart), mandated by those in positions of authority (in the White House, e.g., by the president, chief of staff, or director of legislative liaison), or required by law (e.g., the National Security Council). In contrast, "informal" structures may emerge from habit, convention, practice, or ad hoc initiative. See, e.g., Harold F. Gortner, Julianne Mahler, and Jeanne Bell Nicholson, *Organization Theory: A Public Perspective* (Chicago: Dorsey Press, 1987), 69, 72-75; Hult and Walcott, "Organizational Design," 474.

12. See, e.g., John P. Burke, *The Institutional Presidency* (Baltimore: Johns Hopkins University Press, 1992).

13. During the period examined here, two presidents (Franklin Roosevelt and John Kennedy) died in office. For purposes of discussing institutionalization, it seems reasonable to treat the Roosevelt-Truman and Kennedy-Johnson periods as separate presidencies; although both Truman and Johnson initially continued the organizational arrangements of their predecessors, they later made significant modifications.

14. Casual inspection makes this clear. However, the extent of structural diversity over the 40 years of the early modern presidency is a question we return to in the epilogue.

15. Market structuring should not be confused with an absence of structure. Structurelessness may be defined as a condition in which the doing of a task itself

has not become routine. Market structuring, in contrast, denotes a condition in which doing the task is a routine occurrence, but no predictable structure other than individualistic competition can be specified.

16. This use of the term "differentiation" differs somewhat from that in Walcott and Hult, "Organizing the White House." In the latter, differentiation referred to the reliance on "governance" rather than "management" (i.e., control) structures. Since problems in the White House Office virtually always involve governance issues, we employ differentiation here to refer to the elaboration of governance structures.

17. Hult and Walcott, *Governing Public Organizations,* 38–39; Walcott and Hult, "Organizing the White House," 117.

18. See, e.g., Kernell, "The Creed."

19. Moe, "Politicized Presidency."

20. Richard E. Neustadt, *Presidential Power* (New York: Wiley, 1960).

21. See, e.g., Richard T. Johnson, *Managing the White House* (New York: Harper and Row, 1974); Alexander George, *Presidential Decision-Making in Foreign Policy: The Effective Use of Information and Advice* (Boulder, Colo.: Westview Press, 1980); Erwin C. Hargrove, "Presidential Personality and Leadership Style," in *Researching the Presidency: Vital Questions, New Approaches,* ed. George C. Edwards III, John H. Kessel, and Bert A. Rockman (Pittsburgh: University of Pittsburgh Press, 1993).

22. See also Terry Moe's concerns with emphases on presidents' personal styles. Moe, "Presidents, Institutions, and Theory," 347–52.

23. See Kernell, "The Creed," and Samuel Kernell, "The Evolution of the White House Staff," in *Can the Government Govern?* ed. John E. Chubb and Paul E. Peterson (Washington, D.C.: Brookings Institution, 1989).

24. Nor was the Eisenhower experience an exception. White Houses through Bill Clinton's have struggled with designing workable structures for sorting out the responsibilities of and the relationships between press and communications units and for coping with the seemingly inevitable conflict that erupts between them. On the post-Johnson development of White House communications units, see, e.g., Michael Baruch Grossman and Martha Joynt Kumar, *Portraying the President: The White House and the News Media* (Baltimore: Johns Hopkins University Press, 1981); John Anthony Maltese, *Spin Control: The White House Office of Communications and the Management of Presidential News,* 2d ed. (Chapel Hill: University of North Carolina Press, 1994). On Clinton's early difficulties, see, e.g., Jacob Weisberg, "The White House Beast," *Vanity Fair* 56 (September 1993): 166–71.

25. See Irving L. Janis, *Groupthink,* 2d ed. (Boston: Houghton Mifflin, 1982).

26. For an extended discussion of how factors inside and outside of organizations can affect levels of uncertainty and controversy in decision settings, see Hult and Walcott, *Governing Public Organizations,* ch. 4.

27. Ibid., ch. 5.

28. Ibid., 51; emphasis in original.

29. Our earlier work (Hult and Walcott, *Governing Public Organizations*) used the term "appropriate" rather than "congruent" when discussing the fit between decision setting and organizational structure. Here we are concerned with examining both the normative and the empirical dimensions, with a stress on the latter; in the

earlier work, much of the emphasis was on the former. "Congruence" seems to have fewer value-laden connotations, making it somewhat more straightforward to use when discussing empirical issues.

Using the same term for both normative and empirical purposes requires, of course, that one clearly distinguish between the two. We are decidedly *not* arguing that "whatever structure is, should be." Indeed, examination of the early modern era reveals numerous instances of structuring that is not consistent with the expectations and prescriptions in Table 2.

30. For an illustration of such a use of the governance model, see, e.g., Karen M. Hult, "Governing in Bureaucracies: The Case of Parental Notification," *Administration and Society* 20 (November 1988): 313–33.

31. This is not to argue that congruent structures will always succeed or that incongruent ones will always fail. Moreover, *perceived* congruence—what we hypothesize that designers and decision makers within organizations tend to strive toward—may be grounded in imperfect perception.

32. For elaboration, see Hult and Walcott, *Governing Public Organizations,* ch. 5.

33. Much of the discussion of the cells in Table 2 parallels the more detailed treatment in ibid., 71–77.

34. James D. Thompson, *Organizations in Action* (New York: McGraw-Hill, 1967).

35. Cf. James MacGregor Burns, *Leadership* (New York: Harper and Row, 1978).

36. Walcott and Hult, "Organizing the White House," 115ff.

37. Ibid., 116.

38. Ibid., 116–17.

39. In Stephen Hess, *Organizing the Presidency,* 2d ed. (Washington, D.C.: Brookings Institution, 1988), 70.

CHAPTER 2. CONGRESSIONAL LIAISON

1. See, e.g., Abraham Holtzman, *Legislative Liaison: Executive Leadership in Congress* (Chicago: Rand McNally, 1970); Richard M. Pious, *The American Presidency* (New York: Basic Books, 1979), 187.

2. The distinction between "policy" and "representational" tasks is drawn from Emmette S. Redford and Richard T. McCulley, *White House Operations: The Johnson Presidency* (Austin: University of Texas Press, 1986), 334–37 and passim.

3. This chapter focuses on White House staff participation in the *legislative* phase of policy adoption. Staffers in all early modern White Houses also were involved in policy adoption in a second way: examining legislation once it passed Congress. In the mid-1930s, the Bureau of the Budget (BOB) examined all enrolled bills, with White House staffers providing liaison with the president. Beginning with Eisenhower, the White House began conducting its own separate review, after the BOB had canvassed relevant departments. For further discussion of matters related to the evolution of White House staff involvement in examining bills awaiting the president's signature, see, e.g., Roger W. Jones, Oral History Interview with Jerry

N. Hess, 14 August 1969, Truman Presidential Library; David W. Kendall, Oral History Interview with Don North, 1 December 1970, Columbia University Oral History, Eisenhower Presidential Library; Harold Seidman, Oral History Interview with Jerry N. Hess, 29 September 1970, Truman Presidential Library; Robert J. Spitzer, *The Presidential Veto: Touchstone of the American Presidency* (Albany: State University of New York Press, 1988); Stephen J. Wayne, Richard L. Cole and James F. C. Hyde, Jr., "Advising the President on Enrolled Legislation: Patterns of Executive Influence," *Political Science Quarterly* 94 (Summer 1979): 303–17.

4. A significant kind of representational task—responding to members' patronage requests—receives sustained treatment in Chapter 4.

5. Lawrence F. O'Brien, *No Final Victories: A Life in Politics—From John F. Kennedy to Watergate* (Garden City, N.Y.: Doubleday, 1974), 196.

6. Charles Walcott and Karen M. Hult, "Management Science and the Great Engineer: Governing the White House during the Hoover Administration," *Presidential Studies Quarterly* 20 (Summer 1990): 559.

7. *Time,* 19 June 1933, in Newton Files, Hoover Presidential Library.

8. See A Washington Correspondent, "The Secretariat," *American Mercury* (December 1929): 391, in Richey Papers, Box 2, Hoover Presidential Library; William J. Hopkins, Oral History Interview with Raymond Henle, 8 August 1968, p. 14, Oral Histories, Box 16, Hoover Presidential Library.

9. Henle, in Oral History Interview with Hopkins, 8 August 1968, p. 14; Hopkins readily agreed with this assessment.

10. George A. Akerson, Jr., Oral History Interview with Charles Morrissey, 11 March 1969, p. 9, Oral Histories, Box 1, Hoover Presidential Library. Cf. Herbert Hoover, *The Memoirs of Herbert Hoover,* vol. 2, *1920–33: The Cabinet and the Presidency* (New York: Macmillan, 1952), 217; Jordan A. Schwarz, *The Interregnum of Despair: Hoover, Congress, and the Depression* (Urbana: University of Illinois Press, 1970), 7, 11; James L. Sundquist, *The Decline and Resurgence of Congress* (Washington, D.C.: Brookings Institution, 1981), 33, 133.

11. See, e.g., Schwarz, *Interregnum of Despair,* viii; Sundquist, *Decline and Resurgence,* 132.

12. Hanford Thayer, Oral History Interview with Raymond Henle, 19 October 1967, p. 7, Oral Histories, Box 37, Hoover Presidential Library. Thayer was Mac-Lafferty's nephew.

13. For example, MacLafferty Diary, MacLafferty Papers, Box 1, Hoover Presidential Library, entries for December 1931.

14. Ibid., 5 December 1931; cf. 23 March 1932.

15. For example, ibid., 24 June, 12 August 1930.

16. For example, ibid., 15 December 1930, 11 April 1932.

17. See, e.g., Rexford Tugwell, "Diary 1934," in Tugwell Papers, Box 31, Roosevelt Presidential Library.

18. For example, Hopkins to Roosevelt, 29 May 1941, President's Secretary's File, Box 152; Rosenman to Roosevelt, 18 December 1943, President's Secretary's File, Box 184; Rosenman, Folder 1: 1943, President's Official File 5433; all in Roosevelt Presidential Library.

19. See, e.g., Joseph P. Lash, *Dealers and Dreamers: A New Look at the New*

Deal (New York: Doubleday, 1988); Bernard Sternsher, *Rexford Tugwell and the New Deal* (New Brunswick, N.J.: Rutgers University Press, 1964).

20. From the beginning, Press Secretary Stephen Early served as an intelligence source for the president on congressional activities; Early and Corcoran often brought back political intelligence from their interactions on Capitol Hill, and Cohen remained a key information source into 1940. See, e.g., Early to Roosevelt, 23 February 1939, President's Secretary's File, Box 146; Congress Subject File, President's Secretary's File, Box 140; "Corcoran," James Roosevelt Correspondence Files, Box 13; "Cohen," President's Official File 2708; all in Roosevelt Presidential Library; Louis W. Koenig, *The Invisible Presidency* (New York: Holt, Rinehart and Winston, 1960), 283ff. Another de facto White House aide who helped with congressional relations was Charles West, an ex-congressman from Ohio who nominally served as both a special assistant in the Farm Credit Administration and the undersecretary of the interior in the 1930s. Most of West's work involved following particular activities on Capitol Hill at the direction of FDR, Corcoran, or Marvin McIntyre. "West," President's Official File 1578, Roosevelt Presidential Library. When James Roosevelt joined the staff in 1937, he was sometimes asked by FDR to be a troubleshooter for minor administration problems with Congress and to pass on certain information to supportive legislators. James Roosevelt Correspondence Files, Box 56, Roosevelt Presidential Library. When the younger Roosevelt left the White House in 1938, his assistant, James Rowe, took over many of these responsibilities; see President's Secretary's File, Boxes 115 and 148, Roosevelt Presidential Library. Both before and after Samuel Rosenman officially joined the staff as special counsel in 1943, he advised the president on how FDR might deal with congressional leaders and on the sorts of legislative programs that executive branch agencies might pursue; see, e.g., Rosenman to Roosevelt, 22 August 1941 and 18 December 1943, President's Secretary's File, Box 184, Roosevelt Presidential Library.

21. Among the committee's members were Corcoran, Cohen, Press Secretary Stephen Early, White House staffer Charles West, and representatives of the Justice Department and the Democratic National Committee. James Roosevelt Diary, February–March 1937, J. Roosevelt Correspondence Files, Box 57; Early Diary, 1 February 1937; both in Roosevelt Presidential Library; cf. Lash, *Dealers and Dreamers,* 296ff.

22. J. Roosevelt Diary. Cf. Koenig, *Invisible Presidency,* 285ff; James Macgregor Burns, *The Lion and the Fox* (New York: Harcourt, Brace, 1956), 294–315. It was Corcoran, however, who was the president's "chief agent on the Hill." Lash, *Dealers and Dreamers,* 296.

23. Lash, *Dealers and Dreamers,* 307.

24. Burns, *The Lion and the Fox,* 300–301.

25. Several administrative assistants (AAs) served as White House channels to Congress. In addition to James Rowe (who had assisted James Roosevelt before being named an AA), Sherman Minton, a former senator, and James Barnes, a former House member, counted staying in touch with their ex-colleagues among their tasks. On Minton, see, e.g., Rowe to Rosenman, "AAs to the President," 15 March 1941, Rosenman Papers, Box 41; "Minton," PSF, Box 158. Barnes's activi-

ties are detailed in "Barnes," POF 4276. All the materials are housed at the Roosevelt Presidential Library.

26. Rowe to Grace Tully, "Marvin McIntyre," 26 August 1941, Rowe Papers, Box 20, Roosevelt Presidential Library.

27. Roosevelt to McIntyre, 6 September 1941, PSF, Box 152, Roosevelt Presidential Library. Jonathan Daniels evidently helped McIntyre perform this task; see "Daniels," Folder 1: 1935–43, President's Official File 5230, Roosevelt Presidential Library.

28. Roosevelt to McIntyre, 6 September 1941, President's Secretary's File, Box 152; cf. Rowe, "AAs to the President," Roosevelt Presidential Library.

29. Sundquist, *Decline and Resurgence,* 139.

30. Richard Neustadt, "Approaches to Staffing the Presidency: FDR and JFK," *American Political Science Review* 57 (1963): 856.

31. Quoted in Robert Leon Lester, "Developments in Presidential-Congressional Relations: FDR-JFK" (Ph.D. dissertation, University of Virginia, 1969), 44.

32. John Hart, *The Presidential Branch* (New York: Pergamon Press, 1987), 117.

33. Cf. Lester, "Developments in Presidential-Congressional Relations," 44–45.

34. Charles Murphy, in Joint Oral History Interview with Hugh Heclo and Anna Wilson, 20 February 1980, p. 105, Truman Presidential Library. Cf. Ken Hechler, *Working with Truman* (New York: G.P. Putnam's Sons, 1982), 153; William E. Leuchtenburg, *In the Shadow of FDR: From Harry Truman to Ronald Reagan,* rev. ed. (Ithaca, N.Y.: Cornell University Press, 1983), 14; Richard E. Neustadt, "Executive Office Agencies: Discussion," in *The Truman White House: The Administration of the Presidency, 1945–1953,* ed. Francis H. Heller (Lawrence: Regents Press of Kansas, 1980), 228.

35. Seidman Oral History, 29 July 1970, p. 44.

36. See, e.g., Steelman Papers, Box 3; John Steelman, Truman Memoir Interview by William Hillman, David M. Noyes, Francis Heller, and Lee Williams, 8 December 1954, pp. 26, 30, 34, Truman Presidential Library.

37. For example, Enarson to Neustadt, 10 December 1951, Enarson Papers, Box 4; Stowe Papers, Box 3, Truman Presidential Library.

38. Steelman, Truman Memoir Interview, 8 December 1954, p. 4; cf. "Man in an Inner Circle," Vertical File: "White House Staff Advisers," Truman Presidential Library.

39. "Clifford," Secretary File: General File, Truman Presidential Library.

40. Murphy, Joint Oral History, 20 February 1980, p. 102. Cf. Charles Murphy, Oral History Interview with Charles T. Morrissey and Jerry N. Hess, vol. 1, 24 June 1963, p. 253; memos to the president on legislative activity in "Truman," Murphy Papers, Truman Presidential Library.

41. See, e.g., analyses in "Murphy," Secretary File: General File, Truman Presidential Library.

42. Ibid. See also "Truman" in Murphy Papers and Murphy Oral History, vol. 1, 24 July 1963, p. 114.

43. Murphy, Joint Oral History, 20 February 1980, p. 102.

44. See Seidman Oral History, 29 September 1970; Murphy Oral History, vol. 1, 24 June 1963, p. 259; Neustadt, "Some General Observations on Working Relations in the White House Office," in Heller, *Truman White House,* 115.

45. Two other members of Murphy's staff—David Lloyd and David Bell—also undertook Congress-related tasks. Both Lloyd and Bell tracked legislation and offered strategic advice for dealing with congressional committees on particular bills (e.g., Bell to Truman, 9 June 1952, "Bell," Secretary File: General File; Lloyd Papers, Box 1, Folder 1, and Box 8; Truman Presidential Papers). In addition, two junior aides in the counsel's office, Kenneth Hechler and Richard Neustadt, performed more routine tasks such as summarizing pending legislation and members' voting records.

46. See, e.g., Tannenwald to Murphy, 14 May 1952, 28 June 1952, Tannenwald Papers, Box 3, "Chronological File, 1952," Truman Presidential Library.

47. For example, the Neustadt-Kayle memo to Murphy and Stowe, 12 February 1952, Neustadt Papers, Box 2, Truman Presidential Library. A partial exception to these patterns was the Bureau of the Budget, which, as noted, maintained strong ties to both Steelman's and Murphy's staffs.

48. See "Connelly," Secretary File: General File, Truman Presidential Library.

49. Alfred Dick Sander, *A Staff for the President: The Executive Office, 1921–52* (New York: Greenwood Press, 1989), 91.

50. Matthew Connelly, Oral History Interview with Jerry N. Hess, May 1969, p. 22, Truman Presidential Library.

51. Jones Oral History, 14 August 1969, p. 72.

52. Holtzman, *Legislative Liaison,* 233. For the most part, this particular legislative liaison operation was self-contained. On occasion, Maylon and Feeney passed political and policy intelligence to and received it from other White House staffers. On the whole, however, they were not much involved in the liaison activities of the counsel's office. Murphy recalled: "Our shop got along with them very well, but we didn't have a great deal of business with them. We didn't find they were especially effective." Murphy, Joint Oral History, 20 February 1980, p. 102. See also "Feeney," Secretary File, General File, Truman Presidential Library.

53. Hechler, *Working with Truman,* 162.

54. According to Holtzman (*Legislative Liaison,* 236), neither man had ever worked in Congress, although both had been involved in legislative liaison for the military. Lester, "Developments in Presidential-Congressional Relations," 71.

55. Hechler, *Working with Truman,* 171.

56. Stephen Hess, *Organizing the Presidency,* 2d ed. (Washington, D.C.: Brookings Institution, 1988), 66.

57. DDE Diary, 11 February 1953, Box 4, Eisenhower Presidential Library.

58. Cf. Holtzman, *Legislative Liaison,* 236–38; Homer Gruenther, Oral History Interview with John T. Mason, Jr., Columbia University, 23 May 1972, Eisenhower Presidential Library; Lester, "Developments in Presidential-Congressional Relations," ch. 4; Wilton Persons, Oral History Interview with John Luter, Columbia University, 22 June 1970, Eisenhower Presidential Library.

59. OCR staffers included Gerald Morgan, former assistant legislative counsel for the House; Jack Martin, Sen. Robert Taft's administrative assistant until the latter's death in 1953; Edward McCabe, a former counsel for the House Education and Labor Committee; and Homer Gruenther, who had worked for Nebraska senator Wherry. Jack Z. Anderson had been a House member from California and then

served as legislative liaison for the Department of Agriculture, and Earle Chesney had handled members' requests at the Veterans Administration for many years.

60. Bryce Harlow, Oral History Interview with Stephen J. Wayne and James F. C. Hyde, 30 May 1974, p. 4, Eisenhower Presidential Library.

61. On advising the president and passing along information to him, see Ann Whitman's entries on Eisenhower's meetings with various liaison staffers in the Whitman Diary Series—e.g., 10 March 1956, Box 57; 27 February 1958, Box 9; 1 July 1960, Box 11. Staffers also sent advice to the president in writing; see, e.g., "Staff Memos" folders in the DDE Diary Series and the Whitman Files, Administrative Series. OCR staff also reported to the president on pending legislation; see, e.g., Gruenther to Eisenhower, Whitman Diary, 26 February 1954, Box 1, "February 1954," Folder 1; Harlow to Eisenhower, 18 May 1956, Whitman Files, Administrative Series, "Harlow"; Persons's notes on a meeting with the president, 5 May 1958, DDE Diary Series, Box 32, "May 1958—Staff Notes"; Whitman Diary, 29 August 1960, Box 11. These various materials are housed at the Eisenhower Presidential Library.

62. Merlo Pusey, *Eisenhower the President* (New York: Macmillan, 1956), 212. This information not only went to the president but also was circulated to other White House staffers. For a time, legislative news was reported through "Staff Notes," produced by the White House research office (see Chapter 5). Lucille Catlett, who had represented the navy on Capitol Hill, served initially as the unit's legislative expert and produced "Special Legislative Notes" (see White House Office, Staff Research Group, Box 32, "Memos—Inter-Office," Folder 1, Eisenhower Presidential Library). Ultimately, however, she moved to OCR, and "'Staff Notes' went out of the congressional reporting business." Albert Toner, Oral History Interview with Thomas Soapes, 4 March 1977, p. 59, Eisenhower Presidential Library.

63. See, e.g., entries for 25 February, 2 March, and 19 May 1954 in James Hagerty Diary, Box 1; Bernard Shanley Diaries, Box 2, "VI White House Years," Folder 2, 1953; both in Eisenhower Presidential Library.

64. Neil MacNeil, *Forge of Democracy: The House of Representatives* (New York: David McKay, 1963), 254.

65. Throughout his presidency, Eisenhower held regular meetings with Republican leaders in Congress and, less frequently, with the bipartisan leadership group. Liaison aides developed the agenda and briefed the president for these sessions as well as attended them. See, e.g., Martin Records, Box 2; Whitman Diary, passim; White House Office, Office of Staff Secretary, Minnich Series; Hagerty Diary, Box 1; Shanley Diaries, Box 1; DDE Diary, "Staff Memos" folders; all in Eisenhower Presidential Library.

66. Harlow to Eisenhower, Whitman Diary, 27 August 1957, Box 9, "August 1957," Folder 1, Eisenhower Presidential Library.

67. Anderson to Whitman, 26 June 1958, White House Office, Office of the Staff Secretary, Subject Series, White House Subseries, Box 1, "Conferences," Eisenhower Presidential Library.

68. For example, Gruenther to White House Staff, 9 November 1953, Gruenther Records, Box 4; Goodpaster to Persons, 19 April 1956, Special Projects, Box 6; Clarence Randall Journals, 5 August 1957, Box 4, CFEP, vol. 5; all in Eisenhower Presidential Library.

69. The rules on congressional correspondence were repeated with some frequency. See, e.g., DDE Diary, 10 February 1953, Box 4; 20 May 1954, White House Office, Office of Staff Secretary, Box 4; 13 May 1955, 21 February 1957, 2 September 1957, White House Office, Office of Staff Secretary, Subject Series, White House Subseries, Box 1; 11 February 1957, White House Office, Office of Staff Secretary, Minnich Series, Box 1, "Staff Meetings," Folder 3; Eisenhower to Goodpaster, DDE Diary, 2 September 1957, Box 26, "Goodpaster, September 1957"; all in Eisenhower Presidential Library.

70. Gruenther Oral History, 23 May 1972, p. 63. See also, Whitman, 26 October 1953, Box 1, "August–October 1953," Folder 1, Eisenhower Presidential Library; Lester, "Developments in Presidential-Congressional Relations," 94.

71. For example, J. Anderson Diary, 26 January, 9 February, 11 February, 16 March 1957, Box 1; Harlow Oral History, 30 May 1974, p. 5; both in Eisenhower Presidential Library. The sessions also served as a basis for preparing the agenda for the president's meetings with legislative leaders. See Holtzman, *Legislative Liaison,* 259.

72. For example, J. Anderson Diary, 7 December 1955, 7 February 1956.

73. See, e.g., Randall Journal, 22 December 1954, Box 2, Volume 7, p. 5; 5 May 1955, Box 2, vol. 9.

74. J. Anderson Diary, 24 March 1956.

75. Persons to Eisenhower, Whitman Diary, 15 June 1957, Box 9, "June 1957," Folder 3, Eisenhower Presidential Library.

76. See, e.g., White House Office, Office of Staff Secretary, Subject Series, White House Subseries, "Conferences"; Harlow notes on meeting with Senator Gore, DDE Diary, Box 37, "Staff Notes—November 1958"; Randall Journal, 21 March 1955, Box 2, vol. 8; Whitman Diary, passim; Harlow Oral History, Oral History Interview with John T. Mason, Jr., Columbia University, 27 February 1967, p. 37, Eisenhower Presidential Library.

77. Chesney, "a jolly, personable fellow" (Sherman Adams, Oral History Interview with Ed Edwin, Columbia University, 11 April 1967, p. 143, Eisenhower Presidential Library), provided favors to cooperative members of Congress and accompanied legislators on routine presidential visits or on more ceremonial occasions such as bill signings. Gruenther, too, "had a drudge job" (ibid., 141). He assembled and kept most of OCR's records, arranged for special "congressional" White House tours for members' constituents, and on occasion reported back on members' views of particular bills (Homer H. Gruenther Records, Boxes 1, 2, 4–7).

78. Notes on staff meeting, 11 February 1957, White House Office, Office of Staff Secretary, Minnich Series, Box 1, "Staff Meetings," Folder 3.

79. Harlow Oral History, 30 May 1974, p. 3. Harlow was assisted by Chesney, and Gruenther worked with Morgan (cf. Gruenther Oral History, 23 May 1972).

80. Jack Z. Anderson, Oral History Interview with John E. Wickman, November 1970, p. 28; 2 February 1971, p. 63. See also "Legislative Assignments," n.a., n.d., White House Office, Staff Research Group, Box 35, "Contacts and Directories," Eisenhower Presidential Library.

81. Edward McCabe, interview with authors, 12 October 1990.

82. For example, Harlow Oral History, 30 May 1974, p. 7; J. Anderson Diary, 5 August 1957, 16 April 1958. Cf. Goodpaster notes, DDE Diary, Box 32, "Staff

Notes—April 1958," Folder 2; Whitman Diary, 1 June 1959, Box 10, "June 1959," Folder 2.

83. See, e.g., J. Anderson Diary, 5, 9 February, 27 June, 19 July 1957, 27 February 1958; J. Anderson Oral History, November 1970, p. 31; Whitman Diary, 19 March 1958, Box 9; DDE Diary, 27, 31 March 1958, Box 31, "Staff Notes—March 1958," Folder 1. Similarly, McCabe first came to the White House to help handle congressional investigations of executive branch departments, which he had helped conduct as a House staffer (J. Anderson Oral History, 2 February 1971, p. 63; McCabe interview).

84. Adams Oral History, 11 April 1967, p. 140.

85. McCabe interview, 12 October 1990.

86. Persons Oral History, 22 June 1970, pp. 38–39.

87. See ibid., 9 February 1955.

88. See, e.g., Randall Journals, 8 April, 9 December 1954; 1 February, 8 March 1955; 12 June, 3 December 1957.

89. Harlow Oral History, 30 May 1974, p. 11.

90. Holtzman, *Legislative Liaison,* 235.

91. Harlow Oral History, 30 May 1974, p. 38; Persons Oral History, 22 June 1970, p. 43.

92. Fred I. Greenstein, *The Hidden-Hand Presidency: Eisenhower as Leader* (New York: Basic Books, 1982), 147.

93. Anderson Oral History, November 1970, p. 30.

94. See, e.g., Adams Oral History, 11 April 1967, p. 216; 19 June 1970, p. 229; Martin Records, Box 2; Anderson Oral History, November 1970, p. 31; Adams to Persons, Seaton, Martin, Harlow, 19 January 1956, in Harlow Records, Box 4, "HEW."

95. A good example of an issue that Adams took special interest in was the creation of the federal interstate highway system (see, e.g., Whitman Diary, 15 April 1958, Box 10; Hagerty Diary, 21 February 1955, Box 1a). Illustrations of the chief of staff's involvement in controversial issues include Taft-Hartley revision (12 August 1953, White House Office, Office of Staff Secretary, Minnich Series, Box 1, "Misc—T"; Shanley Diaries, "IV White House Days," Box 1, "Folder 2, 1953"), the Bricker Amendment (see, e.g., Hagerty Diary, 23, 27 January 1954, Box 1; 5 January 1955, Box 1a), and farm bills throughout the administration (Shanley Diaries, 7 May 1953, p. 813; Anderson Diary, 7 December 1955, 18 February 1956; Whitman Diary, 5 April 1956, Box 7, and 27 March 1958, Box 9; Anderson to Whitman, DDE Diary, 27 March 1958, Box 31, "Staff Notes—March 1958," Folder 1).

96. See, e.g., memos from the president to Adams, Whitman Files, Administrative Series, Box 1, "Adams."

97. See, e.g., Joseph A. Pika, "White House Boundary Roles: Marginal Men amidst the Palace Guard," *Presidential Studies Quarterly* 16 (1986): 700–715.

98. John Bragdon, "Chapter II: Organization of the White House Staff," 27 January 1961, "Book—Correspondence and Synopsis," Bragdon Papers, Box 2, Eisenhower Presidential Library. It should be noted that Bragdon, who headed a White House public works planning unit, was disgruntled for much of his time in the White House.

99. Bragdon, "Chapter III—The Dangers of a [sic] Absence of a Substantive Organization," 17 April 1961, "Book—Correspondence," Bragdon Papers, Box 2; emphasis in original.

100. Hagerty Diary, 5 January 1955, Box 1a.

101. Jackson Papers, Daily Log, 27 November 1953, Box 56, p. 2. Cf. ibid., 13 March 1954; Stephen E. Ambrose, *Eisenhower the President,* vol. 2 (New York: Simon and Schuster, 1984), 165ff; Greenstein, *Hidden-Hand Presidency.* Indeed, most of the OCR staff opposed any public presidential action condemning McCarthy; see, e.g., Notes, 22 May 1953, White House Office, Office of Staff Secretary, Minnich Series, Box 1, "Miscell—May 1953–June 1955"; Hagerty Diary, 24 March 1954, Box 1; Greenstein, *Hidden-Hand Presidency,* ch. 5.

102. See, e.g., John Hart, "Staffing the Presidency and the Office of Congressional Relations," *Presidential Studies Quarterly* 13 (Winter 1983): 101–10.

103. Only Charles Daly, who had worked mostly as a journalist, "did not come from a background of intensive involvement in Democratic party politics." Holtzman, *Legislative Liaison,* 238–39. Moreover, two members of the OCR staff— Henry Hall Wilson and Richard Donahue—had no experience working in Congress, and Daly and O'Brien had worked there for only short periods. Only Mike Manatos and Claude Desautels had worked in Congress for many years (Manatos in the Senate and Desautels in the House).

104. Two differences in the operations stand out. First, Kennedy's legislative staff paid considerable attention to providing services to members of Congress who supported the administration. It kept careful track of the "favors requested" by and granted to individual members and paid especially close attention to the distribution of public works projects. O'Brien Staff Files, Box 31; MacNeil, *Forge of Democracy,* 261; Daniel M. Berman, *In Congress Assembled: The Legislative Process in the National Government* (New York: Macmillan, 1964), 87; Charles U. Daly, Oral History Interview with Charles T. Morrissey, 5 April 1966, p. 23, Kennedy Presidential Library. Second, the liaison unit dealt directly with the press. In OCR staffer Charles Daly's view, the office's accessibility to the press helped account for the fact that "despite its great vulnerability . . . the liaison operation got belted very seldom and O'Brien even more seldom." Daly Oral History, 5 April 1966, p. 39.

105. Berman, *In Congress Assembled,* 87–88.

106. Stephen Wayne, *The Legislative Presidency* (New York: Harper and Row, 1978), 149.

107. See, e.g., Lawrence O'Brien File, White House Staff Files, Box 31; O'Brien to Kennedy, 10 October 1961, President's Office Files, Legislative Files, Box 50; Sorensen Papers, "Memos Re: Legislation," Legislative Files, Box 58; all in Kennedy Presidential Library. Much of this material was available to other White House aides. It was also edited for sharing with the president. After some experimentation with the format and frequency of the reports, OCR sent Kennedy a report titled "Legislative Items Recommended by the President" on a weekly or biweekly basis. President's Office Files, Legislative Files, Boxes 49–52; President's Office Files, Staff Files: "O'Brien, Lawrence J.," Box 64; "Wilson, Henry Hall," Box 67; all in Kennedy Presidential Library.

108. MacNeil, *Forge of Democracy,* 268.

109. For example, "Mike Manatos," Landis Files, White House Staff Files, Box

19; O'Brien to White House staff, 26 March 1963, White House Central Subject Files, Box 115, Folder FG11-8/FG-400; both in Kennedy Presidential Library.

110. See, e.g., O'Brien Staff Files, Boxes 31, 32.

111. Daly Oral History, 5 April 1966, p. 104; Joseph W. Barr (Assistant to the Secretary of Treasury) to Desautels, 14 May 1962, President's Office Files, Legislative Files, Box 50; O'Brien to Kennedy, "Summary of Agency Reports on Legislation," 14 January 1963, President's Office Files, Legislative Files, Box 52. More generally, see O'Brien Staff Files, Box 32, Kennedy Presidential Library.

112. Daly Oral History, 5 April 1966, pp. 43–44.

113. Cf. Gary King and Lyn Ragsdale, *The Elusive Executive: Discovering Statistical Patterns in the Presidency* (Washington, D.C.: Congressional Quarterly, 1988), 63.

114. See, e.g., Desautels to O'Brien, 24 June 1963; Manatos to O'Brien, 9 February 1961; Wilson to O'Brien, 7 September 1962, in Schlesinger, Jr., White House Files, Box W-8, "Kennedy, John F., Presidency"; Richard K. Donahue to O'Brien, 5 December 1962, White House Central Subject Files, Box 189. More generally, see Manatos Staff Files, Box 64; Wilson Staff Files, Box 67; Henry Hall Wilson Files, "Memos to O'Brien," Boxes 1–3, Kennedy Presidential Library.

115. For example, Daly Oral History, 5 April 1966, p. 10; O'Brien Staff Files, Boxes 31, 64.

116. For example, "The Man on the Hill," *Time,* 1 September 1961, p. 10; O'Brien, *No Final Victories.*

117. Mike Manatos, Oral History Interview with Joe B. Frantz, 25 August 1969, pp. 12, 42, Johnson Presidential Library; Henry Hall Wilson, Oral History Interview with Joe B. Frantz, 11 April 1973, p. 6; Manatos Staff Files, Box 64; Wilson Staff Files, Box 67, Kennedy Presidential Library.

118. Daly Oral History, 5 April 1966, pp. 60–61.

119. Holtzman, *Legislative Liaison,* 263.

120. Ibid.

121. Daly Oral History, 5 April 1966, p. 9. Daly's interpretation of Donahue's emphasis is illustrated by Schlesinger's tendency to consult Donahue before accepting invitations to speak before political groups; see, e.g., White House Central Subject Files, Box 120.

122. Claude Desautels, Oral History Interview with Michael Gillette, 18 April 1980, pp. 4, 5, 13, 18, Kennedy Presidential Library; Desautels Files, passim.

123. For example, Sorensen, note to files, 10 April 1962; Sorensen to White, 5 February 1962; both in Sorensen Papers, Legislative Files, Box 58, "Memos Re: Legislation"; BOB analysis sent to Feldman, 24 May 1961, White House Central Subject Files, Box 111, Kennedy Presidential Library.

124. In 1963, for example, White was heavily involved in administration efforts to keep Congress from terminating the Civil Rights Commission. Finally, fearing that southern opposition to omnibus civil rights legislation would block the indefinite extension of the commission, White and O'Brien decided to ask Nicholas Katzenbach of the Justice Department—"one of the more restrained bomb throwers in the Administration"—to approach Senators Eastland and Russell to ask for a 90-day extension. See, e.g., White to Katzenbach, 11 September 1963, White Staff Files, Box 19, "Civil Rights Commission," Kennedy Presidential Library.

125. See, e.g., White memos to Kennedy, February 1961, President's Office Files, Legislative Files, Box 49; Feldman and O'Brien to Kennedy, 7, 28 August, 25 September 1962, Sorensen Papers, Legislative Files, Box 58.

126. For example, White to Kennedy, 27 February 1961, President's Office Files, Legislative Files, Box 49; White to Kennedy, 16 March 1962, ibid., Box 50; Feldman to Kennedy, 18 April 1961, ibid., Box 49; 21 February 1963, President's Office Files, Staff Files, "Myer Feldman," Box 63.

127. For example, Sen. Paul Douglas to Feldman, 6 May 1963, White House Central Subject Files, Box 113; White to Rep. Melvin Price, 5 June 1962, ibid., Box 189.

128. For example, Dutton to Sorensen, 25 July 1961, White House Central Subject Files, Box 189; cf. Sorensen Papers, "Memos Re: Legislation." Sorensen sometimes received copies of memos also sent to O'Brien; at other times, it was Sorensen who received the originals and O'Brien the copies, or the Sorensen office was apparently the sole recipient.

129. Myer Rashish, Oral History Interview with John F. Stewart, 11 September 1967, p. 34, Kennedy Presidential Library.

130. Joseph Kraft, "Kennedy's Working Staff," *Harper's*, n.d., in Arthur Schlesinger, Jr., White House Files, Box W-9, "Magazine Articles—General," p. 36, Kennedy Presidential Library.

131. Holtzman, *Legislative Liaison*, 239; cf. Berman, *In Congress Assembled*, 87.

132. For example, Califano to Johnson, 26 December 1967, Joseph Califano Office Files, Box 8, "Memorandums to the President"; Califano to Johnson, 8 April 1968, Califano Office Files, Box 17; Califano to Manatos, O'Brien, Wilson, and others, 23 May 1966, White House Central Files, Confidential File, FG 11-5/MC— Papers of LBJ Confidential File, Box 19, "White House Office 1963–66"; all in Johnson Presidential Library. Cf. Redford and McCulley, *White House Operations*, 93; Nigel Bowles, *The White House and Capitol Hill: The Politics of Persuasion* (New York: Oxford University Press, 1987), 30.

133. The few innovations in OCR activity during the Johnson years involved relatively minor tasks—for example, briefing members of Congress about bills and presidential messages that the administration was preparing to send to Capitol Hill and logging all calls made to notify members of federal projects, contracts, and grants to be awarded in their districts. Subject File, Executive FG 11-8-1, Box 71, "William Blackburn," Johnson Presidential Library.

134. Redford and McCulley (*White House Operations*, 233, n. 7) set the number at ten full- and part-time liaison staff based on a 1967 internal memo; King and Ragsdale (*Elusive Executive*, 63) reported six full-time OCR aides.

135. Manatos continued to focus on the Senate, as did O'Brien at least at the outset; see, e.g., "Manatos, Mike," White House Central Files, Subject Files, FG 11-8-1, Boxes 93–94, Johnson Presidential Library. Johnson, as former Senate majority leader, also was quite involved. Manatos recalled that, although LBJ might offer suggestions, the president never directed him to lobby particular senators. Manatos Oral History, 25 August 1969, p. 25. Bowles notes, however, that "Johnson did not intend that Manatos should bargain with Senators as Wilson occasion-

ally did in the House, and as O'Brien did in both chambers." Bowles, *White House and Capitol Hill,* 43.

Other liaison aides paid attention to the House. Wilson remained the chief White House contact with southern members of Congress, though he shared the task with other staffers; Wilson also continued as de facto head of House liaison. When Wilson left in 1967 to become president of the Chicago Board of Trade, Barefoot Sanders replaced him and rather quickly assumed responsibility for the entire liaison operation (although O'Brien remained as its formal head until spring 1968, when he left to run Robert Kennedy's presidential campaign). James Jones took over the task of remaining in contact with southern members of Congress, which he shared with John Gonella, Robert Hardesty, and Sanders. Formally a member of Watson's staff, Jones spent considerable time on legislative liaison, at least until he replaced Watson as appointments secretary in 1968. Sanders to Jones, 2 October 1967, Subject Files, Box 89, "Jones"; 14 November 1967, Sanders to Larry Temple, Subject File, Executive FG 11-8-1, Box 68; both in Johnson Presidential Library. Donahue continued to work with House members representing urban districts, as did his replacement, Charles Roche; Roche focused in particular on members from Massachusetts (his home state) and other northeastern states. William M. Blackburn, Oral History Interview with David McComb, 21 May 1969, p. 17; Sanders Oral History, Interview with Joe B. Frantz, 24 March 1969, tape 1, p. 3. Daly left soon after Johnson took office. His replacements (David Bunn until February 1967, then Irving Sprague) also worked in the House, with Sprague, a Californian, paying special attention to the western states. "David A. Bunn," White House Central Files, Subject File, General FG 11-8-1/Bundy 1/66—, Box 74, Johnson Presidential Library; Claude Desautels, Oral History Interview with Michael Gillette, 18 April 1980, p. 1, Kennedy Presidential Library. Meanwhile, Sherwin Markman maintained contact with House members from the Midwest, and Blackburn was responsible for Texas, Mississippi, and Alabama. Sanders Oral History, 24 March 1969, tape 1, p. 4; Blackburn Oral History, pp. 16–17.

136. See, e.g., Califano to Johnson, 3 February 1967, Subject File, General FG 11-8-1, Box 85, "Robert Hardesty"; Califano to Johnson, 23 February 1967, Califano Office Files, Box 46, "Personnel," Folder 1; both in Johnson Presidential Library. Robert Hardesty was transferred from the writers' unit (see Chapter 10) to OCR, where he ultimately headed a staff of three other writers. Maguire to Watson, 28 July 1967, Maguire Office Files, Box 13, Johnson Presidential Library; Sanders to Johnson, 23 March 1968, Subject Files, "Hardesty."

137. For example, Kintner to Johnson, 22 July 1966, WH 10 Staff Meetings 11/23/63–6/15/66, Confidential Files, Box 99; Califano to Johnson, 24 July 1966, and O'Brien to Watson, 26 April 1967, Subject File, Executive FG 11-8, Box 68; Califano to Johnson, 7 November 1967, Subject File, Executive FG 11-8-1/Califano 7/1/67—, Box 75, "Joseph A. Califano"; all in Johnson Presidential Library.

138. See, e.g., Jones to Watson, 23 May 1966, WH 10 Staff Meetings 11/23/63–6/15/66, Johnson Presidential Library.

139. Wilson Oral History, 11 April 1973, p. 7.

140. Cf. Bowles, *White House and Capitol Hill,* 44.

141. Jake Jacobsen, Oral History Interview with Dorothy Pierce McSweeney, 27 March 1969, tape 3, p. 11, Johnson Presidential Library.

142. Ibid., 160.

143. He, for instance, became a member of the early morning presidential "bedroom detail," accompanied the president on trips, and served as a liaison between LBJ and his speechwriters. Ibid., 12–24 and passim; Redford and McCulley, *White House Operations,* passim.

144. Califano to Johnson, 29 March 1967, White House Central Files, Subject Files, FG 11-8-1, Box 121B, "Wilson, Henry"; Moyers to Johnson, 14 July 1966, Moyers Office Files, Box 12; both in Johnson Presidential Library.

145. See, e.g., reports on weekly meetings of the OCR staff, Subject File, Executive FG 11-8-1, Box 68; Sanders to Jones, 23 May 1967, Subject File, General FG 11-8-1, Box 89, "James R. Jones"; cf. "Sanders, Barefoot," White House Central Files, Subject Files, FG 11-8-1, Box 113; all in Johnson Presidential Library.

146. All these staffers appeared on a list of full- and part-time OCR aides that Sanders sent to Larry Temple on 14 November 1967 (Subject File, Executive FG 11-8, Box 68). Those on the list with reporting responsibilities to Watson can be identified in "Watson, Marvin," White House Central Files, Subject Files, FG 11-8-1, Box 119; see also "Markman, Sherwin," ibid., Box 94; Blackburn Oral History, pp. 2–3. On Pierson's activities as a White House staffer, see Chapter 7 on domestic policy and his Oral History Interview with Dorothy Pierce McSweeney, 19 March 1969, Johnson Presidential Library.

147. Cf. Bowles, *White House and Capitol Hill,* e.g., ch. 6.

148. The direct access of these aides to LBJ can be traced through their memos to the president, typically initialed to indicate that he'd read them. See, e.g., Moyers Office Files, Box 11, "Memos to the President"; McPherson Office Files, Box 53, "Memoranda for the President"; Cater Office Files, Box 13, "Memos to the President." These files, of course, record only written contact. Considerably more in-person and telephone interaction also took place; see, e.g., James J. Best, "Who Talked to the President When? A Study of Lyndon B. Johnson," *Political Science Quarterly* 103 (1988): 531–45.

149. Sanders Oral History, 24 March 1969, tape 2, p. 34. Sanders lamented that LBJ refused to fire Chuck Roche, whose performance was especially unsatisfactory.

150. Cf. Bowles, *White House and Capitol Hill,* ch. 7.

151. On Jenkins, see Redford and McCulley, *White House Operations,* 161. On Watson, see, e.g., Sanders to Watson, 22 July 1967, Subject Files, Box 113, "Sanders"; "Watson, Marvin," White House Central Files, Subject Files, FG 11-8-1, Box 118; O'Brien to Johnson, 27 April 1965, Office of the President File, Box 5, "Jake Jacobsen." Temple's contacts with the Texas delegation can be found in "Temple," White House Central Files, Subject Files, FG 11-8-1, Box 113. All these materials are housed in the Johnson Presidential Library.

152. Watson to Johnson, 10 January 1967, Subject Files, Box 119, "Watson." Other staffers also worked with members from their home states and regions.

153. See, e.g., Redmon to Moyers, 29 October 1965, Moyers Office Files, Box 11.

154. See Califano Office Files, "Memos to the President."

155. See, e.g., Califano to Sanders, Manatos, Gaither, Panzer, Hardesty, 21 January 1968, Califano Office Files, Box 73, "Messages—General"; more generally, see "Califano," Subject Files; Califano Office Files, "Memos to the President";

James Gaither, Oral History Interview with Joe B. Frantz, 24 March 1970, tape 5, p. 13. When the proposal for a cabinet-level Department of Transportation was being considered in Congress, for example, the Califano unit also "cleared all prepared testimony by Administration witnesses and called several of the witnesses in to brief them on exactly what they should say." Patrick Anderson, *The President's Men* (Garden City, N.Y.: Doubleday, 1969).

156. See, e.g., Califano Office Files, Box 16, "Memos for the President—March 1968."

157. Califano to Johnson, 7 November 1967, "Califano," Subject File, Executive FG 11-8-1, Box 75.

158. For example, Sanders to Califano, 13 June 1967, "Sanders," Subject Files, FG 11-8-1, Box 113; Hardesty to Califano, 26 February 1968, Califano Office Files, Box 9, "Memoranda for the President"; Califano to Johnson, 24 July 1966, Subject File, Executive FG 11-8-1, Box 68, "7/21/66."

159. Manatos to Califano, 15 February 1968, Subject File, General FG 11-8-1, Box 93, "Mike Manatos." Cf. Manatos to Califano, 6 February 1967, Subject File, General FG 11-8, Box 70; Bowles, *White House and Capitol Hill,* 51–52.

CHAPTER 3. PRESS RELATIONS AND PUBLICITY

1. Both tasks are part of what Lawrence Jacobs termed the presidential "public opinion apparatus." See Jacobs, "Public Opinion and Policy Making in the U.S. and Britain," *Comparative Politics* 24 (1992): 199–217. As it is used here, presidential emphasis on "public relations" refers to efforts to shape public opinion about, for example, presidential programs, priorities, and performance. Public-relations activities tend to be more focused on the long term than are day-to-day press operations, and they are typically aimed at communication from the president (or, more often, presidential surrogates) that is unmediated by the Washington press corps. This use of the term "public relations" is consistent with the works of, for example, Paul Brace and Barbara Hinckley, *Follow the Leader: Opinion Polls and the Modern Presidency* (New York: Basic Books, 1992); John Anthony Maltese, *Spin Control: The White House Office of Communications and the Management of Presidential News,* 2d ed. (Chapel Hill: University of North Carolina Press, 1994).

2. Cf. Charles Walcott and Karen M. Hult, "Management Science and the Great Engineer: Governing the White House during the Hoover Administration," *Presidential Studies Quarterly* 20 (1990): 557–79.

3. Ashmun Brown, "Minnesota Most Prominent in Hoover's Appointments," *Providence Journal,* 18 March 1929, Akerson Papers, Container 18, Hoover Presidential Library.

4. Cf. Harold Brayman, "Hooverizing the Press," *Outlook and Independent,* 24 September 1930, p. 155; Craig Lloyd, *Aggressive Introvert: A Study of Herbert Hoover and Public Relations Management* (Columbus: Ohio State University Press, 1973).

5. Cf. William C. Spragens, "Transition in the Press Office," in *The Presidency in Transition,* ed. James P. Pfiffner and R. Gordon Hoxie (New York: Center for the Study of the Presidency, 1989), 322.

6. Samuel Kernell, *Going Public: New Strategies of Presidential Leadership,* 1st ed. (Washington, D.C.: CQ Press, 1986), 57.

7. Cf. Walcott and Hult, "Management Science," especially pp. 559, 572.

8. David Burnet, *Herbert Hoover: A Public Life* (New York: Knopf, 1979), 256. Joslin continued Akerson's efforts to "humanize" Hoover in the public's eye, but this did little to open up press access to the president. Walcott and Hult, "Management Science," 560–61.

9. Graham J. White, *FDR and the Press* (Chicago: University of Chicago Press, 1979), 15.

10. Cf. Patrick Anderson, *The President's Men* (Garden City, N.Y.: Doubleday, 1969).

11. See, e.g., Stephen Early, "Memos to Roosevelt," memoranda, Box 23; Early Diary, 1939 entries; both in Roosevelt Presidential Library.

12. Eben Ayers, Oral History Interview with Jerry N. Hess, vol. 1, 12 January 1967, p. 22, Truman Presidential Library; cf. Kevin McCann, Oral History Interview with Ed Edwin, 21 December 1966, p. 56, Eisenhower Presidential Library; Grace Tully, *FDR, My Boss* (New York: Charles Scribner's Sons, 1949), 151.

13. The notion that Roosevelt wanted his aides to be highly competitive is, on the whole, overdone. In certain well-reported policy contexts, FDR did indeed pit his aides against one another, but in others, he did not. In particular, where his secretaries were concerned, the day began with an informal meeting in FDR's bedroom, and the work of the secretaries and the president proceeded cooperatively.

14. Ayers replaced Hassett when the latter was promoted to correspondence secretary.

15. Not all of Truman's White House press relations were organized or conducted by the press secretary's office. James Fitzgerald, a member of the staff of John Steelman, the assistant to the president, dealt routinely with the press on matters pertaining to the work of Steelman's office. This division of labor seems not to have caused serious problems for the administration or the press office, although it did not survive into subsequent administrations. Moreover, Truman was the first to avail himself of a media consultant when he retained J. Leonard Reinsch to advise him on the delivery of radio addresses. In fact, Truman had hoped to name Reinsch as his first press secretary, but he pulled back in the face of criticism and derision from reporters and White House staffers alike, who believed that only a print journalist was a suitable press chief.

16. Ronald T. Farrar, *The Reluctant Servant: The Story of Charles G. Ross* (Columbia: University of Missouri Press, 1969), 191.

17. Charles Ross Diary, 8 October 1946, Box 2, Secretary's Files, Personal File, Truman Presidential Library.

18. Ibid., 1 April 1946.

19. Eben Ayers, Oral History Interview with Jerry N. Hess, vol. 1, 12 January 1967, p. 86, Truman Presidential Library.

20. There are exceptions, of course. One was Short's advice to Truman on how to handle Senator Moody on a number of different policy issues. See memo, Short to Truman, 21 May 1952, Secretary's File, Joe Short Personal File, Truman Presidential Library.

21. Mrs. Joseph H. Short, Oral History Interview with Jerry N. Hess, 16 February 1971, Truman Presidential Library.

22. Peter Lisagor, "A Most Visible and Vital Man," *Nation's Business* 56 (December 1968): 26.

23. Spragens, "Transitions in the Press Office."

24. Anderson, *The President's Men,* 184.

25. James C. Hagerty, *The Diary of James C. Hagerty: Eisenhower in Mid-Course 1954-1955,* ed. Robert H. Ferrell (Bloomington: Indiana University Press, 1983), 193.

26. James Hagerty, Oral History Interview with Ed Edwin, 16 April 1968, pp. 442-43, Eisenhower Presidential Library. See also Bradley H. Patterson, Jr., *The Ring of Power* (New York: Basic Books, 1988), 172-73.

27. For examples, see Charles Walcott and Karen M. Hult, "White House Organization as a Problem of Governance: The Eisenhower System," *Presidential Studies Quarterly* 24 (1994): 334-35.

28. It should be noted that, although the effectiveness of such advice must be a matter of aesthetic judgment, Eisenhower the television personality played to weak reviews from his contemporaries.

29. Samuel Kernell, *Going Public: New Strategies of Presidential Leadership,* 2d ed. (Washington, D.C.: CQ Press, 1993), 71.

30. Anderson, *The President's Men,* 233.

31. William C. Spragens with Carole Ann Terwoord, *From Spokesman to Press Secretary: White House Media Operations* (Washington, D.C.: University Press of America, 1980), 151.

32. Pierre Salinger, *With Kennedy* (Garden City, N.Y.: Doubleday, 1966), 136-37.

33. James J. Best, "Who Talked to the President When? A Study of Lyndon B. Johnson," *Political Science Quarterly* 103 (1988): 531-45.

34. Paul K. Conkin, *Big Daddy from the Pedernales: Lyndon Baines Johnson* (Boston: Twayne, 1986), 181. On the contrast between Moyers and Christian, see, e.g., Henry F. Graff, *The Tuesday Cabinet: Deliberation and Decision on Peace and War under Lyndon B. Johnson* (Englewood Cliffs, N.J.: Prentice Hall, 1970), 21.

35. See, e.g., Graff, *The Tuesday Cabinet.*

36. Stephen Hess, *Organizing the White House,* 1st ed. (Washington, D.C.: Brookings Institution, 1976), 98.

37. Ibid.

38. George Christian, *The President Steps Down: A Personal Memoir of the Transfer of Power* (New York: Macmillan, 1970), 12.

39. Elizabeth S. Carpenter, Oral History Interview with Joe B. Frantz, 27 August 1969, p. 41, Johnson Presidential Library.

40. Hess, *Organizing the White House,* 98.

41. Walt Rostow, quoted in Spragens, *From Spokesman to Press Secretary,* 155.

42. Graff, *The Tuesday Cabinet,* 21.

43. See Kernell, *Going Public,* 68-69; Dick Kerschten, "Life in the White House Fish Bowl," *National Journal,* 31 January 1981, p. 180.

44. Ibid.

45. See, e.g., Larry Berman, "Johnson and the White House Staff," in *Exploring the Johnson Years,* ed. Robert A. Divine (Austin: University of Texas Press, 1981), 187–213.

46. Kernell, *Going Public,* chs. 1–2 and passim.

47. Public-relations activities predate the early modern presidencies. Scholars have traced such efforts as far back as McKinley, and they are clearly evident as early as Wilson. On the history of presidential public-relations activities, see, e.g., Robert C. Hilderbrand, *Power and the People: Executive Management of Public Opinion in Foreign Affairs, 1897–1921* (Chapel Hill: University of North Carolina Press, 1981); Elmer Cornwell, *Presidential Leadership of Public Opinion* (Bloomington: Indiana University Press, 1966); Jacobs, "Public Opinion"; Maltese, *Spin Control,* ch. 1.

48. See Lloyd, *Aggresssive Introvert.*

49. Ibid.

50. Ibid., 171; cf. Martin L. Fausold, *The Presidency of Herbert C. Hoover* (Lawrence: University Press of Kansas, 1985), 157ff.

51. MacLafferty Diary, 10 November 1930, Hoover Presidential Library.

52. Ibid., 14 November 1930.

53. Ibid., 25 November 1931, pp. 6, 8.

54. See, e.g., ibid., 12 February, 24, 25 March, 14, 29 April, 6 May 1932.

55. Betty Houchin Winfield, "The New Deal Publicity Operation: Foundation for the Modern Presidency," *Journalism Quarterly* 61 (1984): 40.

56. Michael Baruch Grossman and Martha Joynt Kumar, *Portraying the President: The White House and the News Media* (Baltimore: Johns Hopkins University Press, 1981), 22; cf. Winfield, "New Deal Publicity," 41.

57. Richard W. Steele, *Propaganda in an Open Society: The Roosevelt Administration and the Media, 1933–41* (Westport, Conn.: Greenwood, 1985), 9, 15.

58. Ibid., 9.

59. Cornwell, *Presidential Leadership of Public Opinion,* 225.

60. Lawrence R. Jacobs, "A Social Interpretation of Institutional Change: Public Opinion and Policy Making in the Enactment of the British National Health Service Act of 1946 and the American Medicare Act of 1965" (Ph.D. dissertation, Columbia University, 1990), 61; on Early's involvement, see, e.g., Steele, *Propaganda in an Open Society,* 15.

61. Early to Howe, 2 November 1934, in Cornwell, *Presidential Leadership of Public Opinion,* 212.

62. See, e.g., Casey to Early, 11 June 1942 (and similar memos in February, July, September, October, November 1942), President's Official File 3800, Casey, Folder 1, 1934–42, Roosevelt Presidential Library.

63. Maltese, *Spin Control,* 8–9.

64. Anderson, *The President's Men,* 79.

65. Steele, *Propaganda in an Open Society,* 90.

66. Alfred Dick Sander, *A Staff for the President: The Executive Office, 1921–1932* (New York: Greenwood Press, 1989), 51.

67. Steele, *Propaganda in an Open Society,* 68.

68. Draft, Sherwood foreword to Rosenman book, 1 August 1952, in Rosenman Papers, Box 17, "Working with Roosevelt," Roosevelt Presidential Library.

69. See, e.g., "A Difference of Opinion," *Colliers,* n.d., attached to correspondence from Samuel Rosenman to Robert Sherwood, July 1944, Rosenman Papers, Box 4, Roosevelt Presidential Library.

70. Grossman and Kumar, *Portraying the President,* 24.

71. Hechler memo, 16 April 1951, in Murphy Papers, "Hechler," Truman Presidential Library.

72. Stowe to Murphy (passing on Hechler memo), 20 September 1950, in Murphy Papers, "Hechler."

73. Elsey to Truman, 9 February 1951, Secretary File: General File, "Elsey," Truman Presidential Library. Perhaps the best documented public-relations discussions involving the Truman White House were those that took place in the so-called Ewing Group, which began meeting in early 1947 after the disastrous (from the president's perspective) congressional elections of 1946. According to Oscar Ewing (who was the administrator of the Federal Security Agency), the main purpose of the biweekly meetings was "to make Truman popular." Oscar R. Ewing, Oral History Interview with J. R. Fuchs, 29 April 1969, Truman Presidential Library.

74. Farrar, *Reluctant Servant,* 236.

75. See, e.g., Short to Truman, 20 April 1951, Secretary File: General File, "Short, Joe," Truman Presidential Library.

76. On Harriman's activities, see, e.g., White House Official File 370, "Harriman" and Theodore Tannenwald Papers, Box 1, Diaries. On Steelman's activities, see, e.g., White House Official Files 791, "Steelman." All these materials are housed at the Truman Presidential Library.

77. See Charles W. Jackson Papers, Boxes 20 and 21, Truman Presidential Library.

78. Shanley Diaries, Box 1, "IV White House Days," Folder 3, March 1953, p. 761, Eisenhower Presidential Library.

79. Ibid., Box 2, pp. 937, 957.

80. Ibid., Box 2, "VI White House Years," 21 December 1953, p. 1350.

81. Richard Pfau, *No Sacrifice Too Great: The Life of Lewis L. Strauss* (Charlottesville: University Press of Virginia, 1984), 147.

82. Among those who gave such speeches were Chief of Staff Sherman Adams, Appointments Secretaries Thomas Stephens and Bernard Shanley, economic staffers Gabriel Hauge and Don Paarlberg, and foreign policy advisers Clarence Randall and Nelson Rockefeller. Harking back to Stephen Early, Press Secretary James Hagerty for a time sought approval rights of staffers' acceptance of invitations and of speech drafts. See, e.g., Charles Masterson to Howard Pyle, 4 May 1955, Masterson Records, Box 8; Shanley Diaries, 26 May 1954, 19 February 1955, Box 3, pp. 1564, 1742.

83. Shanley Diaries, Box 2, "IV White House Days," Folder 5, 5 June 1953, p. 911; cf. DDE Diary, 16 June 1953, Box 4, Eisenhower Presidential Library.

84. C. D. Jackson Papers, 29 June 1953, Box 56, Daily Log, Folder 1, Eisenhower Presidential Library.

85. Howard K. Pyle and Charles Masterson, Oral History Interview with Ed Edwin, 23 May 1967, pp. 67–68, Columbia University Oral History, Eisenhower Presidential Library. Cf. Stanley M. Rumbough, Jr., Oral History Interview with

John T. Mason, Jr., 27 July 1967, Columbia University Oral History, Eisenhower Presidential Library.

86. See, e.g., Rumbough to staff, April 1954, White House Office, Office of Staff Secretary, Box 6, "Staff Secretary File 1954"; "Executive Branch Liaison Office Fact Papers," White House Central Files, Official File 72-a-2, Box 310; both in Eisenhower Presidential Library. Cf. Rumbough Oral History, 27 July 1967, pp. 20, 21ff, 30.

87. See, e.g., "Executive Branch Liaison Office Fact Papers"; Masterson Records, Box 8, Eisenhower Presidential Library. The "Fact Papers" were discontinued when Masterson left the White House in 1956. Pyle and Masterson Oral History, 23 May 1967, p. 24.

88. Shanley Diaries, Box 2, "VI White House Years, Folder 5, 1954, p. 1572.

89. James Hagerty Diary, 6 December 1954, Box 1a, Eisenhower Presidential Library.

90. Shanley Diaries, Box 3, "VII White House Years," Folder 1, 11 February 1955, p. 1732. Officially, Pyle's duties were to work with Harlow "as one of the President's liaison representatives with the departments and agencies," focusing especially on federal-state relations. Press release, 22 January 1955, White House Central File, Official File 72-a-2, Box 288, "Pyle," Eisenhower Presidential Library. White House internal documents, however, listed his responsibility as "public relations (political impact)." Goodpaster to Adams, 25 March 1955, White House Office, Office of the Staff Secretary, Box 4, "Organization of the White House Staff 1953–56 (2)," Eisenhower Presidential Library.

91. Hagerty, *Diary,* 168.

92. Charles Masterson to Sherman Adams, 7 January 1955, White House Central Files, Official File 72-a-2, Box 288, "Pyle, Howard," Eisenhower Presidential Library. Cf. Masterson memo to Pyle laying out scope of the latter's new position (27 January 1955, Masterson Records, Box 8, "White House 1955," Eisenhower Presidential Library).

93. See White House Central Files, Official File, 72-a-2, Box 288, "Pyle."

94. See, e.g., Masterson Records, Box 8, "Monday Morning Meetings" and "White House 1955."

95. Pyle and Masterson Oral History, 23 May 1967, pp. 19, 25.

96. Anderson, *The President's Men,* 184. Cf. Wilton Persons, Oral History Interview with John Luter, 24 June 1970, Columbia University Oral History, p. 153, Eisenhower Presidential Library; Homer Gruenther, Oral History Interview with John T. Mason, Jr., 11 January 1972, Columbia University Oral History, p. 100, Eisenhower Presidential Library.

97. John Eisenhower to Dwight Eisenhower, 29 August 1957, Hagerty Papers, Box 9.

98. Ibid.

99. Theodore Sorensen, *Kennedy* (New York: Harper and Row, 1965), 210.

100. Dutton to Kennedy, 28 February 1961, President's Official Files, Staff Files, Box 63, "Dutton, Frederick G.," Kennedy Presidential Library.

101. See President's Official File, Staff Files, Box 63a, "Hays, Brooks," Kennedy Presidential Library.

102. See, e.g., Schlesinger to Kennedy, 8 August 1961, President's Official File,

Staff Files, Box 65, "Schlesinger, Arthur"; Schlesinger to Kennedy, 15 May 1962, ibid., Box 65a.

103. Petersen spent most of his time traveling and speaking; see, e.g., White House Staff Files, Petersen, Box 1, Kennedy Presidential Library. Two members of his staff—Myer Rashish and Carl Levin—helped develop public-relations strategies, including making suggestions for the president's participation in and scheduling speakers supportive of trade expansion; see, e.g., Rashish to Petersen, 27 November 1961; Petersen to Levin, 11 January 1962; Petersen to O'Donnell, Salinger, O'Brien, 13 February 1962; all in ibid. Cf. White House Staff Files, Box 20, Carl Levin File, "Petersen and Rashish Memoranda" and "Petersen, Howard," Kennedy Presidential Library.

104. Stan Opotowsky, *The Kennedy Government* (New York: Dutton, 1961), 36.

105. See, e.g., Grossman and Kumar, *Portraying the President,* 97.

106. See, e.g., Busby Office Files, Box 52, "Memos to Mr. Johnson," Johnson Presidential Library. Cf. Grossman and Kumar, *Portraying the President,* 229.

107. See, e.g., Busby to Johnson, 22 May, 15 June, 21 July 1964, 8 May 1965, Busby Office Files, Box 52.

108. See, e.g., Busby to Carpenter, 7 January and 22 January 1965, Busby Office Files, Box 18, "Memos to Liz Carpenter," Johnson Presidential Library.

109. See White House Central Files, Subject Files, FG 11-8-1, Box 112, "S," Johnson Presidential Library.

110. Busby to Valenti, 22 January 1965, in ibid.; Sinclair to Johnson, 14 January 1965, Busby Office Files, Box 27, "Memos to Valenti."

111. Panzer to Johnson, 2 April 1968, Watson Files, Box 28, "Panzer memos," Johnson Presidential Library.

112. See White House Central Files, Subject Files, FG 11-8-1, Box 104, "Panzer, Fred"; Watson Files, Box 28, "Panzer memos"; Johnson Presidential Library.

113. For example, Panzer to Kintner, 14 April 1967, White House Central Files, Subject Files, FG 11-8-1, Box 104, "Panzer."

114. Panzer to Califano, 24 April 1967, ibid.

115. Eric Goldman, *The Tragedy of Lyndon Johnson* (New York: Knopf, 1969), 226.

116. Jacobs, "Public Opinion," 211.

117. Ibid.

118. On Busby, see, e.g., Busby Office Files, Box 27, "Memos to Valenti"; Busby to Johnson, 11 April 1964, Busby Office Files, Box 53, "Memos to Mr. Johnson April"; Johnson Presidential Library. On Nelson, see, e.g., Goldman, *Tragedy of Lyndon Johnson,* 226. On Redmon, see, e.g., Redmon to Moyers, 28 October 1965, 28 February 1966, Moyers Files, Box 11; 27 May 1966, 27 September 1966, Moyers Files, Box 12; Johnson Presidential Library. On Panzer, see White House Central Files, Subject Files, FG 11-8-1, Box 104, "Panzer, Fred," Johnson Presidential Library. Cf. Bruce E. Altshuler, *LBJ and the Polls* (Gainesville: University of Florida Press, 1990).

119. George Christian, *The President Steps Down: A Personal Memoir of the Transfer of the Power* (New York: Macmillan, 1970), 256.

120. See, e.g., Panzer to Johnson, 4 January 1968, Marvin Watson Files, Box 28, "Panzer memos," Johnson Presidential Library. The pollster, however, often

wanted his own role kept quiet. John P. Burke and Fred I. Greenstein, with the collaboration of Larry Berman and Richard Immerman, *How Presidents Test Reality: Decisions on Vietnam, 1954 and 1965* (New York: Russell Sage, 1989), 192.

121. Divine, *Exploring the Johnson Years,* 195.

122. See, e.g., Kintner to Johnson, 1 June 1967, Charles Maguire Office Files, Box 13, "Chrons—June 1967"; Kintner to Johnson, 2 March 1967, Office of the President File, Box 6, "Robert Kintner"; Johnson Presidential Library.

123. Grossman and Kumar, *Portraying the President,* 165.

124. Marvin Watson not only offered general advice on strategy but also, for example, worked to get favorable editorials inserted into the *Congressional Record.* Domestic policy aides Ben Wattenberg, Douglass Cater, and Harry McPherson joined officials from the Census Bureau and the Bureau of Labor Statistics in compiling a report that demonstrated continued progress by blacks. Wattenberg to Johnson, 23 May 1968, White House Central Files, Subject Files, FG 11-8-1, Box 118, "W," Johnson Presidential Library.

125. Busby to Johnson, 21 July 1964, ibid.

126. McPherson to Johnson, 10 October 1967, McPherson Office Files, Box 53, "Memoranda for the President," Johnson Presidential Library.

127. Goldstein to Johnson, 29 March 1968, Goldstein Office Files, Box 12, "Credibility Gap (Raw Material)"; cf. Goldstein to Johnson, 13 March 1968, ibid., "Misc Memoranda to the President"; Johnson Presidential Library. Similarly, McPherson urged the president to show himself as "just as restlessly eager to change things as anyone else." McPherson to Johnson, 18 March 1968, Executive FG 11-8-1/McPherson.

128. Goldstein to Johnson, 20 January 1968, Goldstein Office Files, Box 12, "Miscellaneous Memoranda to the President." Thus, public-relations specialist Panzer wrote a lengthy memo refuting the charges of a credibility gap and offering advice on how best to combat them. Panzer to George Christian, White House Central Files, Subject Files, FG 11-8-1, Box 104, "Panzer"; see also Watson Files, Box 19, "Credibility Gap."

129. McPherson to Johnson, 13 July 1965, McPherson Office Files, Box 52, "Memoranda for the President."

130. McPherson to Johnson, 1 December 1965, McPherson Office Files, Box 51, "Moyers/Valenti."

131. See McPherson Office Files, Box 53, "Memoranda for the President (1968)."

132. Interview with Joseph Laitin, 27 January 1976, cited in Grossman and Kumar, *Portraying the President,* 97.

133. On the emergence of the Office of Communications in the Nixon White House, see Maltese, *Spin Control,* chs. 2–4. On the office more generally, see, e.g., Samuel Kernell, "The Evolution of the White House Staff," in *Can the Government Govern?* ed. John E. Chubb and Paul E. Peterson (Washington, D.C.: Brookings Institution, 1989), 211–17; Howard Kurtz, "White House Briefings Are Put in the Hands of Stephanopoulos," *Washington Post,* 21 January 1993, p. A6.

134. At the beginning of the Reagan administration, Deputy Chief of Staff Michael Deaver supervised both the press and communications units. After Reagan and Press Secretary James Brady were shot in March 1981, the press operation was

placed within the Office of Communications under the direction of David Gergen. See Maltese, *Spin Control,* 190–97, 250–51.

135. Kurtz, "White House Briefings."

136. See, e.g., Maltese, *Spin Control.*

137. See, e.g., Dick Kirschten, "Communications Reshuffling Intended to Help Reagan Do What He Does Best," *National Journal,* 28 January 1984, pp. 153–57.

138. Concerns about these changes are expressed, for example, by Kernell, *Going Public;* Theodore J. Lowi, *The Personal President: Power Invested, Promise Unfulfilled* (Ithaca, N.Y.: Cornell University Press, 1985); Jeffrey Tulis, *The Rhetorical Presidency* (Princeton, N.J.: Princeton University Press, 1987).

CHAPTER 4. STAFFING THE EXECUTIVE BRANCH

1. See Michael Medved, *The Shadow Presidents: The Secret History of the Chief Executives and Their Top Aides* (New York: Times Books, 1979), 41–44.

2. Martin L. Fausold, *The Presidency of Herbert C. Hoover* (Lawrence: University Press of Kansas, 1985), 46.

3. Donald J. Lisio, *Hoover, Blacks, and Lily-Whites: A Study of Southern Strategies* (Chapel Hill: University of North Carolina Press, 1985), 159–66.

4. A Washington Correspondent, "The Secretariat," *American Mercury* (December 1929): 385–95.

5. See Walter W. Liggett, *The Rise of Herbert Hoover* (New York: H. K. Fly, 1932), 349; Fausold, *Presidency of Herbert C. Hoover,* 45–46.

6. Letter, French Strother to G. R. Parker, 1930, Strother Papers, Box 2, Hoover Presidential Library. On Newton's general lack of influence in the White House, see, e.g., William J. Hopkins, Oral History Interview with Raymond Henle, 8 August 1968, Hoover Presidential Library.

7. James MacGregor Burns, *Roosevelt: The Lion and the Fox* (New York: Harcourt, Brace and World, 1956), 187.

8. Alfred B. Rollins, Jr., *Roosevelt and Howe* (New York: Knopf, 1962), 375. Frankfurter's protégés were known, of course, as "hot dogs."

9. Ibid., 371.

10. Ibid., 389.

11. Civil Service Commission to Farley, n.d., Howe Papers, Box 67, Roosevelt Presidential Library.

12. Julian N. Friant to Margaret Durand, 20 December 1934, Howe Papers, Box 66, Roosevelt Presidential Library.

13. Form letter from Howe to Members of Congress, governors, and others, 1934, Howe Papers, Box 70, Roosevelt Presidential Library.

14. See Sidney M. Milkis, "The Presidency and Political Parties," in *The Presidency and the Political System,* 3d. ed., ed. Michael Nelson (Washington, D.C.: CQ Press, 1990), 353–58. See also Milkis, *The President and the Parties: The Transformation of the American Party System since the New Deal* (New York: Oxford University Press, 1993), chs. 5, 6.

15. James Roosevelt entered the White House in January 1937 as an administrative assistant, was promoted to secretary that July, and formally served until Octo-

ber 1938, although his effective service ended some months earlier due to illness. Evidence of his involvement in patronage is especially clear in his correspondence with FDR. See James Roosevelt Correspondence, Box 56, Roosevelt Presidential Library.

16. Rowe began his White House career as "special executive assistant" to Jimmy Roosevelt in January 1938. When he took over JR's duties at the end of that year, he signed himself "Executive Officer." In July 1939, Rowe became one of FDR's original administrative assistants. His duties included legislative and administrative liaison—work clearly relevant, but not limited, to patronage. He left the White House at the end of 1941.

17. Edward J. Flynn, *You're the Boss* (New York: Viking, 1947), 153. Quoted in Milkis, "The Presidency," 355.

18. Memo, FDR to Marvin McIntyre, 6 September 1941, President's Secretary's File, Box 152, Roosevelt Presidential Library.

19. On this process and Rowe's insistence on FDR's primacy in the selection process, see memos, Rowe to James Mathews (DNC Secretary), 17 September and 29 September 1941, Rowe Papers, Box 10, Roosevelt Presidential Library.

20. See Rowe Papers, Box 11, "Dollar-a-Year-Men," especially memo, Rowe to Hopkins, re: Arthur Bunker, 14 July 1941, Roosevelt Presidential Library. By this time, Roosevelt had rejected 15 men, conveying no reasons to the OPM. This could entail particular embarrassment in cases in which the OPM had announced a name to the press before formal clearance with the president.

21. Rowe to FDR, 20 October 1941, President's Secretary's File, Box 184, Roosevelt Presidential Library.

22. Rowe's departure ended any serious White House effort to go beyond conventional patronage brokering. However, Administrative Assistant James Barnes, a former congressman who joined the administration in February 1943, advised in this area. Eugene Casey, a special executive assistant who joined the staff in early 1941, did likewise, sometimes to Rowe's dismay.

23. See G. Calvin Mackenzie, "The Paradox of Presidential Personnel Management," in *The Illusion of Presidential Government,* ed. Hugh Heclo and Lester Salamon (Boulder, Colo.: Westview Press, 1981), 132.

24. Alfred Dick Sander, *A Staff for the President: The Executive Office, 1921–1952* (New York: Greenwood Press, 1989), 55. See also Mackenzie, "The Paradox," 132–34.

25. Milkis, "The Presidency," 358.

26. See Rowe Papers, Box 7, especially Rowe to FDR, 9 April 1941, Roosevelt Presidential Library.

27. The failure of Rowe and McReynolds to agree simply created the need for more governance, since no continuing structure could deal routinely with such problems. FDR's intervention was congruent with the decision setting, since both policy goals and technology (i.e., who would control the decision) were in dispute, and FDR was clearly a legitimate decision maker.

28. According to BOB Director Smith's diary, McReynolds was fired by Truman aide Edward McKim after Truman became convinced that McReynolds had "double-crossed" him on a pay bill. See Ayers Papers, Box 19, "Presidential Staff," Folder 1, Truman Presidential Library. Appointments Secretary Matthew Connelly

also recalled that McReynolds had a nepotism problem—nine relatives on the government payroll. Connelly, Oral History Interview with Jerry N. Hess, 30 November 1967, p. 187, Truman Presidential Library.

29. See, e.g., memo, Zimmerman to HST, 10 July 1946, Zimmerman Papers, Box 35, Truman Presidential Library.

30. Several memos from Zimmerman to Vaughan can be found in the Zimmerman Papers, Box 35, Truman Presidential Library. Zimmerman's attentions were a distinct change for Vaughan, who had been the object of Schoeneman's contempt.

31. Hassett to Matt Connelly, March 1947, White House Official File 740, "Zimmerman," Truman Presidential Library. Deputy Press Secretary Eben Ayers attributed Zimmerman's relatively brief White House tenure to the latter's being seen as "throwing his weight around a little bit." Ayers, Oral History Interview with Jerry N. Hess, vol. 2, 15 August 1969, p. 340, Truman Presidential Library.

32. See the comments of former Agriculture Secretary Charles F. Brannan in Francis H. Heller, ed., *The Truman White House: The Administration of the Presidency 1945-1953* (Lawrence: Regents Press of Kansas, 1980), 5–8, as well as those of former Commerce Secretary W. Averell Harriman in ibid., 11, 25.

33. Cabell Phillips, "The 'Inner Circle' at the White House," *New York Times Magazine,* 24 February 1946, Vertical File, "White House Staff Advisers," Truman Presidential Library.

34. The fullest description of Dawson's work can be found in Thomas Jonathan Weko, "'A Good Man Is Hard to Find': Presidents and Their Political Executives" (Ph.D. dissertation, University of Minnesota, 1991), 62–65. See also Dawson, Oral History Interview with James R. Fuchs, 8 August 1977, especially pp. 12–49, Truman Presidential Library.

35. Weko, "A Good Man," 64–65.

36. "Donald Dawson," in Heller, *Truman White House,* 49–50.

37. Dawson Oral History, 8 August 1977, p. 21. Later, in the early McCarthy era, Dawson and Friedman each functioned for a time as chair of the White House Loyalty Board (which affected only White House personnel), though later much of the responsibility for this onerous business was placed in the lap of administrative assistant (later special counsel) Charles Murphy. See Charles S. Murphy, Truman Memoir Interview, 19 November 1954, Truman Presidential Library.

38. This was the abortive "Operation Best Brains," a proposal, generated by a committee of assistant secretaries, to expand the White House personnel staff and extend its search for talent for appointive positions. Dawson evidently saw this less as an opportunity for political control than as a chance to recruit better people. The plan was killed by opposition from party and cabinet officials who found it insufficiently sensitive to partisan interests. See Weko, "A Good Man," 66–73.

39. Memo, Dodge to Eisenhower, 17 November 1952, Ann Whitman Files, Administration Series, Box 12, 1952-53, Folder 5, Eisenhower Presidential Library.

40. See John W. Macy, Bruce Adams, and J. Jackson Walter, *America's Unelected Government: Appointing the President's Team* (Cambridge, Mass.: Ballinger, 1983), 26. In fact, a preinaugural study by the McKinsey management consulting firm had identified 131 key jobs and a slate of people to fill them, thus providing the resources for an even more aggressive White House patronage role. This chance was largely missed, however. See Weko, "A Good Man," 77–78.

41. See Sherman Adams, *Firsthand Report: The Story of the Eisenhower Administration* (New York: Harper and Brothers, 1961), 76–80; Weko, "A Good Man," 78–80.

42. See Weko, "A Good Man," 81–86.

43. Willis to Adams, 1 June 1953, White House Central Files, Official File 72-a-2, Box 289, Eisenhower Presidential Library.

44. Weko, "A Good Man," 87–90. The administration also created a system of "political personnel officers" in each agency and began to press the Civil Service Commission to be more responsive to departmental requests for reclassification.

45. Weko, "A Good Man," 90–92. Note that this plan was less ambitious, from a White House standpoint, than Truman's "Best Brains," because it left the recruiting to the politicians, not the presidential staff.

46. Harlow to Adams, 2 April 1955, White House Central Files, General File, Box 284, Eisenhower Presidential Library.

47. Bernard Shanley Diaries, 10 August 1953, Box 2, "V White House Years," Folder 2, p. 1139, Eisenhower Presidential Library.

48. Percival Brundage (BOB) to Adams, n.d., White House Central Files, Official File 72-a-2, "Office of the Special Assistant to the President for Personnel Management," Eisenhower Presidential Library.

49. Executive Order 10729, White House Central Files, Official File 72-a-2, Box 310, "Office of the Special Assistant to the President for Personnel Management," Eisenhower Presidential Library.

50. Siciliano to Adams, 24 October 1957, Siciliano letter of resignation, 15 October 1959, White House Central Files, Official File 72-a-2, Box 310, "Office of the Special Assistant to the President for Personnel Management," Eisenhower Presidential Library. When Siciliano resigned, he was replaced by Eugene Lyons, whose work did not differ significantly from his predecessor's.

51. G. Calvin Mackenzie, *The Politics of Presidential Appointments* (New York: Free Press, 1981), 22.

52. See Weko, "A Good Man," 106–14; Mackenzie, "The Paradox," 22–26.

53. Lawrence F. O'Brien, *No Final Victories: A Life in Politics—From John F. Kennedy to Watergate* (New York: Doubleday, 1974), 119; see also Weko, "A Good Man," 116–22. Weko would add O'Brien aide Richard Donahue to the list of active participants.

54. Weko, "A Good Man," 118.

55. Kennedy White House Aide, quoted in ibid., 118.

56. Weko, "A Good Man," 118–22; Mackenzie, "The Paradox," 27.

57. Quoted in Macy et al., *America's Unelected Government,* 27.

58. See ibid., 27–30; Weko, "A Good Man," 123–31.

59. Macy et al., *America's Unelected Government,* 30–31.

60. Charles U. Daly, Oral History Interview with Charles T. Morrissey, 5 April 1966, p. 50, Kennedy Presidential Library.

61. Weko, "A Good Man," 131–36. Indeed, as was the case in prior administrations, neither Fenn and Dungan, the White House aides formally charged with patronage responsibilities, nor such informally powerful players as O'Brien and O'Donnell had anything like a monopoly on advice to or influence on the president in the making of appointments.

62. Mackenzie, "The Paradox," 31.

63. See memoranda of conversation between O'Donnell and David Bell (BOB), 20 and 22 March 1961, White House Central Subject Files, Box 111, Kennedy Presidential Library.

64. Nevertheless, a vestige of the Office of the Special Assistant for Personnel Management continued under Maguire and actually survived him in the White House, lasting into the early Johnson administration, working on "special projects." See John W. Macy, Jr., Oral History Interview with David G. McComb, 26 April 1969, pp. 4–5, Johnson Presidential Library.

65. Milkis, "The Presidency," 359–63.

66. Richard L. Schott and Dagmar S. Hamilton, *People, Positions, and Power: The Political Appointments of Lyndon Johnson* (Chicago: University of Chicago Press, 1983), 12–13.

67. Dungan, Oral History Interview, 18 March 1969, p. 18, Johnson Presidential Library, quoted in Schott and Hamilton, *People, Positions, and Power,* 13.

68. Schott and Hamilton, *People, Positions, and Power,* 13.

69. Emmette S. Redford and Richard T. McCulley, *White House Operations: The Johnson Presidency* (Austin: University of Texas Press, 1986), 137.

70. Schott and Hamilton, *People, Positions, and Power,* 14.

71. John Macy Interview, 14 December 1976, quoted in ibid., 15.

72. In fact, Macy had two offices, one in the White House for his patronage work, another at the Civil Service Commission. His attempt to bring all White House patronage activities into his office meant the elimination of the Office of Congressional Relations's patronage staff (Davies's staff) as well as the remnants of the civil service liaison staff.

73. The staff numbered two "desk officers," an assistant for each desk officer, a specialist in boards and commissions, plus support staff. Macy describes it in his Oral History, 26 April 1969, p. 9.

74. Ibid., 7–9. Weko describes the Macy staff's relationship with the departments as generally excellent, in part because they shared similar goals concerning competence and commitment to policy goals. Weko, "A Good Man," 152–57.

75. Macy Oral History, 26 April 1969, p. 9.

76. Ibid., 17–20; Schott and Hamilton, *People, Positions, and Power,* 15–23. Macy also handled paperwork for judicial appointments, although these continued to originate in the Justice Department, with White House liaison located outside the patronage staff. Macy Oral History, 26 April 1969, p. 8.

77. Weko, "A Good Man," 149–51; Milkis, "The Presidency," 361.

78. Milkis, "The Presidency," 359–63.

79. See Schott and Hamilton, *People, Positions, and Power,* 19–24. They quote congressional liaison aide Mike Manatos, for instance, as complaining that the Macy group produced mostly "eggheads" rather than "practical politicians. . . . They were mostly people who just had the great IQs, a lot of the intelligence, no question about the qualifications for the slots that John was selecting them for. But I thought that a lot of them . . . were just not very practical people."

80. Ibid., 17–19.

81. Weko, "A Good Man," 161.

82. Weko argues that, "in the main, Watson's efforts were amateurish" and lim-

ited by the small size of his staff to making the final judgment on a few key appointments." Ibid., 163. Bill Moyers, on the other hand, contended that Watson's domination of the final stage in the appointments process had serious, detrimental effects on the administration, due to Watson's narrow focus on loyalty. Schott and Hamilton, *People, Positions, and Power,* 25-26.

83. Schott and Hamilton, *People, Positions, and Power,* 28. Kinter, whose White House career lasted just over a year, had little impact on appointments.

84. See, e.g., Terry M. Moe, "The Politicized Presidency," in *The New Direction in American Politics,* ed. John E. Chubb and Paul E. Peterson (Washington, D.C.: Brookings Institution, 1985); Richard P. Nathan, *The Administrative Presidency* (New York: Wiley, 1983); Richard W. Waterman, "Combining Political Resources: The Internalization of the President's Appointment Power," in *The Presidency Reconsidered,* ed. Richard W. Waterman (Itasca, Ill.: Peacock, 1993).

CHAPTER 5. WHITE HOUSE–EXECUTIVE BRANCH RELATIONS

1. Neustadt in Jerry Kluttz, "The Federal Diary: Criticism of President, White House Staff Gives Clue to Change," *Washington Post,* 30 December 1960, Vertical File, "White House Staff Advisers," Truman Presidential Library.

2. A significant amount of staff time during the period examined here was devoted to encouraging executive branch agencies to integrate their workplaces and to end discrimination in the programs they administered. Because these activities tended to reflect White House efforts to respond to the demands of external interests rather than the interests of presidents in monitoring programs, they are discussed in Chapter 6.

3. "To Be Third White House Secretary," *Minneapolis Tribune,* 15 March 1929, Akerson Papers, White House Secretary Files, Container 15, Hoover Presidential Library. Newton's assignment did not include independent regulatory agencies such as the ICC, FCC, and Tariff Commission.

4. White House press release quoted in ibid.

5. On the Hoover administration's reliance on commissions and committees, see, e.g., Charles Walcott and Karen M. Hult, "Management Science and the Great Engineer: Governing the White House During the Hoover Administration," *Presidential Studies Quarterly* 20 (1990): 564-65. On Strother's and Hastings's activities, see Strother Papers, Box 2, and Hastings Papers, Box 2, Hoover Presidential Library. After Strother left in May 1931, Hastings took over his liaison tasks. For most of 1932, Hastings was technically on leave from the White House, charged with following up on the findings and resolutions of the White House Conference on Child Health.

6. Hastings collected data on various questions of interest to Hoover, which put him in frequent touch with the executive branch agencies. For example, on 31 August 1930, the president asked Hastings for data on each department's federal construction expenditures (Hastings Papers, Box 2). In 1931, press secretary Theodore Joslin surveyed departments, commissions, and bureaus on their actions to combat the depression. Although public relations was probably the primary objec-

tive, he followed up on many of the "progress reports" (Joslin Papers, Container 3, Hoover Presidential Library).

7. George Hastings seemingly disagreed. "Apparently it never occurred to the Great Engineer, Organizer and Executive to have one competent Secretary representing him, and give him enough assistants, responsible and reporting to him and not the President, to do the heavy, exacting work of the executive offices." Hastings, "Secretarial Stupidity," n.d., Hastings Papers, Box 9, p. 6. This perhaps represents the first serious call for a strong, unified staff in the White House. It also overestimates the utility of formal hierarchy in the job of executive branch liaison.

8. See the reports Howe received on the activities of, for example, the Civilian Conservation Corps, Works Progress Administration, Federal Trade Commission, and Labor and Justice Departments in Howe Papers, Boxes 66, 70, 72, 74, 81, 84, Roosevelt Presidential Library.

9. Kenneth S. Davis, *FDR, The New Deal, 1933–1937: A History* (New York: Random House, 1986), 285.

10. See Howe Papers, Boxes 74, 85.

11. Ibid., Box 72.

12. Ibid., Box 92. Howe paid special attention to Arthurdale, an experimental community in Reedsville, West Virginia, in which Eleanor Roosevelt had a strong interest; cf. Davis, *FDR,* 373ff. On the Civilian Conservation Corps, see Patrick Anderson, *The President's Men* (Garden City, N.Y.: Doubleday, 1969), 14–17. Howe's efforts to dominate the subsistence home program were less than successful; finally, full responsibility was given to Rexford Tugwell in the Resettlement Administration. Anderson, *The President's Men,* 16–17; Joseph P. Lash, *Eleanor and Franklin: The Story of Their Relationship* (New York: New American Library, 1973); Harold L. Ickes, *The Secret Diary of Harold L. Ickes,* vol. 1 (New York: Simon and Schuster, 1953), 129, 206–7, 254.

13. Stephen Early Diary, 19 June 1934, Roosevelt Presidential Library.

14. Robert Sherwood, *Roosevelt and Hopkins: An Intimate History* (New York: Harper, 1948), 287. See also, e.g., Hopkins Papers, Box 93, "McIntyre"; President's Official File, 1560, "Corcoran," Roosevelt Presidential Library; Louis W. Koenig, *The Invisible Presidency* (New York: Holt, Rinehart and Winston, 1960), 321. Tommy Corcoran also was involved; he served as a channel to the president for administrators and "toil[ed] below decks to keep the administrative machinery of the New Deal in efficient shape." Koenig, *Invisible Presidency,* 265.

15. These were not located directly in the White House, but in what would later be formally designated the Executive Office of the President.

16. According to Tugwell, for example, Interior Secretary Harold Ickes grew irritated at Richberg's "self-satisfied air," and Secretary of Labor Frances "Perkins's New England resistance to rules of all kinds [was] incorrigible." Rexford Tugwell, Diary and Notes, 12 December 1934, Tugwell Papers, Box 31, "Diary 1934," Roosevelt Presidential Library.

17. For example, ibid.

18. Even so, James MacGregor Burns argued that the EC and NEC served at least "one great function": "they exposed the heads of thirty or forty agencies firsthand to Roosevelt's contagious drive and enthusiasm. . . . Roosevelt almost single-

handedly gave pace and direction to the New Deal battalions." *The Lion and the Fox* (New York: Harcourt, Brace, 1956), 174.

19. J. P. Harris, "Confidential Memo on the National Emergency Council," 15 August 1936, President's Committee on Administrative Management Files, Box 13, pp. 4–5, Roosevelt Presidential Library.

20. William Y. Elliott, "The President's Role in Administrative Management," in ibid., 21.

21. On complaints about Civilian Conservation Corps work hours, see Howe Papers, Box 74; on the requests of conductors for a National Recovery Administration employment code, see Howe Papers, Box 96.

22. See Howe Papers, Box 96. The Veterans Administration provided food and housing, and Howe helped secure money from Congress to help pay the veterans' ways home and offered them Civilian Conservation Corps jobs.

23. Harris, "Confidential Memo on the NEC," 4–5; cf. Elliott, "The President's Role," in ibid., 21.

24. Early Diary, 14 March 1934.

25. See President's Secretary's Files, Box 194, Roosevelt Presidential Library.

26. Early to Roosevelt, 16 October 1934, Early Papers, Memos, Box 24, "Edwin M. Watson," Roosevelt Presidential Library; FDR noted his approval of the arrangement at the end of the memo.

27. Harris, "Confidential Memo on the NEC," 4–5. Similarly, Corcoran, in addition to his other activities, worked to mediate conflicts among top executive branch officials such as Ickes and Hopkins. Koenig, *Invisible Presidency,* 278.

28. For example, BOB Director Douglas sought to balance the budget and wanted to hire government employees; "brains trusters" wanted to create more public works jobs. See Theodore C. Wallen, *New York Herald Tribune,* 1 July 1933, in Tugwell Papers, Box 31, "6/1933–5/1934," p. 67, Roosevelt Presidential Library.

29. Burns, *The Lion and the Fox,* 322.

30. See, e.g., Drew Pearson and Robert S. Allen, "Washington Merry-Go-Round," 1934, in Tugwell Papers, Box 38.

31. See James Roosevelt, *Affectionately, FDR* (New York: Harcourt, Brace, 1959).

32. Ibid., 48.

33. See letter, Margaret J. Lawson (a Miami woman who sent an unidentified, undated clipping critical of J. Roosevelt) to James Roosevelt, 23 April 1938, J. Roosevelt Correspondence, Box 2; James Roosevelt Diary, Roosevelt Presidential Library.

34. J. Roosevelt Diary, 21 October 1937.

35. Paul Mallon, King Features article, 24 October 1936, in J. Roosevelt Correspondence, Box 8.

36. Rodney Dutcher, columnist, column (no title, n.d.), in ibid.

37. Rowe to J. Roosevelt, 28 September 1938, J. Roosevelt Correspondence, Box 59, "James Rowe." Rowe seemed to be referring in part to the younger Roosevelt's insistence that agency heads come to see him rather than vice versa, which exacerbated the resistance to White House direction. At the same time, Rowe expressed concern that the younger Roosevelt shied away from imposing White House guidance by not insisting that such meetings actually take place. Finally,

Rowe believed that this particular use of hierarchy was too vulnerable to manipulation from below.

38. See President's Secretary's Files, Box 115, Roosevelt Presidential Library. At first, the arrangement caused additional problems, given Rowe's relatively low status; see, e.g., Early to F. Roosevelt, 23 February 1939, Early Papers, Memoranda, "Roosevelt," Box 23.

39. See, e.g., J. Roosevelt Correspondence, Boxes 2 and 12.

40. J. Roosevelt Diary, 21 March 1938.

41. Rowe to Samuel Rosenman, "AAs to the President," 15 March 1941, Rosenman Papers, Box 41, pp. 2–3, Roosevelt Presidential Library.

42. See, e.g., Currie to F. Roosevelt, 28 September 1939, President's Secretary's File, Box 115. Currie was a professional economist whose duties also involved serving as White House liaison with the Federal Reserve, the Federal Deposit Insurance Corporation, the Securities and Exchange Commission, and lending agencies, as well as with statistical economic units. F. Roosevelt to Currie, 20 July 1939, President's Official File 3719, "Currie." Later he was detailed to the Foreign Economic Administration.

43. Rowe, "AAs to the President," p. 2. Rowe, for example, reported to FDR that some high-level appointees (such as Leon Henderson of the Priorities Board) were frustrated with what they perceived as the president's "placating business. . . . [They] feel you have given away too much, that you do not know what is going on, and most important, that you have left yourself without any protection whatsoever because the OPM [Office of Production Management] executive order has decapitated every person whose first loyalty was to you." Rowe to F. Roosevelt, 23 January 1941, President's Secretary's File, Box 152.

44. Grace Tully, *FDR My Boss* (New York: Charles Scribner's Sons, 1949), 142. Cf. Hopkins Papers, Box 209; President's Official Files 4117, "Hopkins," Folder 1, 1944. Pa Watson, who in 1939 became a secretary to the president as well as military aide, also was involved in wartime liaison (although his main responsibility was serving as appointments secretary). He was a main channel between the president, on the one hand, and the War Department and the services, on the other. Until Adm. William D. Leahy was named chief of staff to the commander in chief (see Chapter 8), for example, the Joint Chiefs of Staff communicated to the president mostly through Watson. Sherwood to Rosenman, 7 January 1952, Rosenman Papers, Box 13, p. 2.

45. George McJimsey, *Harry Hopkins: Ally of the Poor and Defender of Democracy* (Cambridge, Mass.: Harvard University Press, 1987), 151.

46. See, e.g., Early's description of Hopkins's duties, 21 January 1944, President's Official File 4117, "Hopkins," Folder 1.

47. Sherwood, *Roosevelt and Hopkins*, 202.

48. Stephen Hess, *Organizing the Presidency*, 2d ed. (Washington, D.C.: Brookings Institution, 1988), 37.

49. Ibid., 38.

50. Rosenman officially joined the staff in September 1943 as "a general assistant in seeing that Presidential policy directives are carried out by administrative agency [sic]." President's Official File 5433, "Rosenman," Folder 1: 1943. Rosenman had performed this task long before he formally became a staffer. Arthur

Krock observed in May 1942: "If you want to alarm any member of the Administration from the Cabinet level down just whisper in his ear one of two dreaded sentences: 'Sam Rosenman is in town' or 'The Chief has an executive order on his desk that affects you.' Either whisper is likely to pale the cheek of the most favored of administrators." "The Executive Order as a Deadly Weapon," *New York Times,* 22 May 1942, p. 20.

51. McJimsey, *Harry Hopkins,* 325.

52. "Washington Outlook," *Report for the Business Executive,* 31 August 1944, p. 1, in President's Official File 4117, "Hopkins," Folder 1: 1944.

53. See President's Official File 5433, "Rosenman."

54. F. Roosevelt to Wayne Coy, 2 August 1941, President's Secretary's File, Box 147. Coy reported on his actions to Hopkins (e.g., Coy to Hopkins, 18 August 1941, Coy Papers, Box 8, Roosevelt Presidential Library). Similarly, Currie took on a variety of special assignments for Roosevelt or for Hopkins (see President's Secretary's File, Box 115; President's Official File 3719, "Currie"). Much of Jonathan Daniels's work as an administrative assistant involved handling the problems of government personnel overseas and racial problems in agencies. Fred W. Shipman, Report on the White House Executive Office, 1943, Roosevelt Presidential Library; Jonathan Daniels, *White House Witness: 1942-45* (Garden City, N.Y.: Doubleday, 1975).

55. Richard E. Neustadt, "Approaches to Staffing the Presidency: Notes on FDR and JFK," *American Political Science Review* 57 (1963): 858.

56. Hess, *Organizing the Presidency,* 38. Byrnes explained his approach to FDR in Byrnes to F. Roosevelt, 26 January 1944, President's Secretary's File, Box 147.

57. Ibid.

58. F. Roosevelt to Byrnes, 9 March 1943, President's Secretary's File, Box 147.

59. Marquis Childs, *I Write from Washington* (New York: Harper and Brothers, 1942), 224.

60. Daniels, *White House Witness,* 17–18.

61. "Presidential Agent," *Time,* 22 January 1945, p. 18, in Rosenman Papers, Box 2.

62. Neustadt, "Approaches to Staffing," 859.

63. Ibid., 860.

64. "Curtiss-Wright, the Whipping Boy," editorial in *Aero Digest,* July 1943, p. 283, in Hopkins Papers, Box 137, Roosevelt Presidential Library.

65. This may help explain why critics of the Truman staff's efforts at executive branch outreach proposed additional structural mechanisms. In 1948, for example, James Rowe and James Forrestal suggested the creation of a liaison secretary to the president to track the numerous interdepartmental committees and to make sure that all available information was brought to the president's attention; ultimately, they thought, such a person could work with the Bureau of the Budget to "rationalize" the committee system and to help the president anticipate possible problems. Rowe and Forestal, draft memo to Truman, 19 November 1948, Secretary File: General File, "Secretaries—The President"; Rowe to Clifford, 2 May 1949, Clifford Papers, Truman Presidential Library. In 1950, Herman Miles Somers, in the concluding chapter to *Presidential Agency: OWMR, the Office of War Mobilization and Reconversion* (Cambridge: Harvard University Press, 1950), made a similar pro-

posal, which Steelman staffer Una Carter dismissed as redundant with Steelman's activities. Carter to Steelman, 26 July 1950, Secretary File: General File, "Steelman."

66. See Alfred Dick Sander, *A Staff for the President: The Executive Office, 1921–52* (New York: Greenwood Press, 1989), 81. Yet Steelman, for example, was formally the White House link between executive agencies and the President's Commission on Higher Education. Truman statement, 12 December 1946, Dallas C. Halverstadt Papers, Box 4, Truman Presidential Library; cf. Steelman to Director of Extension, USDA, 28 January 1947; Steelman to State Department, 5 February 1947; Steelman Papers, Box 1, Truman Presidential Library. Steelman also worked with the Interagency Policy Committee on Rubber (Steelman to Committee members, 11 February 1947, Steelman Papers, Box 1), the Coordinating Committee for Emergency Exports (Krug [Secretary of Interior] to Steelman, 1 May 1947, ibid.), and the Displaced Persons Commission (Harry N. Rosenfield, Oral History Interview with James R. Fuchs, 23 July 1980, pp. 103–4, Truman Presidential Library).

67. Their assignments typically reflected their substantive responsibilities. As part of his work on labor-management dispute resolution, for instance, Harold Enarson was in contact with the Economic Stabilization Agency as well as the National Security Resources Board; see Enarson Papers, Box 4, Truman Presidential Library. Charles Jackson, who was involved with the Advertising Council and dealt generally with businesses, had close links with the Commerce Department and was involved with its Travel Advisory Committee. Jackson Papers, Box 17, Truman Presidential Library. Similarly, reflecting his own relationships with business, Robert Turner maintained contact with, among others, the Departments of Commerce, Agriculture, and State; see, e.g., Turner Papers, Box 2, Chronological Files, "1948," Truman Presidential Library. Milton Kayle developed ties with agencies working in mobilization, health, labor, and natural resources. Murphy Papers, "Kayle," Truman Presidential Library.

68. Clark Clifford, Oral History Interview with Jerry N. Hess, 23 March 1971, p. 10, Truman Presidential Library. Cf. Leigh White, "Truman's One Man Brain Trust," *Saturday Evening Post,* 4 October 1947, p. 30, in Eben Ayers Papers, Box 19, Truman Presidential Library.

69. "The Presidency: Little Accident," *Time,* 15 March 1948, p. 27, in Elsey papers, Box 57, Truman Presidential Library.

70. Clifford Oral History, 23 March 1971, p. 13; 13 April 1971, pp. 71–72.

71. Rosenfield Oral History, 23 July 1980, pp. 103–4.

72. See, e.g., memo on Spingarn's duties, no author or recipient, 8 September 1948, Secretary's Files, General File; Spingarn to Clifford, 15 June 1949, Spingarn Papers, Box 12; Charles Murphy, Oral History Interview with Charles T. Morrissey and Jerry N. Hess, 24 July 1963, vol. 2, p. 96; all in Truman Presidential Library.

73. See Locke Papers, Box 3, "Special Assistant, June 1946–February 1947," Truman Presidential Library.

74. John Steelman, Truman Memoir Interview by William Hillman, David M. Noyes, Francis Heller, and Lee Williams, 18 December 1954, p. 4, Truman Presidential Library. Naval aide Capt. Robert L. Dennison advised Truman "on Defense, Budget, Maritime, Veterans and other governmental Affairs." Truman, fitness report on Dennison, 20 January 1953, Secretary's File, General File, "Dennison,"

Truman Presidential Library; cf. Roger W. Jones, Oral History Interview with Jerry N. Hess, 14 August 1969, pp. 44ff., Truman Presidential Library. Meanwhile, Harry Vaughan dealt mainly with veterans' affairs; see, e.g., "Interview with Major General H. H. Vaughan," *U.S. News and World Report,* 26 October 1951, p. 26, in Ayers Papers, Box 20.

75. See Steelman Papers, Box 3. For all the likely temptation in the overheated postwar atmosphere, little questionable White House intervention in agency decision making by Steelman or his staff evidently took place. In late 1947, for example, Turner reported to Steelman on a phone conversation he had had with a man who wanted assistance in getting favorable action on export license applications for "good Democrats" in Chicago: "He proceeded to lecture me for some length about the unsympathetic attitude of the Department of Commerce toward Chicago Democrats, and insisted that there was someone in the White House who would fix the applications. I told him I knew of no such persons. He wound up the conversation somewhat annoyed because I was 'not more cooperative,'" Turner to Steelman, 3 December 1947, Turner Papers, Box 2, Chronological Files, "1947."

76. *American Aviation Daily,* 12 July 1946, in Locke Papers, Box 3; cf. Locke to Connelly, 16 May 1946, Secretary File: General File.

77. *American Aviation Daily,* 7 September 1946, in Locke Papers, Box 3.

78. See, e.g., Vaughan Papers, Box 1, Alphabetical Files, Truman Presidential Library; "Interview with Major General H. H. Vaughan," p. 26; Rufus Jarman, "Washington's Worst Politician," *Saturday Evening Post,* 24 July 1948, p. 62.

79. Drew Pearson, "Washington Merry-Go-Round," *Washington Post,* 7 April 1947, in Ayers Papers, Box 20. In July 1949, Vaughan allegedly interceded with the Commerce Department to issue an export license for a company that in the past had been accused of buying such a license. Vaughan also was accused of having helped a racetrack avoid regulations that favored the construction of veterans' housing. "As Pegler Sees It," 20 July 1949, in Ayers Papers, Box 20.

80. See, e.g., Spingarn to Clifford, 15 June 1949, Spingarn Papers, Box 12; Murphy to Spingarn, 8 August 1949, ibid.

81. Steelman, Truman Memoir Interview, 9 December 1954.

82. Truman, Truman Memoir Interview, 18 December 1954, p. 3; cf. Steelman, Truman Memoir Interview, 9 December 1954.

83. Truman, Truman Memoir Interview, 18 December 1954, p. 4.

84. See Turner Papers, Box 2, Chronological Files, "1947." Turner himself helped fashion a compromise among the army, the State Department, and the Department of Agriculture over the sale of German textiles in the United States. Ibid., "1948."

85. David Stowe, Joint Oral History Interview with Hugh Heclo and Anna Wilson, 20 February 1980, p. 17, Truman Presidential Library.

86. Koenig, *Invisible Presidency,* 35.

87. Ibid.

88. Clarence Randall Journal, 2 August 1957, Box 4, CFEP, vol. 5, p. 9, Eisenhower Presidential Library.

89. See, e.g., Hauge to Morgan, 24 October 1957, White House Central Files, Official Files, 72-A-2, Box 309, "White House Files," Eisenhower Presidential Library.

90. See John Foster Dulles to Adams, 24 February 1953, White House Central Files, General, Box 283, Eisenhower Presidential Library.

91. Eisenhower to Pike, 25 June 1956, White House Central Files, Official Files, 72-A-2, Box 288, "Pike, Thomas Potter."

92. Allen Annable interview with Goodpaster, 25 February 1955, "Space Survey of the Presidency," White House Central Files, Official Files, Box 310. According to Goodpaster, his coordinating work generally focused on security issues, and the White House relied on department heads to do the coordinating on domestic issues. Oral History Interview with Ed Edwin, 25 April 1967, p. 30, Eisenhower Presidential Library. With the formalization of the Joint Chiefs of Staff and the increased role of the National Security Council (see Chapter 8), military aides became less important and returned to their largely ceremonial duties.

93. Anderson, *The President's Men,* 379. Donald Paarlberg claimed that, at least from his vantage point in the Department of Agriculture before joining the White House staff, Adams never meddled. Oral History Interview with Ed Edwin, 17 January 1968, Columbia University, p. 75, Eisenhower Presidential Library. Moreover, White House aide Robert Merriam observed that Adams "always got the President's okay before he pushed cabinet members in a particular direction," even if Adams did not always tell the official that Eisenhower was involved. Oral History Interview with John T. Mason, Jr., 13 January 1969, Columbia University, p. 75, Eisenhower Presidential Library.

94. See "Staff Luncheons," White House Central Files, Official Files, 72-A-2, Box 309. On Shanley's efforts to act as a contact person for executive branch officials, see, e.g., Shanley Diaries, 4 May 1954, Box 2, "VI White House Years," Folder 5, 1954, p. 1536; March 1955, Box 3, "VII White House Years," Folder 3, 1955, Eisenhower Presidential Library. Still later, Robert Merriam, who dealt with interdepartmental relations, and others lunched weekly with staff of noncabinet agencies. See Merriam records, Boxes 7 and 9, Eisenhower Presidential Library.

95. See, e.g., Shanley Diaries, Box 1, "IV White House Days," Folder 1 (early 1953), p. 605.

96. Eisenhower to Harlow, 4 December 1954, White House Central Files, Official Files, 72-A-2, Box 286, "Bryce Harlow."

97. Allen Annable interview with Stephen Benedict, 25 February 1955, "Space Survey of the Presidency," White House Central Files, Official Files, Box 310. Throughout this period, Harlow worked mostly in congressional liaison (see Chapter 2; also Bryce Harlow, Oral History Interview with John T. Mason, Jr., 27 February 1967, Eisenhower Presidential Library, passim; Harlow Records, Boxes 5 and 6; Allen Annable interview with Harlow, 23 February 1955, "Space Survey of the Presidency") and occasionally speechwriting.

98. Hagerty Diary, 18 January 1955, Box 1a, Eisenhower Presidential Library.

99. See White House Personnel Records, 21 June 1955, White House Office, Office of the Staff Secretary, Box 5; "Fred A. Seaton," White House Central Files, Official Files, 72-A-2, Box 289.

100. See, e.g., Seaton memos in the Whitman Diary Series—for example, Box 6, September 1955, Folder 7; cf. Randall Journal, 22 May 1955, Box 2, vol. 9, p. 8.

101. See, e.g., "Seaton," Whitman Files, Administrative Series, Box 33, Eisenhower Presidential Library.

102. Seaton spent considerable time on legislative liaison (for which he had been

hired originally in February 1955) and on more "political" tasks such as speaking on behalf of the administration around the country and offering campaign advice. Indeed, John Bragdon (head of the White House public works planning unit) complained that Seaton was " 'Nothing But' a Politician." John Bragdon, handwritten notes, n.d., "Book—A Look at the White House—General," Bragdon Papers, Box 2, Eisenhower Presidential Library.

103. Carter Burgess to Adams and Persons, re: "Staff Work in the White House," 25 June 1953, White House Office, Office of the Staff Secretary, Box 4.

104. See "White House Staff Operations: Forms and Procedures," attached to memo from Adams to "All Department Heads and the White House Staff," 20 August 1954.

105. Ibid.; cf. Goodpaster Oral History, 25 April 1967, p. 35.

106. Goodpaster to Persons, Morgan, Merriam, and Harlow, 18 October 1958, White House Office, Staff Research Group, Box 36, "Procedures—Research Group," Eisenhower Library; cf. Goodpaster Oral History Interview with Maclyn P. Burg, 20 August 1976, p. 76, Eisenhower Presidential Library.

107. Bradley Patterson, *The Ring of Power* (New York: Free Press, 1988), 51. Similarly, staffer Timothy Stanley referred to the position as a "reporter's job." Oral History Interview with Dr. Thomas Soapes, 28 February 1977, p. 10, Eisenhower Presidential Library.

108. Patterson, *Ring of Power*, 29.

109. See Martin Records, Box 2, Eisenhower Presidential Library.

110. See, e.g., Hagerty Diary, 25 February, 14 March 1955, Box 1a.

111. Edward McCabe, Oral History Interview with Paul L. Hopper, 9 September 1967, Columbia University, p. 36, Eisenhower Presidential Library.

112. McCabe, interview with authors, October 1990.

113. Minnich, Oral History Interview with Maclyn P. Burg, 26 June 1975, p. 115, Eisenhower Presidential Library; cf. Stanley Oral History, 28 February 1977, p. 11.

114. McCabe to Toner, 9 February 1957, White House Office, Staff Research Group, Box 23.

115. Patterson, Oral History Interview with Paul L. Hopper, 19 September 1968, Columbia University, p. 48, Eisenhower Presidential Library.

116. Cf. Phillip G. Henderson, "Organizing the Presidency for Effective Leadership: The Eisenhower Years," *Presidential Studies Quarterly* 17 (1987): 63. For example, there is little to suggest any reemergence of White House involvement in mediation. The only real evidence of such a possibility, evidently lodged in the special counsel's office, was one staffer's reference early in the administration to Sorensen's "analysis and mediating" activities. Alan L. Otten, " 'What Do You Think, Ted?': Theodore Sorensen," in *The Kennedy Circle,* ed. Lester Tanzer (Washington, D.C.: Luce, 1961), 4, 23.

117. See, e.g., Dutton memos to Kennedy, "Dutton, Frederick G.," President's Official Files, Staff Files, Box 63; Reardon memos to Kennedy, "Reardon, Timothy J., Jr.," ibid., Box 64a; Kennedy Presidential Library. In addition, as in past administrations, other staffers took on liaison tasks. The special counsel's office again became important, as it had been under Franklin Roosevelt and Harry Truman.

118. See Dutton to departmental reporters, 2 February 1961, White House Central Staff Files, Box 117; cf. ibid., Box 108; Kennedy Presidential Library.

119. Frederick G. Dutton, Oral History Interview with Charles T. Morrissey, 3 May 1965, pp. 47–49, Kennedy Presidential Library. See also, e.g., Dutton reports to Kennedy in President's Official Files, "Dutton" Staff Files, Box 63.

120. Patterson, *Ring of Power,* 52.

121. Dutton Oral History, 3 May 1965, p. 58.

122. Dutton to Kennedy, 19 July 1961, President's Official Files, "Dutton" Staff Files. On Dutton's meetings with the "little cabinet," see, e.g., memo on a subcabinet meeting on the problems of small business, 25 April 1961; Dutton to Lawrence O'Brien, 12 April 1961, White House Central Staff Files, Box 117. When Reardon took over, he assumed many of these responsibilities.

123. See Dutton to Kennedy, 20 February 1961, in President's Official Files, "Dutton" Staff Files, Box 63.

124. Reardon to Kennedy, 27 April 1962, "Reardon" Staff Files, Box 64a; the files contain other examples as well.

125. See, e.g., Jake Jacobsen, in Emmette S. Redford and Richard T. McCulley, *White House Operations: The Johnson Presidency* (Austin: University of Texas Press, 1986), 65.

126. Douglass Cater, Oral History Interview with David G. McComb, 8 May 1969, p. 22, Johnson Presidential Library.

127. Although Maguire's name does not appear with the other two as "cabinet secretary" in Redford and McCulley's listing of White House staffers (*White House Operations,* 54), he is referred to by that title elsewhere in the book (e.g., pp. 144, 153). In any case, Maguire himself reported that when Kintner left the White House in June 1967, Maguire "inherited the title" of cabinet secretary. Charles Maguire, Oral History Interview with Dorothy Pierce McSweeny, 19 August 1969, p. 28, Johnson Presidential Library.

128. See, e.g., Busby to Watson, 8 June 1965, Busby Office Files, Box 27, "Memos to Marvin Watson"; "Robert E. Kintner," Subject Files, General FG 11-8-1, Box 92; Charles Maguire, Office Files, Box 13; Johnson Presidential Library.

129. Johnson's order of 13 July 1965 is referred to in Loyd Hackler to Maguire, 26 June 1967, Subject File, General FG 11-8-1, Box 85, "Loyd Hackler," Johnson Presidential Library.

130. Califano to White House staffers, 22 June 1967, Subject Files, Executive FG 11-8, Box 68.

131. Califano to Johnson, 3 August 1967, Charles Maguire, Office Files, Box 13, "Chronological—August 20–October 26, 1967," Johnson Presidential Library.

132. Maguire to Johnson, 4 October 1967, ibid.

133. Maguire to Temple, 14 December 1967, White House Central Files, Subject Files, FG 11-8-1, Box 13, "T," Johnson Presidential Library. Maguire was plainly happy to give up the task: "My own role has been that of rewrite man with the Califano office. Frankly, I have found much work involved in tightening up the summaries they have sent me . . . Happy Benzedrine." Ibid. Later, William Blackburn in Appointments Secretary Marvin Watson's office took over some of the summarizing of agency reports. Blackburn, Oral History Interview with David McComb, 21 May 1969, p. 13, Johnson Presidential Library.

134. See Valenti to Johnson, 27 December 1964, "Valenti, Jack, 1963–64," Special Files—Office of the President, Box 12; Califano to Johnson, 21 October 1965, White House Central Files, Subject Files, FG 11-8-1, Box 70; Johnson Presidential Library.

135. Linda L. Fisher, "Presidential Power and Policy" (paper presented at the annual meeting of the Southern Political Science Association, 1987), 17; cf. Anderson, *The President's Men,* 306, 321ff.

136. In July 1964, for example, LBJ named Lee White his liaison with federal agencies dealing with drug abuse, trafficking, and rehabilitation. "Statement of the President," Press Release, 15 July 1964, White House Central Files, Subject Files, FG 11-8-1, Box 94, "Markham, Dean," Johnson Presidential Library. Similarly, the president later assigned associate special counsel DeVier Pierson to be the White House liaison to the Task Force on Communications Policy. Douglass Cater and Harry McPherson to Johnson, 17 August 1967, McPherson Office Files, Box 53, "Memoranda for the President, 1967," Johnson Presidential Library.

137. Moyers to Celebrezze (HEW Secretary), 26 January 1965, Subject File, Executive FG 11-8-1/Cater 11/23/63—, Box 77, "Douglass Cater," Johnson Presidential Library.

138. See, e.g., Celebrezze to Johnson, 7 June 1966, ibid.; Cater Office Files, Box 13, "Memos to the President"; Johnson Presidential Library.

139. Cater to Johnson, 19 September 1967, Cater Office Files, Box 17, "Memos to the President."

140. See, e.g., Joseph A. Califano, Jr., *A Presidential Nation* (New York: Norton, 1975), 31–32.

141. See James C. Gaither, Oral History Interview with Dorothy Pierce, 17 January 1969, p. 5, Johnson Presidential Library; John P. Roche, Oral History Interview with Paige Mulhollan, 16 July 1970, p. 51, Johnson Presidential Library; Fisher, "Presidential Power and Policy," 17.

142. For example, Gaither, like Cater, focused on HEW programs (although he tracked poverty and general welfare, not just education and health); Matthew Nimetz served on an HEW task force on prescription drugs; and Fred Bohen tracked urban affairs issues, which largely involved HUD (one of McPherson's responsibilities).

143. Cater Oral History, 8 May 1969, p. 21; cf. Blackburn Oral History, 21 May 1969, p. 15.

144. Califano, *A Presidential Nation,* 23.

145. For example, McPherson writes about the "Great Veterans' Hospital Caper," where the president assigned him to react to the firestorm generated by LBJ's announced closure of 11 veterans' hospitals "where standards of care were poor, buildings were outmoded, or the patient load was small." Harry McPherson, *A Political Education: A Washington Memoir* (Boston: Houghton Mifflin, 1988), 281; cf. McPherson Office Files, Box 52, "Memoranda for the President (1965)." At McPherson's suggestion, Johnson appointed a committee to examine the proposed closings. Ultimately, the committee recommended, and LBJ agreed, that nine of the hospitals should be kept open. McPherson followed the process throughout; later, he did the same regarding efforts to close several Public Health Service hospitals, a move that HEW officials bitterly opposed.

146. Gaither to Califano, 15 May 1968, Califano Office Files, Box 17, "Memos for the President"; Gaither to Califano and Cater, 16 May 1968, Subject File, General FG 11-8-1, Box 84, "James C. Gaither."

147. William Chapman, "Inter-Agency Harmony Is Kintner's Job," *Washington Post,* 2 April 1966, in McPherson Office Files, Box 22, "White House Staff," Johnson Presidential Library.

148. William D. Carey, "Presidential Staffing in the Sixties and Seventies," *Public Administration Review* 29 (1969): 454.

149. Califano, *A Presidential Nation,* 33.

150. See, e.g., Califano to Johnson, 3 January 1968, Califano Office Files, "Memorandums to the President, 1/68."

151. See, e.g., Richard Nathan, *The Plot That Failed: Nixon and the Administrative Presidency* (New York: Wiley, 1975); Richard Nathan, *The Administrative Presidency* (New York: Wiley, 1983).

CHAPTER 6. LOOKING BEYOND WASHINGTON

1. A third possible instance, White House involvement in election campaigning, will not be detailed, both because it failed to attain even the minimal structuring of the first two examples and because it has been dealt with thoroughly elsewhere. The best source is Sidney M. Milkis, *The President and the Parties: The Transformation of the American Party System since the New Deal* (New York: Oxford University Press, 1993). The one real example of White House structuring for campaign activities is the activity of "poll cat" Fred Panzer in the Johnson administration. See Chapter 3 for a discussion of Panzer's work.

2. The Office of Public Liaison formalized the stepped-up group outreach activities of Charles Colson and his staff under Richard Nixon. See Joseph A. Pika, "Interest Groups and the Executive: Presidential Intervention," in *Interest Group Politics,* ed. Allan J. Cigler and Burdett A. Loomis (Washington, D.C.: Congressional Quarterly, 1983); Pika, "The Nixon White House and the Mobilization of Bias" (paper presented at the annual meeting of the Midwest Political Science Association, 1989). On interest group liaison in the Executive Office of the President in more recent presidencies, see, e.g., Mark A. Peterson, "The Presidency and Organized Interests: White House Patterns of Interest Group Liaison," *American Political Science Review* 86 (1992): 612–25.

3. George Christian, *The President Steps Down: A Personal Memoir of the Transfer of Power* (New York: Macmillan, 1970), 16–17. Cf. Stephen Hess, *Organizing the Presidency,* 2d ed. (Washington, D.C.: Brookings Institution, 1988), 94ff.

4. Pika, "Interest Groups and the Executive," 316.

5. On White House "centralization," see Terry M. Moe, "The Politicized Presidency," in *The New Direction in American Politics,* ed. John E. Chubb and Paul E. Peterson (Washington, D.C.: Brookings Institution, 1985). A good summary of the growth in groups and group demands can be found in Mark A. Peterson and Jack L. Walker, "The Presidency and the Nominating System," in *The Presidency and the Political System,* 3d ed., ed. Michael Nelson (Washington, D.C.: Congressional Quarterly, 1990).

6. Pika, "Interest Groups and the Executive," 212.

7. Cf. Joseph A. Pika, "Interest Groups and the White House under Roosevelt and Truman," *Political Science Quarterly* 102 (1987): 650.

8. Among the constituencies with which early modern White Houses established ties were religious groups. The Roosevelt White House was the first to include an explicit staff connection to a particular religious group, the U.S. Jewish community. Since FDR, White House staffs have included aides who maintained contact with religious organizations. However, staff liaison responsibilities were largely minor and mostly unrelated to aides' other assignments. White Houses paid even less regular attention to a variety of other groups, including veterans, consumers, and the "intellectual community."

9. Donald J. Lisio, *Hoover, Blacks, and Lily Whites: A Study of Southern Strategies* (Chapel Hill: University of North Carolina Press, 1985), 239ff.

10. See, e.g., ibid., 87ff. Similarly, many black leaders believed that presidential aide Walter Newton appealed to southern whites in his political activities; his colleague French Strother was perceived to be actively hostile toward the NAACP. Ibid., 201. In fact, Newton ultimately worked hard (though unsuccessfully) to "convince Hoover that the northern vote was important to his reelection and that he needed to mend political fences with black leaders." Ibid., 252.

11. In 1934, for instance, presidential secretary Louis Howe received correspondence on patronage appointments for blacks and an appeal from the Order of Sleeping Car Conductors to encourage the National Recovery Administration to get them an employment code under the National Industrial Recovery Act. On the patronage requests, see, e.g., Joseph L. Johnson (of the DNC) to Howe, 7 December 1934, Howe Papers, Box 86, Roosevelt Presidential Library. On Howe's contacts with the Order of Sleeping Car Conductors, see ibid., Box 96.

12. Joseph P. Lash, *Eleanor and Franklin* (New York: New American Library, 1973), 608-9, 769. Cf. Donald R. McCoy and Richard T. Ruetten, *Quest and Response: Minority Rights and the Truman Administration* (Lawrence: University Press of Kansas, 1973), 7.

13. Eleanor Roosevelt, for example, served as the intermediary between White and Donald Richberg of the National Emergency Council when the former protested the wage differentials for southern blacks in NRA programs. Lash, *Eleanor and Franklin,* 671-72.

14. Harry Ashmore, "Presidents and Civil Rights: Public Philosophy or Pragmatism," *Virginia Papers on the Presidency,* vol. 11 (Lanham, Md.: University Press of America, 1983), 37; McCoy and Ruetten, *Quest and Response,* 8-9. After Roosevelt took these steps, the march was called off.

15. Philleo Nash, in *The Truman White House: The Administration of the Presidency, 1945-53,* ed. Francis H. Heller (Lawrence: Regents Press of Kansas, 1980), 54, 77.

16. As is almost always the case in White Houses, the specialization of civil rights activities was incomplete, and staffers other than those in the Minorities Office became involved. Especially supportive of civil rights goals in the Truman White House were members of the special counsel's staff. Special Counsel Clark Clifford, for example, maintained contact with civil rights groups in 1949 during congressional consideration of legislation creating the Fair Employment Practices

Commission and prohibiting poll taxes. William C. Berman, *The Politics of Civil Rights in the Truman Administration* (Columbus: Ohio State University Press, 1970), 161. Clifford's aide George Elsey and administrative assistant (and Clifford's successor) Charles Murphy were also frequently engaged in civil rights matters. Administrative Assistant Stephen Spingarn authored much of the administration's civil rights legislation.

17. The unit's name is Nash's; in Heller, *Truman White House,* 54.

18. Ibid.

19. Nash and Niles worked largely autonomously, and Nash mainly reported to Niles to keep him informed and to convey information to be communicated to the president. Disagreements between the two were rare, though they did not always see eye to eye on particular tactics. For instance, Nash favored presidential action to desegregate at least northern national guard units, and Niles urged no action. Finally, Special Counsel Clark Clifford had to intervene, essentially backing Nash. See McCoy and Ruetten, *Quest and Response,* 110–11.

20. Niles maintained contact with groups such as the NAACP, tried to arrange for Truman to meet with black ministers, and offered the president "very effective political advice" on dealing with minority groups. Matthew J. Connelly, Oral History Interview with Jerry N. Hess, May 1969, p. 193, Truman Presidential Library. For his part, Nash worked even more closely with blacks and black groups and maintained his agency contacts from the Roosevelt administration. On Niles's activities more generally, see, e.g., White House Office File 502, "Niles"; correspondence with civil rights groups, Niles Papers, Box 27; Alfred Steinberg, "Mr. Truman's Mystery Man," *Saturday Evening Post,* 24 December 1949, in Eben Ayers Papers, Box 19. On Nash, see, e.g., his telephone contacts with black organizations in Nash Papers, Box 38; his correspondence with civil rights groups in Nash White House Office Files, Box 4; and more of his general correspondence on racial matters in Elsey Papers, Box 103, "Nash." All these materials are housed at the Truman Presidential Library.

More generally, the Minorities Office's "method of operation . . . involved a series of networks at inside agency levels, much below the cabinet level, simply to keep track of what was going on." Heller, *Truman White House,* 63. Sometimes, Nash and Niles also became involved in troubleshooting on racial matters. Nash, for instance, handled complaints about racially motivated efforts by an American Bar Association panel to discredit federal trial examiners; followed up (with the assistance of Richard Neustadt in the special counsel's office) on HHFA (Housing and Home Finance Agency) efforts to provide public housing to blacks in Chicago; and, at the NAACP's request, investigated the case of three airmen convicted of rape and murder on Guam. On the allegations about the ABA panel, see, e.g., Nash to Charlie Houston (a Washington lawyer), 29 March 1949, Nash Files, Box 61. Nash's work with Neustadt to secure public housing can be found in Neustadt to Nash, 5 June 1950, Neustadt Papers, Box 1. Finally, Nash's involvement in the Guam case can be traced in Murphy Papers, "Truman." Similarly, Niles, prompted by a member of Congress, intervened to get information from the War Department for the mother of a black soldier shot by MPs during the war who had been denied a pension; see Rep. Chester Bowles to Niles, 14 November 1949, Niles Papers, Box 3.

21. See Nash, White House Office Files, Box 7.

22. See, e.g., Nash, "Memorandum for Files," n.d., in Elsey Papers, Box 103, "Philleo Nash"; Murphy to Nash, 1 December 1951, Murphy Papers, "Truman." See also Nash in Heller, *Truman White House,* 222–23; Pika, "Interest Groups and the White House," 664.

23. See, e.g., Ashmore, "Presidents and Civil Rights."

24. McCoy and Ruetten, *Quest and Response,* 17–19.

25. Thus, Correspondence Secretary William Hassett sent Niles and Nash memos "addressed to the 'Department of National Headaches.' " Nash in Heller, *Truman White House,* 77.

26. Memo, no author, 26 February 1953, White House Office, Office of Staff Secretary, Minnich Series, Box 1, "Misc A1," Eisenhower Presidential Library. Cf. Maxwell Rabb, Oral History Interview with Steven Lawson, 6 October 1970, Columbia University, Eisenhower Presidential Library.

27. See, e.g., Goodpaster to staff, 25 April 1955, White House Office, Office of Staff Secretary, "Org (7)," Box 4; William Hopkins, Oral History Interview with Maclyn Burg, 3 February 1975, p. 192, Eisenhower Presidential Library.

28. Rabb Oral History, 6 October 1970, p. 23.

29. Ibid., 24.

30. Ibid., 4.

31. Robert Frederick Burk, *The Eisenhower Administration and Black Civil Rights* (Knoxville: University of Tennessee Press, 1984), 30ff. Similarly, Rabb joined in efforts to persuade developer William Leavitt to end segregation in planned communities like Levittown; see, e.g., Whitman Diary, 5 January 1957, Box 7, Folder 2, "January 1957," Eisenhower Presidential Library.

32. Burk, *Eisenhower Administration,* 70; cf. E. Frederic Morrow, *Black Man in the White House* (New York: Coward-McCann, 1963), 27–30. Rabb also worked with the President's Committee on Contract Compliance (which he was pivotal in forming) and the President's Committee on Government Employment Policy. On his involvement with the Contract Compliance Committee, see, e.g., Bernard Shanley Diaries, 5 August 1953, Box 2, "V White House Years," Folder 3, August 1953; White House Office, Office of the Staff Secretary, Minnich Series, Box 1, "Miscellaneous—C (2) March–December 1953," 1 September 1953, Eisenhower Presidential Library. Rabb's activities with the Committee on Government Employment Policy can be traced in White House Central Files, Official File, 72-A-2, Box 288, Eisenhower Presidential Library; according to Burk (*Eisenhower Administration,* 71–74), the committee was very weak compared with the Truman-created committee it replaced.

33. See, e.g., Arthur Flemming (HEW) to Eisenhower, 14 August 1958, DDE Diary, Box 35, Staff Memos, August 1958, Folder 2, Eisenhower Presidential Library.

34. The first African American staffer in the White House also was employed during the Eisenhower years. Lois Lippman was initially a secretary in Chief of Staff Sherman Adams's office and then worked for Nelson Rockefeller and others. At least at first, she had a difficult time—some secretaries and their bosses alike refused to work with her. See Robert J. Donovan, *Eisenhower: The Inside Story* (New York: Harper, 1956), 154ff.

35. Morrow, Oral History Interview with Ed Edwin, 31 January 1968, pp. 53–54, Columbia University Oral History, Eisenhower Presidential Library.

36. Burk, *Eisenhower Administration,* 83.

37. See, e.g., Morrow, *Black Man,* 56–57 and passim.

38. Cf. James Hagerty, Oral History Interview with Ed Edwin, 6 February 1968, p. 248, Eisenhower Presidential Library.

39. On Morrow's activities, see, e.g., Morrow Oral History, 31 January 1968, pp. 35–36, 41; 15 April 1968, pp. 100, 119–21; Siciliano to Eisenhower, 24 June 1958, DDE Diary, Box 33; Morrow Papers, Series A69-33, Eisenhower Presidential Library.

40. Clarence Randall Journal, 1 December 1959, Box 5, CFEP, vol. 13, pp. 4–5, Eisenhower Presidential Library.

41. Morrow, *Black Man,* 300.

42. E. Frederic Morrow, Oral History Interview with Dr. Thomas Soapes, 23 February 1977, p. 23, Eisenhower Presidential Library.

43. Robert F. Burk, *Dwight D. Eisenhower: Hero and Politician* (Boston: Twayne, 1986), 160. It took over six years of "struggling . . . year in and year out," for example, to convince the president to meet with black leaders; Eisenhower "didn't feel any good could come out of it." Morrow Oral History, 31 January 1968, pp. 35–36.

On Eisenhower's general reticence on civil rights issues, see also Burk, *Eisenhower Administration;* Stephen E. Ambrose, *Eisenhower: The President* (New York: Simon and Schuster, 1984), 304–9, 406–23, 497–99, and passim; Chester J. Pach, Jr., and Elmo Richardson, *The Presidency of Dwight D. Eisenhower,* rev. ed. (Lawrence: University Press of Kansas, 1991), ch. 6. For a more positive assessment of Eisenhower's accomplishments in the civil rights arena, see, e.g., Michael S. Mayer, "The Eisenhower Administration and the Desegregation of Washington, D.C.," *Journal of Policy History* 3 (1991): 24–41.

44. Burke Marshall (who was assistant attorney general from 1961 to 1965), however, called Louis Martin of the Democratic National Committee Kennedy's "most important black adviser." Marshall, "Congress, Communication, and Civil Rights," in *Portraits of American Presidents,* vol. 4, *The Kennedy Presidency: Seventeen Intimate Perspectives of John F. Kennedy,* ed. Kenneth W. Thompson (Lanham, Md.: University Press of America, 1985), 74. See also Louis Martin, "Presidents and Civil Rights: Organizational Policy-Making," in *Virginia Papers on the Presidency,* vol. 17 (Lanham, Md.: University Press of America, 1984), 47–66.

45. See, e.g., Dutton to Kennedy, 9 February 1961, in Myer Feldman, White House Staff Files, General File, Box 5, "Civil Rights," Folder 2, Kennedy Presidential Library.

46. See Harris L. Wofford, White House Staff Files, Kennedy Presidential Library; Wofford, *Of Kennedys and Kings: Making Sense of the Sixties* (New York: Farrar, Straus and Giroux, 1980), 124; Frank Reeves, Oral History Interview with John F. Stewart, 29 March 1967, Kennedy Presidential Library.

47. Wofford to Kennedy, 29 May 1961, President's Official File, Staff Files, Box 67, "Wofford, Harris," Kennedy Presidential Library. On Wofford's outreach activities more generally, see, e.g., Harris L. Wofford Papers, White House Staff

Files, "Civil Rights—Misc"; Wofford Oral History Interview with Larry Hackman, 3 February 1969, Kennedy Presidential Library.

48. Reeves Oral History, 29 March 1967, p. 29.

49. Wofford, *Of Kennedys and Kings,* 134, 136.

50. Lewis J. Paper, *John F. Kennedy: The Promise and the Performance* (New York: Da Capo, 1975), 79. Cf. Wofford Oral History, 22 May 1968, p. 58; Wofford, *Of Kennedys and Kings,* 145ff.

51. Wofford, *Of Kennedys and Kings,* 145.

52. See, e.g., the notes on subcabinet group meetings on 14 April, 16 June, 19 July 1961 in Harris L. Wofford Papers, White House Staff Files, Box 14, "Subcabinet Group on Civil Rights," "Subcabinet Correspondence," Folder 2, Kennedy Presidential Library.

53. "Proposed Agenda for Subcabinet Meeting," 19 May 1961, ibid., Folder 1. Wofford noted, too: "The dynamics of the subcabinet group worked to put pressure on any agency that was dragging its feet." *Of Kennedys and Kings,* 146.

54. Subcabinet group to agencies, 24 May 1961, Wofford White House Staff Files, Box 11, "Subcabinet Group on Civil Rights."

55. On Dutton's involvement, see, e.g., Wofford to Dutton, 22 April 1961, Dutton to Wofford and Reeves, 5 June 1961, in Wofford White House Staff Files, Box 14, "Subcabinet Group on Civil Rights," "Subcabinet Correspondence," Folder 1. Other evidence of his involvement can be seen in Dutton to Wofford, 19 July 1961, ibid., Folder 2; Wofford to Dutton, 9 November 1961, ibid., Folder 4; Dutton to agencies, September 1962, ibid., Folder 3. See also the group's minutes in ibid., Folder 2.

56. Indeed, according to Wofford, a major problem was "to keep [Dutton's] attention and claim as much of his time as possible." Wofford, *Of Kennedys and Kings,* 145. On the operation of the group, see, e.g., Deirdre Henderson to Reeves and Wofford, 17 May 1961, Wofford White House Staff Files, Box 14, "Subcabinet Group on Civil Rights," "Subcabinet Correspondence," Folder 2; Wofford to Dutton, 19 October 1961, White House Central Staff Files, Box 108. More generally, see Wofford White House Staff Files, Box 14, "Subcabinet Group on Civil Rights."

57. See White to Subcabinet Group on Civil Rights, 15 May 1962, Wofford White House Staff Files, "Subcabinet Correspondence," Folder 5; White to Macy et al., 28 September 1962, ibid., Folder 6. The subcabinet group file ends in late September 1962, suggesting that the group was far less active under White.

58. For example, both Wofford and White tracked the success of the Plans for Progress program in ending employment discrimination and opening up job opportunities for minorities. Wofford Staff Files, "Civil Rights—Misc."; Lee C. White, White House Staff Files, Box 23, "Plans for Progress Program," Kennedy Presidential Library. White also served as the liaison to the President's Committee on Equal Opportunity in the Armed Forces as well as the Committees on Equal Employment Opportunity and Equal Housing Opportunity. White, Staff Files, Box 23, "President's Committee on Equal Opportunity in the Armed Forces"; Hobart Taylor (President's Committee on Equal Employment Opportunity) to White, 6 August 1963, Sorensen Papers, Subject Files, Box 30, Kennedy Presidential Library; see also White to Walter Jenkins, 27 November 1963, FG 11-8-1/White, Box 121A, Johnson Presidential Library. White also received much information on civil rights

activities and problems around the country and corresponded with interested and aggrieved group representatives. Lee C. White, White House Staff Files, Civil Rights Files, Boxes 19, 23, Kennedy Presidential Library.

Other liaison activities were more ad hoc. In 1962, for example, Wofford reported to the president on the reaction of southern educational institutions to an HEW antidiscrimination clause for institutions participating in National Education Defense Act programs. Wofford to Kennedy, 23 January 1962, President's Official File, Staff Files, Box 67, "Wofford, Harris"; only six of the 28 institutions involved withdrew. Similarly, White tracked efforts by HEW, the National Science Foundation, and the Atomic Energy Commission to ensure that no discrimination took place in the teacher training, fellowship, and research grant and equipment programs they sponsored. Alan Waterman (Director of NSF) to White, 13 June 1962; William L. Taylor to White, 2 August 1963; White, White House Staff Files, Civil Rights Files, Box 19, "Education."

59. Wofford Oral History, 3 February 1969, p. 147.

60. Reeves Oral History, 29 March 1967, p. 28. More informally, Reeves worked to get blacks appointed throughout the executive branch. He claimed some success in "opening up" the IRS and, with help from Dutton, in encouraging the Coast Guard to recruit more blacks.

61. Wofford to Sorensen, Goodwin, Dutton, and Marshall, 11 September 1961, Wofford Papers, Box 8, "President's Committee on Equal Employment Opportunity."

62. Wofford, *Of Kennedys and Kings,* 147.

63. See, e.g., Wofford Oral History, 3 February 1969, pp. 154ff.

64. Arthur Schlesinger, Jr., for example, tracked the first-semester progress of James Meredith at the University of Mississippi, reporting his intelligence to Appointments Secretary Kenneth O'Donnell and Justice Department officials; see Arthur Schlesinger, Jr., White House Files, Box WH-15, "Mississippi Situation," Kennedy Presidential Library. Indeed, Schlesinger considered himself to be a contact for black groups. Schlesinger to Bill Moyers, 29 November 1963, White House Central Files, Subject Files, FG 11-8-1, Box 112, "S," Johnson Presidential Library. In addition, Andrew Hatcher, the associate press secretary, kept up his contacts in the black community, with Theodore Sorensen often drafting his frequent speeches on civil rights; see, e.g., White House Central Staff Files, Box 117; Sorensen speech draft, 18 June 1962, Sorensen Papers, Subject Files, Box 30, Kennedy Presidential Library.

65. Even Wofford claimed to have spent "almost half" of his time on Peace Corps matters. Wofford Oral History, 22 May 1968, p. 66.

66. Ibid., 58.

67. Ibid., 3 February 1969, p. 128.

68. Paper, *John F. Kennedy,* 79; cf. Wofford, *Of Kennedys and Kings,* 136.

69. Wofford, *Of Kennedys and Kings,* 133.

70. Paper, *John F. Kennedy,* 80.

71. Wofford, *Of Kennedys and Kings,* 133. Cf. Carl M. Brauer, *John F. Kennedy and the Second Reconstruction* (New York: Columbia University Press, 1977).

72. See, e.g., Dutton to Wofford, 14 September 1961, Wofford Papers, Box 8,

"President's Committee on Equal Employment Opportunity"; Wofford Oral History, 3 February 1969, p. 154; Reeves Oral History, 29 March 1967, p. 29.

73. Wofford Oral History, 22 May 1968, p. 58; cf. Reeves Oral History, 29 March 1967, p. 28.

74. Cf. Wofford, *Of Kennedys and Kings,* 172.

75. Busby to Valenti, 13 July 1964, Busby Office Files, Box 27, "Memos to Valenti," Johnson Presidential Library. Similarly, later in 1964, Busby urged that the date for the White House Civil Rights Conference be changed from 22 November, "thus permitting the Conference to deal with the present more than with the past." Busby to Valenti, 2 September 1965, ibid.

76. See, e.g., White House Central Files, Subject Files, FG 11-8-1, Box 121A, "White, Lee," Johnson Presidential Library.

77. According to Alexander, he "always tried to see to it that the President would have as much contact with other blacks who would state their position . . . in as direct a fashion as was possible." Clifford Alexander, Oral History Interview with Joe B. Frantz, 1 November 1971, p. 29, Johnson Presidential Library. On Alexander's activities more generally, see ibid.; Ruth McCawley to Harry McPherson, 30 June 1967, Pierson Files, Box 27, "Misc/McPherson's Office"; Subject File, Executive FG 11-8-1, Box 71, "Clifford Alexander," Johnson Presidential Library.

78. Johnson note on memo from McPherson, 12 May 1966, McPherson Office Files, Box 52, "Memoranda for the President (1966)." Clifford Alexander was not much more successful: LBJ never responded to his memo arguing that the Plans for Progress program was "bullshit . . . an empty kind of promise." Alexander Oral History, 1 November 1971, p. 42.

79. Steven F. Lawson, "Mixing Moderation with Militancy: Lyndon Johnson and African-American Leadership," in *The Johnson Years,* vol. 3, *LBJ at Home and Abroad,* ed. Robert A. Divine (Lawrence: University Press of Kansas, 1994), 83.

80. John Steelman, Truman Memoir Interview by William Hillman, David M. Noyes, Francis Heller, and Lee Williams, 8 December 1954, p. 24, Truman Presidential Library. There is some support for such an allegation, but it is not clear that the White House always initiated such relations. For example, in 1934, presidential secretary Louis Howe wrote to Secretary of Labor Frances Perkins that he was "regarded as a very great friend of labor . . . , and I find them appealing to me in all their troubles." Howe to Perkins, 5 February 1934, Howe Papers, Box 82, Roosevelt Presidential Library. Throughout the administration, Eleanor Roosevelt was a channel for trade union representatives. Lash, *Eleanor and Franklin,* 769.

81. The administrative assistants, however, did not monopolize labor liaison. Once Samuel Rosenman arrived as special counsel, for example, he too kept in touch with various labor groups; see, e.g., President's Official File 5433, "Rosenman," Folders 2 (1944) and 3 (1945), Roosevelt Presidential Library.

82. See President's Official File 4046, "Tobin," Roosevelt Presidential Library.

83. Tobin to Roosevelt, 23 August 1940, ibid. Cf. Rowe to Rosenman, "AAs to the President," 15 March 1941, Rosenman Papers, Box 41, p. 3, Roosevelt Presidential Library.

84. Coy, for example, fielded and passed on complaints from labor leaders and communicated often with Philip Murray, CIO president; see Coy Papers, Box 13,

Roosevelt Presidential Library. In personnel matters, however, Rowe wanted the administration to distance itself from labor, apparently fearing the response of the CIO. Rowe to Mathews ["Labor Board"], 17 September 1941, Rowe Papers, Box 10, Roosevelt Presidential Library. Coy tried—mostly futilely—to get labor leaders to direct their recommendations for representatives on various boards to the secretary of labor. Coy to Marvin McIntyre, 23 December 1941, Coy Papers, Box 11.

85. See President's Official Files 4847, "Niles," Roosevelt Presidential Library.

86. Appointments Secretary Marvin McIntyre attracted considerable press comment in 1935 for his presence in the hotel suite of Bernard Robinson, the lobbyist for the Associated Gas and Electric System: "The official explanation for this pseudo-treason apparently is that [McIntyre] is the presidential scout and liaison man with whatever enemies happen to be current in the administration." Paul Mallon, "What's What behind News in Capital," *Washington Star,* 17 August 1935, Early Papers, Box 23, "McIntyre," Roosevelt Presidential Library.

87. Currie to Roosevelt, 2 June 1942, President's Staff Files, Box 115, Roosevelt Presidential Library.

88. Steelman, Truman Memoir Interview, 9 December 1954.

89. On Steelman's contacts with labor leaders, see, e.g., White House Office File 791, Steelman, "1950–53," Box 1550; Secretary's File: General File, "Steelman," Truman Presidential Library. His contacts with business leaders can be found in White House Office Files, Steelman, "Alphabetical Files." Steelman described his involvement in mediating labor disputes in his Truman Memoir Interview, 8 December 1954.

90. David Stowe, Oral History Interview with William D. Stilley and Jerald L. Hill, 18 March 1976, p. 12, Truman Presidential Library.

91. See, e.g., Enarson Papers, Box 4, Truman Presidential Library.

92. Jackson's ties can be seen in, e.g., Jackson to Secretary of Commerce Sawyer, 4 May 1949; Herbert A. Wilkinson (Chair, Commerce Department Travel Advisory Committee) to Jackson, 10 May 1949; Jackson to Steelman, 30 March 1950; Jackson Papers, Box 17, Truman Presidential Library. On Turner's ties, see, e.g., Turner Papers, Box 2, Chronological Files, Truman Presidential Library. In addition, Steelman aide Dallas C. Halverstadt served as liaison to the movie industry. His charge was to "work with government agencies and inter-agency committees in planning and development of message films . . . [and to act] as consultant on non-theatrical films intended for wide public usage"; see his job description in Halverstadt Papers, Box 1, Truman Presidential Library.

93. The Ad Council was established in May 1942 as the War Advertising Council. Initially, it was placed in the Office of War Intelligence (OWI). Since Administrative Assistant Lowell Mellett apparently was responsible for White House liaison with all sorts of information and advertising sources during the Roosevelt years, he likely dealt in some way with the Ad Council. OWI was abolished in August 1945, and its advertising and movie liaison work was transferred to the Office of War Mobilization and Reconversion (OWMR). Full responsibility for government liaison with the Ad Council came to the White House when OWMR was abolished in June 1947. On the history of the council, see, e.g., memo on the functions of Lambie's staff, DDE Files, Office of the Staff Secretary, Subject Series, White House Subseries, Box 1, Eisenhower Presidential Library.

94. Jackson Papers, Boxes 13, 23; Gibson Papers, Box 2, Truman Presidential Library.

95. For example, Clifford to Truman, 13 August 1948, Secretary File: General File, "Clifford."

96. Lloyd to Clifford, 24 January 1949, Lloyd Papers, Box 1, Folder 1, Truman Presidential Library.

97. See, e.g., Lloyd Papers, Box 1.

98. In addition to meeting with labor leaders, Rabb handled requests for invocation of the Taft-Hartley Act and monitored dock strikes; see, e.g., Randall Journal, 22 November 1954, Box 2, vol. 6, p. 1; Rabb to Whitman, Whitman Diary, 5 August 1954, Box 3, "August 1954," Folder 2; Allen Annable, "Conversation with Maxwell M. Rabb," 25 February 1955, White House Central Files, Office Files, Box 310, "Space Survey of the Presidency."

99. See, e.g., Hauge to Eisenhower, 3 May 1954, Whitman Files, Administrative Series, Box 18, "Hauge," 1952–55, Folder 5; Whitman Diary, 13 March 1958, Box 9, "March 1958," Folder 1. For example, with assistant staff secretary Arthur Minnich and Special Counsel Gerald Morgan, Hauge provided intelligence on the status of particular strikes. Hauge to Eisenhower, 29 June 1955, Whitman Files, Administrative Series, Box 18; White House Office, Staff Research Group, Box 23, "Submissions to Staff Notes."

100. Shanley countered: "These men were not for us but the important thing was that the working men throughout the country realized these men had an entree to the White House and the President." See Shanley Diaries, Box 3, "VII White House Years," 1955, Folder 1, p. 1787, Eisenhower Presidential Library.

101. Staff minutes, 29 January 1953, White House Central Files, General, Box 183.

102. Burk, *Dwight D. Eisenhower,* 155.

103. See, e.g., Lambie office memo, February 1955; Lambie Oral History Interview with Ed Edwin, 30 January 1968, Columbia University Oral History, Eisenhower Presidential Library; *Advertising News* profile of Lambie, White House Central Files, Official File 72-A-72, Box 286, Eisenhower Presidential Library.

104. See Lambie Papers, Box 43.

105. Peterson, "Presidency and Organized Interests," 615ff.

106. See entries in Randall's Journal: for example, 12, 17 March 1954, Box 1, vol. 1; 29 October 1957, Box 4, CFEP, vol. 6, p. 6.

107. On Anderson's involvement, see, e.g., Anderson notes on the White House visit of a representative of the American Farm Bureau Federation, 2 July 1957, Whitman Diary, Box 9, "July 1957," Folder 2; Anderson to Whitman, 2 July 1957, DDE Diary Series, Box 25, Staff Memos, July 1957, Folder 2; Anderson to Whitman, 13 January 1959, DDE Diary, Box 38, Staff Notes, January 1959, Folder 1. Harlow was involved less regularly, but see, e.g., Harlow Records, Box 4, "Agriculture." On Martin, see, e.g., Martin to Whitman, 21 July 1954, Whitman Diary, Box 2, "July 1954," Folder 4. Finally, examples of Shanley's interactions with representatives of farm groups can be seen in Shanley notes on a presidential meeting with a member of the National Council on Farm Cooperatives, 20 January 1955, Whitman Diary, Box 4, "January 1955," Folder 2; Shanley Diaries, Box 2, "IV White House Days," May 1953, pp. 853ff.

108. Robert Keith Gray, *Eighteen Acres under Glass* (London: Macmillan, 1962), 268.

109. Ibid. These efforts were largely successful. The Institute of Life Insurance and the National Association of Life Underwriters initially provided monies for the fight for a balanced budget and solicited additional support from groups such as the National Taxpayers Association, the American Farm Bureau Federation, and the National Retail Merchants Association. Ibid., 269.

110. Ibid., 268.

111. Theodore C. Sorensen, *The Kennedy Legacy* (New York: Macmillan, 1969), 78.

112. "TCS Draft," Reardon memo to cabinet members, 27 July 1962, Sorensen Papers, Subject Files, Box 29.

113. See, e.g., Kaysen to Schlesinger, 27 July 1961, Arthur Schlesinger, Jr., White House Staff Files, Box WH-16, "National Security Council"; Feldman to Kennedy, 7 March 1963, President's Official Files, Staff Files, Box 63, "Feldman, Myer"; Kenneth O'Donnell and David Powers, *Johnny, We Hardly Knew Ye: Memories of John Fitzgerald Kennedy* (Boston: Little, Brown, 1970), 252; Pierre Salinger, *With Kennedy* (Garden City, N.Y.: Doubleday, 1966), 70.

114. See, e.g., Valenti to Johnson, 5 December 1964, Special Files, Office of the President, Box 12, "Valenti," 1963–64; Kintner to Moyers, Watson, O'Brien, Califano, Cater, McPherson, Wilson, Semer, Rostow, 16 May 1966, White House Central Files, Confidential File, FG 11-5/MC—Papers of LBJ Confidential File, Box 19, "White House Office 1963–66," Johnson Presidential Library.

115. See Kintner memo to Moyers et al., 16 May 1966. Johnson's request was made at Cabinet Secretary Robert Kintner's suggestion; Kintner feared that the president might be "whipsawed" by a lack of coordination in contacts. Kintner to Johnson, 13 May 1966, Confidential Files, White House 10 Staff Meetings, 1963–66, Johnson Presidential Library.

116. Kintner to Moyers et al., 16 May 1966.

117. Christian, *President Steps Down*, 11.

118. See, e.g., White House Central Files, Subject Files, FG 11-8-1, Box 118, "Watson, Marvin."

119. See, e.g., General FG 11-8-1, "McPherson"; McPherson Office Files, Box 45, "White House Speeches and Meetings," Folder 1; ibid., Box 53, "Memoranda for the President (1967)."

120. See Subject File, General FG 11-8-1, Box 92, "Robert E. Kintner."

121. Representatives of the National Council of Farm Cooperatives, the National Grange, and the Farm Workers Union described Feldman's job as "Agricultural Staff Liaison" and praised his work highly; see Kenneth D. Naden (Executive Vice President of the National Council of Farm Cooperatives) to Johnson, 4 February 1965, Subject File, General FG 11-8-1, Box 70. Pierson's involvement can be traced in Pierson Files, Box 31, "Memoranda to Agencies" and "Presidential Memoranda." In addition, McPherson communicated regularly with representatives of farm groups such as the National Grange and the National Council on Agricultural Life and Labor. General FG 11-8-1/McPherson 9-6-67—7/31/68.

122. "Joseph A. Califano," Subject File, General FG 11-8-1/Bundy 1/1/66—,

Box 74, Johnson Presidential Library; George E. Reedy, *The Twilight of the Presidency,* rev. ed. (New York: New American Library, 1987), 84.

123. See, e.g., Subject File, Executive FG 11-8-1/Califano 7/1/67—, Box 75, Johnson Presidential Library.

124. The discussion that follows emphasizes the "systematic presidential liaison with state and local officials." David M. Welborn and Jesse Burkhead, *Intergovernmental Relations in the American Administrative State: The Johnson Presidency* (Austin: University of Texas Press, 1989), 50. Contact with state and local officials, of course, also took place as part of the formulation and implementation of particular policies; these subjects are examined in Part II.

125. Ibid., 20. After this initial meeting, the governors began meeting annually on their own.

126. Ibid., 2–4.

127. Ibid., 53.

128. Ibid., 293.

129. W. Brooke Graves, *American Intergovernmental Relations, Their Origins, Historical Development and Current Status* (New York: Scribner's, 1964), 886; cf. Bradley Patterson, *The Ring of Power* (New York: Free Press, 1988), ch. 16, p. 360, n 2.

130. Graves, *American Intergovernmental Relations,* 886.

131. See, e.g., Shanley Diaries, Box 2, "V White House Years," Folder 1, July 1953, p. 990.

132. On Adams's contacts with governors, see, e.g., Shanley Diaries, Box 1, "IV White House Days," May 1953, p. 799; ibid., "VI White House Years," Folder 3, 18 December 1953, pp. 1338–39; Wilton Persons, Notes on Staff Meeting, 6 November 1957, DDE Diary Series, Box 28, "November 1957 Staff Notes"; Homer Gruenther Records, Box 10, Eisenhower Presidential Library.

133. Special Counsels Bernard Shanley and Gerald Morgan, for instance, met with governors, typically during ceremonial occasions or to discuss specific pieces of federal legislation. Throughout the administration, legislative relations aide Homer Gruenther handled routine information gathering relevant to intergovernmental liaison, such as collecting sketches of newly elected governors and keeping files of natural disasters; see Gruenther Records, Boxes 1 and 10.

134. See, e.g., Pyle to Eisenhower, 18 May 1955, Whitman Files, Administrative Series, Box 29, "Pyle," Folder 2; White House Central Files, Official File 72-A-2, Box 288, "Pyle"; Howard K. Pyle and Charles Masterson, Oral History Interview with Ed Edwin, 11 May 1967, Columbia University; James Reston, *New York Times,* 9 March 1955, in White House Central Files, General, Box 285, Eisenhower Presidential Library.

135. Fred Seaton took over Pyle's work as liaison with executive branch departments and agencies. White House Personnel Records, 21 June 1955, White House Office, Office of Staff Secretary, Box 5, Eisenhower Presidential Library.

136. Even so, Pyle met with and passed on intelligence from state and local officials; he also helped organize and served as White House representative on the Federal-State Joint Action Committee (the forerunner of the Advisory Committee on Intergovernmental Relations), which brought together several governors and cabinet members. On Pyle's intergovernmental liaison activities generally, see, e.g., Whitman Files, Adminis-

trative Series, Box 29, "Pyle"; Pyle to Adams, "Subject: Status of My Replacement," 27 June 1958, White House Central Files, Official File 72-A-2, Box 289, "Warrington, Wayne," Eisenhower Presidential Library. His involvement with the Federal-State Joint Action Committee is discussed in Pyle Oral History, 11 May 1967, p. 7; Robert Merriam, Oral History Interview with John T. Mason, Jr., 3 March 1969, Columbia University, pp. 182–85, Eisenhower Presidential Library.

137. Sherman Adams, Oral History Interview with Ed Edwin, 11 April 1967, p. 148, Columbia University Oral History, Eisenhower Presidential Library.

138. "Meyer Kestnbaum," 11 July 1955, White House Central Files, Official File 72-A-2, Box 286.

139. Adams Oral History, 11 May 1967, p. 149.

140. Ibid., 150.

141. See the 23 May 1958 description of Merriam's position in White House Office, Office of Staff Secretary, Box 4; cf. Merriam Oral History, 13 January and 3 March 1969.

142. Merriam to Persons, 18 January 1961 (a report on a conversation about Merriam's White House activities that Merriam had had with Kennedy staffer Fred Dutton), in Merriam Papers, Box 1, "Part I: The Presidency: A Unique American Institution," Eisenhower Presidential Library.

143. Merriam Oral History, 3 March 1969, p. 184.

144. Ibid., 185; Merriam to Persons, 18 January 1961; Pyle Oral History, 11 May 1967, p. 9.

145. "Conversation with Wilton Persons," 7 March 1955, Allen Annable, "Space Survey for the Presidency," White House Central Files, Official File 72-A-23, Box 310.

146. See, e.g., Pyle to Adams, "Status of My Replacement"; Merriam Records, Box 5, "Federal-State Action Committee."

147. See Randall Journal, 16 July 1957, Box 4, CFEP, vol. 5, 1957.

148. Jean Appleby, "The Office of Intergovernmental Relations: The Study of an Organization" (master's thesis, University of Virginia, 1980), 18.

149. See Brooks Hays, Oral History Interview with Joe B. Frantz, 6 October 1971, p. 1, Johnson Presidential Library.

150. Dutton to Kennedy, 15 February 1961, President's Official File, Staff Files, Box 63, "Dutton, Frederick G."

151. Ibid. Dutton also served as liaison to the ACIR (see, e.g., Appleby, "Office of Intergovernmental Relations," 18; Dutton to Kennedy, 8 May 1961, President's Official File, Staff Files, Box 63, "Dutton"; appointment as staff representative to the Governors' Conference, 20 June 1961, White House Central Staff Files, Box 116) and solicited the help of city and county officials in fighting economic problems (Dutton to Kennedy, 28 February 1961, President's Official File, Staff Files, Box 63, "Dutton").

152. In one case, Dutton alerted Kennedy to the possibility of a federal highway project leading to the condemnation of the homes of "leading Negro citizens" in Alabama. Dutton to Kennedy, 25 September 1961, President's Official Files, Staff Files, Box 63, "Dutton."

153. See Lee C. White, White House Staff Files, Box 18, "White House Regional Conferences," Kennedy Presidential Library.

154. See "Hays, Brooks," President's Official Files, Staff Files, Box 63a, Kennedy Presidential Library.

155. See, e.g., ibid.; Hays Oral History, 6 October 1971, p. 2; Brooks Hays, *Politics Is My Parish* (Baton Rouge: Louisiana State University Press, 1981), 230.

156. Hays to Kennedy, 15 May 1963, President's Official Files, Staff Files, Box 63a, "Hays."

157. Hays, *Politics Is My Parish,* 230.

158. Lee C. White, White House Staff Files, Box 18, "White House Regional Conferences."

159. Ibid., "White House Conference on Community Development."

160. Subject File, General FG 11-8-1, Box 85, "Brooks Hays," Johnson Presidential Library; Hays Oral History, 6 October 1971, p. 16.

161. See, e.g., Ivan Sinclair to Bill Moyers, n.d., Moyers Files, Box 133, "Ivan Sinclair Memos"; Horace Busby to Juanita Roberts, 12 January 1965, Busby Office Files, Box 20, "Memos for Juanita Roberts," Johnson Presidential Library.

162. For example, July 1964 memos between Dungan and the mayor of El Paso, Texas, over federal subsidies, Subject File, General FG 11-8-1, Box 81, "Ralph Dungan," Johnson Presidential Library.

163. Note to Johnson on Valenti's draft of Marvin Watson's job description, 22 December 1964, Office of the President File, Box 13, "Marvin Watson," Johnson Presidential Library.

164. Moyers to White, Cater, Busby, Goodwin, Watson, and Hopkins, 30 January 1965, Special Files, Office of the President File, Box 8, "Bill Moyers, 1963, 64, 65," Johnson Presidential Library.

165. See, e.g., White House Central Files, Subject Files FG 11-8-1, Box 118, "Watson, Marvin," Johnson Presidential Library.

166. Johnson handwritten note on Moyers memo to White et al., 30 January 1965; cf. Welborn and Burkhead, *Intergovernmental Relations,* 51.

167. Wellborn and Burkhead, *Intergovernmental Relations,* 51.

168. See C. Farris Bryant, Oral History Interview with Joe B. Frantz, 5 March 1971, Johnson Presidential Library.

169. Ibid., 52. The OEP directors, for example, led the so-called Flying Feds, high-level executive branch officials who visited state capitals to discuss problems with federal grant programs and arranged White House meetings between officials of the National Governors Conference and the president. See Donald H. Haider, *When Governments Come to Washington: Governors, Mayors, and Intergovernmental Lobbying* (New York: Free Press, 1974), 118, 123, 293ff, and passim.

170. Appleby, "Office of Intergovernmental Relations," 21. Not everyone approved of spinning intergovernmental outreach out of the White House Office. In February 1967, for example, Charles Smith, staff director of the Senate Subcommittee on Intergovernmental Relations, proposed the naming of a special assistant for intergovernmental relations. Charles Smith to Watson, 14 February 1967, Subject File, Executive FG 11-8, Box 68. Similarly, governors complained that the OEP, unlike the vice president's office, "was not one of the major powers [in] the White House." Appleby, "Office of Intergovernmental Relations," 30. In contrast, local officials generally were pleased with the new arrangement. Ibid., 25ff. That local officials were more pleased with their reception from the Johnson administration

than were their state-level counterparts probably also reflected the historically closer ties between mayors and the Democratic Party; governors, in contrast, "found the Republican party to be generally more favorably inclined" to their goals. Haider, *When Governments Come to Washington,* 105ff.

171. For example, domestic policy aide Douglass Cater worked with Bryant in contacting governors to solicit their support for elements of the president's 1967 health and education message; see, e.g., Cater to Johnson, 28 February 1967, Cater Office Files, Box 12, "Memos to and from George Christian and Daily Press Contacts, Jan. 1967–June 1968," Johnson Presidential Library. Jake Jacobsen spoke with several governors about the release of federal highway funds that had been withheld; see Jacobsen note to files, 9 April 1967, Subject File, General FG 11-8-1, Box 86, "Jake Jacobsen," Johnson Presidential Library. Meanwhile, Jack McNulty of the speechwriting staff became a specialist of sorts in drafting comments on intergovernmental issues; see, e.g., Charles Maguire Office Files, Box 13, "Chron—August 20–October 26, 1967," Johnson Presidential Library.

CHAPTER 7. DOMESTIC AND ECONOMIC POLICY

1. Ben W. Heineman, Jr., and Curtis A. Hessler, *Memorandum for the President: A Strategic Approach to Domestic Affairs in the 1980s* (New York: Random House, 1980). Although analysts frequently treat "economic" and "domestic" policy separately, we look at them together; this seems warranted, given their interdependence and substantive similarities. Whether they constitute a coherent *organizational* domain, however, is a question open to empirical examination.

2. Examination of White House staff participation in the sorts of economic policy that involve U.S. trade relations and international economic assistance is postponed until Chapter 9. Not only did such policy receive special attention in the Eisenhower and Kennedy White Houses, but it was separated organizationally from the rest of economic policy.

3. More recent domestic policy staffs have received greater attention from scholars. See, e.g., John H. Kessel, *The Domestic Presidency: Decision-Making in the White House* (Belmont, Calif.: Wadsworth, 1975); Margaret Jane Wyszomirski, "The Roles of a Presidential Office for Domestic Policy," in *The Presidency and Public Policy Making,* ed. George C. Edwards III, Steven A. Shull, and Norman C. Thomas (Pittsburgh: University of Pittsburgh Press, 1985).

4. Robert C. Wood, "When Government Works," *The Public Interest* (Winter 1970): 39–51.

5. For example, Douglass Cater in the Johnson White House was virtually an in-house advocate for HEW's programs and for health, education, and social welfare policies.

6. Cf. Kessel, *Domestic Presidency.*

7. See, e.g., Martha Derthick, "Defeat at Fort Lincoln," *The Public Interest* (Summer 1970): 3–39.

8. On LBJ's monitoring of public housing production, for example, see Karen M. Hult, *Agency Merger and Bureaucratic Redesign* (Pittsburgh: University of Pittsburgh Press, 1987).

9. See, e.g., Stephen Hess, *Organizing the Presidency,* 2d ed. (Washington, D.C.: Brookings Institution, 1988); Richard T. Johnson, *Managing the White House* (New York: Harper and Row, 1974).

10. A host of sources supports such an observation. For example, on FDR, see Richard E. Neustadt, "Approaches to Staffing the Presidency: Notes on FDR and JFK," *American Political Science Review* 57 (1963): 853; on Truman, see Alfred Dick Sander, *A Staff for the President: The Executive Office, 1921–52* (New York: Greenwood Press, 1989), 81; on Eisenhower, see Peri E. Arnold, *Making the Managerial Presidency: Comprehensive Reorganization Planning, 1905–1980* (Princeton, N.J.: Princeton University Press, 1986), 161; on JFK, see Fred Dutton to Raymond R. Sullivan, 1 March 1961, White House Central Files, Subject Files, Box 115, Kennedy Presidential Library; and on Johnson, see Emmette S. Redford and Richard T. McCulley, *White House Operations: The Johnson Presidency* (Austin: University of Texas Press, 1986), 49, 61.

11. This follows the logic of Herbert A. Simon, *Administrative Behavior,* 3d ed. (New York: Free Press, 1976).

12. The focus is on noncrisis policy settings, when decision makers (at least in principle) have time to deliberate over policy responses and strategies. During domestic crises —for example, school desegregation in Little Rock, the urban riots of the 1960s—presidents had to react almost immediately, and normal channels and routines were ignored.

The Johnson White House tried to systematize response by making Joseph Califano the "crisis coordinator." Carroll Kirkpatrick, "Important Great Society Roles Go to Johnson's Newest Aides," *Washington Post,* 24 August 1965, in Harry McPherson Office Files, Box 22, Johnson Presidential Library. Califano typically worked in a collegial-consensual structure with other top staffers (notably Special Counsel Harry McPherson and Press Secretary George Christian) and executive branch officials. The responsibility for follow-up, however, belonged to Califano. See, e.g., Subject File, Executive FG 11-8-1/Califano, Box 75, Johnson Presidential Library; Harry McPherson, *A Political Education: A Washington Memoir* (Boston: Houghton Mifflin, 1988), 357–59; Redford and McCulley, *White House Operations,* 125–26.

13. In David Burner, *Herbert Hoover: A Public Life* (New York: Knopf, 1979), 221.

14. Strother Papers, Box 2; Hastings Papers, Box 2; Hoover Presidential Library.

15. Martin L. Fausold, *The Presidency of Herbert C. Hoover* (Lawrence: University Press of Kansas, 1985), 41–42.

16. Roger W. Jones, Oral History Interview with Jerry N. Hess, 14 August 1969, Truman Presidential Library.

17. Neustadt, "Approaches to Staffing," 857.

18. See, e.g., Joseph Lash, *Eleanor and Franklin* (New York: New American Library, 1973), 609, 618, 669, 671, and passim.

19. President's Official File, OF 5443 "Rosenman," Roosevelt Presidential Library. Cf. Hess, *Organizing the Presidency,* 36.

20. Sander, *Staff for the President,* 73.

21. Ibid., 85.

22. See Chapter 10 for elaboration.

23. On Ross, see, e.g., Charles Ross Diary, Box 2, Secretary's Files, Personal Files, Truman Presidential Library. By most accounts, Short was far less influential than Ross; still, see, e.g., Short to Truman, 21 May 1952, Secretary's File, Personal File, "Short, Joe," Truman Presidential Library.

24. See, e.g., Jones Oral History, 14 August 1969; Harold Seidman, Oral History Interview with Jerry N. Hess, 29 September 1970, Truman Presidential Library; Charles S. Murphy, in *The Truman White House: The Administration of the Presidency 1945–53,* ed. Francis H. Heller (Lawrence: University Press of Kansas, 1980), 73.

25. James F. C. Hyde and Stephen Wayne, "White House–OMB Relations," in *The Presidency: Studies in Public Policy,* ed. Steven A. Shull and Lance T. LeLoup (Brunswick, Ohio: King's Court Communications, 1979), 141.

26. This was a significant increase in staff size; under Rosenman and Clifford, the counsel's staff never included more than two additional professionals.

27. Charles S. Murphy to Donald S. Dawson, 3 August 1949, Murphy Papers, Personal File, Truman Presidential Library.

28. Clark Clifford, Oral History Interview with Jerry N. Hess, 16 April 1971, pp. 71–72, Truman Presidential Library.

29. Nonetheless, Eisenhower's first counsel—Bernard Shanley—drafted legislation and organized meetings with policy advisers; see, e.g., Shanley Diaries, "Preface," p. 12; "IV: 'The White House Days,'" pp. 598, 743–45, 853, and passim; Eisenhower Presidential Library.

30. Hyde and Wayne, "White House–OMB Relations," 141.

31. Phillip G. Henderson, *Managing the Presidency: The Eisenhower Legacy— From Kennedy to Reagan* (Boulder, Colo.: Westview Press, 1988), 25.

32. For example, Andrew Goodpaster to Staff, 25 April 1955, White House Office, Office of the Staff Secretary, Box 4, "Organization (7)"; "Contacts and Directories," White House Office, Staff Research Group, Eisenhower Presidential Library.

33. See, e.g., Hagerty Diary, 25 February, 24 March 1954; James Hagerty, Oral History Interview with Ed Edwin, Columbia University, 16 April 1968, p. 481, Eisenhower Presidential Library.

34. See, e.g., Peter Lisagor, in Oral History Interview of George Herman, Lisagor, and Mary McGrory with Fred Holborn, 4 August 1964, p. 79, Kennedy Presidential Library.

35. Hess, *Organizing the Presidency,* 86.

36. Joseph G. Bock, "The National Security Assistant and the White House Staff, 1947–84: Foreign Policy Implications" (Ph.D. dissertation, American University, 1985), 69.

37. Hyde and Wayne, "White House–OMB Relations," 142.

38. Joseph Kraft, "Kennedy's Working Staff," *Harper's* (n.d.): 29–36, in Arthur Schlesinger, White House Files, Box W-9, "Magazine Articles, General," Kennedy Presidential Library.

39. President's Official Files: Staff Files, Box 63, "Feldman, Myer"; "Areas of Responsibility of the Counsellors in the Office of the Special Counsel to the President," no author, no date, Sorensen Papers, Subject Files, Box 31, "Counsel's Office," Kennedy Presidential Library.

40. "Areas of Responsibility," President's Official Files: Staff Files, Box 67, "White, Lee C.," Kennedy Presidential Library.

41. Kraft, "Kennedy's Working Staff," 31.

42. Hess, *Organizing the Presidency,* 85; Nicholas Lemann, "The Unfinished War," *Atlantic Monthly* (December 1988): 44–46.

43. For details, see, e.g., Califano Office Files, Johnson Presidential Library; Redford and McCulley, *White House Operations,* 89–96.

44. George Christian, *The President Steps Down: A Personal Memoir of the Transfer of Power* (New York: Macmillan, 1970), 13.

45. "White House Staffing as of October 18, 1967," attached to Memo, William J. Hopkins to Marvin Watson, FG 11-8 White House Central File: Subject Files, Box 68, Johnson Presidential Library.

46. The term "system manager" is Redford and McCulley's (*White House Operations,* 83).

47. On Gaither's activities, see, e.g., James C. Gaither, Oral History Interview with Dorothy Pierce, 19 November 1968, tape 1, University of Texas Oral History Project, Johnson Presidential Library; Joseph A. Califano, Jr., *A Presidential Nation* (New York: Norton, 1975)

48. "White House Staffing"; Califano, *Presidential Nation,* 40.

49. Gaither Oral History, 15 January 1969, p. 2.

50. Redford and McCulley, *White House Operations,* 96. Similarly, Harry McPherson called Califano the "number one domestic man." Oral History Interview with T. H. Baker, Johnson Presidential Library, 16 January 1969. Bradley Patterson contends that Califano was "in effect the domestic policy chief." Patterson, *The Ring of Power: The White House Staff and Its Expanding Role in Government* (New York: Basic Books, 1988), 130–31.

51. McPherson to Donald Furtado, 3 August 1967, Executive FG 11-8-1/ McPherson; "Memoranda For the President, 1968," McPherson Office Files, Box 53, Johnson Presidential Library.

52. McPherson Oral History, 8 April 1969, tape 2, p. 13.

53. Christian, *President Steps Down,* 14.

54. Pierson Papers, Box 31, "Memoranda to Agencies"; McPherson to Furtado, Johnson Presidential Library.

55. See Chapter 3.

56. Gaither Oral History, 19 November 1968, tape 2, p. 2; cf. Califano, *Presidential Nation,* 40.

57. Seidman Oral History, 29 September 1970, p. 14.

58. Hyde and Wayne, "White House–OMB Relations," 143.

59. Cf. Roger B. Porter, "The President and Economic Policy: Problems, Patterns, and Alternatives," in *The Illusion of Presidential Governance,* ed. Hugh Heclo and Lester M. Salamon (Boulder, Colo.: Westview Press, 1981), 217.

60. FDR to Currie, 20 July 1939, President's Official Files, OF 3719 "Lauchlin Currie"; memos, Currie to FDR, President's Secretary's File, Box 115; Roosevelt Presidential Library.

61. Coy Papers, Box 13.

62. Rowe to Rosenman, "AAs to the President," 15 March 1941, Rosenman Papers, Box 41, p. 3, Roosevelt Presidential Library.

63. Samuel I. Rosenman, *Working with Roosevelt* (New York: Harper and Brothers, 1952), 337, 356.

64. Steelman's aides, for example, heard appeals on price control decisions (Steelman Personal Papers, Box 1) and worked on wage stabilization (e.g., Harold Enarson Personal Papers, Box 3) and manpower issues (e.g., Steelman to White House Staff, 18 September 1950). Steelman himself spent a great deal of time mediating private labor-management disputes (e.g., Truman Memoir Interviews, 8 December 1954; Charles Murphy, Oral History Interview with Charles T. Morrissey and Jerry N. Hess, 15 July 1969, p. 317). All cited materials are lodged in the Truman Presidential Library. In addition, Steelman aide Harold Enarson processed disputes referred from the Federal Mediation and Conciliation Service and the National Mediation Board (Neustadt in F. Heller, *Truman White House,* 98).

65. Murphy Papers; Susan M. Hartmann, *Truman and the 80th Congress* (Columbia: University of Missouri Press, 1971), 44, 87.

66. For example, Sander, *Staff for the President,* 175; Edwin Nourse, *Economics in the Public Service: Administrative Aspects of the Employment Act* (New York: Harcourt, Brace, 1953), 134; Leon H. Keyserling in F. Heller, *Truman White House,* 187–88.

67. Sander, *Staff for the President,* 179; Keyserling in F. Heller, *Truman White House,* 187.

68. Sander, *Staff for the President,* 176.

69. See, e.g., Richard E. Neustadt Personal Files, Box 1; Milton P. Kayle, Oral History Interview with Neil Johnson, 9 November 1952, Truman Presidential Library. Cf. Robert C. Turner in F. Heller, *Truman White House,* 58.

70. See, e.g., Sherman Adams, Oral History Interview with Douglas Scott, 19 June 1970, p. 249; Clarence Randall Journals, Box 2, "Volume VI," p. 10; Eisenhower Presidential Library.

71. Fred I. Greenstein, *The Hidden-Hand Presidency: Eisenhower as Leader* (New York: Basic Books, 1982), 120.

72. Shanley Diaries, p. 623.

73. For example, Rabb handled requests for the invocation of the Taft-Hartley Act and monitored dock strikes. Allen Annable, "Conversation with Maxwell M. Rabb," 25 February 1955, White House Central Files, Office File, Box 310, "Space Survey of the Presidency," Eisenhower Presidential Library.

74. Shanley Diaries, pp. 12, 598, 624, 873, 920ff; Notes, 12 August 1953, "Miscellaneous—T, January 1953–June 1954," White House Office, Office of the Staff Secretary, Minnich Series, Box 1, Eisenhower Presidential Library.

75. For example, Hauge to Eisenhower, 29 June 1955, Whitman Files, Administration Series, Box 18, Eisenhower Presidential Library.

76. John Hart, *The Presidential Branch* (New York: Pergamon Press, 1987), 55.

77. For example, Theodore C. Sorensen, *The Kennedy Legacy* (New York: Macmillan, 1969), 237; Walter W. Heller, "John F. Kennedy and the Economy," in *Portraits of American Presidents,* vol. 4, *The Kennedy Presidency: 17 Intimate Perspectives of John F. Kennedy,* ed. Kenneth W. Thompson (Lanham, Md.: University Press of America, 1985).

78. For example, Porter, "President and Economic Policy," 97, 112.

79. W. Heller, "John F. Kennedy and the Economy," 154, 155.

80. Ibid. On Califano, see also Redford and McCulley, *White House Operations,* 113.

81. Redford and McCulley, *White House Operations,* 117-19.

82. For example, Patrick Anderson, *The President's Men* (New York: Doubleday, 1969), 306.

83. Redford and McCulley, *White House Operations,* 113.

84. "Joseph A. Califano," Subject File, General FG 11-8-1/Bundy 1/1/66—, Box 74, Johnson Presidential Library; George E. Reedy, *The Twilight of the Presidency: From Johnson to Reagan,* rev. ed. (New York: New American Library, 1987), 84.

85. For example, Subject File, Executive FG 11-8-1/Califano 7/1/67—, Box 75, Johnson Presidential Library.

86. For example, Califano Office Files; James E. Anderson, "Presidential Management of Wage-Price Policies: The Johnson and Carter Experiences," in Edwards, Shull, and Thomas, *Presidency and Public Policy Making,* 178-89.

87. John Robson in J. Anderson, "Presidential Management," 189.

88. Margaret Jane Wyszomirski, "A Domestic Policy Office: Presidential Agency in Search of a Role," *Policy Studies Journal* 12 (1984). 716.

CHAPTER 8. NATIONAL SECURITY POLICY

1. This chapter focuses on White House structuring for defense policy and for handling those aspects of foreign policy that do not explicitly involve trade or economic assistance. Governance structures relevant to foreign economic policy are discussed in Chapter 9.

2. Washington, having grown used to the assistance of military aides, continued to have one or two assigned to him once he became president. Many, though not all, of his successors followed this practice. From Grant through Harding, the military aide to the president was attached to the Office of Public Buildings and served mainly as superintendent of public buildings and grounds; after that, the military aide was directly attached to the White House, with no upgrading of the job. See Harold H. Roth, "The Executive Office of the President: A Study of Its Development with Emphasis on the Period 1939-1953" (Ph.D. dissertation, American University, 1958), 211ff.

3. Ibid., 211.

4. Clark Clifford, with Richard Holbrooke, *Counsel to the President: A Memoir* (New York: Random House, 1991), 60-61.

5. Johnson did, however, develop the "Tuesday lunch" as a regular, informal opportunity to meet with top administration officials. As Vietnam became more clearly a threat to his presidency, he convened the "Wise Men," a gathering of senior statesmen, to advise him on policy. See ibid., ch. 26.

6. Robert E. Sherwood, *Roosevelt and Hopkins: An Intimate History,* vol. 1 (New York: Harper and Brothers, 1948), 328.

7. See Lubin to Hopkins memo, President's Secretary's File, Box 115, Roosevelt Presidential Library.

8. The best summary of Hopkins's activities is found in George McJimsey,

Harry Hopkins: Ally of the Poor and Defender of Democracy (Cambridge, Mass.: Harvard University Press, 1987), chs. 10–23.

9. Herman Miles Somers, *Presidential Agency: OWMR, the Office of War Mobilization and Reconversion* (Cambridge, Mass.: Harvard University Press, 1950), 10.

10. Ibid., 43.

11. William D. Leahy, *I Was There: The Personal Story of the Chief of Staff to Presidents Roosevelt and Truman Based on His Notes and Diaries Made at the Time* (New York: McGraw-Hill, 1950), 96.

12. Leahy largely controlled the flow of military information to FDR, and when the president left Washington, Leahy went along. He met with Roosevelt every day at 9:45 A.M. See ibid., 96–101.

13. "The White House Team: Loyalty, Not Brilliance, Is Their Long Suit," *Kiplinger Magazine,* May 1948, pp. 27–30, Vertical File, "White House Staff Advisers," Truman Presidential Library. By all accounts, Leahy was one of Truman's most respected advisers. Military aide Harry Vaughan described Leahy's style: "When aroused on some matter that came under his authority or challenged his very strong convictions, he became a typical blue water 'Sea Dog' . . . and gave the impression that he was taking his stand on the bridge of his flagship and was ready to 'damn the torpedoes.' " Vaughan Memoir, p. 174, Vaughan Papers, Box 2, Truman Presidential Library.

14. The most complete account of Clifford's time in the White House is his own in *Counsel to the President,* chs. 3–14. Clifford's foreign affairs activities are covered in chs. 6–9.

15. Ibid., pp. 109–13. He recounts that both Admiral Leahy and Secretary of State Byrnes were somewhat miffed at not being asked to do the report themselves. Leahy, however, was cooperative; Byrnes was not.

16. Ibid., ch. 8.

17. George Elsey, note to files, Elsey Papers, Box 95, Truman Presidential Library.

18. Clifford, *Counsel to the President,* 162–64.

19. It should be noted that the executive secretaries of the NSC—Souers, then Lay—were not national security assistants. They were not White House staff members and, although they did play a liaison role between the NSC and the president, they did not view themselves as policy advisers. A detailed description of the NSC operation under Truman can be found in James S. Lay, Jr., and Robert H. Johnson, *Organizational History of the National Security Council during the Truman and Eisenhower Administrations* (monograph written for the Senate Subcommittee on National Policy Machinery, Washington, D.C., 1960).

20. Examples of such correspondence can be found in the Elsey Papers, Box 67, "General File 1951," Truman Presidential Library.

21. By this time, Leahy had also resigned.

22. See Souers Papers, Box 1, Truman Presidential Library.

23. Roger W. Jones, Oral History Interview with Jerry N. Hess, 14 August 1969, p. 44, Truman Presidential Library.

24. See Secretary's File, General File, "Dennison," Truman Presidential Library.

25. Press release, 16 June 1950, Murphy Papers, "Harriman," Truman Presidential Library.

26. Richard Neustadt, Joint Oral History Interview of Neustadt, Charles Murphy, David Stowe, and James Webb with Hugh Heclo and Anna Wilson, 20 February 1980, p. 75, Truman Presidential Library. Melvyn P. Leffler concurs that "Harriman's principal task, at least initially, was to coordinate policy and ease tensions between the Defense and State departments." Leffler, *A Preponderance of Power: National Security, the Truman Administration, and the Cold War* (Stanford, Calif.: Stanford University Press, 1992), 313.

27. Walter Isaacson and Evan Thomas, *The Wise Men: Six Friends and the World They Made* (New York: Simon and Schuster, 1986), 509. Yet Budget Director James Webb recalled that the main motivation lay in the fact that Harriman was tired of living in Paris, so Webb and others contrived to create a job for him at home, finding a policy rationale for it later. Joint Oral History Interview, 20 February 1980, pp. 75–76.

28. W. Averell Harriman, Oral History Interview with Bernard W. Poirier, 10 January 1980, p. 9, Truman Presidential Library.

29. For instance, Harriman spent much of the summer of 1951 in Teheran, mediating a dispute between the governments of Iran and Britain. Leffler, *Preponderance of Power,* 423–24. Harriman also tried to act as a buffer between President Truman and General MacArthur, with little success. But he did not involve himself much in strategy. According to Walter Isaacson and Evan Thomas, "He saw his own role more as a fixer than as a strategist." Isaacson and Thomas, *Wise Men,* 540.

30. Alfred Dick Sander characterized Harriman as "almost a member of the State Department" in *A Staff for the President* (New York: Greenwood Press, 1989), 317. Harriman sat in on the secretary's morning staff meetings and had access to all department information.

31. Ibid., 318.

32. Isaacson and Thomas, *Wise Men,* 540.

33. Lincoln Gordon, Oral History Interview with Richard D. McKinzie, 22 July 1975, p. 158, Truman Presidential Library.

34. Ibid., 136–37.

35. When Harriman was appointed, the BOB undertook discussions as to what his role should be. Some, including William Sheppard of State, seemed to think that Harriman should become a "more aggressive and wide-ranging Souers," focusing on policy making as well as implementation. Sander, *Staff for the President,* 316. But without Harriman replacing Souers, this could not happen, and Truman evidently did not want a potential policy maker or a spokesperson in this position. See Joseph G. Bock, *The White House Staff and the National Security Assistant: Friendship and Friction at the Water's Edge* (New York: Greenwood Press, 1987), 12–14.

36. The OCB was created to replace the existing Psychological Strategy Board, on the grounds that psychological warfare was inseparable from other elements of policy and implementation. The most important new element from a governance perspective was the link to the White House. See Lay and Johnson, *Organizational History,* 38–42.

37. The Planning Board, a renaming of what had been the "Senior Staff" un-

der Truman, consisted of top officials representing State, Defense, the Joint Chiefs, and the CIA. They were nominated by their agencies but needed approval by the president and, under the new Eisenhower system, by the special assistant for national security as well. In effect, it was a structure consisting of stakeholder representatives who were also experts in the field of national security. They were assisted by career staff, as had been the case under Truman.

38. For a full discussion of the NSC reorganization as well as Cutler's duties, see Lay and Johnson, *Organizational History,* 22–33.

39. Ibid., 33.

40. As author of the report that initially defined the responsibilities of the national security assistant, Cutler was especially sensitive to the formal definition of the role.

41. Clarence Randall Journal, 30 July 1957, Box 4, CFEP, vol. 5, 1957; 24 December 1957, Box 4, CFEP, vol. 7; Eisenhower Presidential Library. In the latter entry, Randall cites Appointments Secretary Robert Gray as complaining that Cutler was adding unnecessarily to Eisenhower's burdens by "rushing to the President all the time."

42. See, e.g., Gray's description of his work in his Oral History Interview with Paul L. Hopper, Columbia University, 19 July 1967, pp. 270–73, Eisenhower Presidential Library. In terms of Kevin Mulcahy's taxonomy of national security assistants, the role under Cutler et al. metamorphosed from that of a highly restrained administrator, which it had been under Truman's proto-NSAs Souers and Lay, into that of a coordinator, or process manager. But the NSA had not yet become a true counselor or evaluator of policy alternatives. See Kevin V. Mulcahy, "Presidential Management Styles and National Security Policy-Making," in *Grand Strategy and the Decisionmaking Process,* ed. James C. Gaston (Washington, D.C.: National Defense University Press, 1992), 125–28.

43. C. D. Jackson Papers, Box 58, Daily Log, 11 January 1958, Eisenhower Presidential Library.

44. This analysis helped shape John F. Kennedy's reforms of the system. A good, brief summary of these events (with conclusions more favorable to Eisenhower than to Jackson) is found in Phillip G. Henderson, *Managing the Presidency: The Eisenhower Legacy—From Kennedy to Reagan* (Boulder, Colo.: Westview Press, 1988), 123–27.

45. See, e.g., Richard Tanner Johnson, *Managing the White House* (New York: Harper and Row, 1974), 3–4.

46. See Charles Walcott and Karen M. Hult, "White House Organization as a Problem of Governance: The Eisenhower System," *Presidential Studies Quarterly* 24 (1994): 327–39.

47. One also needs to evaluate the performance of the Eisenhower NSC system in responding to specific issues or crises. Here, recent observers have tended to give it far better marks than its contemporary critics would have expected. Phillip Henderson, for instance, reviewed the administration's response to the 1954–55 crisis over Quemoy and Matsu, small islands off the Chinese shore, as "a case of multiple advocacy," or properly structured and executed collegial-competitive decision making. Henderson, *Managing the Presidency,* 105–15. The term "multiple advocacy" was coined by Alexander George. See, e.g., George, *Presidential Decisionmaking in*

Foreign Policy (Boulder, Colo.: Westview Press, 1980). Similarly, Burke and Greenstein's extensive account of the administration's decision process in addressing the 1954 fall of the French in Vietnam reaches essentially the same conclusion, crediting Cutler in particular with effective process management. See John P. Burke and Fred I. Greenstein, with the collaboration of Larry Berman and Richard Immerman, *How Presidents Test Reality: Decisions on Vietnam, 1954 and 1965* (New York: Russell Sage, 1989), especially ch. 12.

48. See, e.g., I. M. Destler, *Presidents, Bureaucrats, and Foreign Policy: The Politics of Organizational Reform* (Princeton, N.J.: Princeton University Press, 1972), 19ff; Henderson, *Managing the Presidency*, 85–87.

49. C. D. Jackson's work included advising on "psychological warfare," writing foreign policy speeches, and serving as one of Eisenhower's leading "idea men" in the area of foreign policy. His work with the OCB was not a principal element of his White House role. See "Coordination of Operations in the Field of National Security," memo, William Jackson to Eisenhower, 31 December 1956, Whitman Files, Administration Series, Box 22, "William Jackson," Folder 1, p. 7, Eisenhower Presidential Library.

50. Rockefeller was less an idea man and more a mobilizer of the talents of others. His major policy contribution, the Open Skies plan, was developed at a conference at Quantico, Virginia. See Sherman Adams, *Firsthand Report: The Story of the Eisenhower Administration* (New York: Harper and Brothers, 1961), 91. Rockefeller's White House downfall, leading to his leaving at the end of 1955, was his inability to get along with John Foster Dulles and Herbert Hoover, Jr., of the State Department.

51. Henderson, *Managing the Presidency*, 86–87.

52. See memo, William Jackson to Adams, 2 April 1956, White House Office, Office of the Staff Secretary, Box 2, "William Jackson," Eisenhower Presidential Library. See also Henderson, *Managing the Presidency*, 87–88.

53. Elsewhere, we call such complex structural arrangements "governance networks." See Karen M. Hult and Charles Walcott, *Governing Public Organizations: Politics, Structures, and Institutional Design* (Pacific Grove, Calif.: Brooks/Cole, 1990), ch. 7.

54. Jackson to Adams, 2 April 1956.

55. Dulles to Eisenhower, 14 January 1957, Whitman Files, Administration Series, Box 22, "William Jackson," Folder 1, Eisenhower Presidential Library.

56. Lay and Johnson, *Organizational History*, 41–42.

57. Henderson, *Managing the Presidency*, 89. This was in line with Rockefeller's suggestion, and also with a recommendation William Jackson had made to Eisenhower. Jackson to Eisenhower, 31 December 1956. One negative consequence was to downgrade Harr's role somewhat, leaving him frustrated enough to think about resigning. Clarence Randall Journal, 7 January 1960, Box 6, CFEP, vol. 14, Eisenhower Presidential Library.

58. Quoted in Henderson, *Managing the Presidency*, 89.

59. Sherman Adams, Oral History Interview with Ed Edwin, 11 April 1967, p. 155, Eisenhower Presidential Library.

60. Clarence Randall Journal, 15 December 1955, Box 3, vol. 11, 1955, Eisenhower Presidential Library.

61. Stephen E. Ambrose, *Eisenhower, the President* (New York: Simon and Schuster, 1984), 401.

62. During this period, Dulles also believed that Stassen was exceeding his negotiating authority. A memo from Dulles to Stassen, 4 June 1957, for instance, instructs Stassen, "You will notify Mr. Zorin at the earliest possible moment that the memorandum you submitted to him [concerning a moratorium on nuclear testing] was not only informal and unofficial, but had no approval in its submitted form either by the President or the State Department, and that there are some aspects of the memorandum to which this government cannot agree at this moment." Whitman Files, Administration Series, Box 35, "Stassen," 1957, Folder 2, Eisenhower Presidential Library.

63. Stassen's difficulties with Dulles and others in the administration are recounted in Ambrose, *Eisenhower,* 401–4, 447–48.

64. L. Arthur Minnich, Oral History Interview with Paul Hopper, 21 July 1967, p. 7, Eisenhower Presidential Library.

65. Andrew Goodpaster, "Organizing the White House," in *The Eisenhower Presidency: Eleven Intimate Portraits of Dwight D. Eisenhower,* ed. Kenneth W. Thompson (Lanham, Md.: University Press of America, 1984), 66.

66. G. Gray Oral History, 19 July 1967, p. 273. Gray stated: "I've never known a man whom I worked with more easily, or affectionately. . . . I have the highest personal regard for him."

67. In this respect, the staff secretariat greatly resembled the cabinet secretariat. See Chapter 11 and also Charles Walcott and Karen M. Hult, "White House Organization as a Problem of Governance: The Eisenhower System," *Presidential Studies Quarterly* 24 (1994): 335–36.

68. Minnich Oral History, 21 July 1967, p. 13.

69. The Planning Board was not formally abolished, but it was effectively done away with through the device of never calling a meeting.

70. Theodore Sorensen, *Kennedy* (New York: Harper and Row, 1965), 281.

71. Quoted in Bromley K. Smith, *Organizational History of the National Security Council during the Kennedy and Johnson Administrations* (monograph written for the National Security Council, Washington, D.C., 1987), 15. The hyperbole is perhaps forgivable, though it must be noted that the idea of a *team* of Hopkinses is probably a contradiction in terms.

72. Ibid., 3–9. Neustadt suggested to Kennedy that he consolidate a number of offices, including those of the national security assistant and the special assistant for the OCB. Walt Rostow, who became deputy special assistant for national security under Kennedy, was principally responsible for fine-tuning the organizational changes. Ibid., 10ff.

73. See Henderson, *Managing the Presidency,* 127.

74. See Smith, *Organizational History,* 6; Henderson, *Managing the Presidency,* 129.

75. Mulcahy, "Presidential Management Style," 125.

76. G. Gray Oral History, 19 July 1967, p. 272.

77. See Smith, *Organizational History,* 10–12. The intention to rely on State in lieu of the OCB is clear in a memo from Bundy to Senator Jackson, cited in ibid., 40.

78. See Carnes Lord, *The Presidency and the Management of National Security* (New York: Free Press, 1988), 71. Lord also points out that the strength of Secretary of Defense McNamara, plus Bundy's and Kennedy's "inclinations," led the NSC staff to occupy itself mainly with foreign, rather than defense, policy. See also Bundy to JFK, 4 April 1961, President's Official File, Staff Files, Box 62, "Bundy, McGeorge," Kennedy Presidential Library; Bundy noted that assistant secretaries of state seemed to be overloaded, and "thus it has repeatedly been necessary to bring even small problems to you and still smaller ones to the White House staff, while more than once the ball has been dropped simply because no one person felt a continuing clear responsibility."

79. After the Bay of Pigs, the Situation Room was created in the White House to monitor all national security–related developments in the world. It was under Bundy's supervision and was directed by one of Bundy's staff. See Smith, *Organizational History*, 37–38.

80. Bock, *White House Staff*, 46; his emphasis.

81. Bundy, interview by Bill Lawrence (ABC television), 14 July 1963, White House Central Staff Files, Box 116, Kennedy Presidential Library.

82. Walt Rostow, Oral History Interview with Richard Neustadt, 11 April 1964, p. 40, Kennedy Presidential Library.

83. Ibid., 43. Latin America tended to be the responsibility of, among others, White House staffers Richard Goodwin and Arthur Schlesinger, Jr.

84. Smith, *Organizational History*, 21–22.

85. Ibid., 43.

86. Ibid., 47–48.

87. Maxwell D. Taylor, *Swords and Plowshares* (New York: Norton, 1972), 198–99.

88. See Bock, *White House Staff*, 41–53; for a similar analysis but a more critical conclusion, see Henderson, *Managing the Presidency*, 123–34.

89. Taylor, *Swords and Plowshares*, 195.

90. Ibid., 197.

91. Ibid., 199.

92. Ibid., 199–200.

93. Ibid., 7.

94. This story is told in detail in Chester Bowles, *Promises to Keep: My Years in Public Life, 1941–1969* (New York: Harper and Row, 1971), chs. 22–28.

95. On the creation of this job and Sorensen's role, see ibid., 364–68.

96. Ibid., 368.

97. Ibid., 430–34.

98. See Bock, *White House Staff*, 67. Appointments Secretary Marvin Watson has been blamed for this, but Bock points out that Watson never cut off anyone whom Johnson did not want cut off.

99. Bill Moyers reputedly wanted the job, and Rostow was not favored by Johnson's more liberal advisers.

100. Bock, *White House Staff*, 67.

101. For a full listing, see Smith, *Organizational History*, 67.

102. David Halberstam, *The Best and the Brightest* (New York: Random House, 1969).

103. Patrick Anderson, *The President's Men* (Garden City, N.Y.: Doubleday, 1968), 339–47.

104. Ibid., 341.

105. Bock, for example, questions Moyers's influence (*White House Staff,* 68–70).

106. That is the observation of scholars such as Bock (*White House Staff,* 72–75) and Lord (*Presidency and Management*), as well as the conclusion of Burke and Greenstein's examination of Vietnam decision making in 1965 (*How Presidents Test Reality,* especially ch. 12).

107. Such questions give rise to enduring controversies. In the case at hand, for instance, Larry Berman tends to blame Johnson's leadership. Berman, *Planning a Tragedy: The Americanization of the War in Vietnam* (New York: Norton, 1982). Burke and Greenstein, in *How Presidents Test Reality,* argue, for the most part, to the contrary.

CHAPTER 9. SPECIALIZED POLICY STRUCTURES

1. Although our main interest is analyzing White House staff "structures" rather than units, the discussion that follows often refers to "units," since one trait that many of these specialized policy initiatives tended to share was relative self-containment within the White House.

2. On the evolution of consumer representation in the White House, see, e.g., Joan Lucco, "Representing the Public Interest: Consumer Groups and the Presidency," in *The Politics of Interests: Interest Groups Transformed,* ed. Mark P. Petracca (Boulder, Colo.: Westview Press, 1992), 242–63. On White House structuring for consumer affairs during the Kennedy and Johnson presidencies, see, e.g., "Consumers Advisory Council," Myer Feldman, White House Staff Files, General File, Box 7, Kennedy Presidential Library; and "Memos for Mrs. Esther Peterson," Horace Busby Office Files, Box 20; "Betty Furness," White House Central Files, Subject File General FG 11-8-1, Box 83; Betty Furness, Oral History Interview with David G. McComb, 10 December 1968; Johnson Presidential Library.

3. As used here, foreign economic policy encompasses both foreign trade and foreign aid.

4. Two of FDR's original "Brain(s) Trust," Raymond Moley and Rexford Tugwell, played minor roles in the foreign economic policy arena. Each functioned briefly as virtual White House staff while employed as assistant secretaries of state and agriculture, respectively. Indeed, Moley's only significant venture into foreign economic policy proved fatal to his continuation as a Roosevelt aide. His misfortune occurred at the London Economic Conference in mid-1933, when his efforts as a delegate to orchestrate a compromise between those favoring international currency stabilization and those seeking greater policy leeway for each country were publicly torpedoed by a "bombshell" message from Roosevelt himself. That embarrassment, coupled with intrigue on the part of his immediate superior, Secretary of State Cordell Hull, humiliated Moley enough to provoke his departure from government. See Arthur Schlesinger, Jr., *The Coming of the New Deal* (Boston: Houghton Mifflin, 1958), ch. 13.

Tugwell mainly confined himself to domestic matters such as conservation policy and the reorganization of the Department of Agriculture. However, he did dabble in foreign matters, including a small role in preparing the U.S. position for the ill-fated London conference. Bernard Sternsher, *Rexford Tugwell and the New Deal* (New Brunswick, N.J.: Rutgers University Press, 1964), 342; see also Tugwell Diary and Notes, 26 April 1933, Tugwell Papers, Box 30, Roosevelt Presidential Library.

5. The White House role of Harry Hopkins, discussed in Chapter 8, included some foreign economic matters, with heavy emphasis on lend-lease. But Hopkins's tasks were so numerous and varied that he could not be regarded as a specialist—in this or anything else.

6. James Rowe to Samuel Rosenman, 15 March 1941, Rosenman Papers, Box 41, "FDR Public Papers," Roosevelt Presidential Library.

7. Roger J. Sandilands, *The Life and Political Economy of Lauchlin Currie: New Dealer, Presidential Adviser, and Development Economist* (Durham, N.C.: Duke University Press, 1990), 133–36.

8. Roosevelt to Currie, 19 January 1945, President's Secretary's File, Box 147, Roosevelt Presidential Library. Currie also was instructed to "inform yourself on current thinking in British government circles on post-war commercial policy and exchange and financial matters and, if time permits, to inform yourself on current conditions in Italy."

9. Details of Turner's work can be seen in the Turner Papers, Box 2, Chronological Files, Truman Presidential Library. His work did not change materially when he moved into the White House.

10. Turner to Steelman, 18 February 1948, Turner Papers, Box 2, Chronological Files, "1948." Beginning in March 1948, Turner was assisted by Marjorie Belcher, who stayed on after Turner left full-time White House service. Belcher's main task was to wrap up the loose ends of the commodity, materials, and stockpiling issues carried over from OWMR. She "also processed Tariff Commission recommendations under the injury provisions of the Reciprocal Trade Act—documents which came to Steelman for reasons long forgotten by all concerned." Richard Neustadt, untitled essay in Francis H. Heller, ed., *The Truman White House: The Administration of the Presidency, 1945–1953* (Lawrence: Regents Press of Kansas, 1980), 98.

11. Secretary's File, General File, "Gray," Truman Presidential Library.

12. See the Gray Papers, Box 1, Truman Presidential Library, for details on his staff operation.

13. See internal staff memos, May–July 1950, Gray Papers, Box 2.

14. Forty pages of agency comments on the draft were collected and can be found in ibid., Box 1.

15. The study was provoked by allegations of administration wavering in the implementation of the free-trade policies that had initially been recommended by the Randall Commission (see below).

16. Dodge and his staff were funded from a congressional "special projects" appropriation. In this capacity, Dodge became, along with Clarence Randall, one of the first White House aides with both a specialty in foreign economic policy and an open-ended tenure in the White House.

17. Dodge, paraphrased by Clarence Randall, Randall Journal, Box 3, vol. 13, 1 June 1956, p. 10, Eisenhower Presidential Library.

18. Ibid.

19. William Jackson, paraphrased in Randall Journal, Box 3, vol. 13, 1 June 1956, p. 10.

20. See Hauge to Goodpaster, 6 April 1955, White House Office, Office of the Staff Secretary, Box 4, Eisenhower Presidential Library.

21. See Sherman Adams, *Firsthand Report: The Story of the Eisenhower Administration* (New York: Harper and Brothers, 1961), 382–86. This issue was highly controversial, since the Republican Old Guard in Congress, led by Senate Majority Leader William Knowland, along with elements of organized labor, favored greater protectionism.

22. Randall Journal, 8 April 1954, Box 1, vol. 2, 1954. With these expanded duties came an expanded staff, now including two additional detailees from BOB (Dave McEachron and "Hutch" Hutchinson). Staff director Macy was replaced in July 1954 by John Stambaugh.

23. The working group, which, among other things, provided outlines for presidential speeches, included Hauge, staff secretary Andrew Goodpaster, economic policy assistant Stephen Benedict, and three members of Randall's staff, C. Edward Galbreath, John Stambaugh (who succeeded Macy in July 1954), and Henry Wallich.

24. Randall was convinced that Stassen was "on the march as an empire builder," as well as "unpredictable and altogether unsound" in the field of economics. Randall Journal, April 1954, Box 1, vol. 1, 1954.

25. Ibid.

26. Ibid., January–April 1956, Box 3, vol. 13, 1956.

27. Ibid., 2 December 1955, Box 3, vol. 11, 1955.

28. Ibid., 16 August 1956, Box 3, CFEP, vol. 1, 1956. Although Randall had retired from Inland on 1 April 1956, he was still only half-time in the White House. He largely succeeded in making the CFEP a more proactive instrument by leading it to anticipate policy disputes. For example, in 1959, Randall convened the CFEP to discuss trade with the Soviet Union in advance of a meeting between Eisenhower and Soviet Foreign Minister Mikoyan. Randall to Wilton Persons, 9 January 1959, White House Office, Office of the Staff Secretary, Box 5, "Randall," Eisenhower Presidential Library. This meeting revealed Secretary of Commerce Lewis Strauss to be unalterably opposed to any such trade—contrary to the views of the majority. Randall reported this to Persons for Eisenhower's information, warning that Strauss was likely to try to see the president about the issue.

29. See Randall Journal, June 1957, Box 4, CFEP, vol. 4, 1957.

30. This law became the foundation of the government's agricultural commodity assistance program. The assignment of credit for proposing and enacting PL-480 was a matter of controversy. Most contemporary sources give the lion's share to Sen. Hubert Humphrey.

31. His assistant for most of his White House tenure was James Lambie. Lambie worked half-time for Francis and half-time as liaison with the Advertising Council.

32. Food for Peace differed from PL-480 in that it was expressly intended as foreign aid rather than as food surplus disposal. Its primary clients were to be foreign countries rather than American farmers. Again, Hubert Humphrey was a moving force behind the idea. See Peter A. Toma, *The Politics of Food for Peace:*

Executive-Legislative Interaction (Tucson: University of Arizona Press, 1967), especially pp. 42-43.

33. Francis to Bryce Harlow, 16 December 1959, Lambie Papers, Box 4, "Francis—Chronological, 1959," Eisenhower Presidential Library.

34. Adams, *Firsthand Report,* 390-91.

35. Ideas such as distributing the surplus food under United Nations auspices even attracted Sherman Adams's support but could not get past Dulles. Ibid., 391.

36. George McGovern, *Grassroots: The Autobiography of George McGovern* (New York: Random House, 1977), 84.

37. Executive Order, 24 January 1961, White House Central Staff Files, Box 121, "Food for Peace," Kennedy Presidential Library.

38. McGovern, *Grassroots,* 86. Much of the substantive work accomplished by McGovern and his staff of five to six professionals involved working with the agriculture committees of the Congress; see White House Central Staff Files, Box 189, Kennedy Presidential Library. McGovern and his aides had relatively few contacts with the rest of the White House staff, although science adviser Jerome Wiesner did assist in their work with Congress.

39. See, e.g., McGovern to Kennedy, 12 May 1961, White House Central Staff Files, Box 121, "Food for Peace"; McGovern to Orville Freeman (Secretary of Agriculture), 12 December 1961, White House Central Staff Files, Box 121, "Food for Peace," Kennedy Presidential Library. See also McGovern, *Grassroots,* 85-86.

40. See White House Central Staff Files, Box 121, "Food for Peace," Kennedy Presidential Library.

41. The idea of handling this through the White House originated with Myer Rashish, at the time a special assistant to George Ball at the State Department. Rashish recalls that he proposed the strategy in order to resolve conflict between State and Commerce over the bill and to give status to the effort. See Rashish Oral History Interview with John F. Stewart, 11 September 1967, p. 13, Kennedy Presidential Library. This marked the first use of special projects for the sole purpose of working to pass legislation.

42. "Petersen-O'Brien Meeting Agenda," n.d., Feldman Papers, White House Staff Files, General File, Box 26, "Trade Expansion Act of 1962, 2/62-11/62 and Undated," Kennedy Presidential Library.

43. Rashish Oral History, 11 September 1967, p. 14.

44. Ibid., 15.

45. Ibid.

46. Overall, in Rashish's judgment, the staff's work was "haphazard." Ibid., 21.

47. In fact, despite the hierarchy, Petersen's leadership was not especially obtrusive, in part because he was frequently away promoting the act.

48. Emmette S. Redford and Richard T. McCulley, *White House Operations: The Johnson Presidency* (Austin: University of Texas Press, 1986), 43.

49. Ibid., 57.

50. See Goldstein Office Files, Box 1, "Balance of Payments," Johnson Presidential Library.

51. Califano to LBJ, 20 September 1967, White House Central Files, Subject File, General File, Box 85, "Ernest Goldstein"; on balance of payments, see Gold-

stein to LBJ, 9 November 1967, White House Central Files, Subject File, General File, Box 85, "Ernest Goldstein," Johnson Presidential Library.

52. Rostow to (Secretary of the Treasury) Henry Fowler, 13 March 1968, White House Central Files, Subject Files FG 11-8-1, Box 106, "Rostow, Walter P.," Johnson Presidential Library.

53. See, e.g., John Hart, *The Presidential Branch* (New York: Pergamon Press, 1987), 57-58. Designated as members of the CIEP were the secretaries of state, treasury, agriculture, commerce, and labor; the director of the Office of Management and Budget; the chair of the Council of Economic Advisers; the national security assistant; the executive director of the Domestic Council; and the U.S. trade representative.

54. Ibid., 63.

55. On *Sputnik* as a triggering factor, see, e.g., David Z. Beckler, "The Precarious Life of Science in the White House," *Daedulus* 103 (1974): 117; William R. Nelson, *The Politics of Science* (New York: Oxford University Press, 1968), pt. 2 introduction, p. 108.

56. W. Henry Lambright, *Presidential Management of Science and Technology: The Johnson Presidency* (Austin: University of Texas Press, 1985), 25 and passim.

57. Cf. Meg Greenfield, "Science Goes to Washington" (from *The Reporter,* 26 September 1963), in Nelson, *Politics of Science,* 133.

58. Cf. Beckler, "Precarious Life of Science," 122.

59. Cf. ibid.; James Everett Katz, *Presidential Politics and Science Policy* (New York: Praeger, 1978), 8; Lambright, *Presidential Management,* 185.

60. Lambright, *Presidential Management,* 186; cf. Wiesner in Greenfield, "Science Goes to Washington," 138.

61. Lambright, *Presidential Management,* 185.

62. Katz, *Presidential Politics,* 124.

63. James P. Killian, Oral History Interview with Stephen White, 16 November 1969, Columbia University Oral History, p. 53, Eisenhower Presidential Library.

64. Beckler, "Precarious Life of Science," 119.

65. See, e.g., Katz, *Presidential Politics,* 152; Lambright, *Presidential Management,* 9; Charles S. Maier, introduction to *A Scientist in the White House,* by George B. Kistiakowsky (Cambridge, Mass.: Harvard University Press, 1976), lx.

66. Cf. Beckler, "Precarious Life of Science," 46; James R. Killian, Jr., *Sputnik, Scientists, and Eisenhower: A Memoir of the First Special Assistant to the President for Science and Technology* (Cambridge, Mass.: MIT Press, 1977), 255.

67. See, e.g., Maier, introduction, lix; George Kistiakowsky, Oral History Interview with Thomas Soapes, 17 November 1976, p. 18, Eisenhower Presidential Library; Killian, *Sputnik.*

68. Maier, introduction, lix; cf. Nelson, *Politics of Science.*

69. Donald F. Hornig, Oral History Interview with David G. McComb, 4 December 1968, p. 19, Johnson Presidential Library.

70. Katz, *Presidential Politics;* Hart, *Presidential Branch,* 88.

71. Katz, *Presidential Politics,* 8; Hart, *Presidential Branch,* 88.

72. National Science Foundation Report 62-37, "Scientific Activities in Government 1940-62," in Nelson, *Politics of Science,* 56; cf. White House Office Files, 791, Steelman, "1945-1949," Box 1549, Truman Presidential Library.

73. Aides Files, James E. Webb, Box 8, n.d., Truman Presidential Library.

74. Cf. Beckler, "Precarious Life of Science," 117.

75. NSF Report 62-37, in Nelson, *Politics of Science,* 57.

76. See, e.g., Hart, *Presidential Branch,* 88; NSF Report 62-37, in Nelson, *Politics of Science.* According to Beckler, however, the SAC gained some influence under Eisenhower when it was included in the discussion of ways to decrease the risk of a surprise Soviet attack against the United States. Beckler, "Precarious Life of Science," 117.

77. David Beckler in Killian Oral History, 8 April 1970, p. 268.

78. See, e.g., "Staff Notes August 1959," DDE Diary Series, Box 43, Eisenhower Presidential Library; Kistiakowsky Oral History, 17 November 1976, p. 4; Killian, *Sputnik,* 244.

79. Kistiakowsky Oral History, 17 November 1976, p. 4.

80. In addition, Killian and Kistiakowsky occasionally were involved in discussions of science education, research and development, and National Science Foundation funding. Toward the end of the administration, Kistiakowsky was drawn into more "domestic" science issues, such as the concern with radiostrontium levels in wheat and the controversy over the contamination of cranberries by pesticides. See Christopher J. Bosso, *Pesticides and Politics: The Life Cycle of a Public Issue* (Pittsburgh: University of Pittsburgh Press, 1987), 96–100.

The size of the science adviser's staff varied between about 18 and 21, with Kistiakowsky reporting six "technical aides" in 1960 and Richard Neustadt (for the Kennedy transition team) classifying eight of Kistiakowsky's staff as "professional." On the first numbers, see Staff list, n.d., White House Office, Office of Staff Secretary, Box 4, "Killian"; Note to file, 7 December 1959, White House Office, "Office of Special Assistant for Science and Technology," Box 13. On the second, see Kistiakowsky, *Scientist in the White House;* Richard E. Neustadt, "The Science Adviser: First Steps," 4 January 1961, Sorensen Papers, Subject Files, Box 18, Kennedy Presidential Library.

For the most part, the unit seemed to operate as a collection of specialists who, according to Kistiakowsky, acted as "co-equals, each within his area of responsibility." Kistiakowsky Oral History, 17 November 1976, p. 3. For details on the staff, see, e.g., "WH—Miscell [October 1957–December 1960]," White House Office, Office of Special Assistant for Science and Technology, Box 17; Killian Oral History, 16 July 1960; Kistiakowsky Oral History, 17 January 1976.

81. See, e.g., Whitman Files, Administration Series, Box 23, "James R. Killian, Science Adviser" and "George B. Kistiakowsky, Science Adviser," Eisenhower Presidential Library; Kistiakowsky Oral History, 17 November 1976, pp. 5, 89, and passim. See also Killian Oral History, 1 February 1970, pp. 109ff, 16 February 1970, pp. 143ff, and 16 July 1970, passim.

Another of Killian's responsibilities was overseeing the revitalization of the U.S. space program. He was convinced that the space agency should be directed by civilians and focus primarily on nonmilitary space exploration. After legislation making NASA the successor to the National Advisory Committee for Aeronautics was passed in July 1958, Killian worked with Chief of Staff Sherman Adams to find top appointees for the new agency and, at the president's request, organized the initial meetings of the National Aeronautics and Space Council. See. e.g., Killian Oral

History, 1 February 1970, p. 109; "Staff Notes—September 1958," DDE Diary Series, Box 36, Eisenhower Presidential Library.

82. In conjunction with their national security responsibilities, the science advisers participated in a range of executive branch structures. For example, they attended meetings of the cabinet, National Security Council, Operations Coordination Board, and Planning Board and consulted with other bodies. The science adviser also was a member of the Committee of Principals, along with the secretaries of state and defense, the chair of the Atomic Energy Commission, and the director of the CIA; this committee "considered policy problems arising from our negotiations with the United Kingdom and the Soviet Union on a treaty to cease the testing of nuclear weapons." Kistiakowsky speech to the meeting of the Montreal Section of the Chemical Institute of Canada, 19 October 1960, White House Central Files, Official File 72-a-2, Box 311, "Office of the Special Assistant to the President for Science and Technology," Folder 5.

83. Killian Oral History, 16 July 1970, p. 320; Kistiakowsky speech to Chemical Institute of Canada, 19 October 1960.

84. Killian Oral History, 16 November 1969, pp. 54, 114.

85. Ibid., 8 December 1969, p. 78. For his part, Kistiakowsky reported being involved in discussions about ways to cut military spending and hearing appeals from those who would be hurt by the cuts. Kistiakowsky, *Scientist in the White House,* passim.

86. NSF Report 62-37, in Nelson, *Politics of Science;* Kistiakowsky to Eisenhower, 18 May 1960, Whitman Files, Administration Series, "Kistiakowsky," Folder 1.

87. Kistiakowsky Oral History, 17 November 1976, p. 19.

88. See, e.g., "WH—Miscellaneous [October 1957–December 1960]," White House Office, Office of the Special Assistant for Science and Technology, Box 17, Folder 1; Arthur Larson/Malcolm Moos Files, Box 3, Eisenhower Presidential Library.

89. Kistiakowsky Oral History, 17 November 1957, pp. 4, 14. Similarly, Killian recalled that National Security Assistant Bobby Cutler was "without selfish motives of any kind." Killian Oral History, 22 March 1970, p. 243; cf. Hart, *Presidential Branch,* 90. Kreidler remembered close ties between the science unit and the Bureau of the Budget, a relationship, according to Killian, of "confidence and collaboration." Kreidler and Killian in Killian Oral History, n.d., p. 262.

90. Killian Oral History, 1 February 1970, p. 124.

91. Ibid., 9 November 1969, p. 1.

92. Ibid., p. 3.

93. Kistiakowsky Oral History, 17 November 1976, p. 16.

94. Ibid., p. 17.

95. For example, White House Central Subject Files, Box 121, "Office of Science and Technology"; "Wiesner, Jerome B.," President's Official Files, Staff Files, Box 67; Richard Goodwin to Kennedy, 25 March 1961, President's Official Files, Staff Files, Box 63, "Goodwin, Richard W."; notes on meeting with President on disarmament, 1 August 1962, President's Official Files, Staff Files, Box 64a, "O'Donnell, Kenneth P.," Kennedy Presidential Library. Cf. Alan L. Otten

" 'What Do You Think, Ted?': Theodore Sorensen," in *The Kennedy Circle,* ed. Lester Tanzer (Washington, D.C.: Luce, 1961), 23.

96. See, e.g., Dutton to James Webb (NASA), 15 August 1961, White House Central Subject Files, Box 121, "Office of Science and Technology"; Sorensen Papers, Subject Files, Box 38, "Space," Kennedy Presidential Library.

97. Katz, *Presidential Politics,* 143.

98. On Wiesner's participation in NSC meetings, see, e.g., Arthur Schlesinger, Jr., White House Files, Box WH-16, "National Security Council"; Sorensen Papers, Classified Subject Files, Boxes 49–56, "National Security Council," Kennedy Presidential Library. The science adviser's chairmanship of the PSAC and the Federal Council for Science and Technology is stated in Wiesner to Kennedy, 23 January 1961, White House Central Subject Files, Box 204. According to Kistiakowsky, the Federal Council became a "better working unit" during this period. Kistiakowsky Oral History, 17 November 1976, pp. 19–20.

99. Greenfield, "Science Goes to Washington," 135.

100. Killian, *Sputnik,* 244.

101. See White House Central Subject Files, Box 121, "Office of Science and Technology."

102. Cf. Maier, introduction, lixff.

103. Kistiakowsky Oral History, 17 November 1976, pp. 20–21.

104. Hart, *Presidential Branch,* 90. Sorensen, however, believed that Kennedy "used the Bundy staff, the science and budget advisers, and other aides as a check on McNamara's authoritative powers of persuasion." Theodore C. Sorensen, *The Kennedy Legacy* (New York: Macmillan, 1969), 87.

105. See, e.g., White House Central Subject Files, Box 121, "Office of Science and Technology"; White House Central Subject Files, Box 204; Wiesner Staff Files; Beckler, "Precarious Life of Science," 122.

106. Neustadt, "The Science Adviser," 1.

107. See American Chemical Society, "White House Superstructure for Science" (from *Chemical and Engineering News* 42 [19 October 1964]: 78-92), in Nelson, *Politics of Science,* 107.

108. See Maier, introduction, lix; R. Gordon Hoxie, " 'To Promote the Progress of Science . . .': Considerations for the President," in *The Presidency in Transition,* edited by James P. Pfiffner and R. Gordon Hoxie (New York: Center for the Study of the Presidency, 1989), 295; Lambright, *Presidential Management,* 185.

109. Meanwhile, Hornig's staff grew to 25 professionals, who continued to operate as specialists. See, e.g., Hornig Oral History, 4 December 1968, pp. 24, 34, and passim; cf. Lambright, *Presidential Management,* 185.

110. On Hornig's involvement in space policy, see, e.g., Horace Busby Office Files, Box 19, "Memos for Dr. Hornig"; "Donald F. Hornig," Subject File General FG 11-8-1, Box 85; Johnson Presidential Library.

111. See, e.g., Douglass Cater to Johnson, 9 February 1965, Cater Office Files, Box 13, "Memos to the President"; Joseph Califano to Johnson, 13 February 1968, Califano Office Files, Box 9, "Memoranda for the President"; Califano to Johnson, 31 May 1967, Califano Office Files, Box 73, "Trucking Strike"; Johnson Presidential Library. See also Hornig Oral History, 4 December 1968.

112. Lambright, *Presidential Management,* 14.

113. Horace Busby to Johnson, 21 September 1965, White House Central Subject File, Box 70, "FG 11-8-1 2/1/65–9/30/65"; Califano Office Files, Subject File, General FG 11-8-1, Box 85 "Donald Hornig." According to Lambright, "these horizontal relations were key to vertical influence with the President." Lambright, *Presidential Management,* 186.

114. See "Donald F. Hornig," White House Central Files, Subject File General FG 11-8-1, Box 85.

115. Lambright, *Presidential Management,* 9.

116. Ibid., 175.

117. Charles Horsky, Oral History Interview with Charles T. Morrissey, 7 August 1964, pp. 5ff., Kennedy Presidential Library. This should not suggest, however, that the Eisenhower White House completely ignored the District of Columbia. In 1956, for example, Eisenhower met with Sherman Adams and Special Counsel Gerald Morgan to discuss the possibility of home rule in the District. Whitman Diary, 21 April 1956, Box 7, Eisenhower Presidential Library. Among Robert Merriam's responsibilities as deputy assistant for intergovernmental affairs was Washington, D.C. Merriam Papers, Box 1, "Part II: An Overview of the Presidency," pp. 26–27, Eisenhower Presidential Library. Nevertheless, the District of Columbia was not the primary concern of anyone in the White House.

118. See, e.g., White House Central Subject Files, Boxes 111 and 118, Kennedy Presidential Library.

119. Charles Horsky Oral History, 7 August 1964, p. 5.

120. Ibid., 6.

121. See ibid., 13–20.

122. See, e.g., ibid; "Horsky, Charles A.," President's Official Files, Staff Files, Box 64, Kennedy Presidential Library.

123. See, e.g., Cater to Johnson, 1 August 1967, Cater Office Files, Box 17, "Memos to the President"; Califano to Johnson, 30 December 1967, "Legislative Program Development Procedures," Matthew Nimetz Office Files, Box 15; Johnson Presidential Library.

124. See, e.g., Califano memos to Johnson, in Califano Office Files, Box 17, "Memos for the President, April 1968."

125. Bragdon to Wilton Persons, 5 March 1959, Bragdon Papers, Box 3, "Public Works Planning Unit (Old)." Cf. notes on meeting of Bragdon, Sherman Adams, Persons, and Andrew Goodpaster, 6 October 1955, in Bragdon Papers, Box 3, "Comprehensive Planning," Folder 1; "Major General John S. Bragdon," White House Central File, Official File 72–a-2, Box 286. All these materials are housed at the Eisenhower Presidential Library.

126. Stans to Persons, 24 May 1960, White House Central Files, Official File 72–a-2, Box 286, "Bragdon."

127. Bradley H. Patterson, Jr., *The Ring of Power: The White House Staff and Its Expanded Role in Government* (New York: Basic Books, 1988), 272.

128. Bragdon to Persons, 5 March 1959, Bragdon Papers, Box 3.

129. See, e.g., Bragdon Papers, "Finding Aid," Eisenhower Presidential Library.

130. Bragdon, Draft: "The Interstate Limited Access 90/10 Federal Aid System with Special Reference to Toll Financing and Intra-City Routing," 15 June 1961, Bragdon Papers, Box 2, "Book—Correspondence and Draft on Interstate System Financing," Eisenhower Presidential Library.

131. See ibid., pp. 12, 26, and passim.

132. Handwritten notes, n.d., Bragdon Papers, Box 2, "Book—A Look at the White House—General."

133. See Myer Feldman, White House Staff Files, General File, Box 13, "Mental Retardation," Kennedy Presidential Library.

134. See, e.g., ibid.; Eunice Shriver, Oral History Interview with John Stewart, 7 May 1968, Kennedy Presidential Library.

135. See Elmer Staats to Feldman, 20 October 1962, in Feldman Staff Files, "Mental Retardation."

136. See "Office of the Special Assistant to the President for Mental Retardation," White House Central Subject Files, Box 122, Kennedy Presidential Library.

137. See Michael Begab, Oral History Interview with John F. Stewart, 21 March 1968, pp. 9, 12, Kennedy Presidential Library.

138. Donald Stedman, Oral History Interview with William McHugh, 18 December 1968, p. 31. On Warren's activities, see also Patrick J. Doyle, Oral History Interview with John F. Stewart, 4 March 1968, p. 34, Kennedy Presidential Library; White House Central Subject Files, "Office of the Special Assistant for Mental Retardation"; Feldman, Staff Files, "Mental Retardation." Doyle observed that Warren's chief accomplishment was calling "attention to this problem on the part of medical educators, because the medical educators themselves gave [mental retardation] a low priority. When they saw a man of his stature in this, I think they paid more attention." Doyle Oral History, 4 March 1968, p. 23.

139. Doyle Oral History, 4 March 1968, p. 33. See also Stedman Oral History, 18 December 1968, p. 31.

140. On Doyle's activities, see, e.g., Doyle Oral History, 4 March 1968. Other aides had better-defined jobs. Michael Begab, for instance, had largely administrative responsibilities, and Lois Meng served as the unit's information officer. Begab Oral History, 21 March 1968. Donald Stedman joined the office in June 1963 (at Sargent Shriver's request) to help plan the White House Conference on Mental Retardation, which was designed to push for adoption of some of the panel's recommendations at the state level. This also meant that Stedman worked directly with governors and their staffs, often piggybacking on President Kennedy's meetings with small groups of governors to discuss civil rights. See Stedman Oral History, 18 December 1968. David Ray also did some work at the state level, but his main responsibility was getting Congress to enact legislation, for example, for the construction of facilities for the mentally retarded and for mental retardation planning and programming. See Doyle Oral History, 4 March 1968, p. 29. Cf. Ray to S. Shriver, 26 June 1963; Ray to Feldman, 29 August 1963; Warren to E. Shriver, S. Shriver, Feldman, "Highlights of Staff Activities, 14–18 October 1963"; Feldman Staff Files, "Mental Retardation."

141. See Feldman Staff Files, "Mental Retardation"; White House Central Subject Files, "Office of the Special Assistant for Mental Retardation."

142. See Feldman Staff Files, "Mental Retardation."

143. E. Shriver Oral History, 7 May 1968, p. 28.

144. See, e.g., Doyle Oral History, 4 March 1968, pp. 10, 30.

145. See ibid., 6, 13.

146. Doyle described the nature of the interaction: "We could very often identify

people that had a professional interest in mental retardation. . . . [OCR] could tell us who was approachable, who was a political liability, the ones that were censored because Larry O'Brien was working on them for some other vote." Ibid., 29.

147. Ibid., 5.

148. Ibid., 37.

149. Ibid., 35.

150. Stedman Oral History, 18 December 1968, p. 28. Similarly, Doyle contended that the White House pushed agencies faster and further than they wanted to go. "We were plenty rough . . . because there was a great impatience, especially on the part of the Shrivers. . . . I'm sure that we offended more people than we should have." Doyle Oral History, 4 March 1968, p. 22.

151. See, e.g., Begab Oral History, 21 March 1968, p. 15.

152. Doyle Oral History, 4 March 1968, pp. 19–20.

153. Ibid., 16.

154. Ibid., 13.

155. Cohen to Feldman, 11 October 1963, Feldman Staff Files, "Mental Retardation."

156. Stedman Oral History, 18 December 1968, p. 32.

157. Even so, Doyle believed that, in contrast to the Kennedy administration, LBJ had a more sincere interest in the issue and that staffers such as Douglass Cater and Horace Busby treated it with some importance. Doyle Oral History, 4 March 1968, pp. 13, 39.

CHAPTER 10. WRITING AND SCHEDULING

1. In Arthur Larson, *Eisenhower: The President Nobody Knew* (New York: Charles Scribner's Sons, 1968), 152.

2. Roderick P. Hart, *The Sound of Leadership: Presidential Communication in the Modern Age* (Chicago: University of Chicago Press, 1987), 74.

3. Members of all four administrations have made similar observations concerning the importance of the writing process for setting and examining administration policy, and thus of writers as policy advisers. Bryce Harlow's comment is typical: "the speechwriter in the White House can have a very, very substantial influence on the policy, either by the methodology of presentation of the material, or by the inclusion or exclusion of ideas, and by the fact that he has to work so intimately with the President." Harlow, Oral History Interview with John T. Mason, Jr., 27 March 1967, p. 109, Eisenhower Presidential Library.

4. For Truman, see Matthew Connelly, Oral History Interview with Jerry N. Hess, 30 November 1967, pp. 150–55, Truman Presidential Library; Richard E. Neustadt, "Discussion," in Francis H. Heller, *The Truman White House: The Administration of the Presidency, 1945–1953* (Lawrence: Regents Press of Kansas, 1980), 151. For Kennedy, see Pierre Salinger, *With Kennedy* (Garden City, N.Y.: Doubleday, 1966), 66–67; Arthur Schlesinger, Jr., *A Thousand Days* (Boston: Houghton Mifflin, 1965), 690.

5. In what follows, "minor" speeches refer to less substantive presidential

speeches, such as remarks to visitors to the White House, ceremonial speeches, and messages sent to groups and organizations (e.g., Boys' Nation and the Advertising Council). Note that this use differs from that of Gary King and Lyn Ragsdale, *The Elusive Executive: Discovering Statistical Patterns in the Presidency* (Washington, D.C.: Congressional Quarterly Press, 1988), 260-61.

6. Here, "major" speeches are considered those with policy content. These include what King and Ragsdale (*Elusive Executive,* 260-62) label "major speeches" ("live nationally televised and broadcast addresses to the country that preempt all major network programming") as well as what they call "minor speeches" ("domestic public appearances by presidents other than national addresses and news conferences in which presidents make moderately lengthy policy statements to a major group or forum"). Also included are substantive presidential addresses delivered abroad, presidential messages accompanying legislation submitted to Congress, veto statements and speeches, and statements on public issues.

7. Ibid., 262.

8. "Public appearances" are "nonpartisan appearances by presidents before groups outside the vicinity of Washington, D.C., during which ceremonies take place and nonpolicy remarks are made." Ibid., 273. Similarly, Kennedy and Johnson averaged 219 and 293 "public activities" a year; Truman had an annual average of 130, and Eisenhower 84. "Public activities are defined as including all domestic public appearances by a president, including major speeches, news conferences, minor speeches, Washington appearances, and U.S. appearances, but not political appearances." Ibid., 275.

9. Samuel Kernell, *Going Public: New Strategies of Presidential Leadership,* 2d ed. (Washington, D.C.: Congressional Quarterly, 1993), ch. 2.

10. In Peter Benchley, "Rose Garden Rubbish and Other Glorious Compositions," *Life* 66 (23 May 1969): 66.

11. King and Ragsdale, *Elusive Executive,* 270-75. For instance, John Kennedy gave almost twice as many policy speeches to major groups a month as Richard Nixon did.

12. 1932 Campaign folder, Strother Papers, Box 2, Hoover Presidential Library.

13. See Hastings Papers, Boxes 2, 6; Strother Papers, Box 2; Hoover Presidential Library.

14. Theodore G. Joslin, *Hoover Off the Record* (New York: Doubleday, Doran, 1934), 318-19.

15. Robert L. Sherwood, *Roosevelt and Hopkins: An Intimate History* (New York: Harper and Brothers, 1948), 212.

16. Notes on conversation with Ben Cohen and Tommy Corcoran, 27 April 1949, Samuel Rosenman Papers, Container 18, Roosevelt Presidential Library.

17. Stephen Hess, *Organizing the Presidency,* 1st ed. (Washington, D.C.: Brookings Institution, 1976), 35; James Roosevelt correspondence, Box 57, Roosevelt Presidential Library.

18. Rosenman remained on the New York Supreme Court until October 1943, when he assumed a full-time position as special counsel in the White House. Until then, he commuted to Washington but was there so frequently that he was virtually a staff member.

19. Samuel I. Rosenman, *Working with Roosevelt* (New York: Harper and Brothers, 1952), 177.

20. Hess, *Organizing the Presidency,* 1st ed., 35.

21. Ibid.

22. Rosenman, *Working with Roosevelt,* 10.

23. An exception to this was FDR's treatment of Raymond Moley; see ibid., 104. The president sometimes had more than one person work on a draft, but they evidently knew about each other and did not consider this to be "competition." An example of this working style can be found in a discussion of the preparation of the fourth inaugural address in Halford Ross Ryan, "Roosevelt's Fourth Inaugural Address: A Study of Its Composition," in *American Rhetoric from Roosevelt to Reagan,* 2d ed., ed. Halford Ross Ryan (Prospect Heights, Ill.: Waveland Press, 1987), 28-36.

24. Rosenman, *Working with Roosevelt,* 227–34; Stephen Hess, *Organizing the Presidency,* 2d ed. (Washington, D.C.: Brookings Institution, 1988), 30–31.

25. Grace Tully, *F.D.R., My Boss* (New York: Charles Scribner's Sons, 1949), 95. Accounts by Rosenman and Sherwood portray the same collegial process.

26. Rosenman, *Working with Roosevelt,* 315–20, 510.

27. Hess, *Organizing the Presidency,* 2d ed., 31.

28. These included George Allen (a White House hanger-on and later a director of the Reconstruction Finance Corporation), his assistant Eddie Reynolds, and Appointments Secretary Matthew Connelly. See Connelly Oral History, 30 November 1967, p. 150, Truman Presidential Library.

29. Ibid., 155.

30. James P. Sundquist, Oral History Interview with Charles T. Morrissey, 15 June 1963, p. 8, Truman Presidential Library.

31. See, e.g., Charles Ross Diary, 8 October 1946; Ayers Papers, Box 19; Truman Presidential Library.

32. Neustadt, "Discussion," 151.

33. Murphy, in Heller, *Truman White House,* 37.

34. Theodore Tannenwald, Jr., untitled essay, in ibid., 202.

35. Ibid.

36. Murphy, "Discussion," in Heller, *Truman White House,* 74.

37. See Neustadt, in ibid., 100.

38. Harlow Oral History, 27 March 1967, pp. 108-9. Cf. Hart, *Sound of Leadership,* 86.

39. Bernard Shanley Diaries, p. 1268, Eisenhower Presidential Library.

40. Roderick P. Hart, *Verbal Style and the Presidency: A Computer-based Analysis* (New York: Academic Press, 1984), 86.

41. Harlow Oral History, 27 March 1967, p. 93. In general, Eisenhower emulated the Truman model in the preparation of the State of the Union message.

42. Stephen Ambrose, *Eisenhower: The President* (New York: Simon and Schuster, 1984), 93.

43. Kevin McCann, Oral History Interview with Ed Edwin, 21 December 1966, p. 1, Eisenhower Presidential Library.

44. Harlow Oral History, 27 March 1967, p. 132.

45. See Salinger, *With Kennedy,* 66–67; Schlesinger, *A Thousand Days,* 690.

46. Salinger, *With Kennedy,* 66.

47. Jim Bishop, *A Day in the Life of President Kennedy* (New York: Random House, 1964), 20.

48. Theodore Sorensen, *The Kennedy Legacy* (New York: Macmillan, 1969), 82.

49. See Sorensen Papers, JFK Speech files, Boxes 63, 69, 70, 76, "State of the Union," Kennedy Presidential Library.

50. Patrick Anderson, *The President's Men* (New York: Doubleday, 1969), 220–21.

51. Eunice Shriver, Oral History Interview with John Steward, 7 May 1968, p. 11, Kennedy Presidential Library. As the president's sister, Eunice Shriver had a bit more access and clout than the average advocate.

52. See, e.g., Anderson, *The President's Men,* 342; Moyers Papers, Box 12, Johnson Presidential Library; Harry McPherson, *A Political Education* (Boston: Little, Brown, 1972), 404, 431–39.

53. See, e.g., McPherson, *Political Education,* 431–39.

54. See, e.g., Patrick Anderson's account of the politics behind the preparation of a speech on China in mid-1966 in *The President's Men,* 342–43.

55. For example, Horace Busby to Perry Barber, 8 February 1965, Busby Office Files, Box 18, "Memos for Perry Barber"; Busby to Moyers, 27 July 1964, Busby Office Files, Box 20, "Memos for Bill Moyers"; Johnson Presidential Library. See also Peter Benchley, Oral History Interview with Thomas Harrison Barker, 20 May 1968, p. 9, Johnson Presidential Library.

56. According to writer Peter Benchley, "Bill Moyers tried to get it for awhile and then Joe Califano tried to get it . . . it is my impression that [Johnson] shot down Moyers and Califano and gave it to [Robert] Kintner." Benchley Oral History, 20 May 1968, p. 8.

57. See Kintner to President Johnson, 20 May 1966, 21 July 1966, Confidential Files: WH10 White House Staff Meetings, Johnson Presidential Library; cf. Kintner memo for files, 17 May 1966, Office of the President Files, Box 5, "Robert Kintner," Johnson Presidential Library.

58. Will Sparks to Kintner, 26 January 1967, Johnson Papers, FG 11/5MC, Box 20, "White House Office 1967–," Johnson Presidential Library.

59. Kintner to John Macy, 16 January 1967, Johnson Papers, FG 11-5/MC, Box 20, "White House Office 1967–," Johnson Presidential Library.

60. Kintner to McPherson and Roche, 22 February 1967, White House Central Files, Subject File, Box 68, "FG 11-8 3/1/67–4/20/67," Johnson Presidential Library.

61. For example, Maguire memo for the file, 31 July 1967, Maguire Office Files, Box 13, Johnson Presidential Library.

62. Benchley Oral History, 20 May 1968, p. 8.

63. Ibid., 60c.

64. For elaboration of the structuring of presidential writing from the Nixon through Reagan administrations, see Charles Walcott and Karen M. Hult, "The Evolution of Presidential Writing: An Organizational Analysis" (paper presented at the annual meeting of the American Political Science Association, 1990).

65. Michael Medved, *The Shadow Presidents: The Secret History of the Chief Executives and Their Top Aides* (New York: Times Books, 1979), 19.

66. Ibid., 101.

67. Ibid., 112–16.

68. William J. Hopkins, Oral History Interview with Raymond Henle, 8 August 1968, pp. 10–11, Hoover Presidential Library. See also Medved, *Shadow Presidents,* 189.

69. Charles Walcott and Karen M. Hult, "Management Science and the Great Engineer: Governing the White House during the Hoover Administration," *Presidential Studies Quarterly* 20 (1990): 559. Journalist and Hoover intimate William Hard, in an article that was virtually a paean to Richey, identified Akerson as having charge of appointments early in the administration. William Hard, " 'First Aid' to the President," *New York Herald Tribune,* 5 May 1929, Richey Papers, Box 1, Hoover Presidential Library.

70. Ruth Steadman White Durno, Oral History Interview with Raymond Henle, 4 March 1970, p. 16, Hoover Presidential Library. See also Akerson, speech before the Men's Club of Bronxville, New York, Akerson Papers, Box 18, Hoover Presidential Library.

71. Akerson to Hoover, 5 February 1931, Akerson Papers, Box 18, Hoover Presidential Library.

72. Medved, *Shadow Presidents,* 189.

73. Horace Marden Albright, Oral History Interview with Raymond Henle, 22 September 1967, p. 74, Hoover Presidential Library.

74. Ibid., 68.

75. It appears that Richey retained predominant influence, at least over controversial matters. For instance, when the mother of a convicted radical begged for a chance to plead her case with Hoover, it was Richey who finally refused her. See Donald J. Lisio, *The President and Protest: Hoover, Conspiracy, and the Bonus Riot* (Columbia: University of Missouri Press, 1974), 57–58.

76. Walcott and Hult, "Management Science," 572–73.

77. Ibid.

78. Samuel Rosenman, for instance, commented that McIntyre's "sound judgment about whom the President would see and whom he should not . . . made him particularly valuable." Rosenman, *Working with Roosevelt,* 411.

79. Cf. James MacGregor Burns, *Roosevelt: The Lion and the Fox* (New York: Harcourt, Brace and World, 1956), 152.

80. Rosenman, *Working with Roosevelt,* 411.

81. When Watson died in February 1945, he was replaced on a temporary basis first by Correspondence Secretary William Hassett, then by Press Secretary Stephen Early, who was on the job when FDR passed away.

82. Early to McIntyre, 20 June 1939, Early Memoranda, Box 23, "Marvin McIntyre," Roosevelt Presidential Library.

83. Neustadt, in Heller, *Truman White House,* 105.

84. Harold H. Roth cites Associated Press writer Clark Beach as claiming that Connelly "had more to say than anyone else . . . about where the President should make speeches and what kind of speeches he should make." Roth, "The Executive

Office of the President: A Study of Its Development with Emphasis on the Period 1938-1953" (Ph.D. dissertation, American University, 1958).

85. A good description of Connelly's work is found in Alfred Dick Sander, *A Staff for the President: The Executive Office 1921-1952* (New York: Greenwood Press, 1989), 87–88.

86. William Hopkins, in Heller, *Truman White House,* 72.

87. Hess, *Organizing the Presidency,* 1st ed., 50.

88. When Truman briefly tried to eliminate his larger staff meetings in March 1946 (at Connelly's suggestion), he limited his morning meetings to just Connelly and Press Secretary Charlie Ross. Within about a month, the general staff meeting was reinstated. See Eben Ayers Diary, 25 and 26 March 1946, Box 1, Truman Presidential Library.

89. Hopkins, in Heller, *Truman White House,* 78.

90. Neustadt, in ibid., 116.

91. Ibid., 104.

92. Quoted in Drew Pearson, "Washington Merry-Go-Round," *Washington Post,* 22 March 1952, Ayers Papers, Box 19, Truman Presidential Library.

93. White House colleague Ken Hechler noted that Connelly "usually supported [Treasury Secretary] John W. Snyder on issues that were resolved on conservative versus liberal lines." Hechler, *Working with Truman: A Personal Memoir of the White House Years* (New York: Putnam, 1982), 39.

94. Drew Pearson, "Washington Merry-Go-Round," *Washington Post,* 11 January 1952, Ayers Papers, Box 19, Truman Presidential Library.

95. Clark Clifford, telephone interview with Kenneth Hechler, 9 March 1982, Hechler Papers, Box 6, "Clifford," Truman Presidential Library.

96. See Roth, "Executive Office," 313.

97. Connelly Oral History, quoted in Bradley H. Patterson, Jr., *The Ring of Power: The White House Staff and Its Expanding Role in Government* (New York: Basic Books, 1988), 230.

98. Hechler, *Working with Truman,* 39.

99. Stephens met with Chief of Staff Sherman Adams daily at 7:30 A.M. to go over the daily schedule. See Sherman Adams, *First-Hand Report: The Inside Story of the Eisenhower Administration* (New York: Hutchinson, 1962), 71.

100. Bernard Shanley Diaries, Box 2, Folder 4, p. 880, Eisenhower Presidential Library.

101. Robert J. Donovan, *Confidential Secretary: Ann Whitman's 20 Years with Eisenhower and Rockefeller* (New York: Dutton, 1988), 55.

102. Ibid., 54.

103. See William Bragg Ewald, *Eisenhower the President: Crucial Days, 1951-1960* (Englewood Cliffs, N.J.: Prentice Hall, 1981), 256.

104. Shanley Diaries, Box 3, "VII White House Years," Folder 1, 1955, p. 1787, Eisenhower Presidential Library.

105. Ann Whitman Diary, Box 7, Folder 7, 12 April 1957, Eisenhower Presidential Library.

106. Shanley Diaries, Box 3, "VII White House Years," Folder 4, 24 August 1955, p. 2033.

107. Ibid., 14 November 1955, pp. 2085–87.

108. See, e.g., August Heckscher, Oral History Interview with Wolf von Eckhardt, 10 December 1965, pp. 53–55, Kennedy Presidential Library.

109. Memo, n.d., "Principal White House Professional Staff," Theodore Sorensen Papers, Subject Files, Box 18, Kennedy Presidential Library.

110. Salinger, *With Kennedy,* 65.

111. William Hartigan, Oral History Interview with Charles T. Morrissey, 22 April 1964, pp. 22–23, Kennedy Presidential Library.

112. For instance, in May 1961, O'Donnell sought the advice of Arthur Schlesinger and Richard Goodwin concerning a Cuban refugee group whose members sought to see Kennedy. Schlesinger to O'Donnell, 8 May 1961, Schlesinger White House Files, Box WH-5, "Cuba," Kennedy Presidential Library.

113. Salinger, *With Kennedy,* 374.

114. Nelson handled some liaison duties with Congress and with Eric Goldman, whose main role was to communicate with the intellectual community. Nelson actually recruited Goldman, his former Princeton professor, to the White House. See Eric F. Goldman, *The Tragedy of Lyndon Johnson* (New York: Knopf, 1968), 3–5.

115. Patterson, *Ring of Power,* 231. Patterson points out that in the highly partisan Johnson White House, Jenkins was far from the only link to the party.

116. Hess, *Organizing the Presidency,* 1st ed., 98-99.

117. Ibid., 99.

118. Jack Valenti, Oral History Interview with T. H. Baker, 14 June 1969, pp. 39–41, Johnson Presidential Library.

119. See Emmette S. Redford and Richard T. McCulley, *White House Operations: The Johnson Presidency* (Austin: University of Texas Press, 1986), 23–26.

120. Bunn was replaced by William Blackburn in February 1967. Sherwin Markman, who worked principally in legislative liaison, was technically assigned to Watson; researcher Fred Panzer was also assigned to Watson after June 1967, when Robert Kintner left the White House.

121. Larry Temple, Oral History Interview with Joe B. Frantz, 11 June 1970, tape 2, p. 9, Johnson Presidential Library.

122. See Redford and McCulley, *White House Operations,* 64-68.

123. See Richard L. Schott and Dagmar S. Hamilton, *People, Positions, and Power: The Political Appointments of Lyndon Johnson* (Chicago: University of Chicago Press, 1983), 25.

124. Temple Oral History, 11 June 1970, tape 2, pp. 40ff.

CHAPTER 11. GOVERNING THE WHITE HOUSE STAFF

1. See Charles Walcott and Karen M. Hult, "Organizing the White House: Structure, Environment, and Organizational Governance," *American Journal of Political Science* 31 (1987): 117.

2. A Washington Correspondent, *American Mercury* (December 1929): 385.

3. Charles Walcott and Karen M. Hult, "Management Science and the Great Engineer: Governing the White House during the Hoover Administration," *Presidential Studies Quarterly* 20 (1990): 557-63.

4. Ibid., 573-75.

5. The distinction between strategy and style is notable here. Hoover's personal style—aloof and brooding—did not work especially well in managing a staff. That helps explain why Hoover's secretariat was not especially successful in virtually anyone's estimation.

6. Strictly speaking, Early and McIntyre were initially assistant secretaries. This designation served to emphasize the primacy of Louis Howe among FDR's closest associates. However, this hierarchy was mainly symbolic, since Howe supervised neither Early nor McIntyre.

7. It is interesting to note that Joseph P. Harris and William Y. Elliott, scholars associated with the President's Committee on Administrative Management (the Brownlow Committee) in the mid-1930s, seem to have missed the secretariat's administrative role, or at least chosen to downplay it. In internal commission documents, both identified the secretariat's jobs as scheduling, press and public contacts, and (in Elliott's case), political strategy. See William Y. Elliott, "The President's Role in Administrative Management," p. 18, and Joseph P. Harris, "The Six Assistants," p. 3, in President's Committee on Administrative Management File, Box 13, Roosevelt Presidential Library.

8. When former appointments secretary Marvin McIntyre returned from an illness, he was assigned to legislative and executive liaison tasks during 1941–43. However, his main work during this period can best be described as "political."

9. Erstwhile assistant press secretary William Hassett filled that job, which formally recognized a task he had performed in the White House for years. See Jonathan Daniels, introduction to *Off the Record with F.D.R.: 1942–1945,* by William D. Hassett (New Brunswick, N.J.: Rutgers University Press, 1958), xiii–xiv. Hassett filled the secretarial position vacated by the death of Marvin McIntyre. All early modern presidents had a staff member responsible for overseeing correspondence. For Hoover, Lawrence Richey did this job. FDR had personal secretaries Missy Le-Hand and Grace Tully in charge prior to Hassett's appointment. Hassett continued under Truman, followed by Beth Short. Eisenhower relied on his personal secretary, Ann Whitman. With an annual mail count that was roughly two and a half times that of Eisenhower, Kennedy effectively reinstituted the correspondence secretary, albeit at a lower level of the White House hierarchy, naming Fred Holborn to the position. Johnson assigned the task to a series of aides, none of whom worried about correspondence full time. Over the years, a substantial correspondence staff grew to handle most of the actual work.

10. This is most obvious from the tone of the entries in the diary kept by Press Secretary Steve Early (Roosevelt Presidential Library).

11. Occasionally others, such as (in the early years of the administration) Budget Director Lewis Douglas and adviser Raymond Moley, would attend these meetings. See Stephen T. Early Diary, entries for March 1934, Roosevelt Presidential Library; Arthur Schlesinger, Jr., *The Coming of the New Deal* (Boston: Houghton Mifflin, 1959), 15, 512.

12. Richard Neustadt, "Staffing the President Elect," memo prepared for the Kennedy transition, 30 October 1960, Sorensen Papers, Subject Files, Box 18, Kennedy Presidential Library.

13. Among those tasks were, for instance, Lauchlin Currie's involvement with China, Lowell Mellett's work with the film industry, and William McReynolds's ill-

fated effort to oversee emergency management. Others, however, were closer to the president—e.g., James Rowe (patronage), David Niles (minority relations), and Jonathan Daniels, who performed a wide variety of chores reminiscent of a secretary (and ultimately became one). The best description of the White House during this period is Jonathan Daniels, *White House Witness: 1942-1945* (Garden City, N.Y.: Doubleday, 1975).

14. Ibid., 62.

15. See John Steelman, Truman Memoir Interview with William Hillman, David M. Noyes, Francis Heller, and Lee Williams, 9 December 1954, p. 17, Truman Presidential Library.

16. See the diary of assistant press secretary Eben Ayers for a running account of the growth of the size of these meetings between 1945 and 1949 (Truman Presidential Library). See also David Stowe, Oral History Interview with William D. Stilley and Jerald L. Hill, 18 March 1976, p. 5, Truman Presidential Library.

17. Ayers Diary, entry for 21 April 1947, Box 2.

18. See ibid., especially entries for 25 March and 2 April 1946.

19. Charles Ross Diary, entry for 2 May 1949, Box 2, Truman Presidential Library.

20. William Hopkins, Oral History Interview with Fred Dutton, 3 June 1964, p. 30, Kennedy Presidential Library. See also Hopkins's interview in Francis H. Heller, ed., *The Truman White House: The Administration of the Presidency 1945-1953* (Lawrence: Regents Press of Kansas, 1980), 43-48.

21. George Elsey, "Truman's White House," *Washington Post,* 6 May 1974, Vertical File, Truman Presidential Library.

22. Stowe Oral History, 18 March 1976, p. 13.

23. *Time Magazine,* 15 March 1948, Elsey Papers, Box 57, Truman Presidential Library.

24. Clifford diplomatically recalls little tension with Steelman, noting, "I think that there was maybe some feeling of competition between us, but there shouldn't have been because we were really operating in different areas." Clark Clifford, with Richard Holbrooke, *Counsel to the President: A Memoir* (New York: Random House, 1991), 401. Richard Neustadt recalls it quite differently, referring to "continuous clashes of personality and ambition" as characterizing the relationship. In Heller, *Truman White House,* 102. Clifford's successor, Charles Murphy, remembers his own relationship with Steelman as more "cordial" than Clifford's. Charles Murphy, Oral History Interview with Charles T. Morrissey and Jerry N. Hess, 25 July 1969, vol. 2, p. 440, Truman Presidential Library.

25. Charles Murphy, Richard Neustadt, David Stowe, and James Webb, Joint Oral History Interview with Hugh Heclo and Anna Wilson, 20 February 1980, comments by Stowe (pp. 5, 21) and Murphy (p. 6), Truman Presidential Library.

26. Matthew Connelly, Oral History Interview with Jerry N. Hess, 20 November 1967, p. 214, Truman Presidential Library.

27. Murphy Oral History, 25 July 1969, vol. 2, p. 439.

28. Instances of such teamwork are abundant. Several illustrations can be found, for example, in the papers of Steelman aide Harold Enarson (Box 4, Truman Presidential Library). In one typical example, Enarson discusses a proposal for public hearings on the steel industry with Murphy, Murphy's aide Richard Neustadt, and

Milton Kayle, assistant to Administrative Assistant (and former Steelman staffer) David Stowe. The position they agreed on amounted to a request directed to Steelman, with which he complied.

29. These pre-press conference sessions could have significant policy content, however. See Charles Walcott and Karen M. Hult, "White House Organization as a Problem of Governance: The Eisenhower System," *Presidential Studies Quarterly* 24 (1994): 334-35. Cf. Chapter 3.

30. Sherman Adams, Oral History Interview with Ed Edwin, 12 April 1967, p. 211, Eisenhower Presidential Library; Dwight D. Eisenhower Diary, entry for 3 February 1953, Box 4, Eisenhower Presidential Library.

31. Bernard Shanley Diaries, Box 2, "V White House Years," Folder 2, 1953, pp. 1104, 1313, Eisenhower Presidential Library. The president did not attend either of these meetings.

32. Clarence Randall Journal, Box 3, CFEP, vol. 1, 1956, Eisenhower Presidential Library.

33. Goodpaster to Hagerty et al., January 1959, White House Office, Office of the Staff Secretary, Box 7, "Staff Secretary File," Eisenhower Presidential Library.

34. Samuel Kernell, "The Creed and Reality of Modern White House Management," in *Chief of Staff: Twenty-Five Years of Managing the Presidency,* ed. Samuel Kernell and Samuel L. Popkin (Berkeley: University of California Press, 1986), 222.

35. Sherman Adams, *Firsthand Report: The Story of the Eisenhower Administration* (New York: Harper and Brothers, 1961), 50.

36. Stephen Hess, *Organizing the Presidency,* 2d ed. (Washington, D.C.: Brookings Institution, 1988), 65.

37. However, as we have seen, the extent of this control is commonly overstated. Several staffers, including Andrew Goodpaster, James Hagerty, and congressional relations heads Wilton Persons and Bryce Harlow, had direct access to Eisenhower.

38. Adams, *Firsthand Report,* 50-51.

39. Hess, *Organizing the Presidency,* 65.

40. Cf. ibid., 67.

41. James Rowe to Clark Clifford, 2 May 1949, Clifford Papers, Truman Presidential Library.

42. Hopkins, in Heller, *Truman White House,* 45.

43. Burgess to Sherman Adams and Wilton Persons, 25 June 1953, White House Office, Office of the Staff Secretary, Box 4, "Organization," Eisenhower Presidential Library.

44. Andrew J. Goodpaster, "Organizing the White House," in *The Eisenhower Presidency: Eleven Intimate Perspectives of Dwight D. Eisenhower,* ed. Kenneth W. Thompson (Lanham, Md.: University Press of America, 1982), 65.

45. See Carter Burgess, "Staff Work for the President," a memo circulated to top administration officials in August 1954, Eisenhower Presidential Library. The papers coming out of the president's office included correspondence as well as such things as presidential messages to Congress (Goodpaster, memo for the record, 23 April 1955, White House Office, Office of the Staff Secretary, White House Subseries, Box 1, Eisenhower Presidential Library).

46. Persons to Carroll, 15 September 1953, White House Office, Office of the Staff Secretary, Box 4, Eisenhower Presidential Library.

47. Minnich, notes on meeting of Eisenhower, Burgess, and top staff members, 3 August 1954, White House Office, Office of the Staff Secretary, Minnich Series, Box 1, Eisenhower Presidential Library. Cf. Chapter 5.

48. John Eisenhower, the president's son, also was a Goodpaster assistant, but he dealt mainly with the national security liaison responsibilities that formed the other side of Goodpaster's job.

49. See Frederick G. Dutton, Oral History Interview with Charles T. Morrissey, 3 May 1965, pp. 51–54, Kennedy Presidential Library.

50. Joseph Kraft, "Kennedy's Working Staff," *Harper's Magazine,* Schlesinger Papers, Box W-9, "Magazine Articles—General," p. 30, Kennedy Presidential Library.

51. Harris Wofford, Oral History Interview with Berl Bernhard, 29 November 1965, p. 130, Kennedy Presidential Library.

52. Walt Rostow, Oral History Interview with Richard Neustadt, 11 April 1964, p. 12, Kennedy Presidential Library.

53. Clifford, "Memorandum on Transition," Sorensen Papers, Subject Files, Box 18, Kennedy Presidential Library.

54. Stephen Hess, attributing the success of such informal arrangements largely to the staff's familiarity with and trust in one another, suggested that had there been significant staff turnover in later years, more formal procedures likely would have been required. Hess, *Organizing the Presidency,* 76–77.

55. Kraft, "Kennedy's Working Staff," 36.

56. Hess, *Organizing the Presidency,* 76; Kraft, "Kennedy's Working Staff," 30–31.

57. Dutton Oral History, 3 May 1965, p. 38.

58. Emmette S. Redford and Richard T. McCulley, *White House Operations: The Johnson Presidency* (Austin: University of Texas Press, 1986), 62–67.

59. Ibid., 63.

60. Moyers to Watson, 3 May 1966, Subject File, General File, 11-8-1, Box 92, "Robert E. Kintner," Johnson Presidential Library.

61. Redford and McCulley, *White House Operations,* 63.

62. Ibid.

63. Kintner to Califano, Cater, Christian, McPherson, and Rostow, 12 January 1967, White House Central Files, Johnson Presidential Library.

64. Redford and McCulley, *White House Operations,* 63. The meetings that concerned speechwriting, for instance, provided a forum for writers and others to air their considerable frustration with the manner in which the process was organized.

65. Moyers to Johnson, 14 July 1966, Moyers Files, Box 12, Johnson Presidential Library.

66. Redford and McCulley, *White House Operations,* 65.

67. Perhaps the clearest argument to this effect is made by Richard Tanner Johnson, *Managing the White House* (New York: Harper and Row, 1974).

EPILOGUE

1. The basic structures for public relations and civil service liaison were both highly congruent and stable during much of the early modern presidency. Experimentation with different structures for these tasks during the Eisenhower adminis-

tration produced less congruent structures that did not last. In one of the instances, structuring for civil service liaison, Eisenhower ultimately returned to the kind of structure that FDR and Truman had relied upon.

2. John P. Burke reaches similar conclusions in *The Institutional Presidency* (Baltimore: Johns Hopkins University Press, 1992), 178-94.

3. The major example of nontemporary governance structuring during the Kennedy years was the personnel operation set up by Dan Fenn. Structures for White House involvement in the arts and in mental retardation policy also were put in place during the administration, although, as Chapter 9 indicated, neither survived as activities in the White House Office very far into the Johnson years.

Index